ADVERTISING EXPOSURE, MEMORY, AND CHOICE

ADVERTISING AND
CONSUMER PSYCHOLOGY
A series sponsored by the Society for Consumer Psychology

ADVERTISING EXPOSURE, MEMORY, AND CHOICE

Edited by

ANDREW A. MITCHELL
University of Toronto

LEA LAWRENCE ERLBAUM ASSOCIATES, PUBLISHERS
1993   Hillsdale, New Jersy   Hove and London

Lawrence Erlbaum Associates, Inc., Publishers
365 Broadway
Hillsdale, New Jersey 07642

Library of Congress Cataloging-in-Publication Data

Advertising exposure, memory, and choice / edited by Andrew A.
Mitchell.
    p.   cm. — (Advertising and consumer psychology)
    Includes bibliographical references and index.
    ISBN 0-8058-0685-7
    1. Advertising—Psychological aspects. 2. Consumers' preferences.
  3. Persuasion (Psychology) 4. Consumer behavior. I. Mitchell,
Andrew A., 1939– . II. Series.
HF5822.A26   1992
659.1'01'9—dc20   92-11407
                                      CIP

Printed in the United States of America
10 9 8 7 6 5 4 3 2 1

Contents

v

Preface

The chapters in this volume were originally presented at the eighth annual Advertising and Consumer Psychology Conference held at the Leo Burnett Company, Ltd. in Toronto during May, 1989. The conference was sponsored by the Leo Burnett Company, Ltd., the Marketing Science Institute, and the Division of Consumer Psychology of the American Psychological Association.

The participation of all the authors in the conference is greatly appreciated, as is their considerable effort in the careful preparation of their manuscripts. A special thanks is also extended to Joe Alba, Peter Dacin, John Lynch, and Tom Srull who presented papers at the conference that were not included in the volume.

A number of individuals also expended considerable effort behind the scenes to ensure that the conference was successful. These individuals include David Chalmers, vice president of the Leo Burnett Company, Ltd., for his support and commitment to the conference; Diane Schmalense and Kathy Joscz of the Marketing Science Institute, who have continued to be strong supporters of the conference year after year; and Karen Finlay, a doctoral student at the University of Toronto, who made all the arrangements for the conference and was responsible for making sure that everything ran smoothly. The assistance of Gwen Brawley and two doctoral students, Elizabeth Cowler and Sharmistha Law, in preparing the manuscripts for this volume is also gratefully acknowledged.

Andrew A. Mitchell

Introduction

Andrew A. Mitchell
University of Toronto

Over the last 20 years, considerable progress has been made in advancing our theoretical understanding of the psychological effects of advertising. Early in this period, research focused on identifying mediators of advertising exposure on attitude formation and change. This research has indicated that the number of support and counterarguments generated during exposure to an advertisement (Wright, 1973), attitude toward the ad (Mitchell & Olson, 1981), and beliefs about the advertised product (Lutz, 1975) mediate attitude formation or change.

Later research concentrated on identifying factors that may influence the psychological processes that occur during exposure to advertising and how these psychological processes affect attitude formation and change. One of the proposed models, the Elaboration Likelihood Model (Petty & Cacioppo 1983), for instance, identified message relevance as one of these factors. According to this model, when message relevance is high, individuals will actively process and evaluate the information in the advertisement when forming or changing attitudes. When message relevance is low, individuals will not actively process the information in the advertisement, but will instead rely on peripheral message cues to form or change attitudes.

Other models have identified goals or processing sets as a factor affecting the psychological processes that occur during exposure to advertising. Examples of the different alternative goals or processing sets that have been examined include a brand or advertisement processing set (e.g., Gardner, 1985) and a utilitarian or value expressive set (Park & Young, 1986). Most of this research examining the psychological processes that precede attitude formation or change during exposure to an advertisement is integrated in a review by MacInnis and Jaworski (1989).

Within the last 5 or 6 years, research on the psychological effects of advertising has focused on 5 areas. The first area is the examination of the effect of emotional reactions and mood states that occur during exposure to advertisements. The initial research in this area was directed at developing a typology of the different types of emotional reactions that may be generated by television advertising. Edell and Burke (1986) and Holbrook and Batra (1987) showed consumers a large number of television commercials and asked them to report the emotions that they felt during exposure to each advertisement. These data were then factor analyzed. Both Edell and Burke and Holbrook and Batra found that three orthogonal factors explained these data, however, the three factor solutions that were found differed somewhat. For instance, Edell and Burke found the three emotional dimensions of up-beat feelings, negative feelings, and warm feelings while Holbrook and Batra found the emotional dimensions of pleasure, arousal, and domination.

Burke and Edell (1989), then used a path analytic model to examine the effect of the three types of emotional reactions on brand attitudes and the different mediators of attitude formation and change. This analysis indicated that the effect of the three types of emotional reactions to advertisements on brand attitudes operated primarily through the attitude toward the Ad (A_{ad}) and brand beliefs. There were direct effects on brand attitudes for two of the three types of emotional reactions, but these effects were less important. These results indicate that the previously developed models of advertising effects also seem to explain the effects of emotional advertising.

Other research has induced moods prior to or during exposure to advertising messages. Srull (1984), for instance, demonstrated that moods created prior to exposure to advertising messages would affect attitudes if subjects formed an evaluation of the advertised brand during exposure to advertising, but did not have this effect if subjects formed attitudes after exposure to the advertising message. Other research has indicated that moods created during exposure to advertising messages have an effect on attitudes whether or not the attitudes were formed during exposure to the advertisement (Mitchell, 1987).

The second area of research has focused on A_{ad} construct. Two research issues have dominated this area. The first is understanding how A_{ad} affects brand attitude with different types of processing and, more specifically, is whether A_{ad} affects brand attitudes under high message relevance conditions. If the latter occurs, such findings would be inconsistent with the Elaboration Likelihood Model. The second research issue centers on developing an understanding of the factors that affect attitude toward the ad.

In response to the first issue, MacKenzie, Lutz, and Belch (1986) tested a number of different causal path models of how A_{ad} may affect brand attitudes. The model that provided the best fit to the data was the Dual Mediation model. In this model, A_{ad} has a direct effect on brand attitudes and also an indirect effect through brand cognitions (e.g., support and counterarguments). Homer (1990) tested the same set of models on data from two experiments where subjects were given either a brand or an advertisement processing set instructions. One experiment used television advertisements; the second used print advertisements. Results indicated that the Dual Mediation model provided the best fit whether the subjects were given brand or advertisement processing set instructions or whether television or print advertisements were used.

With respect to the second research issue, Madden, Allen, and Twible (1988) factor analyzed responses to a humorous and a nonhumorous radio advertisement and found support for the notion that both affective and cognitive responses affect attitude toward the ad. They also found differences in the cognitive and affective responses to advertisements based on whether subjects were instructed to focus on the advertisements or not.

Mitchell (1986) demonstrated that affective reactions to an advertisement can have an effect on brand attitudes which is independent of the brand beliefs that are formed. Evidence was also presented that A_{ad} was based on the entire advertisement, rather than just a single component. Miniard, Bhatta, and Rose (1990) found similar results and also demonstrated that A_{ad} had similar effects on brand attitudes under both high- and low-elaboration likelihood.

At a more macro level, MacKenzie and Lutz (1989) developed a model of the antecedent variables that affect A_{ad} and the relationship between A_{ad} and brand attitudes. Ad credibility, ad perceptions, and attitude toward the advertiser were all found to affect A_{ad}, which, in turn, affected brand attitudes and brand perceptions. Ad credibility was also found to directly affect brand attitudes.

The third area of research is the examination of the possible effects of preconscious or subconscious processing of advertising messages. Janiszewski (1988), for instance, presented evidence that the preattentive analysis of a brand name or logo while the consumer focuses attention on other portions of the ad can enhance liking of the brand. Additional studies, have used hemisphere processing theory to examine the effect of different placements of the brand name relative to the focal point of the ad on the evaluation of the brand (Janiszewski, 1990).

In the fourth area of research, a number of studies have examined how the processing of an advertisement may be affected by its structure. Droge (1989), for instance, presented evidence that comparative advertisements tend to be processed under high elaboration likelihood conditions, while noncomparative ads tend to be processed under low elaboration likelihood conditions. Schumann, Petty, and Clemons (1990) examined the effect of the repetition of different types of ad variations on attitudes under conditions of high and low message relevance conditions. As expected, cosmetic variations were most successful under low message relevance conditions, while substantive variations were most successful under high message relevance conditions.

The final area of research is the examination of individual differences in the processing of advertising messages. Cacioppo, Petty, and Morris (1983), for instance, showed that individuals high in need for cognition were more likely to actively process and evaluate the information in a message. This was indicated by the finding that they were more persuaded by strong than weak message arguments, whereas the reverse was true for individuals low in need for cognition.

Snyder and DeBono (1985) examined differences in the effects of informational and image oriented advertisements on high and low self-monitors. They hypothesized that high self-monitors would be more persuaded by image oriented advertisements since they strive to adapt the appropriate behavior in each social situation. Low self-monitors, on the other hand, were hypothesized to be more persuaded by informational advertisements as their behavior tends to be guided more by their attitudes and beliefs. The results of two studies supported these hypotheses.

As indicated by this discussion, most research examining advertising effects has focused on the psychological processes that occur during exposure to advertising and has used attitudes as the primary dependent variable. It has largely ignored that advertising exposure and the eventual effect of that advertising on the selection of a product or a service occur at two different points in time. Consequently, the important role of memory, which links advertising exposure with the actual choice situation has been generally ignored in previous research (for an exception, see Burke & Srull, 1988).

The three chapters in Part I present models that link advertising exposure with the choice situation and thereby, posit a role for memory in models of advertising effects. In Chapter 1, Kevin Keller summarizes the results of a number of studies examining the effect of advertising cues at the point of purchase on brand choice. These studies demonstrate the importance of advertising cues at point of sale on brand evaluations in situations where there is considerable competitive advertising.

William Baker, in Chapter 2, discusses the Relevance Accessibility model, which stresses the necessity of having the same level of involvement during both advertising exposure and the purchase decision. Baker argues that the level of involvement during advertising exposure determines the type of information that becomes associated with the advertised brand (e.g., affective or attribute information), while the type of information that consumers use in making brand choices depends on the level of involvement in the purchase decision. If consumers are highly involved in the decision, they will use attribute information to make a choice. When involvement is low, however, they use only affective information.

In Chapter 3, Nedungadi, Mitchell, and Berger decompose the choice process into three different stages and discuss how the content and accessibility of different types of information may affect each stage. They then argue that advertising will affect the content and accessibility of these types of information. However, advertising may affect each stage differently. In some situations, for instance, advertising may increase the likelihood of choice at one stage while decreasing it at another stage. They then present the results of a study that demonstrates the value of this approach.

The three chapters in Part II represent recent research on the psychological processes in persuasion. In Chapter 4, Herr and Fazio, present a process model of the attitude-behavior relationship. According to the model, attitudes are more likely to predict behavior when attitudes are highly accessible. The authors then contrast this model with Fishbein's attitude theory and combine them into a Two Mode Model which defines the situations when each is likely to operate. The implications of the Two Mode Model of consumer behavior are then discussed based on this analysis.

Zanna, in Chapter 5, examines the issue of message receptivity. He contrasts previous findings in social psychology which indicated that attitudes were very difficult to change with the current information processing perspective which indicates that attitudes are relatively easy to change. He speculates that these different conclusions may be due to the different topics that were studied. The previous research examined high ego involving topics, while the current information processing tends to involve low ego involving topics.

Kardes, in Chapter 6, reviews the results of a series of studies that examine when consumers are most likely to form inferences and when these inferences will affect judgments. The implications of this research for examining advertising effects and the generation of biased inferences are then discussed.

In Part 3, the three Chapters examine the psychological processes that occur during exposure to multiple advertisements for a brand and a review of the recent research on the effect of positive affect in an advertising context and on cognitive processes and structures. In Chapter 7, Edell examines interactions between advertisements in different media. She discusses how the psychological processes during exposure to advertising will be affected by a previous advertising exposure in another media. The implications of these effects on brand equity are also discussed.

Mitchell, in Chapter 8, examines the effects of attitude toward the ad over time and in situations when individuals see two different print messages at two different points in time. The issue examined is whether or not brand attitudes based on attitude toward the ad effects are relatively stable over a 2-week time period and whether the effects of attitude toward the ad from the first message remain after exposure to the second message.

Finally, in Chapter 9, Isen examines different ways that positive affect can influence the effect of advertising on decisions and choices. In addressing this issue, Isen first discusses the results of a number of studies which indicate that a positive affect state during exposure to advertising may influence how consumers categorize and think about the advertised product and how they relate it to other products or services. She then considers how affect experienced at advertising exposure may influence what information is learned, maintained over time and rendered accessible when decisions are made concerning purchase or use.

The three chapters in Part IV, explore the measurement of advertisement effectiveness. In Chapter 10, Deighton and Hoch review the differences between informational and drama advertisements and the advantages and disadvantages of each. They then discuss the elements that are required for effective drama advertising and how to assess whether these elements exist in a particular drama advertisement.

Gengles and Reynolds in Chapter 11 present a methodology for estimating a hierarchical means-end analysis to determine the effectiveness of television commercials. They also demonstrate that advertisements that affect values results in greater attitude change than advertisements that only affect beliefs about product attributes.

In Chapter 12, Rothschild discusses the use of EEG as diagnostic measures of advertising effectiveness. He presents the results of a series of studies that examine the relationship between different physical elements of television commercials and EEG measures. He also examines differences in brain wave patterns for advertisements that received either a high or low score on recall and recognition tests.

REFERENCES

Burke, M. C., & Edell, J. A. (1989). The impact of feelings on ad-based affect and cognition. *Journal of Marketing Research, 26,* 69–83.

Burke, R. R., & Srull, T. K. (1988). Competitive interference and consumer memory for advertising. *Journal of Consumer Research, 15,* 55–68.

Cacioppo, J. T., Petty, R. E., & Morris, K. (1983). Effects of need for cognition on message evaluation, recall and persuasion. *Journal of Personality and Social Psychology, 45,* 371–384.

Dröge, C. (1989). Shaping the route of attitude change: Central versus peripheral processing through comparative versus noncomparative advertising. *Journal of Marketing Research, 26,* 193–204.

Edell, J. A., & Burke, M. C. (1987). The power of feelings. *Journal of Consumer Research, 14,* 421–433.

Gardner, M. (1985). Does attitude toward the ad effect brand attitude under a brand evaluation set. *Journal of Marketing Research, 22,* 192–198.

Holbrook, M. B., & Batra, R. (1987). Assessing the role of emotions as mediators of consumer response to advertising. *Journal of Consumer Research, 14,* 404–420.

Homer, P. M. (1990). The mediating role of attitude toward the ad: Some additional evidence. *Journal of Marketing Research, 27,* 78–86.

Janiszewski, C. (1988). Preconscious processing effects: The independence of attitude formation and conscious thought. *Journal of Consumer Research, 15,* 199–209.

Janiszewski, C. (1990). The influence of nonattended material on the processing of advertising claims. *Journal of Marketing Research, 27,* 263–278.

Lutz, R. J. (1975). Changing brand attitudes, through modification of cognitive structure. *Journal of Consumer Research, 1,* 49–59.

MacInnis, D., & Jaworski, B. J. (1989). Information processing from advertisements: Toward an integrative framework. *Journal of Marketing, 53,* 1–23.

MacKenzie, S. B., & Lutz, R. J. (1983). An empirical examination of the structural antecedents of attitude toward the ad in an advertising pretesting context. *Journal of Marketing, 53,* 48–65.

MacKenzie, S. B., Lutz, R., & Belch, G. (1986). The role of attitude toward the ad as a mediator of advertising effectiveness: A test of competing explanations. *Journal of Marketing Research, 23,* 130–143.

Madden, T. J., Allen, C. T., & Twible, J. L. (1988). Attitude toward the ad: An assessment of diverse measurement indices under different processing "Sets". *Journal of Marketing Research, 25,* 242–252.

Miniard, P. W., Bhatla, S., & Rose, R. L. (1990). On the formation and relationship of ad and brand attitudes: An experimental and causal analysis. *Journal of Marketing Research, 27,* 290–303.

Mitchell, A. A. (1986). The effect of verbal and visual components of advertisements on brand attitudes and attitude toward the advertisement. *Journal of Consumer Research, 13,* 12–24.

Mitchell, A. A. (1987). Current perspectives and issues concerning the explanation of 'feeling' advertising effects. In S. Heckler & D. Stewart (Eds.), *Consumer psychology and advertising* (pp. 127–144). New York: Praeger.

Mitchell, A. A., & Olson, J. C. (1981). Are product attribute beliefs the only mediator of advertising effects on brand attitude? *Journal of Marketing Research, 18,* 318–332.

Park, C. W., & Young, S. M. (1986). Consumer response to television commercials: The impact of involvement and background music on brand attitude formation. *Journal of Marketing Research, 23,* 11–24.

Petty, R. E., & Cacioppo, J. T. (1986). *Communication and persuasion: Central and peripheral routes to attitude change.* New York: Springer-Verlag.

Schumann, D. W., Petty, R. E., & Clemons, D. S. (1990). Predicting the effectiveness of different strategies of advertising variation: A test of the repetition-variation hypotheses. *Journal of Consumer Research, 17,* 192–202.

Snyder, M., & DeBono, K. G. (1985). Appeals to image and claims about quality: Understanding the psychology of advertising. *Journal of Personality and Social Psychology, 49,* 586–597.

Srull, T. K. (1984). Effects of subjective affective states on memory and judgment. In T. C. Kinnear (Ed.), *Advances in consumer research* (pp. 530–533).

Wright, P. L. (1973). The cognitive processes mediating acceptance of advertising. *Journal of Marketing Research, 10,* 53–62.

ADVERTISING EXPOSURE AND CHOICE

1 Memory Retrieval Factors and Advertising Effectiveness

Kevin Lane Keller
Stanford University, California

Of all the elements in the marketing mix, advertising may have the longest delayed effect on sales. Often, a substantial amount of time passes from the time consumers are first exposed to advertising about a specific brand to when they can actually purchase the product. Although most advertising campaigns do not include explicit assumptions about consumer memory performance, it is often implicitly assumed that advertising affects consumers in some way, which may later be manifested in recall and recognition performance that influence brand evaluations and choice. Consequently, the role of memory processes in advertising is of great interest to practitioners and theoreticians alike.

What factors increase the likelihood that consumers' advertising experiences influence their brand evaluations? How can memory performance for communication effects from advertising exposure be improved? Much theorizing about consumer memory for advertising has considered the effect of memory encoding processes (e.g., Greenwald & Leavitt, 1984; Kisielius & Sternthal, 1986); and how ad information is stored in memory (Olson, 1978). A broader view of memory, however, has been stressed by several researchers (e.g., Baker & Lutz, 1987; Burke & Srull, 1988; Hutchinson & Moore, 1984; Keller, 1987; Lynch & Srull, 1982; Mitchell, 1982). The work of these researchers has emphasized three additional points about memory structures and processes in advertising.

1. Many different types of information can be stored in memory as a result of exposure to a target ad and may exhibit different memory properties.
2. The amount and nature of information for other advertised brands in memory can produce interference effects, decreasing the accessibility of target ad information from memory during any later brand evaluations.

3. The amount and nature of externally available information can act as a retrieval cue, increasing the accessibility of target ad information from memory during any later brand evaluations.

Together, these last two points suggest that recall of target ad information is highest when many strongly related external cues are evident and few competing associations exist in memory.

Although this chapter considers all three issues, as well as issues related to memory encoding processes, the primary emphasis is on examining how memory retrieval processes contribute to advertising effectiveness; for example, how communication effects stored during ad exposure are accessed during brand evaluations. Recently, consumer behavior researchers have recognized the importance of considering retrieval processes in memory-based judgments (Alba & Hutchinson, 1987; Baker & Lutz, 1987; Biehal & Chakravarti, 1986; Feldman & Lynch, 1988; Friestad & Thorson, 1990; Keller, 1987, 1991a, 1991b). Toward this goal, this chapter makes a number of points. One of the main points is to show how some general principles that have been useful in conceptualizing encoding processes can also be used to conceptualize retrieval processes. These conceptual frameworks are then employed to identify factors at advertising exposure and the point-of-purchase, which affect advertising recall, and to suggest appropriate strategies to improve recall of communication effects when consumers make their brand evaluations.

This chapter is organized into six sections. The first section describes antecedents and consequences of advertising encoding. It is argued that encoding antecedents can be classified in terms of three factors—*motivation, ability,* and *opportunity*—and that the actual consequences of encoding processes can be characterized in terms of two dimensions—*intensity* and *direction*. The second section defines the different types of communication effects or information stored in memory from ad exposure, termed the *ad memory trace,* distinguishing between ad representation and ad response elements. The third section deals with the accessibility of communication effects from the ad memory trace and outlines how the conceptual frameworks used to understand encoding and retrieval processes are very similar. That is, retrieval antecedents can also be classified according to motivation, ability, and personality factors, and the actual consequences of retrieval processes can also be characterized along intensity and direction dimensions. The fourth section considers advertising and point-of-purchase interactions, identifying circumstances when weak or strong associations to the brand name in memory may lower the accessibility of communication effects from the ad memory trace. The fifth section reviews some of the basic theory and empirical evidence concerning advertising retrieval cues (Keller 1987, 1991a, 1991b). An ad retrieval cue is a technique that can improve consumer memory performance when the brand name is an ineffective cue to the ad memory trace. The sixth and final section provides a chapter summary and a discussion of managerial implications and future research directions.

ENCODING PROCESSES

Background

To understand how ad information is encoded and stored in memory, it is necessary to first make some assumptions about the structure of memory. A functional distinction is made between short-term memory (STM), the temporary repository of information currently accessible to people, which is limited in capacity, and long-term memory (LTM), a relatively permanent repository of information, which is virtually unlimited in capacity (Bettman, 1979; Horton & Mills, 1984). Long-term memory can be represented according to an associative network memory model (Anderson, 1983; Wyer & Srull, 1986). For example, knowledge in LTM can be represented as a network of nodes and links; nodes are stored concepts or information and links are connecting mechanisms that vary in strength. A spreading activation process determines the extent of retrieval in LTM (Collins & Loftus, 1975; Raaijmakers & Shiffrin, 1981; Ratcliff & McKoon, 1988). At any point in time, an information node in STM may be a source of activation because it is either encoded external information or retrieved internal information currently being processed. Activation can spread from these nodes to associated nodes in the LTM network of linked nodes. If the amount of activation that spreads to a node exceeds some threshold level, then the information in that node is recalled. The strength of association between the activated nodes and all linked nodes determines this "spreading activation" and which information is retrieved from LTM.

Encoding information in LTM involves memory control processes, that is, the processes monitoring the flow of information in and out of LTM (Atkinson & Shiffrin, 1968). Some processes are automatic (Hasher & Zacks, 1979) but others are under active control of the individual. Active control processes can determine the organization of information in LTM (Hastie, 1980; Mitchell, 1982; Srull, 1981). Memory control processes (Bettman, 1979; Olson, 1978) include rehearsal (i.e., the allocation of processing effort to keep information active in STM and/or transfer it to LTM), coding (i.e., representing of information in LTM in terms of cognitive symbols such as words or visual images assigned to represent information), and transfer/placement (i.e., the location of information in LTM in terms of the other information to which it is related). Thus, active control processes are important to understand how advertising effects are organized in LTM.

MacInnis and Jaworski (1989) provided a comprehensive model of memory encoding operations in advertising, incorporating a number of prior models. Here, we selectively highlight two key aspects of that conceptualization, which, as will be shown, have significance to retrieval processes: encoding antecedents and encoding consequences.

Encoding Antecedents

Encoding antecedents have been classified according to factors related to a person's motivation, ability, or opportunity to process ad information (Batra & Ray, 1986a; MacInnis, Moorman, & Jaworski, 1990; Petty & Cacioppo, 1986; Roberts & Maccoby, 1973; Schmalensee, 1983; Wright, 1981). *Motivation to process* refers to a person's willingness or desire to expend mental effort and devote mental resources or capacity to processing information from an ad. Consumer processing goals are one example of this factor. Processing goals influence the type of information in an ad that consumers notice, evaluate, or respond to. For example, consumers may desire to evaluate the advertised brand, perhaps because of enduring involvement with the brand or product category, or a more transitory interest, due to an imminent purchase. As will be discussed, consumers may have other goals; in that case, they would direct their processing effort elsewhere.

Ability to process refers to a person's mental resources, which are relevant for processing the information in an ad. A consumer's knowledge structure is one example of a factor that affects the capability to comprehend and receive the intended effects of the ad (Alba & Hutchinson, 1987). Knowledge can be characterized according to its content (e.g., as it relates to the domain of interest), as well as its organization (e.g., in terms of the strength of associations among information nodes in memory). Although closely related, many researchers distinguish ability to process from *opportunity to process,* which refers to the extent to which external conditions are present in the environment conducive to processing information from an ad. Does the medium allow for self-paced processing of ad information (i.e., print as opposed to broadcast media)? To what extent is the program or editorial context and physical setting free of distractions? For example, time pressure has been shown to affect how consumers process ad information (Houston, Childers, & Heckler, 1987; Moore, Hausknecht, & Thamodran, 1986).

Encoding Consequences

Actual encoding processes during ad exposure can be characterized by intensity and direction dimensions (Bettman, 1979; Mitchell, 1981). *Processing intensity* is defined as the amount of mental resources or capacity devoted to encoding information. Processing intensity is a prime determinant of the strength of associations among information in LTM. The levels or depth of processing view

(Craik & Lockhart, 1972; Craik & Tulving, 1975; Lockhart, Craik, & Jacoby, 1976) maintains that more intense or elaborate processing produces more durable memory effects. *Processing direction* refers to the stimuli or objects that receive these mental resources or capacity. During ad exposure, for example, processing may be directed toward the brand claim or the ad execution information.

A person's motivation, ability, and opportunity to process will determine the intensity and direction of that processing. For example, one motivational distinction for processing during ad exposure has been made between consumers who have ad evaluation goals and consumers who have brand evaluation goals (Gardner, Mitchell, & Russo, 1985; Keller, 1991a; Park & Young, 1986). Consumers who view an ad with an ad evaluation goal, where they seek the entertainment value of an ad, may be more likely to direct their processing to executional characteristics of an ad. That is, a person may deeply think about, or be emotionally affected by, an ad but may be focusing that attention on some aspect of the ad not directly related to the brand claims, such as the source or spokesperson of the ad (high-intensity and ad-directed processing). Consumers who view an ad with a brand evaluation goal, where they seek information about the advertised brand, however, may be more likely to direct their processing towards product claims, although they may also critically evaluate the ad execution itself (MacKenzie & Lutz, 1989). That is, a person may carefully consider the claims made about a brand while processing an ad, rendering belief judgments as to its believability, and forming or updating an overall brand attitude (high-intensity and brand-directed processing). Besides motivation, ability considerations can also affect processing direction. For example, Lutz, MacKenzie, and Belch (1983) found that consumers with little product knowledge were more likely to use their reactions to the ad execution itself during ad exposure in forming their evaluations of the advertised brand than were consumers with relatively more product knowledge. Evidently, consumers low in knowledge lacked the ability to process the brand claim information in the ad and directed their processing elsewhere. Finally, as may often be the case, a person has almost no motivation or ability to process the ad and barely attends to either the brand claims or executional information (low intensity processing).

AD MEMORY TRACE

The stored representation of an event in memory, referred to as a *memory trace,* can be conceptualized as a multidimensional collection of elements, features, or attributes (Jones, 1978; Le Voi, Ayton, Jonckheere, McClelland, & Rawes, 1983; Ogilvie, Tulving, Paskowitz, & Jones, 1980; Tulving & Watkins, 1975). Specifically, an *ad memory trace* is defined as the communication effects stored in memory from ad exposure (Hutchinson & Moore, 1984; Keller, 1987), that is, the change in LTM that results from perceptual and encoding processes during ad exposure. Ideally, ad memory trace would be stored with other knowledge about the advertised brand in memory, affecting beliefs and evaluations associated with the brand. There are two types of communication effects that a person may store as elements in the ad memory trace from processing an ad: (a) a representation of the ad itself, and (b) responses that occurred during ad exposure.

Ad Representation Elements

Encoding the original ad information, like encoding any stimulus, will not produce a literal copy of that information in memory. The representation may contain only a subset of the features of the original information (Wyer & Srull, 1986). Two pieces of information are almost always in any ad—the brand name of the product and its accompanying product category, or class. In general, two other basic types of information in an ad will produce two different types of ad representation elements in the ad memory trace (Kotler, 1988): brand-specific and ad-specific elements. *Brand-specific information* is defined in terms of the brand positioning expressed by the ad (i.e., the particular goals or objectives of the ad intended by the advertiser), as well as the more general product associations, which ad exposure may reinforce. Thus, they relate to the appeals, claims, or unique selling proposition made about the brand in the ad. In contrast, *ad-specific information* is defined in terms of the executional information in the ad conveying or communicating the brand positioning (e.g., how the claims are made). That is, they relate to the format, structure, tone, and style of the ad execution.

Ad Response Elements

There are two major types of outcomes from consumer ad processing—affective, or feeling, responses (Silk & Vavra, 1974) and cognitive, or thinking, responses (Greenwald, 1968; Petty, Ostrom, & Brock, 1981; Wright, 1980). Examples of affective response categories are mood states (Gardner, 1985b; Srull, 1987), emotional responses or feelings (Batra & Ray, 1986b; Edell & Burke, 1987; Stayman & Aaker, 1987), and attitude toward the ad (MacKenzie & Lutz, 1989; Mitchell & Olson, 1981). Examples of cognitive response categories are counterarguments, support arguments, source bolstering, and curiosity statements (Wright, 1973), abstractions (Chattopadhyay & Alba, 1988), inferences (Dick, Biehal, & Chakravarti, 1990), and positive and negative reactions about the ad execution itself (MacKenzie & Lutz, 1989). Consumers may form specific reactions to or overall evaluations of either the ad-specific information or the brand-specific information. Finally, these reactions and evaluations can vary in their favorability. In short, consumers may have responses to an ad characterized along the following four dimensions: (a) type (cognitive thoughts or affective feelings),

(b) direction or focus (particular to the brand-specific or ad-specific information), (c) level of abstraction (particular to one aspect of the ad or an overall summary response), and (d) valence (ranging from positive to negative).

A priority in the study of memory factors in advertising is an understanding of the accessibility of different elements of the ad memory trace, for example, which communication effects of the ad memory trace are the most durable and resistant to interference effects and which are the most easily retrieved? In a general sense, accessibility of the ad memory trace will depend on the organization of memory and the retrieval cues that are evident, as will be discussed in detail. One reason that the distinction between ad representation and ad response elements is important is that the two different types of elements in the ad memory trace may vary in their accessibility. A person's evaluative responses to information are often assumed to be more durable and accessible in memory than the actual information itself. As Hertel (1982) noted, ". . . to the extent that reactions and judgments require more cognitive effort (Eysenck & Eysenck, 1979; Tyler, Hertel, McCallum, & Ellis, 1979), are associated with a high degree of internal generation (Raye, Johnson, & Taylor, 1980), or involve self-reference (Rogers, Kuiper, and Kirker, 1977), they will be remembered better than facts," (p. 528). Along these lines, many advertising researchers assert that personal, evaluative responses to ads or products such as affective reactions (Moore & Hutchinson, 1985), inferences (Chattopadhyay & Alba, 1988), intermediate judgments (Kardes, 1986), or overall evaluations (Beattie & Mitchell, 1985; Lichtenstein & Srull, 1985) are more durable in memory than the ad or product information on which they are based. The next section considers in more detail how communication effects are accessed from the ad memory trace.

RETRIEVAL PROCESSES

Background

Retrieval processes are concerned with how information is activated in LTM and transferred to STM. Retrieving information from LTM requires the determination of an entry point or retrieval cue in LTM. The retrieval cue used to enter the network may be generated internally, by the person, or externally, by the environment. Failure to remember stored information occurs because of inability to gain access to information because of ineffective or inappropriate cues. *Interference theory* (Postman & Underwood, 1973) maintains that forgetting information is primarily the consequence of learning related information. In terms of an associative network memory model, additional learned information creates a greater number of links to a node. Therefore, the likelihood of successful retrieval of any one piece of linked information is lower.

Providing proper retrieval cues to activate other linked nodes, however, can often eliminate interference effects in memory. Tulving and Psotka (1971) provided a convincing demonstration of cue-dependent forgetting. Subjects were given a series of categorized word lists. Each list contained 24 words and consisted of four words from each of six categories. Subjects learned the target list of words and were given no intervening lists or from one to five additional lists. Then, subjects recalled as many words from the target list as possible. The more lists which were additionally learned, the poorer was recall. The decline in memory performance was attributable primarily to forgetting entire categories. Subjects also performed a final cued recall test where they were given the six category titles for the original list (e.g., animals). In this instance, recall was basically unaffected by the number of the additional lists learned. Providing cues virtually eliminated the interference effects.

Thus, cues evident at retrieval influence whether or not previously stored information can be accessed from memory (Tulving & Pearlstone, 1966). Information may be available in memory but in the improper retrieval context, it may be inaccessible. What are the most effective types of cues? Tulving (1968, 1972, 1983), maintained that any given event has only one episode and technically occurs just once, proposed the *encoding specificity principle* to explain memory for events. In its broadest form, this principle asserts that "specific encoding operations performed on what is perceived determine what is stored, and what is stored determines what retrieval cues are effective in providing access to what is stored" (Tulving & Thomson, 1973, p. 369).

Tulving and Thomson (1971) provided a convincing demonstration of encoding specificity. Subjects were given a list of weakly associated word pairs at input (e.g., "black train") and assigned to one of two groups for the memory test. During later recall (e.g., for "black"), one group was given the list of weakly associated cues seen at input ("train"). The second group was given strongly associated cues that had not been present at input ("white"). The results showed that the cues present at input or encoding led to higher recall than the generally strongly associated cues, even though the cues at input were otherwise weakly associated. Much research has supported the principle of encoding specificity and the importance of reinstating the encoding context at the time of retrieval (Horton & Mills, 1984). Thus, successful recall depends on the extent of the match between the information at initial encoding and later retrieval.

Although cues generally enhance recall by identifying forgotten information, this may not always be the case (e.g., Alba & Chattopadhyay, 1985a, 1985b, 1986; Hoch, 1984). Part-list cuing suggests that cues may sometimes inhibit recall (Nickerson, 1984; Roediger, 1973, 1974; Rundus, 1973; Slamecka, 1968; Sloman, Bower, & Rohrer, 1991). The implication of this retrieval process is that recall of one of the items associated with a cue lowers the probability of recall for other items associated with that cue. In other words, a person can fixate on certain items and fail to retrieve other items. Thus, one reason for the inability to retrieve otherwise accessible information is that the act of recalling some information inhibits the recall of other similar information. To illustrate, assume that a person is asked to recall all beverages known to him or her. After all beverage names are given and no example is provided from the fruit juice category, providing the person with examples of fruit juices will then stimulate recall of other types of fruit juices. If the person was aware of the fruit juice category, on the other hand, then the provision of a subset of fruit juices may actually inhibit recall of additional types of fruit juices, compared to what would have happened without the cue. In short, the effectiveness of retrieval cues in any situation depends on the following two factors (Roediger, 1974): (a) Retrieval cues improve recall as compared to noncued situations when they allow access to more higher order units (e.g., categories or types of information) than could be recalled unaided; but (b) such cues impair recall to the extent that they provide more information than necessary to gain access to the higher order unit.

One of the main assertions of this chapter is that there are strong theoretical similarities between encoding and retrieval processes, so the conceptual frameworks used to understand the two types of processes are very similar. As Craik noted (1979), "there is growing agreement that retrieval processes are quite similar to encoding processes in many respects and may even be identical. . . ." (p. 84). As previously described, the antecedents to encoding can be defined in terms of motivation, ability, and opportunity factors and actual encoding processes can be characterized according to intensity and direction dimensions. The remainder of this section shows how the antecedents and consequences of retrieval can be conceptualized in a similar manner (see Fig. 1.1).

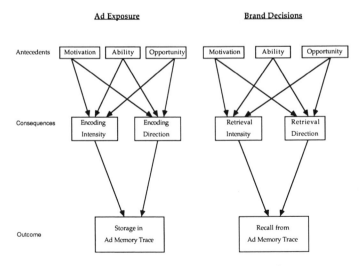

FIG. 1.1. Conceptual equivalence of encoding and retrieval processes for advertising.

Retrieval Antecedents

The antecedents to retrieval, like encoding, can be thought of in terms of motivation, ability, and opportunity factors. *Retrieval motivation* is a consumer's willingness and desire to allocate mental resources to attempt to retrieve information from memory. Generally, factors affecting retrieval motivation are related to characteristics of the person (e.g., goals). In an advertising context, one key factor affecting a person's motivation to retrieve advertising information is its perceived diagnosticity (Feldman & Lynch, 1988). To what extent does a consumer think that advertising information is useful in making his or her decision? Consumers will be more motivated to retrieve ad information when they think that it will help them in their brand evaluations. Baker and Lutz (1987), in their relevance-accessibility model of advertising effectiveness, noted that the perceived relevance of ad information will be a function of consumer involvement when making brand evaluations. *Retrieval ability factors* relate to the capabilities of a consumer to retrieve information from memory if he or she attempts to do so. Ability to retrieve depends on the organization of information in memory and the retrieval cues that are present. In particular, successful recall depends on the extent to which external cues are present in the environment or internal cues can be generated by the person that have strong associations to the target information to be recalled (Lynch & Srull, 1982). Finally, *retrieval opportunity* factors refers to the extent to which external conditions are conducive for retrieval from LTM. To what extent is the retrieval environment free of distractions and time pressure?

Retrieval Consequences

The consequences of retrieval, like encoding, can be thought of in terms of intensity and direction dimensions. *Retrieval intensity* concerns the amount of cognitive effort used to retrieve information from LTM. Thus, it will reflect the number of retrieval attempts that are made and the extent of spreading activation associated with such retrieval attempts (Bjork, 1975). Greater retrieval effort should not only increase the likelihood of successful recall at one time but it has been shown to also produce enhanced memory performance for subsequent recall tasks at a later time (Gardiner, Craik, & Bleasdale, 1973; Gotz & Jacoby, 1974). *Retrieval direction* concerns the particular information in LTM memory that receives this retrieval effort and spreading activation. Thus, it is concerned with the particular entry points in memory from the internal or external retrieval cues.

As with encoding, a person's motivation, ability, and opportunity to retrieve information will determine the intensity and direction of that retrieval. Thus, a person must have motivation, ability, and opportunity to successfully access whatever communication effects have been stored in the ad memory trace. Sufficient retrieval intensity must be forthcoming, but it alone does not ensure successful recall of information. That is, even though a person devotes considerable cognitive effort to recalling a particular piece of information from memory, that attempt may be unsuccessful if the associative links in LTM are such that spreading activation fails to access that information. In an advertising setting, one key issue is whether sufficient retrieval intensity will be correctly directed by consumers to any of the communication effects in the ad memory trace when brand decisions (e.g., evaluations or choices) are made. The next section examines this conceptual framework in more detail to consider how communication effects may be recalled at the point of purchase.

ADVERTISING AND POINT-OF-PURCHASE INTERACTIONS

At the point of purchase, a consumer generally encounters several brands within a product category. The package or product appearance for each brand presents a combination of "new" visual or verbal information to which the consumer has not been exposed outside the store and "old" visual or verbal information, which either reinforces or suggests (i.e., cues) previously encountered information. Even if consumers store communication effects from ad exposure in memory, there is no guarantee that anything from that ad memory trace will play a role during brand evaluations. For example, consumers may have little motivation to retrieve any information from LTM such that low retrieval intensity is forthcoming. They may use stored decision rules based only on information physically present at the point of purchase (e.g., always buy the same brand or the least expensive brand in a product category), ignoring or overlooking any communication effects available in memory.

Nevertheless, consumers often constructively arrive at a purchase decision (Alba, Hutchinson, & Lynch, 1990; Bettman, 1979). As Bettman (1986) noted, "one of the major developments in research on consumer decision processes is the realization that memory and decision processes interact . . . most consumer choices are probably a mixture of memory—and stimulus-based, where some information is available in the choice environment and some are in memory" (p. 263). The memory retrieval environment presented by the package or product information, by influencing recall from memory, will have an important influence on how brand evaluations are made. More specifically, the number and nature of informational cues on the package or product can affect retrieval motivation and ability. They can determine what stored information, beliefs, thoughts, feelings, evaluations, and so forth are retrieved from the ad memory trace and potentially incorporated into brand evaluations.

Retrieval ability, according to the encoding specificity principle, depends on the extent to which there is congruency between the information presented in the ad and on the product, or package. To reinforce or cue advertising, the point-of-purchase (POP) information (e.g., package graphics) should be consistent with

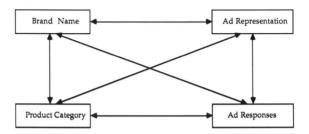

FIG. 1.2.   Organization of ad memory trace in memory.

the ad information. The *ad and POP congruence* is defined as the extent to which the ad and point of purchase contain similar information. One way to ensure a match between the ad and point of purchase, as Bettman (1979) suggests, is to prominently display the package and/or feature the brand name in the ad. To the extent that these pieces of information appear in the ad, they can then function as cues at the POP for communication effects stored in the ad memory trace. The effectiveness of these cues will depend on the strength of their links to the ad representation and ad response elements in the ad memory trace (see Fig. 1.2). The brand name, in particular, may prove to be an ineffective cue to the ad memory trace, however, because of a variety of factors that create weak or strong associations from it to other elements in the ad memory trace.

Accessibility Problems Due to Weak Brand Name Associations

Why might the brand name be a poor cue to communication effects in the ad memory trace? Weak links from the brand name to the ad memory trace may occur because of the nature of the ad itself (either its structure or content), the environment surrounding the ad (e.g., the type and extent of competitive advertising), and the person's motivation and ability to process the ad at encoding.

As an example of an ad structure factor that affects accessibility, consider brand identification strategies with television advertising. Many television ads delay or downplay the identity of the advertised brand (or even product) in an attempt to raise attention levels of consumers during ad exposure. By reducing the brand name prominence, marketers hope to lower the risk that consumers "tune out" the ad because of negative attitudes toward the sponsor or a lack of interest in the ad content. The increased processing intensity from consumers as they seek to identify the advertised brand or product, or follow the action in the ad, would be expected to result in many communication effects stored in the ad memory trace (e.g., the images and main selling point of the ad and consumers' reactions to the ad). Unfortunately, such a brand identification strategy means that relevant, brand-related knowledge is less likely to also be activated and retrieved into STM during ad exposure. Consequently, the ad memory trace may not be correctly incorporated into the brand cognitive structure in LTM, so that weak links would exist between the brand name and the ad memory trace. Consistent with this reasoning, Walker and von Gonton (1989), in a meta-analysis of test scores for 750 commercials, showed that ad recall with a brand name cue was considerably lower, both when the brand name was delayed until the end of the ad, and when the brand name was mentioned less frequently in the ad.

In addition to structural aspects of the ad, such as the location and frequency of brand name mentions, the actual content of the ad may cause weak links from the ad memory trace to the brand name. The use of a well-known spokesperson is often viewed advantageously by advertisers because a rich memory trace often already exists in LTM for that person, containing positive affect, beliefs, and so on. Yet, the links formed during ad exposure in such situations may be between the spokesperson and the product class only, rather than to the advertised brand. Substantial interference and confusion may result. For example, when the popular actor James Garner was advertising for Polaroid, marketing research surveys routinely noted that many interview respondents mistakenly attributed his promotion to their chief competitor, Kodak.

Besides such possible source effects, consider the more general differences between informational (i.e., "thinking") ads and emotional (i.e., "feeling") ads (Kotler, 1988). Loosely defined, informational ads focus directly on the brand and attempt to link to it product-related information, such as the functional benefits or attributes of the product or service, appealing directly to the audience's self-interest. Emotional ads attempt to associate certain positive or negative feelings, images, or attitudes with the brand, either centrally through the ad execution or peripherally by evoking already stored feelings. In distinguishing the effects of these two types of ad content on encoding processes, it may be expected that informational ads evoke more brand-directed processing, and emotional ads evoke more ad-directed processing (Mitchell, 1982). If so, the effects of these ads will differ substantially in terms of what would be stored in memory and how these effects would be linked to other information. In particular, because emotional ads may cause processing directed more at the ad execution information, they may produce an ad memory trace that has weaker links to the advertised brand name. Consistent with this reasoning, Zielske (1982) presented the results of a study that provided ". . . a factual basis for the concern that day-after recall may penalize feeling television commercials relative to thinking commercials" (p. 22). More generally, any "borrowed interest" technique (e.g., music, humor, sex appeals, celebrities), by downplaying the identity of the advertised brand, may create weak links from the communication effects in the ad memory trace to the brand name.

Finally, besides the ad itself, the amount and nature of competitive advertising in the product class can also produce weak brand name links. The presence in memory of communication effects for other ads may cause the ad memory trace for the target ad to be overlooked or confused with other ad memory traces (Burke & Srull, 1988; Keller, 1987, 1991b). For example, a common observation in commercial ad recall studies is that consumers mistakenly associate competitive ads with the target ad, particularly if the market leader is the main competitor (e.g., Philips and GE light bulbs, Lee and Levis jeans, and Polaroid and Kodak cameras). The effect of competitive advertising on consumer recall and evaluations will be considered in greater detail.

A person's motivation and ability to process should also affect the strength of the brand name associations. Concerning processing motivation, Greenwald and Leavitt (1984) conceptualized audience involvement to advertising as consisting of four qualitatively distinct levels. With the two lowest involvement levels, preattention and focal attention, it is doubtful that much of an ad memory trace would be produced and even less likely that any links would be formed to the advertised brand. In contrasting the highest level of involvement, elaboration, from the next highest level, comprehension, Greenwald and Leavitt note that elaboration produces substantial freedom of memory and attitude from the specific details of the original message or its setting, but that comprehension is usually not sufficient to establish easily retrievable memories. Accessibility difficulties arise with comprehension levels of involvement because a message's content is not sufficiently elaborated upon and integrated with existing knowledge. Additional message exposures may, however, enable the attitude object (e.g., the brand) to cue and make retrievable the message arguments. Similarly, Krugman (1977) maintained that advertising for low involvement products consists of the "building or strengthening of picture image memory potential" (p. 8). Motivational considerations may not only affect processing intensity but also processing direction as well. Because many consumers may not be in the market for a product, they may engage in more ad-directed processing. The effect of processing goals on consumer memory and evaluations will be considered in greater detail.

Concerning processing ability, most consumers probably have more generic product knowledge than knowledge specific to particular brands. In other words, they are more likely to know general aspects of the product class (i.e., characteristics that all brands share) rather than the particular attributes or claims advertised by brands within the product category (i.e., characteristics that differentiate brands). For example, a person may know basically how a camera operates, when they are fun to use, and so on, and may also know the brand names of some cameras that are advertised, without really knowing much about the specific characteristics that distinguish advertised brands of cameras. In situations where generic product knowledge exceeds specific knowledge about any particular brand, consumers may be more likely to form stronger links between elements of the ad memory trace and the product category nodes rather than to the brand name nodes. If so, consumers may be confused about which ad information corresponded to which brand within a product category, even though they remember something about advertising in that product category.

Accessibility Problems Due to Strong Brand Name Associations

Thus, for a variety of reasons, weak brand name links to the ad memory trace may exist and pose accessibility problems when the brand name is used as a cue. Although less common, strong associations to the brand name already existing in memory can cause it to be a poor cue for communication effects from the current ad campaign. In situations where there are changes in the marketing program, undesirable part-list cuing effects may occur such that the brand name may not cue the information desired by the advertisers. For example, a change in positioning, a change in target market, and the addition of a new attribute or product use are all situations when consumers may still think about the brand in the "old way" when making brand decisions, which over time have been strongly linked to the brand, and not consider new information now communicated by the ad.

These effects may be particularly evident when the brand name has been chosen to reinforce the initial positioning of the brand. Because the brand name semantically suggests certain product attributes or characteristics, it may be harder for consumers to recall other attributes advertised as a result of a change in marketing strategy. For example, unreported pretests to Keller (1987) showed that based on the brand name alone, CIRCLE laundry detergent had little product meaning to consumers, whereas BLOSSOM laundry detergent suggested to many a product with a fresh scent or fragrance. Presumably, a suggestive brand name would more easily allow for linkages of the suggested attribute to the brand name during ad exposure. Thus, BLOSSOM would be a more effective cue than CIRCLE to an advertised claim of scent. If the brand were to advertise on the basis of another attribute unrelated to scent, for example, cleaning power, then it may be that CIRCLE could be a more effective cue. With BLOSSOM, part-list cuing effects may emerge to the effect that consumers would have difficulty thinking of the brand in another way beside a scented detergent.

ADVERTISING RETRIEVAL CUES

Basic Concepts

Thus, because of weak or strong associations, the brand name or package may be an ineffective cue and consumers may not have the ability to retrieve elements from the ad memory trace. Yet, under many circumstances, it may be desirable to have these communication effects accessible during brand evaluations. To increase the accessibility of the ad memory trace, one approach would be to try to change the ad so that in some way the brand name links to the ad memory trace would be strengthened, for example, by increasing brand name prominence due to the position and frequency of brand name mentions. Another possible approach to increase ad and POP congruence and improve consumers' recall ability would be to put some information from the ad execution itself directly on the product or package. An *advertising retrieval cue* is verbal or visual information originally contained in an ad that is present when a consumer is contemplating a brand decision. Examples of such cues might be the headline from a print ad or a scene from a television ad. For example, Quaker Oats placed a photograph of the "Mikey" character from the popular LIFE cereal ad on the front of the package. By establishing a connection between a brand name product and some parts of the ad at the point of purchase, ad retrieval cues can increase the likelihood that consumers access communication effects stored in LTM (i.e., what the consumer learned, saw, thought, or felt during the ad exposure).

The theoretical rationale for ad retrieval cues is Tulving's (1968, 1972, 1983) encoding specificity principle, which implies that information specific to an ad should be the most effective retrieval cue to communication effects in that ad memory trace. More general cues may fail to elicit specific ad information (Hastie, 1982). That is, Watkins (1979) described the cue overload principle, which postulates that the effectiveness of a retrieval cue for a particular item of information is inversely related to the number of items of information associated with that cue. Thus, a cue associated with many pieces of information is "overloaded" and may be a relatively ineffective cue for any single piece of information. Cue overload suggests that although many brandmark type of items which appear both in ads and on packages (e.g., Keebler Elves, Jolly Green Giant, Pillsbury Doughboy) may be powerful cues to the *general* affect or beliefs for the brand that have been created by a set of ads, their cuing ability for the information from or reactions to any *one* particular ad campaign may be limited.

For recall of specific elements from the ad memory trace, however, the *encoding specificity principle* implies that the more a cue specifically relates to an ad (i.e., is uniquely associated with the ad), the more effective it will be in facilitating the recall of communication effects associated with that ad, assuming these effects have been encoded. The ad retrieval cue should be unique and recognizable. As a simple example, if it is assumed that consumers will recognize a particular visual scene, perhaps due to its distinctiveness, and that the scene will suggest the information presented in or responses generated by the ad, then that visual scene should serve as the basis for the cue. If it is expected that a particular tag line or slogan will be most suggestive, given the manner in which consumers processed the ad, then it should be used as the cue. Three factors will determine the effectiveness of ad retrieval cues on brand evaluations or choice (Keller, 1987):

1. The amount and valence of communication effects encoded and stored in the ad memory trace, thus potentially retrievable during brand evaluations.
2. The strength of the links from the ad memory trace to the cues typically evident during brand evaluations, for example, the brand name or package.
3. The strength of the links from the ad memory trace to the information serving as the ad retrieval cue.

If no communication effects are stored in the ad memory trace, then ad retrieval cues can have little effect because there is nothing to retrieve. If the ad memory trace is easily retrieved with brand name as a cue because of strong links, ad retrieval cues will again have little effect. Ad retrieval cues should have the greatest effect on brand evaluations when a rich ad memory trace is encoded but weak links are formed to the brand name because of motivation, ability, or opportunity considerations at encoding. Because retrieval ability with a brand name cue may then be low, ad retrieval cues may be necessary to access communication effects from the ad memory trace.

Experimental Evidence

Many researchers have noted the potential importance of retrieval cues in the brand choice environment on ad effectiveness (e.g., Bettman, 1979; Hutchinson & Moore, 1984; Lynch & Srull, 1982). In a series of studies, Keller (1987, 1991a, 1991b) examined the effects of advertising retrieval cues on consumer memory and evaluations. The purpose of these studies was to assess the effectiveness of ad retrieval cues and to identify any limiting boundary conditions. Based on the conceptual development previously summarized, the general experimental approach was to create conditions where an ad memory trace would be stored in memory but where weak associative links would exist from it to the brand name. Because weak brand name links imply low retrieval ability, the ad retrieval cue should be able to improve recall of communication effects from the ad memory trace and, assuming these effects were generally positive, lead to more favorable evaluations.

Because the basic methodology was common to all three studies, it is useful to briefly describe the general experimental approach (see Keller, 1987 for a detailed description). In these studies, subjects examined a series of print ads under the guise of a "shopper of the future" cover story. The ads were for fictitious brands from four frequently purchased supermarket product categories (e.g., cereal, laundry detergent, pain relievers, and toothpaste). Each ad was full-page, color-reproduced and had the same basic format, containing a half-page photo, an ad headline, text presenting two main product attribute claims, and four brand name references. Ads were designed to be "good" (i.e., persuasive and likable) or "bad" (i.e., not persuasive or likable). Persuasiveness was related to the strength of the supporting arguments for the claims; likability was related to the affect associated with the ad executions, for example, the valence of ad photos. (See Table 1.1 for a summary description of the ad stimuli, and Fig. 1.3 for an example.)

Because You Care,
Trust Your Clothes To CIRCLE

CIRCLE gently removes tough stains and leaves a fresh scent in all your clothes. It's the laundry detergent the whole family appreciates.

Removes Tough Stains

It contains gentle, effective cleansing proteins which help to remove tough, stubborn stains from all types of clothes. Your whole family will appreciate CIRCLE.

Adds Fresh Scent

CIRCLE also adds a fresh natural scent so your clothes will look good and smell good. It's as if you dried them in the sun.

FIG. 1.3.   Target ad for laundry detergent product class.

TABLE 1.1
Description of Ad Stimuli

Ad Photo	Brand Name/Headline	Product Claims
Cereal		
Young woman jumping in the air	COLONY will have you jumping for joy	Delicious fruit taste High protein
London Bridge	Everyone eats QUEST	From England Costs less
Young woman on scales	MONARCH keeps your life in balance	More fiber Fewer calories
Older man buying a newspaper	Let TRIBUTE start your morning	Tastes good 50-year tradition
Laundry Detergent		
Young family of four hanging clothes	Because you care, trust your clothes to CIRCLE	Removes tough stains Adds fresh scent
Young man staring intently	Because little things matter, use PANORAMA	Convenient to use Biodegradable
Five young people having fun	BARON is the right detergent for today	Works with all fabrics Brightens color
Young woman gazing pensively	SALUTE looks after your wash	Works on delicate fabrics Adds gentle softness
Pain Relievers		
Three adults in stressful sitations	When life takes a turn for the worse, let CHARTER help	More medicine Safe to use
Older man looking annoyed	ATTENDANT is easy to take	Low cost Easy to swallow
Father and son jogging	Let ANGLE reward your extra effort	Works fast Works a long time
Misty, jagged sea coast	DECREE is the tranquil solution	Fights stress Advanced medicine
Toothpaste		
Mother and son smiling	Depend on the protection of HARP	Gently whitens teeth Prevents tooth decay
Polished gold-filled tooth	With DUTY, you don't have to put your money where your mouth is	Low cost Helps prevent decay
Young couple smiling	RITUAL keeps everybody smiling	Freshens breath Whitens teeth
Mountain stream	FLAG is the naturally good toothpaste	All natural Pleasing mint taste

29

After viewing the ads, subjects completed a brief distraction task to clear short-term memory. Next, subjects evaluated a target brand in each product category. As they evaluated each brand, subjects saw a concept board of a mock package front. The brand name and product category were always evident at the top. If present, the advertising retrieval cue was in the lower right-hand corner. The particular ad retrieval cue was either an ad execution cue containing key visuals from the ad (i.e., a reduced version of the picture and headline) or a brand claims cue consisting of the two main claims from the ad (see Fig. 1.4 and Fig. 1.5). Consumers recalled as much as they could about the ad itself and then recalled the responses they had (i.e., thoughts or feelings) while processing the ad. Finally, they provided evaluations of the ad and brand on a variety of scales.

CIRCLE

LAUNDRY DETERGENT

**Because You Care,
Trust Your Clothes to Circle**

FIG. 1.4.   Mock package front for ad execution cue condition for laundry detergent product class.

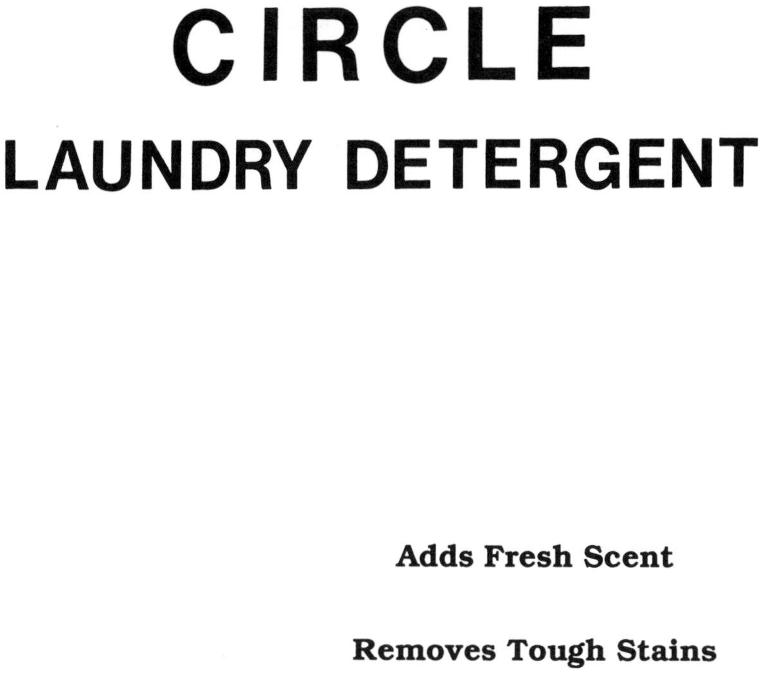

CIRCLE

LAUNDRY DETERGENT

Adds Fresh Scent

Removes Tough Stains

FIG. 1.5.   Mock package front for brand claims cue condition for laundry detergent product class.

The Effect of Advertising Retrieval Cues on Brand Evaluations.   In the first of these studies (Keller, 1987), three factors were manipulated: (a) the presence or absence of ad execution cues; (b) the number of competing ads in the product class (either 1 or 3); and (c) subjects' processing goals during ad exposure (i.e., either to evaluate how likable the ads were or how good the advertised brands were). Because ad exposure was in a "difficult" memory environment (i.e., single exposure, unfamiliar brands, nonsuggestive brand names), it was hypothesized that the presence of ad execution cues would lead to higher recall of brand claims and cognitive responses related to the ad execution and brand claim information and, because the target ads were always good, more favorable ad and brand evaluations. This facilitating effect on recall and evaluations was thought to be particularly likely when subjects lacked the ability to retrieve the ad memory trace because of weak brand name links formed from ad exposure, that is, when consumers were not evaluating the brand or were exposed to many ads within a product category.

The findings showed that the provision of ad execution cues, in addition to the brand name cue, led to greater recall of brand claims and cognitive responses related to the ad execution and, as a consequence, more favorable brand evaluations. A higher number of competing ads produced lower recall of brand claims but did not affect recall of cognitive responses nor, as a result, brand evaluations. Anticipated interactions with the ad retrieval cue and the number of competitive brands advertising in the product class, however, failed to materialize. A higher number of competing ads in the product category appeared to produce "overlapping" ad memory traces, resulting in weak links being produced from both the brand name and ad execution cue to the brand claims in memory. Subjects were not only confused about which claims were associated with which brand name, but also with which claims were associated with which ad execution. Although the ad execution cue did improve recall of brand claims in the high competitive ad condition, as compared to when no ad cue was provided, recall was still lower than when subjects had been cued with fewer competitive ads. Nevertheless, the additional presence of the ad execution cue always improved recall as compared to when only the brand name and product category cues were provided. The processing goal manipulation did not, however, have strong effects on recall or evaluations. In judging ad likability, ad evaluation subjects appeared to devote considerable processing to the brand name so that their recall on the brand name cue alone was as high as brand evaluation subjects who judged the product quality of the advertised brand.

Two follow-up studies extended these findings by exploring in greater depth the boundary conditions moderating the effectiveness of ad retrieval cues. The second study (Keller, 1991a) further examined the moderating effects of consumer processing goals during ad exposure. The third study (Keller, 1991b) further examined the moderating effects of competitive advertising.

Cue Compatibility and Framing in Advertising.   This second study had two main goals. One was to provide a more rigorous test of the encoding specificity properties of ad recall. Specifically, this study more closely examined the effects of processing goals at ad exposure and retrieval cues present during later recall of communication effects and ad and brand judgments. The second goal was to explore the effects of different types of ad retrieval cues, specifically in terms of the extent to which they facilitated and inhibited recall of elements from the ad memory trace. Two factors were manipulated. *Processing goals* during ad exposure were manipulated to involve either ad evaluation (i.e., how interesting and engaging the ads were) or brand evaluation (i.e., how good the advertised brands were). Subjects saw four ads in each of three product categories. The *retrieval cues* present during later recall and judgments always involved the brand name and product category identification, and either no additional cue, an ad execution cue, or a brand claims cue. All three target ads were good.

It was assumed, based on prior research (e.g., Gardner, 1985a; Lutz, MacKenzie, & Belch, 1983; Park & Young, 1986), that subjects with brand evaluation goals would process both ad execution and brand claim information during ad exposure, but subjects with ad evaluation goals would only process ad execution information during ad exposure. Compared to when only the brand name and product category were present, it was predicted that ad retrieval cues would both facilitate and inhibit the recall of elements from the ad memory trace, depending on subjects' processing goals. Ad retrieval cues would help recall of strongly associated information according to encoding specificity cuing effects. Ad retrieval cues would hurt recall of less-strongly associated information according to part-list cuing effects. This facilitation and inhibition would only be present when the cued information had been stored during ad exposure.

Based on this general reasoning, the following hypotheses were made for ad-related and brand-related cognitive responses: An ad execution cue would improve recall of ad-related cognitive responses for both ad and brand evaluation subjects because both groups of subjects should have processed that information (consistent with Keller, 1987), but would decrease recall of brand-related cognitive responses only for brand evaluation subjects because only brand evaluation subjects should have processed that information. Similarly, a brand claims cue would improve recall of brand-related cognitive responses only for brand evaluation subjects because only they should have processed that information, but would decrease recall of ad-related cognitive responses for both ad and brand evaluation subjects because both groups of subjects should have processed that information. In other words, because ad evaluation subjects failed to process brand claim information, they would have an insufficient number of brand-related cognitive responses to allow for any facilitating or inhibiting cuing effects.

It was predicted that ad and brand judgments would resemble the facilitative recall effects. Thus, as long as subjects could access their ad memory trace, even if recall of some specific communication effects were inhibited, it was argued that sufficient recall of other communication effects would enable higher ad and brand judgments. For example, if the ad retrieval cue permitted access to the ad memory trace, it would be more likely that favorable cognitive responses or overall evaluations formed during ad exposure (Lichtenstein & Srull, 1985; Lingle & Ostrom, 1979) could be recalled. Consequently, higher, more confident judgments would be provided with the ad execution cue for both brand evaluation and ad evaluation subjects but with the brand claims cue only for brand evaluation subjects. Because ad evaluation subjects primarily processed ad execution information, however, they would not benefit from a brand claims cue.

The recall and judgment findings almost exactly conformed to those predictions. The different ad retrieval cues improved recall of cognitive responses and led to higher, more confident evaluations depending on the processing goals at encoding. The findings were interpreted in terms of the *cue compatibility principle,* which maintains that successful recall of communication effects from memory (e.g., cognitive responses) is more likely to occur when the type of information contained in retrieval cues is compatible or congruent with the type of information stored during earlier encoding. The findings also supported the notion that although retrieval cues can facilitate recall of strongly-associated information, they can also inhibit recall of other less-strongly associated information in memory, again depending on processing goals at encoding. Finally, additional regression analyses indicated that ad execution cues appeared to increase the relative salience of ad-related cognitive responses in the brand attitudes for both ad and brand evaluation subjects. Thus, ad execution cues affected brand evaluations, not only by affecting the types of communication effects that could be used in brand evaluations, but also by affecting the weights given to those communication effects in brand evaluations.

Memory and Evaluation Effects in Competitive Advertising Environments. The purpose of this third study was to consider how qualitative and quantitative aspects of competitive advertising interacted with ad retrieval cues to affect memory and evaluations from ad exposure. In particular, the effects of the presence and absence of competing ads were explored, as well as the valence of competing ads. Three factors were manipulated: (a) the number of competing ads in the product category (none, one of same valence, one of different valence, or three of different valence); (b) the presence or absence of ad execution cues; and (c) the valence of the target ad (good or bad). The third factor was included to broaden the tests of the hypotheses and increase the generalizability of the findings. All subjects were given brand evaluation instructions at encoding.

It was hypothesized that consumers would have greater ability to recall communication effects from an ad memory trace the more distinctive the ad memory trace was, for example, as compared to ad memory traces for other competing brands in the product category. Specifically, it was argued that recall would decline as the number of competing ads increased and, holding fixed the number of competing ads, when a competing ad was the same valence, as compared to a different valence. Based on Keller (1987), it was predicted that an ad retrieval cue would facilitate recall of communication effects in the presence of competing advertising. It was hypothesized, however, that ad retrieval cues would not improve recall of communication effects with *no* competing ads because the product category itself would serve as an effective retrieval cue. That is, when no other brand beside the target brand advertised in the product category, the ad memory trace would be unlikely to be overlooked or confused.

Given the difficult memory environment, it was argued that ad and brand evaluations would be based on the accessibility and valence of communication effects retrieved from memory (Kisielius & Sternthal, 1986; Reyes, Thompson, & Bower, 1980). If the target ad was seen in a competitive environment containing good and bad ads, confusion or failure to access the ad memory trace would be expected to lead to lower evaluations for a good target ad and higher evaluations for a bad target ad. Because the ad retrieval cue would improve accessibility of communication effects from the ad memory trace in the presence of competitive advertising, however, it would be expected to raise evaluations of a good target ad but lower evaluations of a bad target ad. Again, with no competing ads, the product category itself would function as an effective retrieval cue so that the ad retrieval cue was predicted to have little effect on evaluations.

Although the results were largely consistent with the hypotheses, several exceptions were noted. Specifically, six main findings emerged. The first three findings are concerned with the effects of competitive advertising on recall and evaluations when the ad execution cue was not present (i.e., only brand name and product category identification were provided). First, the number of competing ads lowered recall of brand claims and, to a lesser extent, cognitive responses. Second, with one competing ad, the valence of the competing ad reduced recall of brand claims but did not affect recall of cognitive responses. Specifically, recall of claims was lower when a good target ad was competing with another good ad than with a bad ad, consistent with the notion that evaluative congruence is one dimension of ad distinctiveness. The fact that cognitive responses were more resistant to interference is consistent with much prior research (e.g., Chattopadhyay & Alba, 1988).

Turning to the evaluations, the third finding is that, because competitive advertising appeared to produce confusion about which ad corresponded to the target brand, the presence of a high number of competing ads of different valence produced lower evaluations for a good target ad and higher evaluations for a bad target ad, compared to when there were no competing ads. This finding is important because even though Keller (1987) showed that a lower versus high level of competitive advertising did not affect evaluations, this study showed that a high level of competitive advertising did affect evaluations as compared to when *no* competing ads were present. When there was only one competing ad, however, the valence of the competing ad did not affect evaluations for a good target ad. Overall, it was the case that the pattern for evaluations across the experimental conditions was very similar to the pattern for cognitive responses.

The other three findings are concerned with how the ad execution cue affected consumer memory and evaluations in these different competitive ad environments. The fourth finding is that the ad execution cue improved recall of brand claims only when there was competitive advertising present. With no competitive advertising, the product category itself appeared to function as an effective cue. As with Keller (1987), overlapping ad memory traces again appeared to be present so that no interaction between the ad execution cue and the amount of competitive advertising was present for recall of claims. Thus, ad execution cues were only able to partially offset the interference effects of competitive advertising on recall of brand claims. On the other hand, the fifth finding was that an ad execution cue led to increased recall of cognitive responses for a target ad both in the presence *and* absence of competing ads. Moreover, ad execution cues affected evaluations, both when there were and were not competing ads in the product category.

Motivational and ability considerations may explain why cognitive response recall and evaluations were affected by an ad execution cue, even when there were no competing ads. It may have been that ad execution cues are particularly effective at accessing from memory those cognitive responses generated during ad exposure. In other words, consistent with Tulving's encoding specificity principle (Tulving, 1968, 1972, 1983) the information which served as the basis for cognitive responses may be a particularly good reminder of the specific nature of those responses. It may also have been that the ad execution cues encouraged more extensive, deeper retrieval than would have otherwise been forthcoming. That is, even if subjects had been able to retrieve communication effects without any cues, they may not have been motivated to do so without the inducement of the ad execution cue. Either way, ad retrieval cues could have an effect on recall of cognitive responses and evaluations of a brand with no competing ads.

The sixth finding is that ad execution cues produced higher evaluations for a good target ad but lower evaluations for a bad target ad. In fact, evaluations for a good target ad for those subjects who were given the ad execution cue were not significantly different when there were no competing ads from when there were three competing ads. Methodologically, this provides a stronger demonstration of ad retrieval cue effects than Keller (1987). Managerially, it suggests the common sense notion that ads that evoke negative reactions should not be cued. Note that this finding does not imply that ads evoking negative reactions cannot necessarily "work" and have a delayed effect on persuasion. Prior research exploring the sleeper effect noted that ads initially producing negative affect can, after a delay, produce positive evaluations. A variety of explanations have been provided (e.g., Hannah & Sternthal, 1984; Moore & Hutchinson, 1985; Pratkanis & Greenwald, 1985), basically revolving around attention and memory arguments. For example, the *dissociative cue hypothesis* asserts that initially negative contextual information decays faster in memory than brand related information or brand familiarity (Cook & Flay, 1978). Yet, these theories would suggest that reminding consumers of the negative valence of the original information could produce lower evaluations. Consistent with this reasoning, this study showed that reminding consumers of the content of a bad ad led to lower evaluations.

Three important conclusions can be drawn from these study findings. First, the different types of communication effects encoded during ad exposure and stored in the ad memory trace vary in their sensitivity to contextual effects. Recall of brand claims was more susceptible to interference effects from competing advertising than was recall of cognitive responses. On the other hand, recall of cognitive responses exhibited stronger cue effects than did recall of brand claims. Second, competitive advertising can produce interference effects in memory that affect evaluations of an advertised brand. The additional presence of an ad retrieval cue, however, can help to offset those interference effects. Third, recalled cognitive responses appeared to be an important mediator of brand and ad evaluations. Interference and cue effects for brand evaluations were virtually identical to those for recall of cognitive responses.

DISCUSSION

Summary

This chapter addresses the situation where the objective of the advertiser is for consumers to recall communication effects for the advertised brand (i.e., whatever they learned, saw, thought, felt, etc., during earlier ad exposure(s)) at the point of purchase. The fundamental proposition of this chapter is that both encoding and retrieval factors will affect recall of these communication effects. In support of that proposition, a number of points were made concerning the role of memory retrieval factors in advertising effectiveness. One of the main points of this chapter is that the conceptual frameworks used to understand both encoding and retrieval processes are quite similar. Thus, antecedents to encoding and retrieval processes can be defined in terms of motivation, ability, and opportunity constructs, and the actual outcomes or consequences of encoding and retrieval processes can be characterized in terms of intensity and direction dimensions. The most important implication of these conceptualizations is that successful recall of communication effects will only occur when consumers have sufficient motivation, ability, and opportunity to encode during ad exposure and sufficient motivation, ability, and opportunity to retrieve during later recall attempts.

Another key assertion of this chapter is that the ability to access communication effects from the ad memory trace will depend on how it is organized in memory and the external cues provided. Under many circumstances, the information typically available at the point of purchase (POP), for instance, the brand name, may ineffectively cue the ad memory trace. That is, communication effects may be encoded during ad exposure and successfully stored in an ad memory trace, but this trace may not be strongly associated with the advertised brand. Weak links from the brand name to the ad memory trace may occur because of many factors, for instance, the number and location of brand name mentions in the ad, the executional style of the ad, the amount and nature of competitive advertising, and extent of the person's involvement and knowledge. As a consequence of these weak links, communication effects may be available in memory but inaccessible with the brand name and other cues typically available at the point of purchase.

When weak brand name links exist, ad retrieval cues (i.e., executional information from the ad itself) can improve consumers' ability to retrieve information or responses stored in memory from ad exposure. Three studies were reviewed (see Tables 1.2, 1.3, and 1.4) which show how ad retrieval cues can improve accessibility of communication effects from the ad memory trace. One major conclusion from all three studies is that ad retrieval cues can improve later recall of brand claims and cognitive responses generated during ad exposure and, assuming the ad was well regarded, produce higher brand evaluations. This finding is important because it demonstrates that although advertising may have

TABLE 1.2
Summary of Study 1
(Keller, 1987)

Subjects

    200 members of a local PTA in Durham, North Carolina

Manipulations

    1. Consumer Processing Goals at Encoding

        —Ad evaluation
        —Brand evaluation

    2. Number of Competing Ads in Product Category

        —Two
        —Four

    3. Ad Retrieval Cue

        —No additional cue
        —Ad execution cue

Findings

1. The presence of an ad execution cue increased recall of brand claims and ad-related cognitive responses.

2. The presence of an ad execution cue led to higher ad and brand evaluations.

3. A higher number of competing ads decreased recall of brand claims but had no effect on recall of ad-related cognitive responses.

4. A higher number of competing ads had no effect on ad and brand evaluations.

5. There was no interaction between the ad retrieval cue and competitive ad interference factors for recall of brand claims.

6. The processing goal factor had little effect on recall or evaluations.

---

the potential to impact brand evaluations, it may not do so without the proper cues or reminders at the POP. It should be noted that this finding replicated across four product categories and three samples differing in age, gender, and geographic region.

These studies also identified several boundary conditions as to how advertising retrieval cues operate. For example, the effectiveness of ad retrieval cues on recall depended on a person's processing goals at encoding (Study 2): There must be compatibility between the type of information stored in memory at encoding and the type of information present as cues at retrieval for successful recall of communication effects. The presence or absence of competitive advertising also affected the effectiveness of ad retrieval cues (Study 3): Ad retrieval cues were not necessary for recall of brand claims when there were no other brands advertising in the product category; but even in the absence of competitive ads, however, ad retrieval cues affected both recall of cognitive response and evaluations. When competing ads were present, ad retrieval cues had significant effects on recall of both cognitive responses and claims as well as ad and brand evaluations, offsetting the interference effects. In general, cognitive responses during ad exposure were found to be more durable in memory than the actual ad information itself, for example, brand claims, exhibiting less interference effects (Studies 1 and 3).

Although ad retrieval cues facilitated recall of strongly associated information in memory, they also inhibited recall of less strongly associated information (Study 2). Moreover, ad retrieval cues also affected the salience of, or weight given to, communication effects recalled from memory in brand evaluations. In particular, an ad execution cue increased the importance of subjects' reactions to the ad execution (i.e., ad related cognitive responses) in their brand evaluations (Studies 1 and 2). The effect of ad retrieval cues on the actual level of evaluations depended on all of these factors, as well as the valence of the reactions to the ad

TABLE 1.3
Summary of Study 2
(Keller, 1991a)

Subjects

       103 members of a local PTA in Palo Alto, California or Stanford University staff employees

Manipulations (Note: Subjects saw three competing ads; target ad was always good)

    1. Consumer Processing Goals at Encoding

        –Ad evaluation
        –Brand evaluation

    2. Ad Retrieval Cue

        –No additional cue
        –Ad execution cue
        –Brand claims cue

Findings

    1.   The presence of an ad execution cue increased recall of ad-related cognitive responses for ad and brand evaluation subjects.

    2.   The presence of an ad execution cue decreased recall of brand-related cognitive responses only for brand evaluation subjects.

    3.   The presence of an ad execution cue led to higher, more confident evaluations for both ad and brand evaluation subjects.

    4.   The presence of a brand claims cue increased recall of brand-related cognitive responses only for brand evaluation subjects.

    5.   The presence of a brand claims cue decreased recall of ad-related cognitive responses for both ad and brand evaluation subjects.

    6.   The presence of a brand claims cue led to higher, more confident evaluations only for brand evaluation subjects.

TABLE 1.4
Summary of Study 3
(Keller, 1991b)

Subjects

> 145 upper-division business school students from the University of California at Berkeley

Manipulations   (Note: Subjects were given brand evaluation instructions at encoding)

> 1. Number of Competing Ads in Product Category
>
>> --None
>> --One (same valence)
>> --One (different valence)
>> --Three
>
> 2. Ad Retrieval Cue
>
>> --No additional cue
>> --Ad execution cue
>
> 3. Target Ad Valence
>
>> --Good
>> --Bad

Findings

1. Recall of brand claims and, to a lesser extent, cognitive responses, were significantly lower as the number of competing ads increased.

2. With one competing ad, recall of brand claims for a good target ad was lower when it was competing with a good ad, as compared to a bad ad. The valence of the competing ad did not affect recall of cognitive responses nor evaluations.

3. Evaluations for a good target ad were lower and evaluations for a bad target ad were higher when there were three competing ads, as compared to when there were no competing ads.

4. The presence of an ad execution cue increased recall of brand claims only in the presence of competing ads. Ad execution cues only partially offset the interference effects of competitive advertising on recall of brand claims.

5. The presence of an ad execution increased recall of cognitive responses both in the presence and absence of competing ads. Ad execution cues fully offset the interference effects of competitive advertising on recall of cognitive responses.

6. The presence of an ad execution cue led to higher evaluations for a good target ad and lower evaluations for a bad target ad both in the presence and absence of competing ads. Ad execution cues fully offset the interference effects of competitive advertising on evaluations for a good target ad but only partially offset the interference effects of competitive advertising on evaluations for a bad target ad.

---

itself. Ad retrieval cues led to higher evaluations for good target ads (Studies 1, 2, and 3) but lower evaluations for bad target ads (Study 3).

Implications

The basic managerial implication of the aforementioned research is clear: Marketers must be concerned with the congruence of advertising and point-of-purchase information. Consumers will remember different amounts and types of advertising information and reach different judgments, depending on the retrieval cues provided. Marketers must translate their assumptions as to how consumers process their ads into a hypothetical ad memory trace to decide what information should be present at the POP. If it is the case that consumers do not focus on the brand name or package during ad exposure, weak links may be formed to the desired communication effects stored in memory. In such instances, more explicit cues, such as ad retrieval cues containing actual information from the ad, may be necessary for successful recall. Note that ad retrieval cues are not restricted to the point of purchase and should appear at any point in the decision process where actionable brand decisions are being made that advertising may influence. For example, ad retrieval cues may be important for products, services, or retailers who advertise in the *Yellow Pages* (Lutz, K. A., & Lutz, R. J., 1977), as well as on television, in print, and so forth, because consumers may make the relevant brand decisions while consulting the phone directory. As another example, ad retrieval cues may also be beneficial in accompanying promotions to initiate action by the consumer, for example, with coupons to encourage clipping for the brand.

The use of ad retrieval cues have some important implications for ad copy and media strategies. If ad retrieval cues are used at the POP, the brand name and package presumably can be made less prominent in the ad execution. Thus, greater attention can be paid in the ad to supplying persuasive information and creating positive associations so that consumers have a reason as to why they should buy the brand. In other words, ad retrieval cues allow for creative freedom in the ad execution because the brand name and package do not have to take center stage. In a similar sense, lower frequency levels of ad exposure should be possible when ad retrieval cues are used because the brand name links are being reinforced or made at the point of purchase. In a very basic sense, cues get the ad "in the store" and should be more persuasive than "shelf talkers," or shopping cart ads, which almost necessarily provide less information and must contend with a potentially distracted, inattentive shopper. Finally, copy testing implications follow directly from the previous discussion. If it is assumed that consumers are making in-store decisions, then memory should be tested on the basis of the entire package, which will serve as the informational cue, and not just on the brand name.

Future Research

In a recent review, Jenkins (1979) made the following comments concerning the current state of memory research in cognitive psychology:

> The central theme, then, is that no one . . . thinks that memory is simple anymore. No one is looking for "the one rule" or "the primary rule" that will capture the important variations in memory experiments. Everyone now knows that memory

phenomena are much more complicated and contextually determined than we used to think they were. . . . Our hopes that we could "wrap this field up" in a few years of research are gone. All of the variables interact strongly with each other. . . . Even the most cursory survey of the field is sufficient to reveal that research on human learning and memory is far beyond the stage of announcing simple laws. . . . We are now trying to accept the fact that our field is context sensitive. (pp. 430–431)

Jenkins continued by asserting that memory performance in experimental settings depends on the interaction of variables in four major categories: (a) Characteristics of subjects, (b) the kinds of acquisition conditions provided (e.g., orienting tasks), (c) the nature of the material to be remembered, and (d) the criterial, or dependent, measures employed.

These statements are equally relevant when considering the role of memory in advertising effectiveness. Memory for advertising is clearly complex and a function of many factors. To isolate the memory phenomena of interest, it is often necessary to control these factors in the lab. Because these controls represent a simplification, memory research in advertising, as much as any area of consumer behavior, requires programmatic research efforts, where a series of studies are conducted. Each study must control some factors, while allowing others to vary. Only with such an approach can the richness of memory phenomena be investigated. In that spirit, this chapter described a research program that attempted to further our understanding of memory retrieval factors and advertising effectiveness. In closing, four research questions that represent the next steps in that research program are highlighted. Many other opportunities exist in the study of memory factors in advertising (see Keller 1987 for a more detailed discussion).

First, how do ad retrieval cues work when consumers have low involvement during ad exposure? During brand evaluations? Low involvement at ad exposure may result in weak brand name links because brand information is not activated. Consequently, later retrieval ability may be low. Low involvement during brand evaluations, on the other hand, may result in low retrieval motivation for ad information. Note that the three studies reported were primarily concerned with retrieval ability, in that the experimental task probably ensured that retrieval motivation was fairly high. Advertising retrieval cues could have important effects on retrieval motivation as well. That is, although consumers may have the ability to retrieve elements from the ad memory trace, an advertising retrieval cue can still motivate or encourage more extensive, deeper retrieval. For example, assuming that little retrieval effort or intensity would otherwise be forthcoming, an ad cue may elicit greater recall of the elements of the ad trace most closely linked to it (e.g., ad reactions). The motivational property of ad retrieval cues may be particularly important for low involvement decision settings where consumers may not bother to consider information in memory at all without some type of reminder. In either case, because ad retrieval cues can increase retrieval motivation and ability, they may benefit ad recall and brand evaluations in low involvement settings.

Second, how are the effects of ad retrieval cues moderated by ad repetition? Repetition may differentially influence ad retrieval cue effectiveness: To the extent that repetition leads to stronger brand name links to the ad memory trace and greater incorporation of communication effects into brand knowledge in memory, an ad cue will be less beneficial; but to the extent that repetition leads to greater elaboration of ad information (i.e., more stored communication effects) without affecting brand name links in memory, an ad cue will be more beneficial.

Third, how are the effects of ad retrieval cues moderated by brand name prominence? The point in an ad at which time the brand name first appears (e.g., at the beginning or the end of the ad) may affect processing and ad retrieval cue effectiveness. Delaying brand identification until the end of a television commercial, for example, may increase attention levels during commercial exposure and result in many communication effects stored in the ad memory trace, but also create only weak links from this trace to the brand name.

Fourth, how do retrieval cues work across ads in different media? Edell and Keller (1989) showed how the audio track from a TV ad could be used as a cue on the radio. They defined *radio replay* to occur when a consumer views a TV ad and later hears the audio track from the TV ad as a radio ad. They argued that the outcomes from radio replay depended on the relative extent of comprehension, retrieval, and elaboration processes that consumers undertake during the reinforcing radio ad exposure. They experimentally showed that when subjects heard a radio replay, they did very little critical, evaluative processing and instead appeared to be mentally replaying the TV ad video in their minds. An interesting research question is how consumers process print ads that visually and/or verbally reinforce TV ads. Print ad reinforcement may be an effective way to capture readers' attention and encourage more evaluative brand processing. In other words, initial ad processing on TV may be passive and primarily focused on the ad execution itself but later print reinforcement may cause consumers to consider more carefully the advertised brand claims and form an overall evaluation of the ad and the brand.

ACKNOWLEDGMENTS

For their comments on earlier drafts of this chapter, I thank Sheri Bridges, Meg Campbell, Bruce Clark, Itamar Simonson, Brian Wansink, Rich Yalch, and especially Andy Mitchell. Financial support for the studies reported in this chapter from the Marketing Science Institute, the Institute of Business and Economic Research at the University of California at Berkeley, and a Stanford University Graduate School of Business faculty fellowship provided through the generosity of James and Doris McNamara is greatly appreciated.

REFERENCES

Alba, J. W., & Chattopadhyay, A. (1985a). The effects of context and part-category cues on the recall of competing brands. *Journal of Marketing Research, 22,* 340–349.

Alba, J. W., & Chattopadhyay, A. (1985b). The effects of part-list cuing on attribute recall: Problem framing at the point of retrieval. In E. C. Hirschman & M. B. Holbrook (Eds.), *Advances in consumer research* (Vol. 12, pp. 410–413). Provo, UT: Association for Consumer Research.

Alba, J. W., & Chattopadhyay, A. (1986). Salience effects in brand recall. *Journal of Marketing Research, 23,* 363–369.

Alba, J. W., & Hutchinson, J. W. (1987). Dimensions of consumer expertise. *Journal of Consumer Research, 13,* 411–453.

Alba, J. W., Hutchinson, J. W., & Lynch, J. G., Jr. (1990). Memory and decision making. In H. H. Kassarjian & T. S. Robertson (Eds.), *Handbook of consumer behavior* (pp. 1–49). Englewood Cliffs, NJ: Prentice-Hall.

Anderson, J. R. (1983). *The architecture of cognition.* Cambridge, MA: Harvard University Press.

Atkinson, R. C., & Shiffrin, R. M. (1968). Human memory: A proposed system and its control processes. In K. W. Spence & J. T. Spence (Eds.), *The psychology of learning and motivation: Advances in theory and research* (Vol. 2, pp. 89–195). New York: Academic Press.

Baker, W. E., & Lutz, R. J. (1987). The relevance-accessibility model of advertising effectiveness. In S. Hecker & D. W. Stewart (Eds.), *Nonverbal communications in advertising* (pp. 59–84). Lexington, MA: Lexington Books.

Batra, R., & Ray, M. L. (1986a). Situational effects of advertising repetition: The moderating influence of motivation, ability, and opportunity to respond. *Journal of Consumer Research, 12,* 432–445.

Batra, R., & Ray, M. L. (1986b). Affective responses mediating acceptance of advertising. *Journal of Consumer Research, 13,* 234–239.

Beattie, A. E., & Mitchell, A. A. (1985). The relationship between advertising recall and persuasion: An experimental investigation. In L. F. Alwitt & A. A. Mitchell (Eds.), *Psychological processes and advertising effects: Theory, research and applications* (pp. 129–156). Hillsdale, NJ: Lawrence Erlbaum Associates.

Bettman, J. R. (1979). *An information processing theory of consumer choice.* Reading, MA: Addison-Wesley.

Bettman, J. R. (1986). Consumer psychology. *Annual Review of Psychology, 37,* 257–289.

Biehal, G., & Chakravarti, D. (1986). Consumers' use of memory and external information in choice: Macro and micro perspectives. *Journal of Consumer Research, 12,* 382–405.

Bjork, R. A. (1975). Short-term storage: The ordered output of a central processor. In F. Restle, R. M. Shiffrin, N. J. Castellan, H. R. Lindeman, & D. B. Pisoni (Eds.), *Cognitive theory* (pp. 151–171). Hillsdale, NJ: Lawrence Erlbaum Associates.

Burke, R. R., & Srull, T. K. (1988). Competitive interference and consumer memory for advertising. *Journal of Consumer Research, 15,* 55–68.

Chattopadhyay, A., & Alba, J. W. (1988). The situational importance of recall and interference in consumer decision making. *Journal of Consumer Research, 15,* 1–12.

Collins, A. M., & Loftus, E. F. (1975). A spreading activation theory of semantic processing. *Psychological Review, 82,* 407–428.

Cook, T. D., & Flay, B. R. (1978). The persistence of experimentally induced attitude change. In L. Berkovitz (Ed.), *Advances in experimental social psychology* (Vol. 11, pp. 1–57). New York, NY: Academic Press.

Craik, F. I. M. (1979). Human memory. *Annual Review of Psychology, 30,* 63–102.

Craik, F. I. M., & Lockhart, R. S. (1972). Levels of processing: A framework for memory research. *Journal of Verbal Learning and Verbal Behavior, 11,* 671–684.

Craik, F. I. M., & Tulving, E. (1975). Depth of processing and the retention of words in episodic memory. *Journal of Experimental Psychology, 104,* 268–294.

Dick, A. S., Biehal, G., & Chakravarti, D. (1990). Memory-based inferences during consumer choice. *Journal of Consumer Research, 17,* 82–93.

Edell, J. A., & Burke, M. C. (1987). The power of feelings. *Journal of Consumer Research, 14,* 421–433.

Edell, J. A., & Keller, K. L. (1989). The information processing of coordinated media campaigns. *Journal of Marketing Research, 26,* 149–163.

Eysenck, M. W., & Eysenck, M. C. (1979). Processing depth, elaboration of encoding, memory stores, and expended processing capacity. *Journal of Experimental Psychology: Human Learning and Memory, 5,* 472–484.

Feldman, J. M., & Lynch, J. G., Jr. (1988). Self-generated validity and other effects of measurement on belief, attitude, intention, and behavior. *Journal of Applied Psychology, 73,* 421–435.

Friestad, M., & Thorson, E. (1990). Memory for advertising: The effects of emotional response, encoding strategies, and retrieval cues (Working Paper). Department of Marketing, University of Oregon.

Gardiner, J. M., Craik, F. I. M., & Bleasdale, F. A. (1973). Retrieval difficulty and subsequent recall. *Memory and Cognition, 1,* 213–216.

Gardner, M. P. (1985a). Does attitude toward the ad affect brand attitude under a brand evaluation set. *Journal of Marketing Research, 22,* 192–198.

Gardner, M. P. (1985b). Mood states and consumer behavior: A critical review. *Journal of Consumer Research, 12,* 281–300.

Gardner, M. P., Mitchell, A. A., & Russo, J. E. (1985). Low involvement strategies for processing advertising. *Journal of Advertising, 14,* 4–12.

Gotz, A., & Jacoby, L. L. (1974). Encoding and retrieval processes in long-term retention. *Journal of Experimental Psychology, 102,* 291–297.

Greenwald, A. G. (1968). Cognitive learning, cognitive responses to persuasion, and attitude change. In A. G. Greenwald, T. C. Brock, & T. M. Ostrom (Eds.), *Psychological foundations of attitude* (pp. 147–170). New York: Academic Press.

Greenwald, A. G., & Leavitt, C. (1984). Audience involvement in Advertising: Four levels. *Journal of Consumer Research, 11,* 581–592.

Hannah, D. B., & Sternthal, B. (1984). Detecting and explaining the sleeper effect. *Journal of Consumer Research, 11,* 632–642.

Hasher, L., & Zacks, R. (1979). Automatic and effortful processes in memory. *Journal of Experimental Psychology: General, 108,* 356–388.

Hastie, R. (1980). Memory for behavioral information that confirms or contradicts a personality impression. In R. Hastie, T. M. Ostrom, E. B. Ebbesen, R. S. Wyer, D. Hamilton, & D. E. Carlston (Eds.), *Person memory: The cognitive basis of social perception* (pp. 155–170). Hillsdale, NJ: Lawrence Erlbaum Associates.

Hastie, R. (1982). Consumers' memory for product knowledge. In A. A. Mitchell (Ed.), *Advances in consumer research* (Vol. 9, pp. 72–73). Ann Arbor, MI: Association for Consumer Research.

Hertel, P. T. (1982). Remembering reactions and facts: The influence of subsequent information. *Journal of Experimental Psychology: Learning, Memory, and Cognition, 8*(6), 513–529.

Hoch, S. J. (1984). Availability and interference in predictive judgment. *Journal of Experimental Psychology: Learning, Memory, and Cognition, 10,* 629–662.

Horton, D. L., & Mills, C. B. (1984). Human learning and memory. *Annual Review of Psychology, 35,* 361–394.

Houston, M. J., Childers, T. L., & Heckler, S. E. (1987). Picture-word consistency and the elaborative processing of advertisements. *Journal of Marketing Research, 24,* 359–369.

Hutchinson, J. W., & Moore, D. L. (1984). Issues surrounding the examination of delay effects of advertising. In T. C. Kinnear (Ed.), *Advances in consumer research* (Vol. 11, pp. 650–655). Provo, UT: Association for Consumer Research.

Jenkins, J. J. (1979). Four points to remember: A tetrahedral model of memory experiments. In L. S. Cermak & F. I. M. Craik (Eds.), *Levels of processing in human memory* (pp. 429–445). Hillsdale, NJ: Lawrence Erlbaum Associates.

Jones, G. V. (1978). Tests of a structural theory of the memory trace. *British Journal of Psychology, 69,* 35–367.

Kardes, F. R. (1986). Effects of initial product judgments on subsequent memory-based judgments. *Journal of Consumer Research, 13,* 1–11.

Keller, K. L. (1987). Memory factors in advertising: The effect of advertising retrieval cues on brand evaluations. *Journal of Consumer Research, 14,* 316–333.

Keller, K. L. (1991a). Cue compatibility and framing in advertising. *Journal of Marketing Research, 28,* 42–57.

Keller, K. L. (1991b). Memory and evaluation effects in competitive advertising environments. *Journal of Consumer Research, 16,* 463–576.

Kisielius, J., & Sternthal, B. (1986). Examining the vividness controversy: An availability-valence interpretation. *Journal of Consumer Research, 12,* 418–431.

Kotler, P. (1988). *Marketing management: Analysis, planning, implementation, and control.* Englewood Cliffs, NJ: Prentice Hall.

Krugman, H. E. (1977). Memory without recall, exposure without perception. *Journal of Advertising Research, 12,* 7–12.

Le Voi, M. E., Ayton, P. J., Jonckheere, A. R., McClelland, A. G. R., & Rawles, R. E. (1983). Unidimensional memory traces: On the analysis of multiple cued recall. *Journal of Verbal Learning and Verbal Behavior, 22,* 560–476.

Lichtenstein, M., & Srull, T. K. (1985). Conceptual and methodological issues in examining the relationship between consumer memory and judgment. In L. F. Alwitt & A. A. Mitchell (Eds.), *Psychological processes and advertising effects: Theory, research, and applications* (pp. 113–128). Hillsdale, NJ: Lawrence Erlbaum Associates.

Lingle, J. H., & Ostrom, T. M. (1979). Retrieval selectivity in memory-based impression judgments. *Journal of Personality and Social Psychology, 37,* 180–194.

Lockhart, R. S., Craik, F. I. M., & Jacoby, L. (1976). Depth of processing, recognition, and recall. In J. Brown (Ed.), *Recall and recognition* (pp. 75–102). New York, NY: Wiley.

Lutz, K. A., & Lutz, R. J. (1977). Effects of interactive imagery on learning: Application to advertising. *Journal of Applied Psychology, 62,* 493–498.

Lutz, R. J., MacKenzie, S. B., & Belch, G. E. (1983). Attitude toward the ad as a mediator of advertising effectiveness: Determinants and consequences. In R. P. Bagozzi & A. M. Tybout (Eds.), *Advances in consumer research* (Vol. 10, pp. 532–539). Ann Arbor, MI: Association for Consumer Research.

Lynch, J. G., Jr., & Srull, T. K. (1982). Memory and attentional factors in consumer choice: Concepts and research methods. *Journal of Consumer Research, 9,* 18–36.

MacInnis, D. J., & Jaworski, B. J. (1989). Information processing from advertisements: Towards an integrative framework. *Journal of Marketing, 53,* 1–23.

MacInnis, D. J., Moorman, C., & Jaworski, B. J. (1990). Enhancing consumers' motivation, opportunity, and ability to process brand information from ads: Conceptual framework and field research agenda (Working Paper Series #7). Department of Marketing, University of Arizona.

MacKenzie, S. B., & Lutz, R. J. (1989). An empirical examination of the structural antecedents of attitude toward the ad in an advertising pretest context. *Journal of Marketing, 53,* 48–65.

Mitchell, A. A. (1981). The dimensions of advertising involvement. In J. C. Olson (Ed.), *Advances in consumer research* (Vol. 7, pp. 25–30). Ann Arbor, MI: Association for Consumer Research.

Mitchell, A. A. (1982). Models of memory: Implications for measuring knowledge structures. In K. B. Monroe (Ed.), *Advances in consumer research* (Vol. 8, pp. 25–30). Ann Arbor, MI: Association for Consumer Research.

Mitchell, A. A., & Olson, J. C. (1981). Are product attribute beliefs the only mediator of advertising effects on brand attitudes? *Journal of Marketing Research, 18*, 318–332.

Moore, D. L., Hausknecht, D., & Thamodaran, K. (1986). Time compression, response opportunity, and persuasion. *Journal of Consumer Research, 13*, 85–99.

Moore, D. L., & Hutchinson, J. W. (1985). The influence of affective reactions to advertising: Direct and indirect mechanisms of attitude change. In L. F. Alwitt & A. A. Mitchell (Eds.), *Psychological processes and advertising effects: Theory, research, and applications* (pp. 65–87). Hillsdale, NJ: Lawrence Erlbaum Associates.

Nickerson, R. S. (1984). Retrieval inhibition from part-set cueing: A persisting enigma in memory research. *Memory and Cognition, 12*, 531–552.

Ogilvie, J. C., Tulving, E., Paskowitz, S., & Jones, G. V. (1980). Three-dimensional memory traces: A model and its application to forgetting. *Journal of Verbal Learning and Verbal Behavior, 19*, 405–415.

Olson, J. C. (1978). Theories of information encoding and storage: Implications for consumer research. In A. A. Mitchell (Ed.), *The effect of information on consumer and market behavior* (pp. 49–60). Chicago, IL: American Marketing Association.

Park, C. W., & Young, S. M. (1986). Consumer response to television commercials: The impact of involvement and background music on brand attitude formation. *Journal of Marketing Research, 23*, 11–24.

Petty, R. E., & Cacioppo, J. T. (1986). *Communication and persuasion.* New York: Springer-Verlag.

Petty, R. E., Ostrom, T. M., & Brock, T. C. (Eds.). (1981). *Cognitive responses to persuasion.* Hillsdale, NJ: Lawrence Erlbaum Associates.

Postman, L., & Underwood, B. J. (1973). Critical issues in interference theory. *Memory and Cognition, 1*, 19–40.

Pratkanis, A. R., & Greenwald, A. G. (1985). A reliable sleeper effect in persuasion: Implications for opinion change theory and research. In L. F. Alwitt & A. A. Mitchell (Eds.), *Psychological processes and advertising effects: Theory, research, and applications* (pp. 157–173). Hillsdale, NJ: Lawrence Erlbaum Associates.

Raaijmakers, J. G. W., & Shiffrin, R. M. (1981). Search of associative memory. *Psychological Review, 88*, 93–134.

Ratcliff, R., & McKoon, G. (1988). A retrieval theory of priming in memory. *Psychological Review, 95*(3), 385–408.

Raye, C. L., Johnson, M. K., & Taylor, T. H. (1980). Is there something special about memory for internally generated information. *Memory and Cognition, 8*, 141–148.

Reyes, R. M., Thompson, W. C., & Bower, G. H. (1980). Judgmental biases resulting from differing availabilities of arguments. *Journal of Personality and Social Psychology, 39*, 2–12.

Roberts, D. F., & Maccoby, N. (1973). Information processing and persuasion: Counterarguing behavior. In P. Clarke (Ed.), *New models for communication research* (pp. 269–307). Beverly Hills, CA: Sage.

Roediger, H. L. (1973). Inhibition in recall from cuing with recall targets. *Journal of Verbal Learning and Verbal Behavior, 12*, 644–657.

Roediger, H. L. (1974). Inhibiting effects of recall. *Memory and Cognition, 2*, 261–269.

Rogers, T. B., Kuiper, N. A., & Kirker, W. S. (1977). Self-reference and the encoding of personal information. *Journal of Personality and Social Psychology, 35*, 677–688.

Rundus, D. (1973). Negative effects of using list items as recall cues. *Journal of Verbal Learning and Verbal Behavior, 12*, 43–50.

Schmalensee, D. (1983). Today's top priority research questions. *Journal of Advertising Research, 23*, 49–60.

Silk, A. J., & Vavra, T. G. (1974). The influence of advertising's affective qualities on consumer response. In G. D. Hughes & M. L. Ray (Eds.), *Buyer/Consumer information processing* (pp. 157–186). Chapel Hill, NC: University of North Carolina Press.

Slamecka, N. J. (1968). An examination of trace storage in free recall. *Journal of Experimental Psychology, 76,* 504–513.

Sloman, S. A., Bower, G. H., & Rohrer, D. (1991). "Congruency effects in part-list cuing inhibition," *Journal of Experimental Psychology: Learning, Memory, and Cognition, 17,* 974–982.

Srull, T. K. (1981). Person memory: Some tests of associative storage and retrieval models. *Journal of Experimental Psychology: Human Learning and Memory, 7,* 40–63.

Srull, T. K. (1987). Memory, mood, and consumer judgment. In M. Wallendorf and P. F. Anderson (Eds.), *Advances in consumer research* (Vol 14, pp. 532–539). Provo, UT: Association for Consumer Research.

Stayman, D. M., & Aaker, D. A. (1987). Are all the effects of ad-induced feelings mediated by Aad? *Journal of Consumer Research, 15*(3), 368–373.

Tulving, E. (1968). Theoretical issues in free recall. In T. R. Dixon & D. L. Horton (Eds.), *Verbal behavior and general behavior theory* (pp. 2–36). Englewood Cliffs, NJ: Prentice-Hall.

Tulving, E. (1972). Episodic and semantic memory. In E. Tulving & W. Donaldson (Eds.), *Organization of memory* (pp. 381–403). New York: Academic Press.

Tulving, E. (1983). *Elements of episodic memory.* London, England: Oxford University Press.

Tulving, E., & Pearlstone, Z. (1966). Availability versus accessibility of information in memory for words. *Journal of Verbal Learning and Verbal Behavior, 5,* 381–391.

Tulving, E., & Psotka, J. (1971). Retroactive inhibition in free recall: Inaccessibility of information available in the memory store. *Journal of Experimental Psychology, 87,* 1–8.

Tulving, E., & Thomson, D. M. (1971). Retrieval processes in recognition memory: Effects of associative context. *Journal of Experimental Psychology, 87,* 116–124.

Tulving, E., & Thomson, D. M. (1973). Encoding specificity and retrieval processes in episodic memory. *Psychological Review, 80,* 352–373.

Tulving, E., & Watkins, M. J. (1975). Structure of memory traces. *Psychological Review, 82,* 261–275.

Tyler, S. W., Hertel, P. T., McCallum, M. C., & Ellis, H. C. (1979). Cognitive effort and memory. *Journal of Experimental Psychology: Human Learning and Memory, 5,* 607–617.

Walker, D., & von Gonten, M. J. (1989). Explaining related recall outcomes: New answers from a better model. *Journal of Advertising Research, 29,* 11–21.

Watkins, M. J. (1979). Engrams as cuegrams and forgetting as cue overload: A cueing approach to the structure of memory. In C. R. Puff (Ed.), *Memory organization and structure* (pp. 317–372). New York: Academic Press.

Wright, P. L. (1973). The cognitive processes mediating acceptance of advertising. *Journal of Marketing Research, 10,* 53–62.

Wright, P. L. (1980). Message-evoked thoughts: Persuasion research using thought verbalizations. *Journal of Consumer Research, 7,* 151–175.

Wright, P. L. (1981). Cognitive responses to mass media advocacy. In R. E. Petty, T. M. Ostrom, & T. C. Brock (Eds.), *Cognitive responses in persuasion* (pp. 263–282). Hillsdale, NJ: Lawrence Erlbaum Associates.

Wyer, R. S., Jr., & Srull, T. K. (1986). Human cognition in its social context. *Psychological Review, 93,* 322–359.

Zielske, H. A. (1982). Does day-after recall penalize 'feeling' ads?. *Journal of Advertising Research, 22,* 19–22.

2 The Relevance Accessibility Model of Advertising Effectiveness

William Baker
Ericson Marketing Communications, Nashville, TN

A beer advertising executive kicks back in his chair. The new campaign is a winner. Sales for their premium beer are up. He *knows* why the campaign succeeded. It communicated the beer's superior quality. The creative director for the company's agency also *knows* why it worked. Men relate to the outdoorsy, rugged lifestyle portrayed in the campaign. They want to drink the beer because it makes a statement about "who they are." The marketing research director also *knows* why it worked. It increased top-of-mind awareness of the brand relative to its competitors. "In an undifferentiated product category," he says, "people choose the first beer that comes to mind." The academic consultant to the company also *knows* why it worked. It classically conditioned strong positive feelings to the brand. People are just naturally "drawn" to it when they see it on the shelf. Any one of these reasons are viable. Perhaps each one of them influenced some people. But which reason influenced the most people in the brand's target market?

How can advertisers be confident that they have isolated the key message factor that made their campaign successful or unsuccessful? If they guess wrong, their next campaign could flop. For decades, advertising researchers have chronicled the many ways advertising can influence consumer preferences for products and services. What is less obvious is when each of these ways advertising can work, *will* work. This latter issue is of primary importance to advertising practitioners. Cataloguing all the ways that advertising can work is only half the battle. Strategists also need to know when each of a series of potential strategies is likely to be *most* effective. Ultimately, a list of rules is needed to select the optimal message strategy out of the entire menu of available strategies for any given situation. For example, the rules must determine when the goal of advertising

49

should be to make people feel good, or when its goal need be to inform people why a brand is better than another brand by providing specific, comparative information.

The Relevance-Accessibility Model of Advertising Effectiveness (RAM) is a theory that confronts the issue of maximizing advertising message effectiveness. The RAM presumes that the primary purpose of advertising is to present information that will give a brand a "relative advantage" over competing brand alternatives at the time of brand choice. This relative advantage serves to motivate purchase behavior (see Baker & Lutz, 1987). The RAM establishes guidelines for picking the most effective advertising message strategy from a menu of strategic options. More specifically, because the ultimate measure of advertising effectiveness is brand choice, the RAM is concerned with predicting when a given message strategy is most and least likely to influence brand choice.

This chapter presents the two major assumptions or axioms upon which the RAM is built and the four propositions that transform these assumptions into a theory of advertising effectiveness. The specific "rules" or principles that the RAM offers to pick or predict the best message strategy in a given advertising scenario come from these propositions.

The RAM's first axiom states that elements of the advertising message must be accessible at the time of brand choice to be effective. The key implication of this axiom is that advertising effectiveness is not typically determined by brand attitude formation at the advertising exposure occasion, but by consumer perceptions of remembered elements of the advertising message at the time of brand choice. The second axiom states that advertising information must be relevant to be effective. Breakdowns in advertising effectiveness often occur because advertising is communicating at the wrong *level* of information. Consumer involvement with the choice process is the greatest predictor of the type of information consumers perceive to be relevant or irrelevant at the purchase occasion.

Four propositions flesh out these two axioms. Proposition 1 states that advertising effectiveness is ultimately determined at the point of brand choice. Attempts to study advertising effectiveness at or near the time of advertising exposure are likely to greatly overstate effectiveness. Proposition 2 states that consumers use three levels of information to make brand purchase decisions. These levels are relative performance information, quality cues, and pure affect (feelings). Proposition 3 states that brand response involvement determines the level of information that consumers prefer to use to make their brand choice. When brand response involvement is low, consumers react to the affect evoking qualities of brands. When involvement is moderate, consumers tend to seek quality cues to reassure themselves they are buying a "good" brand. When involvement is high, consumers are motivated to optimize their brand choice by using specific brand information that provides direct evidence of a brand's relative quality. Proposition 4 states that advertising message involvement predicts the level of information that consumers are most likely to efficiently encode at the advertising exposure occasion. Low involvement is associated with the automatic encoding of affect; moderate involvement is linked to the encoding of absolute quality cues and high involvement is characterized by the processing of detailed relative performance information.

The major implication to draw from these propositions is that advertising effectiveness is most likely to be successful when advertising messages communicate at the level of information consumers are most likely to use to discriminate brands at the purchase occasion. Given this, advertising effectiveness will be optimized when consumer advertising message involvement corresponds to brand response involvement. Only then can advertising exposure typically lead to the efficient encoding of the level of information that consumers are motivated to use to make their brand choice. Unfortunately, there are many situations when advertising message involvement is likely to be lower than brand response involvement. When this occurs, breakdowns in advertising effectiveness are likely to occur.

AXIOM 1: ADVERTISING INFORMATION MUST BE ACCESSIBLE TO BE EFFECTIVE

The RAM assumes that advertising can be effective only when the impressions it creates in a consumer's memory are retrieved (accessed) from memory when brand evaluations are made. These impressions may be visual, verbal, or emotional.

The idea that a persuasive communication's effect on evaluation is dependent on the memorability of elements of that communication, but not necessarily on attitude or judgment of that communication made at the time of exposure, is not new (Feldman & Lynch, 1987; Lichtenstein & Srull, 1985; Tversky & Kahnemann, 1973). However, a great deal of current advertising research assumes, sometimes implicitly, that advertising works by influencing brand attitudes or judgments at the time of advertising exposure, which in turn influence choice at a later time. The RAM views brand attitudes, judgments, or preferences formed at the time of advertising exposure as potential mediators of brand choice but no more or less likely to actually mediate brand choice than memory of the actual or mentally transformed advertising message content (e.g., benefit claims, spokespeople endorsements, emotion-evoking music and visuals, etc.).

This assumption is simple, but as the following brief discussion illustrates, predicting the accessibility of advertising information is a very complex issue; there are a multitude of factors to consider.

When a consumer is exposed to advertising, that advertising leaves an impression on memory. Depending on the level of attention a consumer directs at an advertisement, the memory impression it leaves may be very weak and difficult to access at a later time, or it may be very strong and simple to access (Greenwald & Leavitt, 1984). The direction of focus of a consumer's attention influences the elements of the advertising that are most likely to be retrievable. For example, all things equal, if a consumer focuses on the executional aspects of an advertisement such as background scenery or an actor, then that is what is most likely to be remembered. If, on the other hand, the consumer focuses on the message, then that is what is most likely to be remembered.

The impressions left in memory may bear little resemblance to the actual content of advertising. Consumers may misunderstand the contents of a message. For example, they may believe a message claimed that a pain reliever lasts 6 hours, when in fact the message claimed 12 hours. They also may mentally "summarize" a message. For example, while viewing television commercials, consumers may make mental abstractions such as, "my detergent doesn't get my clothes this white," "Honda really handles the curves," or "this ad is stupid." These mental summaries and evaluative reactions are more likely to leave a highly accessible impression than the literal elements of the advertising (Alba & Hasher, 1983; Carlston, 1980; Wright, 1980).

Advertising information that consumers perceive to be meaningful is more likely to be heavily attended than information that is not so perceived (Burnkrant & Sawyer, 1983). For example, advertising that conveys brand benefits that are important to consumers, depicts brand usage situations that make sense to consumers, and portrays lifestyles and living situations with which consumers can relate, is more likely to be perceived as meaningful. Because meaningful information is attended and elaborated more than nonmeaningful information, it is more likely to be accessible at a later time.

There are qualities to information that make it intrinsically more or less accessible. A picture may not always be worth a thousand words, but visual information is typically easier to encode and retrieve from memory than verbal information (see Anderson & Bower, 1980). Unique, distinctive verbal expressions are easier to remember than common expressions (see Berlyne, 1970). Highly arousing, mood-evoking information, something frightening, erotic, or beautiful, is inherently more memorable than flat, nonstimulating information (see Kroeber-Riel, 1979).

"Environmental" factors also exert a major influence on the accessibility of advertising information. Accessibility increases with repetition. If repeated enough, some types of information can be retrieved automatically without effort when a person sees a brand name or package (Bargh, 1984). Accessibility increases in the presence of memory cues (Bettman & Sujan, 1987). A brand name, a brand package, and scenes or characters from an advertisement can all cue the retrieval of other advertising information. Accessibility decreases as the delay between advertising exposure and brand evaluation increases (see Wyer & Srull, 1986). Some qualitative types of information decay in memory at a faster rate than other information (Baker, 1985; Moore & Hutchinson, 1985).

Due to the many motivational (e.g., desire to pay attention to advertising), structural (e.g., advertising copy and execution elements), and environmental (e.g., repetition and delay) factors that influence the accessibility of advertising information, it is difficult at best for any theory to reliably predict one individual's ability to access specific elements of a given advertisement. This is not the intent of the RAM. The intent of the RAM is to predict the relative accessibility of the information inherent in one type of advertising strategy versus other types of advertising strategies in a given situation across a large number of individuals. The model as presented in this chapter emphasizes motivational antecedents.

AXIOM 2: ADVERTISING INFORMATION MUST BE RELEVANT TO BE EFFECTIVE

The RAM further assumes that accessed advertising information must explicitly or implicitly be perceived by the consumer to be relevant at the time of brand choice if it is to have a direct effect on brand choice. *Explicit* recognition of relevance refers to those situations when consumers consciously and deliberately seek out specific information because they believe it to be a more reliable indicator of quality than other information. Information that is explicitly judged to be irrelevant will be discounted in favor of other more relevant information. *Implicit* recognition of relevance refers to the more subtle influences of information that is not sought out, but that can automatically drive behavior unless it is deliberately discounted, influences such as the effects of familiarity (Baker, Hutchinson, Moore, & Nedungodi, 1986) and classical conditioning (Gorn, 1982).

This assumption of relevance is completely consistent with the focus of applied marketing research and many academic models of persuasion and decision making. It is standard marketing research practice to identify the product benefits that are most and least important to consumers when they are making purchase decisions. Techniques to identify the most relevant benefits in a product category range from standard focus group and survey research methodologies to more sophisticated technologies like conjoint analysis and multidimensional scaling. Many academic models of persuasion and decision making also act on the assumption that consumer choice is a function of perceived relative brand performance on one or more product benefits (Lutz & Swasy, 1977; Lynch, Marmorstein, & Weigold, 1988).

One commonality among most applied and academic models of decision making is that they tend to look at relevance from the perspective of relative brand performance across a series of explicit product benefits or attributes. Using these approaches, for example, cars may be evaluated on the basis of styling, speed, comfort, and depreciation. Microwaves may be evaluated on the basis of cooking speed, price, and durability.

The purpose of the RAM is not to predict which of a set of specific performance or value features are most important and most relevant to consumers. The RAM examines relevance from a more general perspective. Its purpose is to predict whether specific relative performance information is likely to be used at all to make brand choices. Like the Elaboration Likelihood Model (Petty & Cacioppo, 1981) and the Percentage Contribution Model (Batra & Ray, 1985), for example, the RAM proposes that consumers base brand choices on different qualitative categories of information, each of which is perceived to be most relevant in different situations.

The RAM presumes that the perceived relevance of various types of information is determined primarily by motivational factors. However, the model also recognizes that there are a number of factors that may make it difficult or impossible for consumers to use the type of information that they may prefer to use in a situation. There are environmental factors such as the availability of the preferred information either externally (e.g., in a store) or internally (e.g., in memory), experienced based factors such as expertise (e.g., the ability to discriminate brands using the desired information), and opportunity based factors such as time (e.g., it may take too much time to choose a brand using the information a consumer would prefer to use) (see Alba & Hutchinson, 1987). A focus of this chapter is on proposing how consumer motivation at the time of brand choice influences perceived informational relevance and how this relates to the issue of maximizing advertising effectiveness.

The bulk of the remaining portion of this chapter is devoted to presenting four major propositions of the RAM. The final part of this contribution outlines the implications of these propositions for maximizing advertising effectiveness.

PROPOSITION 1: ADVERTISING EFFECTIVENESS IS DETERMINED AT THE POINT OF BRAND CHOICE

The RAM presumes that brand purchase decisions typically are not made when people are watching, reading, or listening to advertisements. Given this, the effectiveness of an advertising message strategy must be judged at the brand response occasion (i.e., the point of brand choice), not the advertising exposure occasion (i.e., the point of advertising exposure). Usually, these two occasions are separated by time and space. Typically, advertising message exposure occurs in the home or car, whereas brand choice decisions occur at the point of purchase, usually a store.

Two implications follow directly. First, any persuasive effects of advertising at the advertising exposure occasion may no longer be accessible at the brand response occasion. Second, advertising information that is perceived as relevant at the advertising exposure occasion may not be so perceived at the brand response occasion.

Memory Decay

Any theory of advertising effectiveness that does not consider the effects of the decay of advertising information in memory is likely to overstate the impact of advertising because it exaggerates the memorability of advertising. Consumers are exposed to hundreds of advertisements daily. Their ability to remember advertising information over time is limited. As the time between advertising message exposure and brand choice increases, the ability to remember advertising information deteriorates rapidly (Sawyer & Ward, 1979).

Similarly, any theory of advertising effectiveness that does not consider the memorability of advertising relative to other sources of information at the brand response occasion is likely to overstate the impact of advertising effects on brand choice at the brand response occasion. Advertising does not operate in a vacuum. Consumers can base their brand choice decisions on many sources of information other than advertising such as prior brand usage experiences, package information, and point-of-purchase display information. Advertising must compete with these other sources of information at the brand response occasion. If advertising effectiveness is judged at the time of advertising exposure, then it is likely to be exaggerated because it is being given a contrived advantage over these other sources of information.

Because consumers often make purchase decisions quickly with little deliberate mental effort (Krugman, 1965; Ray et al., 1973), in many choice situations easy to remember, "top-of-mind" information is more likely to be used to make a brand choice than less accessible, more difficult to retrieve information, even if this more difficult to retrieve information is of equal or greater relevance (Feldman & Lynch, 1987; Hoch, 1984; Wyer & Srull, 1986). As the time between the advertising exposure occasion and the brand response occasion increases, the amount of effort it takes to remember and use advertising information relative to other sources of information increases (see Anderson, 1983). So, even if advertising information is not forgotten, if it takes considerable effort to remember it, other more readily accessible information is likely to take its place at the brand response occasion.

Consider an example. Assume that a shampoo advertisement imparts a relative advantage for the shampoo over its competitors, perhaps by a discussion of a critical control ingredient, a professional endorsement of the product, or other aspects of the advertisement. If choice took place at that moment, the consumers it persuaded would choose it.

However, over time, the memory of the commercial will fade considerably. After 2 weeks, many of the consumers originally persuaded may no longer associate any claims in the advertisement to the brand. In this scenario, the advertisement can no longer influence choice unless the consumers made a mental note at the time of advertising exposure to buy the brand, and remembered it (Carlston, 1980; Lingle & Ostrom, 1979). Some consumers may be able to remember the message with considerable effort, but may not be willing to make that effort at the store. In this case, even if the consumers intend to choose a brand that gives extra control, or that is endorsed by professionals, the advertisement is unlikely to influence choice because other information that is more easily accessed such as package information or usage experience memories will be used.

Changes in Informational Relevance

The "pool" of easily accessible information from which to draw to make brand choice decisions is likely to change significantly from the advertising exposure occasion to the brand response occasion because the two environments are very different. At the advertising exposure occasion for a given brand, advertising information for this brand is likely to dominate the pool of easily accessible information because it is an environment where other sources of information are at an extreme disadvantage. There are no packages or point-of-purchase displays that can provide information about competing brands and remind people of prior usage experiences. Advertising information for competing brands is less accessible because advertisements for these brands were not just seen, read, or heard.

Given this, advertising information is more likely to be perceived to be relevant at the advertising exposure occasion than at the brand response occasion. There is less information with which it must compete. There is less information that can render the advertising information irrelevant to the choice decision for consumers. Any theory of advertising effectiveness that does not consider the potential that the perceived relevance of advertising information may be artificially inflated at the advertising exposure occasion because other potentially more relevant information to the consumer is absent or less accessible, is likely to overstate the impact of advertising messages on brand choice.

Consider the shampoo advertisement example again. At the advertising exposure occasion, consumers may report very high purchase intentions for the shampoo because the information on the critical control ingredient or the professional endorser seem relevant and, hence, motivates them to want the brand. At the brand response occasion, however, new information may make this information less relevant and, hence, no longer motivating. They may learn that the shampoo costs twice as much as other brands or has a scent they strongly dislike. They may notice other shampoos that they know through experience provide excellent control, or recall that other brands have control ingredients just as effective as the other advertised brand; or out of the biased context of the advertising exposure occasion, they may remember an advertisement for another brand that is endorsed by someone whose opinion they respect more than the endorser for the other advertisement.

Figure 2.1 summarizes the potential range of change in the potency of advertising effects between the advertising exposure occasion and the brand response

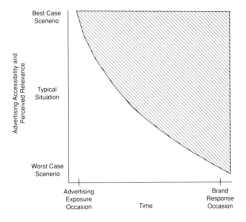

FIG. 2.1. Advertising effects are likely to be most extreme (positive or negative) at the advertising exposure occasion where information accessibility and perceived relevance are likely to be maximized. Over time, accessibility and relevance are expected to decline.

occasion. The shaded area represents the proportion of advertising effects, positive or negative, that remain accessible and relevant to the consumer at the brand response occasion. The top of the figure represents a best case scenario where advertising accessibility and relevance hardly decays between the two occasions. The middle of the graph represents what the RAM would expect to be a more typical situation in which some significant decay in the accessibility and/or perceived relevance of advertising information is expected. The bottom of the graph represents a worst case scenario where there is little or no advertising information accessibility or perceived relevance remaining at the brand response occasion. The goal of advertisers is, of course, to maximize the potential of the best case scenario and minimize the potential of the worst case scenario.

Summary

The RAM proposes that any theory whose purpose it is to predict the effectiveness of advertising on choice behavior must evaluate advertising effectiveness in the context of the brand response occasion, not the advertising exposure occasion. Both the accessibility and the relevance of advertising information are likely to be overstated in the context of the advertising exposure occasion, which means the impact of advertising on brand choice decisions is likely to be overstated. Depending on the evaluation of the advertising message, the impact may he overstated positively (i.e., advertising motivates acceptance of the brand) or negatively (i.e., advertising motivates rejection of the brand).

The accessibility of advertising information is biased in the context of the advertising exposure occasion because its natural tendency to decay in memory between the time of advertising exposure and brand choice is not considered. Also, through the process of output interference, the high accessibility of brand advertising information at the advertising exposure occasion inhibits the ability of consumers to retrieve other information (Alba & Chattopadhyay, 1985).

The relevance of advertising information is overstated in the context of the advertising exposure occasion because other potentially more relevant sources of information that are typically present or highly accessible at the time of brand choice are not so at the advertising exposure occasion.

PROPOSITION 2: CONSUMERS USE THREE LEVELS OF INFORMATION TO MAKE BRAND PURCHASE DECISIONS

The RAM proposes that advertising influences brand choice through the effects of three general levels of information: relative brand performance information, brand quality cues, and pure affect (feelings).

Relative Brand Performance Information. This is the most detailed, most direct information that is available about a brand. It provides explicit, specific "apples to apples" comparisons among competing brands to identify the best of a set of brands. For example, a consumer may decide to compare cars on the basis of performance features such as gas mileage and acceleration, or on the basis of image features such as styling and color before making a purchase decision.

Much of the persuasion research in the 1960s (see Fishbein, 1967) and the 1970s (see Lutz & Swasy, 1977) operated on the assumption that consumers explicitly compare brand alternatives across multiple relevant utilitarian and/or hedonic benefits. Brand choice was expected to be the outcome of a series of complex tradeoffs among brand alternatives. The brand with the greatest relative advantage across all product benefits was expected to be chosen. Other approaches assumed that consumers make explicit comparisons between brand alternatives, but only across the most important benefit they provide, or only until a brand emerged as a clear winner on one key benefit (see Bettman, 1979). The common thread through many of these popular models of persuasion and advertising response is they viewed the consumer as a "rational man," as an information-processing machine similar to a computer. The input to this information-processing machine was assumed to be specific performance information that allows direct comparisons to be made across brands.

Brand Quality Cues. These cues provide descriptive, but indirect information that can be used to make inferences about a brand's quality, but they contain no definitive evidence of a brand's performance relative to other brands. For example, rather than take the time and expend the effort to compare cars on specific features, an individual may take a short cut and buy a car because it is a top seller, produced by a manufacturer that stands for quality or status or luxury, or simply because it possesses one or more attributes that are symbolic of quality (e.g., the door "thuds" when slammed, front wheel drive, fuel-injected engine). Although the reliability of many quality cues may be unshakeable, one might say they provide no more than "circumstantial evidence" of relative quality and performance.

Almost everybody can personally relate to making brand selections using quality cues rather than more specific performance information. The specific persuasive effects of commonly used quality cues such as brand name prestige (Wheatley, Walton, & Chiu, 1982), price (Monroe, 1973), expert endorsement (Sternthal & Dholakia, & Leavitt, 1978), and the sheer number of brand benefits (Alba, 1987) are intuitively obvious and have been demonstrated empirically. Theoretical models predict their usage when consumers do not have the motivation, ability, or opportunity to use more specific information (Chaiken, 1980; Petty & Cacioppo, 1981).

Pure Affect.   This level refers to "free-floating" feelings and emotional responses that are consciously unlinked to any specific brand attributes, benefits, and past promotional (e.g., advertising) or usage experiences, at least at the time of brand choice. Such affect provides no real evidence of either absolute or relative product quality, but consumers may interpret it as such. When individuals make decisions based on pure affect, they are reacting solely to a feeling, not on the information that led to that feeling.

Positive feelings intrinsically motivate approach behavior, negative feelings motivate avoidance behavior (Skinner, 1972; Zajonc, 1980). These naturally reinforcing properties of affect can influence brand choice. The sources of accessed affect may be brand name familiarity (Harrison, 1977), the classical conditioning of affect-evoking stimuli like music or beautiful visuals to a brand through advertising (Gorn, 1982), the affective residue from past usage experiences, or a combination of these and other affective experiences that have come to be associated to a brand over time (Kisielius & Sternthal, 1984).

In the economists' world of the "rational man" making decisions with perfect information, consumers would always use relative performance information to make their brand choices because it is the most reliable, most direct brand information available. Most marketing academics and practitioners agree that this does not happen. In fact, everybody, but economists agree that this does not happen. Even a lot of economists agree that this does not happen.

It is certainly not "irrational" for consumers to make purchase decisions with less than perfect information. We live in an era where brands competing in many product categories are so equal that few, if any, substantive differences exist between them. When product innovations do occur, they are copied quickly. In such product categories many consumers belief that it is a waste of their time to compare brands on the basis of specific performance features. When consumers perceive they do not need specific information to make a brand choice, the motivation to take the time and energy to meticulously compare brand alternatives is low (Burnkrant & Sawyer, 1983; Robertson, 1976).

Another implication of the similarity among brand offerings is that consumers may attempt but fail to find differences among brand alternatives on specific features. For example, consumers may compare two sports cars across several performance features and conclude they are equal. When this happens, they may have no recourse but to use other types of information such as brand quality cues or simple affective reactions to discriminate brands. In the end, one sports car may be chosen over the other because it is from a more prestigious manufacturer (i.e., a brand quality cue), or perhaps more simply because, for some reason unknown to the consumer at the time of choice, he or she is "drawn" to one car over the other (i.e., a purely affective response).

In product classes where real differences do exist, the differences are sometimes difficult to observe. Some consumers do not have the ability to compare brands on specific information, others have the ability but do not have the time to make these comparisons. Many consumers would like to compare automobiles on the basis of specific engine performance features, but do not have the ability. If grocery shoppers took the time to specifically compare every brand alternative on the shelf before making every purchase, they would never get out of the store. In both cases, circumstances force them to make decisions on the basis of other types of information.

Table 2.1 summarizes the type of evidence each level provides about a brand's quality or performance. It also provides examples of each. Relative performance

TABLE 2.1
The Levels of Information Approach

Level of Information	Evidence Provided	Examples
Relative performance information	Direct evidence of relative quality or performance on one or more product attributes	34 miles per gallon 0 to 60 in 7.1 sec Pain relief that lasts twice as long as any other brand
Quality cues	Indirect evidence of absolute or relative quality or performance	The leading seller for 20 years Two out of three doctors recommend Good Housekeeping Seal of Approval
Affect	No tangible evidence of quality or performance	Facilitation of the exposure effect through repeated brand name and package exposure Heartwarming scenes of family togetherness

information provides direct, concrete evidence of a brand's performance that may be used to make explicit interbrand comparisons. For example, the knowledge that an analgesic delivers pain relief twice as long as any other leading brand, permits a consumer to make a reliable relative performance judgment about the brand in question. Quality cues provide only indirect evidence of a brand's quality or performance. Relative performance judgments cannot be made from the information; the information is more reassuring than reliable. For example, the knowledge that an analgesic is recommended by two out of three doctors implies that the brand is good, but it is not concrete evidence of relative superiority. Affect provides no tangible evidence of quality or performance, it simply makes consumers feel comfortable with a brand. This comfort can be imparted to the brand, for example, through repeated exposure to the brand name or by associating the brand name to affect-evoking situations.

An Extended Example

The potential influence of all three levels of information on brand choice can be illustrated through the following example. Imagine the following TV commercial for a brand of shampoo. A young, alluring woman brushes her long beautiful hair in a luxurious penthouse suite filled with classical music. The woman explains that her shampoo has made her hair thick and manageable. A graphic demonstrates that the shampoo contains more of a critical control ingredient than other shampoos. An announcer states that the shampoo is preferred by professional hairdressers three to one over the leading shampoo. As the commercial ends, a handsome young gentleman arrives at the penthouse.

All three types of information are included in this commercial. The commercial may be persuasive for many different reasons. Some motivated viewers may form specific relative performance beliefs about the shampoo and use them at the point of purchase to choose the brand. For example, the graphics display may persuade them that the shampoo provides more control than other brands, or the theme of the commercial may persuade them that using this shampoo will improve their social life more than other shampoos.

Other viewers may be persuaded on the basis of the brand quality cues it communicates. One brand quality cue is the credibility of the woman. Viewers may believe that a beautiful woman with beautiful hair is a credible source whose recommendations should be considered. Another brand quality cue is the fact that 75% of surveyed professional hairdressers prefer the shampoo. Many viewers may find this to be reassuring evidence that the shampoo is of high quality.

Finally, some viewers may not remember any specific information from the commercial, but may be persuaded by the affective "residue" generated by the beauty, atmosphere, and music in the commercial. The beautiful woman, luxurious penthouse, sensuous music, and handsome man may have combined to associate a very strong, positive feeling to the brand that influences brand choice when they see the brand on the shelf in the supermarket.

A Brand Loyalty Caveat

The RAM operates under the assumption that consumers do not have strongly formed preferences for a brand at the time of choice. In these cases, prior preferences are likely to override the usage of raw information (i.e., relative performance beliefs, quality cues, and affect) and be the primary determinant of purchase behavior. Situations where prior preferences are expected to dominate brand choice are not expected to be common for the following reasons. First, consumer durables (e.g., automobiles, major appliances) are modified frequently, but purchased infrequently. Due to the changes in brand characteristics and the potential presence of new brands, prior preferences become "obsolete" (Biehal & Chakravarti, 1986). Second, there are so few differences between many consumer nondurables (e.g., packaged foods, household cleaners, etc.) that there is little or no basis on which to form strong preferences (see Lastovicka & Bonfield, 1982). The ability of couponing, rebates, and other discounting strategies to constantly "switch" consumers from brand to brand in these product categories indicates the absence of strong performance-based preferences.

Summary

A central proposition of the RAM is that consumers can discriminate brands by using three types of information—relative performance information, quality cues, and pure affect. The key implication of this proposition is that advertising strategists need to know which type of information their consumer target market is most likely to use when making purchase decisions in a given product category. In any given product category, advertising strategists need to know if their target is most likely to deliberately compare brand alternatives across performance dimensions, employ brand quality cues, or rely on simple affective reactions to base their brand choice decision.

The information type that is most likely to be used by the targeted consumers for a given brand in a given product category needs to be emphasized in advertising messages for that product category. If most targeted consumers for a given brand of shampoo buy shampoos on the basis of simple affective reactions, then the goal of advertising should be to associate positive feelings to the brand. Communicating relative performance information is a waste of advertising copy if that type of information is not expected to be used by consumers at the point of purchase and is only likely to inhibit advertising effectiveness. Conversely, if targeted consumers buy shampoos on the basis of relative performance information, then the commercial should stress information capable of persuading consumers that the brand is superior on one or performance dimensions and de-emphasize elements of the ad that generate only positive feelings.

PROPOSITION 3: BRAND RESPONSE INVOLVEMENT DETERMINES CONSUMERS' PREFERRED LEVEL OF INFORMATION

Brand Response Involvement

Simply put, *involvement* refers to the intensity of mental effort (Cohen, 1982). *Brand response involvement* (BRI) is the degree of mental effort expended by the consumer while making a brand choice. When BRI is high, consumers are motivated to think intently about their brand choice; they are motivated to ex-plicitly search for information and compare brand alternatives. At the other extreme, when BRI is very low, consumers are not motivated to think about their brand choice; they have little desire to either seek information or to compare brand alternatives.

Two major antecedents of brand response involvement are perceived product differentiation and perceived product risk (Kapferer & Laurent, 1985; Robertson, 1976). Perceived product differentiation refers to the degree consumers believe there are performance differences between the brand alternatives in a product category. As perceived product differentiation increases, the probability of mak-ing a "nonoptimal" brand choice increases. For this reason, increased differ-entiation is expected to lead to increased brand response involvement. For exam-ple, if a consumer believes there are performance differences between the brands of shampoo on a supermarket shelf, he or she is more likely to spend time seeking information and considering the brand alternatives than if he or she believes that all shampoos are the same.

Perceived product risk refers to the probability that a nonoptimal brand choice has negative consequences. The consequences may be economic, perhaps the loss of thousands of dollars that result from choosing the wrong automobile. They may be social, perhaps the peer ridicule that results from buying the wrong style of clothing. Or, they may be utilitarian, perhaps from buying a microwave that is missing a useful feature such as automatic cooking programs.

Perceived high product differentiation does not necessarily lead to high per-ceived product risk. In other words, there may be a perceived high probability of making a nonoptimal choice, but no serious consequences of such a choice, no serious economic, social, or utilitarian injury. For example, some consumers may perceive there are many differences between shampoos' color, smell, con-trol, price, and so forth, but they may also believe that a less than ideal choice will lead to little consequence because even the worst shampoo alternative will perform adequately. In this case, perceived high product differentiation is not expected to lead to the highest level of BRI.

Also, high perceived product risk is not necessarily caused by high product differentiation. Some product categories trigger high product risk because of their social, utilitarian, and/or economic magnitude. However, brands within these product categories may not be significantly differentiated. People, for example, may believe there are very serious consequences associated with a "wrong" choice in a product category, but may also believe there is little chance of a "wrong" choice because most brand alternatives in their consideration set are very similar. Choosing the wrong pain reliever may have very serious utilitarian consequences, but people are not likely to meticulously choose a pain reliever unless they believe there are real performance differences between the alternatives in their consideration set. Perceived high product risk is not expected to lead to the highest level of brand response involvement unless it is also associated with high perceived product differentiation.

BRI Influences How People Make Brand Choice Decisions

Brand response involvement is a cornerstone of the RAM because it is presumed that as BRI changes, different levels of information are sought by consumers at the brand response occasion, and others are avoided or ignored. The RAM proposes that BRI is the primary determinant of the level of information that consumers seek to make brand choices. What follows is a discussion of three levels of BRI and how the RAM predicts they correspond to the three levels of information described in Proposition 2.

High BRI Leads to "Optimization."   The highest level of BRI is most likely to occur when consumers perceive both high product differentiation and high product risk. That is, they believe there are major differences between brand alternatives and they believe a nonoptimal brand choice will have serious negative consequences. This situation motivates them to want to optimize their brand choice; they want to make the best decision possible and are willing to expend the mental effort required to make the best choice.

Optimization is characterized by consumers choosing what they believe to be the best of a considered set of brands. Assuming consumers have the ability and opportunity to explicitly compare brand alternatives, it makes sense that if consumers wish to optimize their brand choice they will seek the most specific information available that permits direct "apples to apples" comparisons between brand alternatives. When consumers are highly involved in the purchase decision, the RAM presumes they will seek the highest level of information (relative performance information) to make their brand choice. Optimizing consumers are willing to spend the time and effort to read package information, recall brand information from memory, talk to salespeople, read *Consumer Reports,* and so on.

Highly differentiated product categories with considerable economic, social, and utilitarian risk to many consumers are likely to include automobiles, homes, durable appliances, and clothing. Purchase decisions made to support hobby (coins, stamps, etc.) and sporting interests (skiing, tennis, golf, etc.) are also likely to be made in a state of high BRI.

Within a given product category, consumers may be motivated to optimize for different reasons. Referring to the shampoo example, some consumers may be highly involved because they want to buy the shampoo with the best control, others may want the shampoo that is least likely to sting their eyes, others may want the best-smelling shampoo. Whatever the cause, a person that is optimizing his or her shampoo brand choice will explicitly compare shampoo alternatives on the specific performance dimensions that he or she believes to be important.

Much of the consumer persuasion and decision-making literature in the 1960s and 1970s explicitly or implicitly assumed that consumers optimize purchase decisions. The plethora of multiattribute expectancy value models experimented with during this period cast consumers as sophisticated decision makers calculating complex tradeoffs across brand alternatives on several utilitarian and/or social attributes (Ryan & Bonfield, 1975; Toy, 1982). These approaches lost popularity as "all purpose" models of decision making as the concept of involvement-driven decision strategies grew in popularity (Ray et al., 1973) and because empirical tests have demonstrated that much simpler predictors of behavior often perform as well as compensatory models (Kraft & Granbois, 1973).

However, advertising research in consumer involvement has found that consumers do tend to use more specific performance or product-related advertising message information when consumer involvement is high. Such research supports the idea that consumers do not always optimize, but they are most likely to attempt to optimize when they are in a state of high involvement. That is, consumers are most likely to evaluate brands on the basis of specific product-related information when consumer involvement is high (see MacKenzie, Lutz, & Belch, 1986; Ray et al., 1973; Robertson, 1976; Wright, 1980).

Moderate BRI Leads to "Satisficing."   When consumers perceive significant product differentiation, but little product risk, or perceive significant product risk, but little product differentiation, BRI is likely to be moderate.

In the first case, consumers perceive a high probability, but no serious negative consequences of an nonoptimal brand choice. For example, a man may believe that microwaves vary in how quickly they cook food, but he may also believe all microwaves cook food fast enough for his purposes. Or, a woman may believe that some conditioners leave hair more manageable than others, but she may also believe the three or four brands in her consideration set all leave her hair sufficiently manageable. Assuming that the man is buying a microwave primarily to cook food fast and the woman is buying the conditioner primarily to leave her hair manageable, there is no real reason for the man or the woman to optimize their brand choices. Both do not perceive any serious consequences of a nonoptimal purchase. As a result, the marginal effort required to optimize is not worth the marginal gain in product performance.

In the second case, consumers perceive serious consequences of a wrong choice, but little chance that a wrong chance will be made. For example, the purchase of a sports car has very high social risk to a young man who wants to improve his image among his peers. However, the three cars that remain in his consideration may all be very popular among his peers. Or, a woman buying a mink coat perceives serious economic consequences if she buys the "wrong" mink coat simply because they cost thousands of dollars. However, the three coats she has to choose from all cost about the same. Assuming that in both examples there are no other major perceived differences across the alternatives on risky dimensions, there is no reason for the man or the woman to optimize his or her brand choice. Again, the marginal effort required to optimize is not worth the marginal gain in performance.

When consumers believe there is no benefit to be gained from putting extreme mental energy into their purchase decision, BRI is likely to be moderate and optimization is not likely to occur. However, due to the high perceived risk or high perceived differentiation associated with the purchase, consumers need to feel comfortable that they are making a satisfactory brand choice. In this scenario, consumers are expected to seek information to reassure themselves that they are making a good selection.

When BRI is low, the RAM presumes that people make satisficing brand decisions. Satisficing is characterized by consumers selecting the first acceptable brand, not necessarily the best of a considered set of brands. The RAM expects that people will typically use quality cues to select a brand when they are satisficing. Quality cues include a prior satisfactory usage experience, a credible spokesperson's endorsement, a friend's recommendation, the knowledge that a brand is a top seller or the professional image generated by high quality advertising. The knowledge that a brand possesses a key desired ingredient (e.g., aceteminophen, no salt, no sugar), or feature (e.g., automatic cooking programs, self-cleaning, permanent press, etc.), or that a brand is linked to a particular lifestyle (e.g., BMWs and "yuppies") or usage situation (e.g., Michelob and "the night") can also be quality cues. Whatever the quality cue, it must provide quick reassurance or reinforcement that the brand is good and that the brand is a satisfactory choice.

Different individuals are likely to use different quality cues to determine acceptability. In the case of shampoo, some consumers may buy a brand name that they trust, others may take the advice of a spokesperson, others may buy the most expensive brand, and others may take the first brand they see that has a special ingredient or performance claim they desire.

Whatever the case, a satisficing brand decision typically takes significantly less time and effort to make than an optimizing brand decision, primarily because multiple brands are not explicitly compared across one or more performance features. Consumers are not motivated to thoroughly search through their memory or the purchase environment to find quality cues. They are "cognitive misers" and do not want to expend much mental effort to make their choice (Wyer & Srull, 1986). Consumers are likely to choose the first acceptable brand that comes to mind. This means that brands linked with easy to remember quality cues are more likely to be chosen than brands whose quality cues are less accessible. When a consumer target market is expected to be satisficing, then, marketers must not only associate persuasive quality cues to their brand, they must make their quality cues more memorable than other brands' quality cues (see Hoch, 1984; Wright & Rip, 1980).

The link between the use of quality cue type information and lower levels of involvement is well established in both the advertising and social psychology literature. Experiments involving the Elaboration Likelihood Model and similar approaches have repeatedly shown that people less involved with an issue will tend to use peripheral cues such as the credibility of a spokesperson to evaluate an issue rather than specific message arguments (Chaiken, 1980; Petty & Cacioppo, 1981). Other research has shown that consumers less involved with advertising tend to evaluate products on the basis of the appeal of the advertising execution rather than the product related message arguments (Baker, 1985; MacKenzie, Lutz, & Belch, 1986).

Very Low BRI Leads to "Indifference."   When BRI is very low, buyers perceive little or no product differentiation and little or no product risk. There is a low perceived probability of a "wrong" brand choice and trivial consequences if a wrong brand choice is made.

If there are no serious perceived economic, social, or utilitarian risks in a product category and no perceived performance differences between brand alternatives in the product category, there is little reason for a consumer to expend any significant deliberate mental effort when making the brand choice. It is as if there are no real choices, no real alternatives from which to choose.

In this situation, consumers are expected to be "indifferent." Indifferent purchase decisions are characterized by consumers selecting the first brand that comes to mind. If there are multiple salient brand alternatives as in a supermarket shopping situation, indifference purchase decisions are characterized by consumers selecting the brand in the set with which they feel most comfortable. Indifferent decisions are expected to typically be driven by simple affective reactions toward brands that come to mind effortlessly at the time of brand choice.

For example, if a woman believes there are no differences among shampoos and no serious negative consequences associated with the choice of a "nonoptimal" brand of shampoo, then her purchase choice is likely to be influenced by simple affective reactions. Few, if any, deliberate brand comparisons are evaluation of quality cues accompany the decision process. While scanning a shelf of brand alternatives, she is likely to pick the shampoo that makes her feel most comfortable, the shampoo that evokes the most positive emotional reaction. These feelings may be created by the look of the package, by the familiarity of the brand name or by images that advertising has associated to the brand. She does not deliberately bring these feelings to mind, they automatically come to mind when she sees the brand.

When BRI is very low, decisions are made as quickly as possible. As a result, factors like shelf position, point-of-purchase (POP) displays and package designs are predicted to have their strongest influence on purchase.

The RAM predicts that the free-floating affect that drives purchase decisions when involvement is very low can result from effects of affective classical conditioning (Gorn, 1982) and the exposure effect (Zajonc, 1980). Other research predicts that these types of effects are most likely to influence brand choice when consumer involvement in the purchase process is at its lowest level (Krober-Riehl, 1979, 1984; Nord & Peter, 1980; Obermiller, 1985).

Table 2.2 summarizes the defining characteristics of optimizing, satisficing, and indifferent consumer behavior. These characteristics include consumer choice goals, information level sought, the extent of information search, and the

TABLE 2.2
Characteristics of Optimizing, Satisficing, and Indifference

Issue	Optimizing	Satisficing	Indifference
Brand response involvement	High	Low moderate	Very low
Consumer choice goal	Buy the best of a considered set of brands	Buy the first acceptable brand	Buy any brand
Information level sought	Relative performance	Quality cues	Affect
Extent of search	Sufficient to explicitly compare brands across performance dimensions	Sufficient to reassure self that brand is satisfactory	No deliberate information search
Decision process	Compensatory or multiple stage noncompensatory strategy	Simple inference drawn from quality cue	Recognition of liking
Appropriate advertising strategy	Credibly persuade consumers of brand superiority on one or more key performance dimensions	Link brand with a quality cue more accessible to consumers than other brands' quality cues	Facilitate automatic recognition and affect retrieval upon brand exposure

decision process. The advertising strategy the RAM expects will most likely influence consumers employing each of these behavioral "routes" is also listed.

Summary

Three types of purchase behavior have been identified and linked to BRI: optimizing, satisficing, and indifference. Each type of purchase behavior corresponds to a different decision-making process. Each decision-making process is associated with a different level of information: relative performance information, quality cues, and affective reactions.

The advertising implications are straightforward. For any given product category, strategists need to identify the expected level of BRI of their consumer target market and produce advertising that communicates that level of information. When consumers optimize, present relative performance information about key product benefits. When consumers satisfice, present memorable, credible quality cues. When consumers are indifferent, build package and brand awareness and link positive feelings to the brand.

In the case of shampoo, if consumers are expected to optimize, then an advertisement presenting specific performance information that allows direct comparisons with other brands has the best chance of directly influencing brand choice. If consumers are satisficing, then an advertisement that uses a credible quality cue such as a famous model is most likely to be effective. If consumers are making "indifferent" decisions, then an advertisement that builds brand name familiarity and associates good feelings to the brand is most likely to be effective.

If advertising is produced that is not communicating the "correct" level of information, then the RAM predicts that the impact of advertising at the point of purchase will suffer. If shampoo purchasers are optimizing at the point of brand choice and advertising presents simple quality cue type information, or if shampoo purchasers are operating indifferently and advertising presents relative performance information, then advertising is less likely to be effective because the advertising is communicating an inappropriate level of information; it is communicating information that is not likely to be used at the time purchase decisions are made.

PROPOSITION 4: ADVERTISING MESSAGE INVOLVEMENT PREDICTS THE LEVEL OF INFORMATION LEARNED

Advertising Message Involvement

Advertising messages that communicate the "correct" level of information, the level of information consumers are expected to use at the brand response occasion, are not necessarily effective. Simply because an advertisement contains relative performance information, for example, does not mean that a consumer exposed to the advertisement will remember that information or the implications of that information at the time of brand purchase.

One reason a consumer may not remember the relative performance information in an advertising message is because the message may not have been "processed" in a manner that could lead to the efficient "storage" of the relative performance information in memory. For example, simply because an automobile commercial contains the results of a braking test among three cars does not mean that those results will be remembered by a consumer exposed to the advertisement. The consumer may not have paid sufficient attention to the relative performance information to store it in memory in a manner that would make it readily "accessible" when he or she is in the process of purchasing a car. Generally, consumers must mentally rehearse and perhaps simplify complex information in order to remember its meaning at a later time (see Alba & Hutchinson, 1987).

The RAM predicts that consumer motivation to attend, comprehend, and integrate advertising message information into memory at the time of advertising exposure is a primary determinant of the level of information that consumers will "take away" from the advertisement had been likely to remember at the time brand decisions are made (Greenwald & Leavitt, 1984).

Advertising message involvement (AMI) refers to consumer motivation to attend, comprehend, and integrate advertising message information into memory at the time of advertising exposure. As AMI increases, the cognitive effort expended by the consumer to process the contents of an advertising message increases (Gardner, Mitchell, & Russo, 1985).

AMI Antecedents

There are many factors that are likely to influence a consumer's AMI level. Advertisers are not helpless. There are tactics they can employ to increase consumers' motivation to attend to advertising. One critical factor is information meaningfulness (Burnkrant & Sawyer, 1983). If advertisers are going to include specific performance information in advertising, then it needs to be information about benefits that are most important to consumers. If the message is going to include quality cues, then it needs to discuss quality cues that people perceive to be reliable predictors of quality. If the message goal is to make people feel good, then the visual (e.g., people, situations, scenery) and audio (e.g., music) tactics used to create positive emotions must be ones that are most likely to touch chords among the advertiser's customer target market.

Advertisers can also employ certain executional tactics to increase AMI. Unique, vivid visuals, sounds and dialogue are more likely to capture and hold attention than common ordinary executions (Berlyne, 1970; Reyes, Thompson, & Bower, 1980). And executions that are emotionally intense are more likely to grab attention than emotionally flat executions (Silk & Vavra, 1974).

Despite these tactics, there are several factors that influence AMI that are at least partially out of the control of advertisers. As a result, advertisers cannot necessarily influence the AMI level at which an advertisement will be processed. This has strong implications for advertising effectiveness. Four relatively uncontrollable antecedents of AMI include (a) anticipated brand response involvement, (b) the extent to which the consumer perceives a need for additional information before making purchases in the product category, (c) the consumer's interest in the advertised product category, and (d) consumer distraction at the time of advertising message exposure.

If consumers typically behave "indifferently" at the point of purchase because they do not perceive any differentiation or risk associated with purchases in that product class, then there is no logical reason why those people would bother deliberately attending to quality cue or relative performance type advertising information in that product category. Unless an advertiser can somehow increase a consumer's belief that there are differences between brands or that there is social, utilitarian, or economic risk associated with purchases in the product category, it is likely to be very difficult to get people to attend to and learn information at a higher level than what they expect to use when they make their brand choice. Take the shampoo example. People that do not believe there are any differences between shampoos may enjoy looking at the beautiful actress in the advertisement and they may listen to the background music, but they are less likely to pay much attention to the specific message information. People that do believe there are differences, people that do associate risk with purchases in the product category are more likely to focus their attention on the message.

Many people may be likely to make their brand choices in a product category by either "optimizing" or "satisficing," but they still may not be likely to expend much energy attending to specific performance or quality cue type information in advertising if they do not believe they need additional information before they make their brand choice (Burnkrant & Sawyer, 1983). Some people may believe they have learned all the information they need to make a brand choice through their prior experience with using brands in the product category. Other people may simply believe that they do not need advertising information before they make their brand choice, perhaps because they find it to be less credible than other information (Smith & Swinyard, 1983). These people may believe they will need information before they make their choice, but that they can get it at the point of purchase through package information, salesmen, or some means other than advertising. Unless advertisers unleash messages that convince the former group that they do need additional information or convince the latter group that they are giving them valuable information that they cannot get elsewhere, these people are not likely to deliberately attend and learn advertising message information.

Another factor that may prevent people who are likely to optimize or satisfice at the time of brand choice from learning relevant information in advertising is lack of interest in the product category. Although interest in any given product category changes from one individual to the next, some product categories tend to be inherently interesting to people, others are not. Interest alone can influence the degree of attention paid to advertising (Kapferer & Laurent, 1985). Automobile, home electronics, and clothing advertisers benefit from the high interest many people have in their categories. This high interest increases the likelihood that people will pay attention to their advertising. Battery, paper towel, and condiment advertisers are likely to be hurt by the intrinsically low interest many people have in their product categories. These advertisers must work harder to develop creative executions to draw consumers' attention toward their advertising messages.

Finally, distractions at the time of advertising message exposure can direct consumers' attention away from advertising. People do not watch television or listen to the radio in isolation. Commercial time can also be conversation time, reading time, snack time, and so on.

Figure 2.2 summarizes why AMI is likely to be lower than BRI, particularly when BRI is high. In the best case scenario, AMI and BRI correspond because consumers' need for information, product class interest, and the perceived meaningfulness of advertising message content are all high, and there no competing goals at the time of advertising exposure. When this occurs, advertising has a higher likelihood of succeeding because information relevant to the brand choice is likely to be learned at the advertising exposure occasion. In the worst case scenario, all four antecedents serve to lower AMI relative to BRI. When this occurs, advertising is less likely to be effective because information relevant to the brand choice is not likely to be learned. When these antecedents suggest that AMI will be lower than BRI, advertisers must either lift AMI through the use of unique, compelling executional tactics, or consider marketing tactics other than advertising.

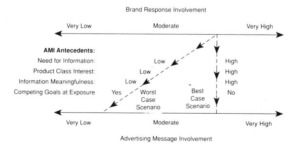

FIG. 2.2. The antecedents of advertising message involvement other than brand response involvement create a strong potential that advertising message involvement will be *lower* than brand response involvement.

AMI Effects

The RAM predicts that AMI is a primary determinant of the level of information that consumers most effectively encode in memory at the time of advertising message exposure and, hence, remember at the time brand purchase decisions are made.

High AMI. High product class interest, high expected BRI and a strong perceived need for information are all expected to contribute to high AMI. When AMI is high, consumers are expected to focus their attention on AMI that facilitates the specific comparison of the brand relative to its competitors. Message information relating to specific product attributes and benefits is likely to be attended. Lower level information is likely to be used to judge the credibility of the specific performance information, but not to directly evaluate the brand. Consumers are expected to process the advertisement in a manner that will allow the formation of relative performance beliefs either at the time of advertising exposure or at the time of brand choice (e.g., better feature, better product).

If consumers believe that no information in the advertising message is pertinent to the formation of relative performance beliefs, then consumer attention to the message is likely to "switch off" (Greenwald & Leavitt, 1984), or worse, consumers may have a strong negative reaction that may transfer to the brand (Petty & Cacioppo, 1981). Think about a commercial for a sports car. The RAM predicts that highly involved consumers will focus their attention on those aspects of the advertising message that will help them to form specific performance beliefs about the car. If a consumer is most concerned with the social implications of car ownership, then he or she will seek out information in the advertisement that will help gauge the social status of this sports car relative to others. If the consumer is most concerned with the utilitarian aspects of sports car ownership, he or she will seek out message information on, for example, the relative acceleration or handling of this car versus other sports cars. If the advertisement has no information that can be used to form relative performance beliefs, then the person is likely to either withdraw his or her attention from the ad, or worse, become frustrated and react negatively to the ad, and perhaps the car. The advertisements for Nissan's Infiniti that did not show the automobile are likely to have frustrated many people.

Moderate AMI. Lower product interest, expected BRI, and/or perceived need for information are expected to contribute to moderate AMI. When AMI is low, consumers are likely to be motivated to comprehend the advertising message, but not to analyze and integrate the implications of specific message claims with other brand-related or competitive information in memory (Krugman, 1965). Consumers are not expected to seek out specific relative performance information or expend the cognitive effort to transform message information into relative performance beliefs. Instead they are more likely to attend to quality cue type information and make absolute mental judgments or summaries about the ad (e.g., good ad, good spokesperson), the brand's benefits (e.g., the brand has this feature, this feature is good), and the product in general (e.g., good brand). They are not expected to make relative judgments about the advertisement (e.g., better ad, better spokesperson) or the brand (e.g., better brand, better feature) because they are not expected to deliberately relate or integrate brand information in the advertisement with information about other brands (see Alba & Hasher, 1983; Fiske, 1982).

Recall the shampoo example. The RAM asserts that consumers exhibiting a low level of AMI are most likely to attend to quality cues. They are neither motivated to learn "details" about the brand because they are not interested in such information nor do they expect to ever use it. It is easier to draw a quick evaluative inference from this type of information than it is from more specific performance information. Assume that Jacqueline Bissett is the actress in the ad. Both Jacqueline Bissett's credibility and the hairdresser's endorsement are easily understood and have direct evaluative implications. If a consumer wants to get a "quick read" of the brand from the advertising message, it makes more sense to attend to the quality cues.

Quality cue type information is also more likely to be remembered than specific attribute claims when one is not motivated to deeply process and integrate the contents of an advertisement into memory because simple, novel information is easier to remember than complex, common information (Alba & Hutchinson, 1987). Quality cue information is often more novel than specific performance information. Many shampoos have hair control ingredients, but only one brand can be endorsed by Jaqueline Bissett. Consider product classes that debate ceaselessly about who has the most of a given benefit, for example, the amount of pain reliever in aspirin, the fiber content of cereals, the acceleration rate of sports cars. It is difficult even for a motivated consumer to remember each brand's specific claims on these common benefits. The barrage of claims interfere with each other in memory and make it difficult for consumers to learn and access it (Hoch, 1984; Keller, 1987). It is easier to remember the general themes of advertisements in these product classes than it is to remember the values of the debated benefits (e.g., the milligrams of pain relief offered by Bayer, Excedrin, Tylenol, etc.) because the themes are generally more novel, more arousing and, hence, easier to efficiently encode into brand memory than the factual content (Anderson & Bower, 1980).

Very Low AMI.   Very low product interest, anticipated BRI, and/or little or no perceived need for brand information are likely to lead to very low AMI. Strong distractions at the time of advertising exposure can also lead to very low AMI even if these other conditions are not present. The RAM presumes that when AMI is very low, there is no motivation to attend to brand information in the advertising message. Consumers are not expected to expend any mental effort to comprehend the message nor are they expected to intentionally generate any absolute or relative mental summaries or judgments of the brand or any of its benefits.

Consumer attention to any executional themes is expected to be purely a function of their novelty and affective qualities. As a result, the only type of brand information that is likely to be remembered is simple affective reactions to executional elements of the advertising that became effortlessly associated to the brand name through repeated exposure (Bargh, 1984; Zajonc, 1980).

Consumers exhibiting very low AMI while watching the shampoo commercial are not expected to attend deliberately to any message elements. As a result, memory for specific claims, whether they be quality cues or relative performance information is expected to be poor. If, however, viewers found the music, luxurious setting, or the model's beauty highly arousing, or if they were constantly exposed to be brand name, it is possible that positive feelings could become linked to the brand automatically. Consumers may not be able to explain accurately the reason(s) why their perceptions became more positive.

Summary

The RAM proposes that consumer AMI is a strong predictor of the level of information that is most likely to be attended, comprehended, and integrated into brand memory at the time of advertising message exposure and, hence, accessible to the consumer at the brand response occasion.

When AMI is high, consumers prefer to attend to relative performance type information. As a result, it is the level of information that is likely to be most accessible at the brand response occasion. When AMI is low, quality cue type information is most likely to be attended and efficiently encoded into memory at the advertising exposure occasion and thus, be more accessible at the brand response occasion. And, when AMI is very low, inherently interesting executional elements of advertising are all that is likely to be attended at the advertising exposure occasion and, as a result, remembered at the time of brand choice.

The major implication of the effects of AMI is that advertising effectiveness cannot be completely controlled by advertisers. An advertising message may contain the correct level of information, information that is more relevant than anything the consumer could find at the point of purchase, information that the consumer would seek at the point of purchase; but if the consumer is not attending and integrating this information into memory at the time of advertising message exposure, the advertisement is not likely to influence brand choice because the "correct" level of information is not likely to be efficiently stored into memory.

Well-designed advertisements can fail because AMI and BRI have different antecedents. Two of AMI's "uncontrollable" antecedents—product category interest and the perceived need for information—create the potential that AMI will be different, usually lower, than BRI. When this happens, advertising is less likely to be effective because the "correct" level of information is less likely to be attended to and stored into memory at the advertising exposure occasion. For example, a consumer may use a satisficing strategy at the point of purchase, but due to a low perceived need for information and/or low product category interest, that consumer may have not paid sufficient attention to a well-designed ad containing reliable quality cues when he or she was exposed to it. As a result, the ad is ineffective. Other information will drive the brand choice decision at the point of purchase.

ADVERTISING EFFECTIVENESS

Four Prerequisites to Effective Advertising

The RAM identifies four necessary and mutually sufficient conditions that advertising must meet to have the highest probability of directly influencing brand choice.

The first condition is *information availability*. Before advertising can have any opportunity to influence brand choice, it must leave an imprint on consumer memory (Kisielius & Sternthal, 1984). Advertisements must be presented at times and in places where consumers will be exposed to their contents. Advertisements must also affect consumer attention in a way that the message, not just the execution, will be attended, comprehended, and stored into memory. If a consumer is not exposed to an advertisement, or if a consumer is exposed to an advertisement but neither attends or comprehends the message, then advertising has next to no chance of being effective.

The second condition is *level relevance*. Advertising effects are level relevant if there is a one-to-one correspondence between the level of information sought by the consumer to discriminate brand alternatives at the POP (i.e., pure affect, quality cues, or relative performance information) and the level of information encoded into memory at the time of advertising exposure. If, for example, consumers are seeking quality cues at the POP and quality cues were encoded into memory at the time of advertising exposure, then advertising effects are level relevant. If, on the other hand, consumers are making brand selections on the basis of relative performance information, but encoded advertising effects are limited to simple affective information, then advertising is not level relevant.

Two requirements must be met to maximize the likelihood that advertising effects in memory will be level relevant. First, advertisements need to be designed to emphasize the "correct" level of information as determined by expected consumer BRI. Second, consumer AMI needs to correspond to BRI.

Using the shampoo commercial example, if an advertisers' consumer target market is expected to satisfice at the time of brand choice, then advertising effects are most likely to be level relevant if the shampoo advertising emphasizes quality cues rather than pure affective information or specific performance information. The quality cue information may be an expert endorsement or survey research evidence that three out of four hairdressers recommend its critical control ingredient. Level relevance will be maximized if this commercial is processed at the middle level of AMI. At this level of involvement, consumers are expected to be most likely to attend to the quality cue type information in a manner that it will be accessible at the brand response occasion.

The third condition is *relative accessibility*. Relative accessibility refers to the probability that level relevant advertising effects will be accessed at the time of brand choice. Level relevant advertising effects may be available in memory, but the amount of effort required to retrieve them relative to other sources of information such as past usage experiences or package information can inhibit their retrieval at the POP.

The relative accessibility of level relevant information is a direct function of how easily that information can be retrieved at the POP relative to other accessible level relevant information such as package information or past usage experiences. Relative accessibility is influenced both by nonmotivational (e.g., message design factors, repetition, package or POP tie-ins) and motivational (e.g., consumer effort to attend, comprehend, and integrate the advertising message into memory) factors.

The Relative Accessibility of Advertising Information Becomes Increasingly Important as Brand Response Involvement Decreases.   As BRI decreases, consumers are expected to expend less effort to search their memories for relevant information. When BRI is high, consumers are motivated to deliberately search for relevant information regarding every brand in their consideration set. When BRI is low, consumers are only expected to search until they access a quality cue that allows them to confidently select a brand. When BRI is very low, consumers are not expected to deliberately try to recall any information from memory. According to the RAM, then, relative accessibility is a more critical issue to advertisers promoting brands to consumers that are not involved in the purchase process.

The third condition is *relative relevance*. Assuming that an advertising effect in memory is level relevant, its relative relevance is its perceived ability to better, more reliably discriminate brand alternatives than other level relevant information such as package information, salesperson advice, usage experience memories, and so on. Within each of the three levels of information, the RAM supposes that consumers encode, access, and use information they perceive to be most reliable and to avoid and discount implications of less important information.

The Relative Relevance of Advertising Information Becomes Less Important as Brand Response Involvement Decreases. Optimizing consumers are expected to take the effort to locate and use the information they believe to be the most reliable discriminator of brand alternatives; relative relevance is important. Satisficing consumers seek only a reliable brand discriminator, not necessarily the best discriminator; relative relevance is less important. Indifferent consumers do not deliberately seek or use any information to base brand choice, relative relevance is not considered.

Maximizing Advertising Effectiveness

Within the context of the RAM, several steps can be taken to meet the conditions just outlined. The first two steps are unique to the RAM, but are also consistent with much of the consumer involvement literature. The next three steps are not unique to the RAM but are cast within the context of the RAM's major propositions.

Step 1. Advertising strategists need to correctly predict the BRI of the targeted consumers. This knowledge will reveal which level of information needs to be emphasized in advertising. Brand response involvement can be predicted by studying its primary antecedents, particularly perceived product risk and product differentiation. For example, in the case of paper towels, if strategists learn that their target consumers perceive little or no substantive differences between brand alternatives and no serious negative consequences associated with a nonoptimal purchase, then they can conclude that BRI is very low.

Step 2. Advertising messages must communicate level relevant information. If BRI is expected to be high, then the advertising message should communicate relative performance information. If it is expected to be very low, then it should build brand and package awareness and effectively associate pure affect to the brand. For example, if the consumer target for a new sports car is expected to be in a state of high BRI during the automobile purchase process, then to impact directly on brand choice, advertising needs to contain information on factors such as acceleration, braking, handling, styling, comfort, status, and so on, relative to other sports car alternatives. If the consumer target for paper towels is expected to be in a state of very low BRI during the purchase process, then to impact directly on brand choice, advertising need only increase brand name and package familiarity and associate good feelings to the brand.

Step 3. Advertising messages must communicate relatively relevant information. Once the level of information the target market is expected to use to make the brand choice is identified, research is needed to identify the best quality cue, the most important performance benefit, and/or the most arousing, compelling execution to associate affect to the brand. In the case of the sports car, if BRI is expected to be high, then research needs to determine which performance dimension is the most important to communicate through advertising.

Step 4. The advertising message must be designed to maximize its relative accessibility to the consumer target market. Tactics that strategists can use to improve relative accessibility include communicating the message in a novel and arousing manner, repeating the message throughout the advertisement, communicating the message through multiple sensual modes (words, sounds and pictures), focusing consumer attention on the message, not the execution, and heavy repetition schedules.

Maximizing the relative accessibility of advertising information is not something that advertisers can control completely. Advertisers can influence it by designing relevant advertising messages with compelling executions, but they cannot control consumer AMI at the time of advertising exposure.

The Principle of Optimal Advertising Contribution

The RAM presumes that advertising effectiveness is most likely to be maximized when Steps 1–4 just listed are accomplished and consumer AMI corresponds to consumer BRI. When consumer AMI and BRI correspond, advertising has the best chance of being effective because the level of information that is sought by the consumer at the time of brand choice is most likely to correspond to the most accessible advertising effects in memory.

For example, if a consumer's BRI is moderate when selecting a shampoo, then the RAM predicts that the person is most likely to seek a quality cue to select a brand at the POP (e.g., top-selling brand name). If the consumer also experienced moderate AMI when exposed to the shampoo commercial, then the persuasive effect of the quality cues presented in the advertisement are most likely to be highly accessible at the brand response occasion (e.g., spokesperson credibility). When both AMI and BRI are moderate, quality cues are most likely to be sought at the brand response occasion and the effects of quality cues in the advertising message are most likely to be highly accessible at the brand response occasion.

If, on the other hand, the consumer experienced very low AMI when exposed to the advertisement, then the advertisement is expected to have a significantly lower chance to influence consumer choice because the quality cue information in the message is expected to be less accessible at the point of purchase. The consumer is not expected to have deliberately attended to the quality cue infor-

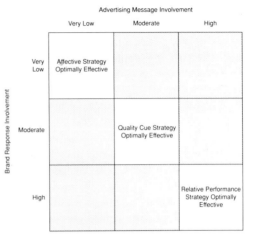

FIG. 2.3. The Principle of Optimal Advertising Contribution states that advertising has the highest probability of success when the informational focus of advertising corresponds to the level of information consumers are most likely to seek at the brand response occasion and encode at the advertising exposure occasion.

mation in the advertising. The advertising effect that is more likely to be accessible in this situation, free-floating affect, is expected to be perceived as less relevant to the consumer. Rather than base a choice on advertising information in this situation, the consumer is expected to use a quality cue from some other information source.

Figure 2.3 summarizes the implications of the Principle of Optimal Advertising Contribution for advertising message strategy. When AMI and BRI are both expected to be very low, an advertising strategy that efficiently links affect to the brand is predicted to be optimally effective. When both types of involvement are moderate, an advertising strategy that effectively communicates a quality cue is expected to be optimally effective; and when both AMI and BRI are high, an advertising strategy that credibly presents relative performance evidence is likely to be optimally effective. In each of these three scenarios, the stated strategy is expected to be most effective because the level of information consumers are expected to use to make their choice at the brand response occasion corresponds to the level of information that is most likely to be efficiently encoded into memory at the time of advertising exposure. This type of match between information sought and information encoded is less likely in all those cells where AMI and BRI do not correspond.

AN EMPIRICAL TEST OF THE PRINCIPLE OF OPTIMAL ADVERTISING CONTRIBUTION

An experiment was conducted at the University of Florida to test some of the basic implications of the RAM. The experiment tested three hypotheses relating to the four propositions of the model and the Principal of Optimal Advertising Contribution.

Hypothesis 1:   Both AMI and BRI directly influence the effect of advertising on brand choice.

If correct, the major implication of Hypothesis 1 is that theoretical perspectives that study advertising effectiveness from the point of view of the advertising exposure occasion or the brand response occasion, but not both, are incomplete.

Hypothesis 2:   When AMI and BRI correspond, the advertising message contents most likely to mediate brand choice is the one that focuses on the level of information typically associated with that degree of involvement.

Hypothesis 2 tested one dimension of the Principle of Optimal Advertising Contribution. As shown in Fig. 2.3, it predicts, for example, that when both AMI and BRI are very low, an advertising strategy focusing on associating affect to a brand will be more effective than a strategy emphasizing quality cue or relative performance information.

Hypothesis 3:   Message content that focuses on one of the three levels of information is more likely to mediate choice when both AMI and BRI correspond to that level of information than when only AMI or BRI or neither corresponds to that level of information.

Hypothesis 3 tests the other dimension of the Principle of Optimal Advertising Contribution. Looking at Fig. 2.3, it predicts, for example, that an advertising strategy employing relative performance information will be more effective when both AMI and BRI are high then when only one or the other is high, and especially when neither is high. When AMI or BRI, but not both are high, than there is more likely to be a breakdown in either the accessibility of relative performance information (low or moderate AMI) or the perceived relevance of relative performance information (low or moderate BRI). When both AMI and BRI are not high, then there is even more likelihood of a breakdown in both the accessibility and perceived relevance of relative performance information, lowering further the probability it will be used to discriminate brands.

Experimental Design and Methodology

The experiment was conducted at the University of Florida. The subjects were 258 introductory marketing students. A 3×3 between-subjects design manipulating AMI and BRI was employed.

Subjects were told that the primary purpose of the study was to evaluate an old-time radio show, the "Lone Ranger," that was being considered for programming on a local radio station. They were also told that potential sponsors were also interested in reactions to the program's advertising. The AMI manipulation was embedded in these instructions. The experimental stimuli were three radio ads for three different brands of motor oil. One advertisement contained superior relative performance information (i.e., better fuel economy, longer engine life), one contained superior quality cue type information (i.e., A. J. Foyt endorsement), and one contained superior affect producing information (i.e., Beach Boys musical theme). During the course of the show, each ad was repeated three times. Advertisements for three clothing stores were also included and repeated twice each during the program. Three brand names, Purity, Easyride, and Austin were counterbalanced across each message type. The order of presentation of each message type was also counterbalanced. After the presentation, subjects completed a memory test related to the AMI and were excused. Subjects returned after a 1-day delay. At this time, they answered several questions related to the experimental pretense. Afterward, the BRI manipulation was applied. Questions pertaining to the experimental hypotheses followed.

The AMI manipulation was applied immediately prior to the presentation of the "Lone Ranger" episode. Advertising message involvement was varied by manipulating subjects' attentional focus at the show and/or the advertisements and their need for information. In the high AMI condition, participants were told that a free-recall test immediately after the presentation would test their memory of the motor oil and clothing store advertising information presented during the show; participants scoring 90% or better would be rewarded $5. In the moderate AMI condition, participants were told that a recognition test of both advertising and "Lone Ranger" episode content would follow the presentation; participants scoring 80% of higher would earn $1. In the low AMI condition, participants were told that a free-recall test about the "Lone Ranger" episode, but not advertising, would follow the presentation; participants scoring 90% or higher would be rewarded $5. All advertising-related memory test questions dealt with the clothing store advertisements. This prevented a test-caused learning effect of motor oil advertising content.

Brand response involvement was manipulated by varying the consequences of an unsatisfactory motor oil brand choice. In the high BRI condition, participants were rewarded $5 if they could accurately identify the "highest quality motor oil" from the three brands advertised during the show. In the moderate BRI condition, participants were told two of the three advertised motor oils were high quality. They were given $1 if they could avoid choosing the lower quality motor oil and correctly answer two other questions about the clothing store advertising. In the low BRI condition, participants saw a list of brands in 12 product categories. They were asked to choose a brand that they "liked" from each category. Motor oil was one of the 12 categories. In each condition, participants had 1 minute to perform the assigned task.

Prior to the experiment, a series of pretests were conducted. One pretest was performed to select three brand names with relatively equivalent credibility, familiarity, valence, and quality associations. Purity, Easyride, and Austin were chosen. Pretests were run to identify a song about cars that evoked strong positive affect ("409" by the Beach Boys was selected.), to select the race car driver with the highest name recognition and credibility (A. J. Foyt was selected), and to uncover important performance benefits associated with motor oil (better fuel economy and longer engine life were selected). Finally, a pretest was conducted to confirm that every advertising message was the superior performer at its designated level of information. The affective ad evoked more positive feelings than any other ad; the quality cue ad was rated to have the most credible spokesperson, and the relative performance information ad was rated to have the most cogent arguments.

The dependent variable used to test each of three hypotheses was motor oil brand choice, more specifically, the advertising appeal associated to the chosen motor oil brand. Experimental results were analyzed using chi-square and logit analyses. Other measures included involvement manipulation checks, motor oil brand preference, and advertising recall.

Experimental Results

Both the AMI and BRI manipulations were successful. Advertising message involvement was measured primarily by a number of factor-analyzed semantic differentials that loaded on a single dimension that may be called *attentional intensity*. The BRI semantic differential battery loaded on a single dimension that was labeled *decision-process intensity*. Significant differences emerged between each level of AMI and BRI.

Hypothesis 1 was strongly supported. There were strong, significant main effects of AMI and BRI on message strategy effectiveness as measured by brand choice. Given the strong main effects of both AMI and BRI, the proposition that advertising effectiveness is affected at both the advertising exposure occasion and the brand response occasion was supported. The implication is that models of advertising effectiveness must not limit themselves to either the advertising exposure occasion or the brand response occasion; consumer behavior activity at each occasion must be modeled.

Hypotheses 2 was also supported. Each advertising message type was most effective in its respective involvement correspondence cell. The "indifferent" appeal was significantly more effective than either the quality cue or relative performance information appeal when both AMI and BRI were very low. The satisficing appeal was significantly more effective than either other appeal in the moderate involvement correspondence cell and the optimizing appeal was the significantly more effective in the high involvement correspondence cell.

Finally, Hypothesis 3 was supported. Each advertising message appeal was also significantly more effective in its respective correspondence cell than in those cells where there was limited (one type of involvement corresponded to appeal) or no involvement correspondence (neither type of involvement corresponded to appeal). For example, the optimizing appeal was significantly more effective in the high involvement correspondence cell than in those cells where either AMI or BRI, but not both were high, and in those cells where neither AMI or BRI were high.

The Principle of Optimal Advertising Contribution was supported. The experimental results are consistent with the notion that to be maximally effective, (a) advertising must communicate at the level of information consumers prefer to use at the brand response occasion as determined by BRI and (b) AMI and BRI must correspond.

Summary

The RAM of advertising effectiveness has several key implications for the planning and implementation of advertising strategy. First, it stresses the importance for advertisers to understand more "global" aspects of consumer decision making, not just tactical methodologies such as benefit segmentation. In order to develop a sound advertising strategy, advertisers must first be able to ascertain what level of information consumers are likely to be using when they make purchase decisions. Second, it asserts that advertisers need to focus on BRI as the critical input to determine whether to pursue an affective, quality cue, or attribute-based advertising strategy.

By studying the antecedents of AMI and BRI, the RAM offers a means to predict those situations when advertising is most and least likely to be able to directly influence brand choice. In situations where AMI and BRI can be expected to be relatively equal, advertising has the greatest opportunity to directly impact on choice. In those situations when AMI is expected to be less than BRI, advertising has less opportunity to directly influence brand choice. Effective advertising in this latter situation requires more expert manipulation of the controllable antecedents of AMI (e.g., highly relevant message content and unique, arousing executional elements). In this situation it may be prudent to "downgrade" advertising's role to influence consideration rather than choice. It may be best advised for other elements of the marketing mix such as packaging, POP, sales promotion, distribution intensity, and shelf-space dominance to take greater priority than advertising.

REFERENCES

Alba, J. W., & Chattopadhyay, A. (1985). The effects of context and part-category cues on the recall of competing brands. *Journal of Marketing Research, 22,* 340–349.

Alba, J. W., & Hasher, L. (1983). Is memory schematic? *Psychological Bulletin, 93,* 203–231.

Alba, J. W., & Hutchinson, J. W. (1987). Dimensions of consumer expertise. *Journal of Consumer Research, 14,* 1–27.

Alba, J. W., & Marmorstein, H. (1987). The effect of frequency knowledge on consumer decision-making. *Journal of Consumer Research, 14,* 14–25.

Anderson, J. R. (1983). A spreading activation theory of memory. *Journal of Verbal Learning and Verbal Behavior, 22,* 261–295.

Anderson, J., & Bower, G. (1980). *Human associative memory.* Hillsdale, NJ: Lawrence Erlbaum Associates.

Anderson, J. R., & Reder, L. M. (1979). An elaborative processing explanation of depth of processing. In L. S. Cermak & F. I. M. Craig (Eds.), *Levels of processing in human memory* (pp. 224–241). Hillsdale, NJ: Lawrence Erlbaum Associates.

Baker, W. E. (1985). *Advertising generated brand evaluation: A memory based information processing perspective.* Unpublished master's thesis, University of Florida, Gainesville.

Baker, W. E., & Lutz, R. J. (1987). The relevance-accessibility model of advertising effectiveness. In S. Hecker & D. W. Stewart (Eds.), *Nonverbal communication in advertising* (pp. 59–84). Lexington, MA: Lexington Books.

Baker, W. J., Hutchinson, J. W., Moore, D., & Nedungadi, P. (1986). Brand familiarity and advertising: Effects on the evoked set and brand preference. In R. J. Lutz (Ed.), *Advances in consumer research* (pp. 637–42). Provo, UT: Association for Consumer Research.

Bargh, J. A. (1984). Automatic and conscious processing of social information. In R. M. Sorrentino & E. T. Higgins (Eds.), *Handbook of cognition and social learning* (pp. 1–43). New York: Guilford Press.

Batra, R., & Ray, M. (1985). How advertising works at contact. In L. F. Alwitt & A. A. Mitchell (Eds.), *Psychological processes and advertising effects: Theory, research, and application* (pp. 13–43). Hillsdale, NJ: Lawrence Erlbaum Associates.

Berlyn, D. E. (1970). Novelty, complexity, and hedonic value. *Perception and Psychophysics, 8,* 279–285.

Bettman, J. R. (1979). *An information processing theory of consumer choice.* Reading, MA: Addison-Wesley.

Bettman, J. R., & Sujan, M. (1987). Effects of framing on evaluation of comparable and noncomparable alternatives by expert and novice consumers. *Journal of Consumer Research, 14,* 141–154.

Biehal, G., & Chakravarti, D. (1986). Consumers' use of memory and external information in choice: Macro and micro perspectives. *Journal of Consumer Research, 12,* 383–405.

Burnkrant, R. E., & Sawyer, A. G. (1983). Effects of involvement and message content on information processing intensity. In R. J. Harris (Ed.), *Information processing research in advertising.* Hillsdale, NJ: Lawrence Erlbaum Associates.

Carlston, D. E. (1980). Events, inferences, and impression formation. In R. Hastie, T. M. Ostrom, E. B. Ebbesen, R. S. Wyer, D. L. Hamilton, & D. E. Carlston (Eds.), *Person memory: The cognitive basis of social perception* (pp. 89–119). Hillsdale, NJ: Lawrence Erlbaum Associates.

Chaiken, S. (1980). Heuristic versus systematic information processing and the use of source versus message cues in persuasion. *Journal of Personality and Social Psychology, 39,* 752–766.

Cohen, J. B. (1982). *Involvement: Separating the state from its causes and effects* (Working Paper #33). University of Florida.

Feldman, J. M., & Lynch, J. G., Jr. (1987). Self-generated validity and other effects of measurement on belief, attitude, intention and behavior. *Journal of Applied Psychology, 73,* 421–35.

Fishbein, M. (1967). A consideration of beliefs, and their role in attitude measurement. In M. Fishbein (Ed.), *Readings in attitude theory and museum.* New York: Wiley.

Fiske, S. (1982). Schema-triggered affect: Applications to social perception. In M. S. Clark & S. T. Fiske (Eds.), *Affect and cognition.* Hillsdale, NJ: Lawrence Erlbaum Associates.

Gardner, M. P. (1985). Mood states and consumer behavior: A critical review. *Journal of Consumer Research, 12,* 281–300.

Gardner, M. P., Mitchell, A. A., & Russo, J. E. (1985). Low involvement strategies for processing advertising. *Journal of Advertising, 14,* 4–12.

Gorn, G. J. (1982). The effects of music in advertising on choice behavior: A classical conditioning approach. *Journal of Marketing, 46,* 94–101.

Greenwald, A. G., & Leavitt, C. (1984). Audience involvement in advertising, four levels. *Journal of Consumer Research, 9,* 132–40.

Harrison, A. A. (1977). Mere exposure. In L. Berkowitz (Ed.), *Advances in experimental social psychology.* New York: Academic Press.

Hoch, S. J. (1984). Availability and interference in predictive judgment. *Journal of Experimental Psychology: Learning, Memory, and Cognition, 10,* 649–662.

Kapferer, J-N., & Laurent, G. (1985). Consumer involvement profiles: A new practical approach to consumer involvement. *Journal of Advertising Research, 25,* 48–55.

Keller, K. L. (1987). Memory factors in advertising: The effect of advertising retrieval cues on brand evaluation. *Journal of Consumer Research, 14,* 316–333.

Kisielius, J., & Sternthal, B. (1984). Detecting and explaining vividness effects in attitudinal judgments. *Journal of Marketing Research, 21,* 54–64.

Kraft, F. B., Granbois, D. H., & Summers, J. O. (1973). Brand evaluation and brand choice: A longitudinal study. *Journal of Marketing Research, 10,* 235–41.

Kroeber-Riel, W. (1979). Activation research: Psychological approaches in consumer research. *Journal of Consumer Research, 5,* 240–250.

Kroeber-Riel, W. (1984). Emotional product differentiation by classical conditioning. In M. E. Holbrook & B. Hirschman (Eds.), *Advances in consumer research* (Vol. 11, pp. 538–543). Ann Arbor, MI: Association for Consumer Research.

Krugman, H. E. (1965). The impact of television advertising: Learning without involvement. *Public Opinion Quarterly, 29,* 349–356.

Lastovicka, J. L., & Bonfield, E. H. (1982). Do consumers have brand attitudes? *Journal of Economics Psychology, 2,* 57–75.

Lichtenstein, M., & Srull, T. K. (1985). Conceptual and methodological issues in examining the relationship between consumer memory and judgment. In L. F. Alwitt & A. A. Mitchell (Eds.), *Psychological processes and advertising effects: Theory, research and application* (pp. 113-128). Hillsdale, NJ: Lawrence Erlbaum Associates.

Lingle, J. H., & Ostrom, T. M. (1979). Retrieval selectivity in memory-based impression judgments. *Journal of Personality and Social Psychology, 37,* 180–194.

Lutz, R. J., & Swasy, J. L. (1977). Integrating cognitive structure and cognitive response approaches to monitoring communication effects. In W. D. Perrault (Ed.), *Advances in consumer research* (Vol. 4, pp. 363–371). Atlanta, GA: Association for Consumer Research.

Lynch, J. G., Jr., Marmorstein, H., & Weigold, M. (1988). Choices from sets including remembered brands: Use of recalled attributes and prior overall evaluations. *Journal of Consumer Research, 15,* 34–42.

MacKenzie, S. B., Lutz, R. J., & Belch, G. E. (1986). The role of attitude toward the ad as a mediator of advertising effectiveness: A test of competing explanations. *Journal of Marketing Research, 23,* 130–143.

Monroe, K. (1973). Buyers' subjective perception of price. *Journal of Marketing Research, 10,* 70–80.

Moore, D. L., & Hutchinson, J. W. (1985). The influence of affective reactions to advertising: Direct and indirect mechanisms of attitude change. In L. Alwitt & A. A. Mitchell (Eds.), *Psychological processes and advertising effects: Theory, research, and application.* Hillsdale, NJ: Lawrence Erlbaum Associates.

Nord, W. R., & Peter, J. P. (1980). A behavior modification perspective on marketing. *Journal of Marketing, 44,* 36–47.

Obermiller, C. (1985). Varieties of mere exposure: The effects of processing style and repetition on affective response. *Journal of Consumer Research, 12,* 17–30.

Petty, R. E., & Cacioppo, J. T. (1981). *Attitudes and persuasion: Classic and contemporary approaches.* Dubuque, IA: Brown.

Ray, M. L., Sawyer, A. G., Rothschild, M. L., Roger, M., & Reed, J. B. (1973). Marketing communications and the hierarchy of effects. In *New models for mass communications research* (pp. 117–136). Beverly Hills, CA: Sage.

Reyes, R. M., Thompson, W. C., & Bower, G. H. (1980). Judgmental biases resulting from differing availabilities of arguments. *Journal of Personality and Social Psychology, 39,* 2–12.

Robertson, T. S. (1976). Low commitment consumer behavior. *Journal of Advertising Research, 16,* 19–24.

Ryan, M. J., & Bonfield, E. H. (1975). The fishbein extended model and consumer behavior. *Journal of Consumer Research, 2,* 118–136.

Sawyer, A. G., & Ward, S. (1979). Carry-over effects in advertising communication. *Research in Marketing, 2,* 259–314.

Silk, A. J., & Vavra, T. G. (1974). The influence of advertising's affective qualities on consumer response. In G. D. Hughes & M. L. Ray (Eds.), *Buyer/consumer information processing* (pp. 157–86). Chapel Hill, NC: University of North Carolina.

Skinner, B. F. (1972). *Beyond freedom and dignity.* New York: Alfred A. Knopf.

Smith, R. E., & Swinyard, W. R. (1983). Attitude-behavior consistency: The impact of product trial versus advertising. *Journal of Marketing Research, 20,* 257–267.

Sternthal, B., Dholakia, R., & Leavitt, C. (1978). The persuasive effect of source credibility: Tests of cognitive response. *Journal of Consumer Research, 4,* 252–260.

Toy, D. R. (1982). Monitoring communication effects: A cognitive structure/cognitive response approach. *Journal of Consumer Research, 9,* 66–76.

Tversky, A., & Kahnemann, D. (1973). Availability: A heuristic for judging frequency and probability. *Cognitive Psychology, 5,* 207–32.

Wheatley, J. J., Walton, R. G., & Chiu, J. S. Y. (1982). The influence of prior product experience, price, and brand name on quality perception. In W. Perrault (Ed.), *Advances in consumer research* (Vol. 4, pp. 72–77). Ann Arbor, MI: Association for Consumer Research.

Wright, P. L. (1980). Message-evoked thoughts: Persuasion research using thought verbalizations. *Journal of Consumer Research, 7,* 151–75.

Wright, P., & Rip, P. (1980). Product class advertising effects on first time buyers' decision strategies. *Journal of Consumer Research, 7,* 176–88.

Wyer, R. S., Jr., & Srull, T. K. (1986). Human cognition in its social context. *Psychological Review, 93,* 322–359.

Zajonc, R. B. (1980). Feelings and thinking preferences need no inferences. *American Psychologist, 35,* 151–75.

3

A Framework for Understanding the Effects of Advertising Exposure on Choice

Prakash Nedungadi
Andrew A. Mitchell
Ida E. Berger
University of Toronto

Although advertising may have a variety of effects on consumers (e.g., Lavidge & Steiner, 1961; Palda, 1966), firms generally advertise to influence brand choice. Thus, an advertising campaign that increases awareness or improves attitudes will be only partially successful if it does not ultimately lead to an increase in sales. Most theoretical research examining advertising effects at the individual level, however, rarely considers the impact of advertising exposure on the brand choice process (for an exception, see Baker & Lutz, 1988). In fact, research on individual-level advertising effects and brand choice have largely proceeded independently of each other.

Most theoretical research on advertising effects has used brand attitude as the critical dependent variable. Recent research in this area has focused on the role of mediating variables (such as cognitive responses and attitude toward the ad) in influencing brand attitudes (e.g., MacKenzie, Lutz, & Belch, 1986; Mitchell, 1986), under different processing conditions (e.g., Homer, 1990). This approach has provided a well-developed, theoretical understanding of how persuasive messages affect attitude formation and change (e.g., MacInnis & Jaworski, 1989; Petty & Cacioppo, 1986). In extending this understanding to brand choice, researchers have generally assumed that a shift in brand attitudes is both neces-sary and sufficient for a change in purchase behavior. However, for a number of reasons, the effects of advertising exposure on brand attitudes may not translate to brand choice.

First, a number of variables have been identified as moderators of the rela-tionship between attitudes and behavior (see Zanna & Fazio, 1982, for a compre-hensive review). These variables include attitude accessibility, attitude confi-dence, attitude clarity, the amount of information about the attitude object, and the degree of consistency between cognitive and affective attitude components. Second, changes in behavior have recently been shown to occur without shifts in attitude (e.g., Berger & Mitchell, 1989; Nedungadi, 1990). Berger and Mitchell used advertising repetition to produce changes in brand choice by increasing attitude accessibility, whereas Nedungadi used brand primes to change brand accessibility and to directly influence brand choice probabilities. In both cases, choice probabilities were changed without any change in brand attitudes. Finally, the processes underlying attitude formation and change are often qualitatively different from those involving a choice between competing brands. Whereas attitude judgments generally involve responses to one brand or issue at a time, choice requires discrimination between brands, even when they are very similar (e.g., Bettman, Johnson, & Payne, 1990; Payne, 1982).

Although research on advertising effectiveness has only perfunctorily considered implications for choice, the settings typically used to examine the brand choice process (e.g., brand by attribute information displays) are not conducive to the consideration of advertising effects (e.g., Bettman & Park, 1980; Payne, 1976; Russo & Dosher, 1983). The effects of advertising exposure on choice must operate through memory. However, most of the choice research focused entirely on the use of externally available information and did not consider the effects of memory (Lynch & Srull, 1982).

Consequently, it is our view that any valid and useful theory of advertising effectiveness must bridge these two related streams of research and examine the effect of advertising exposure not only on attitudes, but also on the choice process. Toward this end, this chapter develops a conceptual framework to examine how advertising exposure may influence the choice process. First, we present an overview of the consumer choice process and analyze its various subprocesses or stages. Next, we identify those factors that are critical to a brand successfully "passing" through each choice stage, until it is finally chosen. Then we examine how ad exposure may influence information use at each choice stage and discuss the role of two important contextual factors on choice. Finally, we present the results of a study designed to examine the value of the proposed framework in developing a theoretical understanding of advertising exposure on brand choice.

THE CONSUMER CHOICE PROCESS

A conceptualization of the choice process that aims to account for ad effects must include a number of aspects. First, it must incorporate the use of previously obtained information including knowledge about brands, their attributes, and attitudes. Second, it must allow for the use of memory. In many brand choice situations, consumers generate some brand information from memory, rather than relying solely on externally available information. Third, it must be dynam-

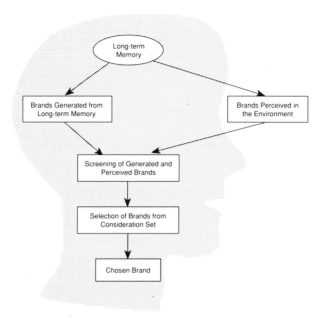

FIG. 3.1. The three stages or subprocesses in the choice process.

ic. Consumers retrieve and use different information and choose different brands on different choice occasions. Finally, it must take account of contextual factors in the choice situation.

By providing subjects with external information about fixed sets of hypothetical brands, the choice process studies referred to previously were unable to incorporate these elements of choice. In order to account for these aspects, we conceptualize the choice process as consisting of the following three stages or subprocesses as illustrated in Fig. 3.1 (see also Nedungadi, 1987).

1. *Generation of Alternatives.* This process involves the retrieval of brands from long-term memory and the recognition of brands in the external purchase environment. It results in a set of alternatives being "brought to mind," and considered in short-term or working memory. Implicit in this process is a "stopping rule" that determines when to stop generating alternatives.

2. *Consideration of Alternatives.* Within this process, the alternatives in working memory are quickly screened for acceptability. This screening process is seen as being very perfunctory; serving to eliminate only unknown, inappropriate, or disliked brands. For instance, a consumer might generate a brand of soft drink (Coke) that he or she finds inappropriate for the current situation (morning break). The consumer is unlikely to consider this brand for long, and will thus drop it from working memory and from further consideration.

3. *Selection of an Alternative.* This last process is the one that has received the most attention by choice researchers. At this stage one or more of the many heuristics or decision rules (e.g., affect-referral, lexicographic, elimination-by-aspects) reported in the literature may be used to compare and evaluate the remaining brands for choice (cf. Bettman, Johnson, & Payne, 1991).

In most choice situations, these processes will not occur in the strict, ordered sequence this discussion suggests. For instance, the consumer might retrieve and consider a few brands, then drop some from consideration while continuing to hold others in short-term or working memory, then decide to retrieve a few more brands, and so on, before making a final choice. We believe, however, that it is useful to decompose the choice process into these discrete stages because the evidence suggests the processes and the factors affecting the processes will be very different at each stage. For instance, previous choice research suggests that consumers may use noncompensatory heuristics in the consideration stage for screening brands, and more compensatory heuristics in the selection stage for arriving at a final choice (e.g., Bettman, 1979; Wright & Barbour, 1975). Likewise, Nedungadi (1990) presented evidence that brand accessibility may play the primary role during the generation stage, whereas preference may be more important during the selection stage of choice. Notably, a distinction between these various choice stages also permits an examination of the factors that may help a brand advance from one choice stage to the next.

FACTORS INFLUENCING EACH CHOICE STAGE

Generation of Alternatives

In order to be generated or "brought to mind," a brand must be accessible. *Accessibility,* as the term is used here, includes both a brand's retrievability from long-term memory and its recognizability in the external purchase environment. According to most associative network models of memory (e.g., Anderson, 1983a; Humphreys, Bain, & Pike, 1989; Raaijmakers & Shiffrin, 1981), the strength of association between various information items will determine the likelihood that activation will spread from one item to the other.

Accordingly, the current contents of working memory will cue, and bring to mind other associated information from long-term memory. Further, recently retrieved or recognized items will act to guide subsequent retrieval or recognition. Information that is relevant will be further processed, whereas irrelevant information will be allowed to "fade" from working memory (Alba, Hutchinson, & Lynch, 1991; Nedungadi, 1987). In general, at least two types of cues could render a brand accessible on a particular choice occasion.

Product Categories or Subcategories as Cues.   In many consumer situations, categories or subcategories are most likely to serve as cues for the retrieval of brands. For example, feeling thirsty might bring to mind the category of soft drinks and this category may be strongly associated with specific subcategories (e.g., "colas"). Strongly associated subcategory members (e.g., "Coke") are now likely to be retrieved (cf. Crowder, 1976), or recognized (e.g., Baker, Hutchinson, Moore, & Nedungadi, 1986; cf. Jacoby & Brooks, 1984).

Category structure may be flat, with direct linkages between the brand and the category, or hierarchical, with subcategories linking brands to the category. A consumer who eats frequently at "McDonald's" is likely to bring this outlet to mind spontaneously (without accessing the subcategory of "burger places") when selecting a fast food outlet for lunch. The frequency, recency, and saliency of brand instantiation within the product category are critical to accessibility (e.g., Barsalou, 1985, Kintsch & Young, 1984). Evidence also suggests that typical members of the category are recalled more quickly and more often when the category serves as cue (Nedungadi & Hutchinson, 1985; Rosch & Mervis, 1975; Ward & Loken, 1986).

Decision Criteria or Goals as Cues.   Barsalou (1983, 1985) examined the properties of "goal-derived" categories, or categories that are constructed to meet specific goals (e.g., places to go for a winter vacation). In contrast to taxonomic categories (e.g., restaurants, soft drinks), specific goals are likely to serve as cues in such categories. Thus, retrieval will be guided, not by typicality of a brand within the category, but by the strength of the association between category-specific goals and the brand or the attributes of the brand. Thus, when selecting alternatives for a "winter vacation," the consumer may retrieve alternatives that "have warm weather" and are "located on the ocean."

The usage situation is a special example of a goal-derived category (Nedungadi, 1987; Ratneshwar & Shocker, 1991). Ratneshwar and Shocker showed that retrieval of brands in specific usage situations is strongly guided by situation-specific typicality (vs. taxonomic typicality). It is likely that categories that are often encountered as part of frequent usage contexts will become well entrenched in memory, and may be cued by established context-specific decision criteria (Nedungadi, 1987; cf. Barsalou & Ross, 1986).

When product categories or subcategories serve as cues, the organization of alternatives in memory determined retrieval, whereas when decision criteria or goals are used as cues, the alternatives are generally constructed based on the characteristics of the choice situation. On many choice occasions, these various retrieval cues may act in unison, allowing the consumer to generate a relatively small, conscribed set of brands for further consideration.

Consideration of Alternatives

In order to be considered a brand must be acceptable. It is quite possible that some of the brands accessed during the generation stage are inappropriate or unacceptable. A store at which the consumer recently encountered rude service may be extremely salient and may thus be generated. Or, a disliked brand may be suggested by a friend (or primed by an advertisement) during the choice process. Such alternatives can be eliminated by the consumer with very little processing. Thus, the screening stage allows the consumer to drop these brands from working memory and from further consideration. Two factors are hypothesized as being important in determining brand acceptability.

Brand Attitudes Must be Accessible and Positive.   If accessible, overall brand attitudes are likely to be the quickest and easiest way in which a consumer can assess the acceptability of a brand (cf. Jamieson & Zanna, 1989; Sanbonmatsu & Fazio, 1990). Once the attitude is accessed, brands with negative attitudes can be dropped from consideration. Thus, brands must possess accessible and positive attitudes in order to pass the consideration stage of choice.

The Relevant Brand Attribute Values Must be Accessible and Appropriate.   In some instances, it is not the brand's overall attitude that is pertinent, but its possession of situationally relevant attribute values. Thus, it is not the overall performance of a restaurant that may be most critical during lunch, but its "closeness" or its "speed of service." This reasoning is consistent with previous choice literature that suggests that noncompensatory decision rules (e.g., lexicographic) are more likely to capture the initial, screening stage of the choice process.

Thus, when situationally relevant attributes are used to screen brands for consideration, the brand must possess appropriate values on these attributes. In addition, the value of the attributes for the brand must be accessible to the consumer.

In may situations the generation and consideration stages of the choice process will be almost simultaneous during choice. For instance, an individual may generate and consider "restaurants I like for lunch" or "restaurants I like that are close by"). Thus attitudes or attributes may allow consumers to generate and screen brands simultaneously. Our separation of the two stages is primarily intended to differentiate the factors that influence accessibility from those that affect the acceptability of brands.

Selection of an Alternative

In order to be selected, a brand must be preferred. In this final stage of the choice process, the consumer uses specific criteria to select from the brands in working memory. The consumer is now evaluating, not the full set of available brands, but a constrained, consideration set for choice. Although a number of decision criteria might be used at this stage, we focus on the use of individual attribute and overall attitude information. If more than one brand is being considered at this stage, the preferred brand will probably be the one with the highest value on the decision criteria used, relative to other brands in the consideration set.

A number of researchers have suggested that when some overall summary judgment or attitude about an object is available in memory, it is likely to be used in preference to specific features or attributes (e.g., Hastie & Park; Lingle, Geva, Ostrom, Leippe, & Baumgardner, 1979; Lingle & Ostrom, 1979). This reasoning is consistent with the use of simplifying heuristics (e.g., affect referral; Wright, 1975) to arrive at a judgment. However, a number of studies have found greater use of attribute information, although attitude information was available (e.g., Biehal & Chakravarti, 1983, 1986; Lynch, Marmorstein, & Weigold, 1988).

Feldman and Lynch (1988) proposed a theoretical framework that identifies when various alternative inputs to a decision are likely to be used. According to their framework, the relative use of individual attribute and overall attitude information depends on (a) the relative accessibility of overall attitudes versus individual attribute values, and (b) the relative perceived diagnosticity of each of these information elements. Here, diagnosticity refers to the degree to which the use of each type of information is perceived to result in selection of the "best" alternative.

The Feldman and Lynch (1988) framework appears able to account for a number of findings in the area (Alba et al., 1991). In a study of mixed choice tasks; Lynch et al. (1988) found that subjects made use of individual attribute information to arrive at a judgment, although attitudes were accessible, specifically because these attitudes did not help discriminate among the considered brands (i.e., they were not diagnostic). However, when diagnostic, overall evaluations were used in preference to specific attribute information.

Thus, when accessible and diagnostic, attitude information is likely to be used by the consumer during the selection stage of the choice process, in order to choose among brands in the consideration set. This is because retrieval and use of an overall summary evaluation is likely to be simpler than the use of information on a number of individual attributes of the brand. However, in a number of instances, attitude information may be inaccessible (e.g., Baumgardner, Leippe, Ronis, & Greenwald, 1983; Keller, 1987, 1991) or nondiagnostic (e.g., Biehal & Chakravarti, 1983, 1986; Lynch et al., 1988). Attitude information is particularly likely to be nondiagnostic if the context in which the current decision is being made is dissimilar to the context in which the original attitude was formed. In such instances, consumers are likely to compute brand evaluations based on the accessible diagnostic attribute information about the brands.

Thus, the following two factors are seen to be important in determining selection from a consideration set of brands:

First, the brand must have the highest overall attitude, when brand attitudes are likely to be accessible and diagnostic for choice. For instance, when attitudes are relevant for the choice situation and there are clear differences in consumers' liking for the brands, the brand must possess the highest attitude among brands in the consideration set.

Second, the brand must have the most appropriate value on relevant attributes, when brand attitudes are nondiagnostic or inaccessible. For instance, when the stored attitude is irrelevant for the current choice situation or when there are a number of equally well-liked brands, the brand must perform best on the salient or important attributes used to discriminate between brands and arrive at a choice.

Summary

Our discussion of the factors that influence brand choice serves to underscore the importance of considering variables other than brand attitude when examining advertising effectiveness. In our framework, there are three stages to the choice process—generation of brands, consideration of brands, and selection of a brand for purchase. Three types of information—brand, attitude, and attribute—and two dimensions of this information—accessibility and value—are seen as primary in determining the progress of a brand through each choice stage. Thus, the accessibility of brand, attitude, and attribute information and the value of brand attitudes and attributes are all believed to contribute to the final probabilities of brand choice.

EFFECTS OF ADVERTISING EXPOSURE

Research on advertising effects indicates that advertisements can directly influence all of the three types of information and the two dimensions of this information that affect the different stages of the choice process. First, advertisements can alter the content of brand information stored in memory. This includes the brand name, the value and valence of brand attribute beliefs, and the valence of brand attitudes. Second, advertising can affect the representational structure of brand information and thereby the accessibility of the brand, its attributes and its attitude.

Content and Valence of Information

There is considerable evidence that advertising can form and change the content and value of brand attributes and attitudes in memory. Several studies have indicated that the type of processing (i.e., under memory vs. evaluation instructions, brand vs. nonbrand processing) that occurs during advertising exposure influences the kind of information that is processed and stored. For instance, individuals who execute a nonbrand processing strategy are more likely to recall structural details of the advertisement, and less likely to recall information about product attributes, (Gardner, Mitchell, & Russo, 1985); (Lichtenstein & Srull, 1985). When later asked to form an evaluation of the advertised brand, they must retrieve information about the ad from memory. On the other hand, individuals who execute a brand processing strategy form inferences about the brand, recall more information about the brand, and are more likely to form or recall overall brand evaluations.

Other research, using a multiattribute attitude framework to examine the effect of advertising exposure, indicates that advertisements can affect the formation or evaluation of product attribute beliefs and consequently attitude formation (e.g., Mitchell, 1986; Mitchell & Olson, 1981) or change (e.g., Lutz, 1975). For instance, Mitchell and Olson showed subjects ads for different brands of facial tissue, that contained either photographs or simple headlines and found that subjects formed very different beliefs and attitudes toward the different advertised brands. Similarly, Lutz (1975) showed that advertising messages could be used to change product attribute beliefs and the evaluations of these beliefs.

The Accessibility of Information

Recent research, both in social cognition and marketing, suggests that advertising may also affect memory structure, and thus the accessibility of information in memory. Research in social cognition suggests that the number of linkages formed between information elements about a person is based on the amount of elaboration or processing conducted at the time of encoding (Hamilton, Driscoll, & Worth, 1989; Srull, 1981; Srull, Lichtenstein, & Rothbart, 1985). As the number of linkages increases, information accessibility increases and information is more likely to be recalled. In addition, the strength of these linkages depends on the recency or frequency with which they are activated (e.g., Anderson, 1983b). A brand attitude may also be conceptualized as a piece of information in memory that is linked to related brands and attributes (e.g., Fazio, 1986). Consequently, the continued activation of an attitude will increase its accessibility (e.g., Fazio, Powell, & Herr, 1983).

There is emerging evidence that advertising, through executional elements or through repeated exposure, can influence both the number of linkages in a brand structure and the strength of these linkages. A number of studies indicate that frequent or very recent exposure to a brand name may increase its accessibility (Nedungadi, 1990; Ray & Sawyer, 1971). In addition, frequent or recent executional presentation of a brand within a particular usage situation may create a relatively strong association between the brand and the situation (Ratneshwar & Shocker, 1991). Finally, advertising repetition that induces the activation of brand information has been shown to increase both the accessibility of product attribute beliefs (Berger, 1987) and attitudes (Berger & Mitchell, 1989).

Repeated reference to specific product characteristics leads to an increase in their salience and influence in subsequent judgments. The "problem framing" literature provides examples where manipulations of attribute accessibility (either perceptual salience or memorability) leads to a change in the influence of the attribute during evaluation (e.g., Gardner, 1983; MacKenzie, 1986; Wright & Rip, 1980). For instance, Gardner (1983) showed that increasing the prominence of an important attribute in an ad headline served to increase both its memorability and its effect on brand evaluations.

Finally, there is also evidence that exposure to advertisements for similar products may lead to interference, thereby, inhibiting recall of ad details (e.g., Burke & Srull, 1988). For instance, Burke and Srull find that advertising for competing brands inhibited recall of advertising information in both proactive and retroactive interference situations. It was argued that this occurred because an increase in the number of similar advertisements in memory reduced the likelihood that any one advertisement could be recalled.

In summary, research on advertising effects and current models of memory indicate that advertising can be effectively used to alter the content/valence and accessibility of brand information in memory. As discussed, all of these factors can have important influences on the probability of brand choice.

CONTEXTUAL AND TASK FACTORS

A number of factors, other than advertising exposure, could affect the amount and type of information used at each stage of the choice process. In this chapter we focus on two critical factors: the motivation and opportunity to process information and the type of choice task-memory-based or stimulus-based.

Motivation and Opportunity

The consumer's motivation and opportunity to process information will determine the amount of effort expended during the choice process. In our framework, this has an important effect on: (a) the amount of information retrieved and processed for choice, and (b) the willingness to retrieve less accessible information.

Motivational intensity will affect all three stages of the choice process. It will affect the first stage by determining the appropriate stopping rule for brand generation. Very low levels of motivation will cause the consumer to retrieve only the most accessible brands, whereas high levels of motivation will cause the consumer to actively "search" for brands that may be less accessible. At the second and third stages, motivational intensity will affect the number of criteria used by the consumer to consider and select brands. Low levels of motivation will favor the use of an overall attitude, when it is accessible. If motivation is high, consumers will attempt to use the most diagnostic information available, even when it takes effort to access.

Lynch et al. (1988) suggested that motivational intensity will also affect the (cumulative) diagnosticity threshold at which the consumer is willing to stop using further information (although it may still be diagnostic). Only at high levels of motivational intensity are consumers likely to consider all diagnostic information that is available.

Similarly to motivational intensity, the opportunity to process information also will act to constrain the brand, attribute, or attitude information used by consumers during choice. With little opportunity, consumers will use the most accessible information, even if it is not diagnostic. With increases in opportunity, consumers will use diagnostic information, even if it is inaccessible. For instance, studies by Jamieson and Zanna (1989) and Sanbonmatsu and Fazio (1990) indicate that when individuals are under time pressure to make a decision, they will rely on previously formed attitudes even if they are not diagnostic. When given more time to make a decision, they will retrieve and process more information and frequently make different decisions.

In summary, differences in motivation and opportunity may cause a tradeoff between the accessibility and diagnosticity of information, assuming they are unrelated. As motivation or opportunity increase, the consumer is likely to access more brands, attributes, and attitudes, and make use of both overall attitude and attribute information for choice. With little motivation or opportunity they will evaluate only those alternatives that are highly accessible using only criteria that are also highly accessible.

Memory-Based, Stimulus-Based, and Mixed-Choice

It is now well recognized that memory-based choices, which rely on information retrieval from long-term memory (e.g., deciding which supermarket to shop at), involve qualitatively different processes than stimulus-based choices, where all information is externally available (e.g., deciding which cereal to buy when in the cereal aisle at the supermarket). Implications of this distinction for our framework center around the difference between retrieval and recognition processes, and the importance of information accessibility to each.

Importantly, the distinction between memory and stimulus-based processes will apply to all three stages of the choice process. In theory, recognition does not require the generation of alternatives, and thus stimulus-based choices have no need for the first stage of the choice process. In addition, a "pure" stimulus-based choice will not resort to memory at all, but will use externally available brand and attribute information to arrive at judgments. Conversely, a pure memory-based choice will only draw on information from long-term memory. Clearly, most choice decisions are likely to be "mixed" in their use of information, both within stages (e.g., Lynch et al., 1988) and across different stages of choice. Thus, for instance, a consumer interested in purchasing breakfast cereal may simply go to the appropriate aisle in the supermarket and use recognition processes to generate a consideration set. The consumer may then rely entirely on memory to make a choice or may use a combination of unit pricing information from the shelf in conjunction with recalled information about the nutritional value of considered brands in order to arrive at a choice. In most instances, the importance of information accessibility is likely to increase with increasing reliance on memory for choice.

However, accessibility (perceptual salience or brand familiarity) is also likely to play a role in determining which of many external items the consumer recognizes, or pays attention to (see Alba et al., 1991, for an excellent discussion). In typical shopping situations, the large number of available alternatives precludes a pure stimulus-based examination of each, and forces the consumer to focus attention on a small subset of brands (cf. Dickson & Sawyer, 1986; Hoyer, 1984). In a recent study, Fazio, Powell and Williams (1989) had subjects choose from a display of 10 brands in which 5 were in the front row and 5 in the back row after measuring their attitude accessibility for each brand. The results indicated the probability of choosing a product from the front row increased as attitude accessibility decreased, whereas the reverse occurred for the back row. When subjects' attitudes were accessible, there was no significant effect of row placement on choice probabilities. These results were interpreted as indicating that as brand attitudes became less accessible, behavior was more likely to be guided by physical salience.

Summary

To recapitulate, research in psychology and consumer behavior indicates that the content and accessibility of brand-related information in memory will determine the probability that a particular brand will be selected. The effect of these different types of (brand, attribute, and attitude) information will differ at each of the three stages of the brand choice process. Further, a number of contextual and task factors will affect the relative influence of these different types of brand-related information on choice.

Although advertising has been shown to affect the content and accessibility of each of these different types of information, the influence of advertising exposure is unlikely to be restricted to just one type of brand-related information. For instance, exposure to a well-liked ad may increase both the accessibility of the advertised brand and the valence of attitude. Similarly, exposure to an ad that favorably changes the perceived attribute values on important attributes will also increase the attitude valence of that brand. In both of these situations, the effect of the changes will be to increase the likelihood that the brand will be selected in a particular purchase situation. In some situations, however, an ad could alter information accessibility and content such that it has opposite effects on choice. For instance, advertising repetition has been shown to increase the accessibility of the advertised brand (e.g., Ray & Sawyer, 1971; Sawyer & Ward, 1979), information about the advertised brand (Berger, 1987) and attitudes toward the advertised, however, after a point, advertising repetition also decreases attitude valence (e.g., Cacioppo & Petty, 1979; Calder & Sternthal, 1980). Consequently, repetitions may increase the likelihood that the brand will be retrieved or recognized at the generation of alternatives stage, but may decrease the likelihood that it will be considered, or selected for choice. One of the strengths of the framework presented here is its ability to tease apart these different effects of advertising on the choice process. In the next section we describe an experiment that was designed to take advantage of the strengths of our framework and to examine the effects of advertising repetition on the different stages of the brand choice process.

RESEARCH GOALS AND STRATEGY

We now discuss the results of an experiment that was designed to examine the value of our framework for understanding the effects of advertising exposure on choice. Our goals were to design a study that examined the effects of advertising exposure (a) on different types of information at different stages of the choice process, (b) under different choice contexts, and (c) on both the advertised brand and on competing brands. Accordingly, we:

1. Manipulated advertising repetition. Advertising repetition has been shown to increase accessibility of the brand (e.g., Ray & Sawyer, 1971; Sawyer & Ward, 1979) information about the brand (Berger, 1987) and brand attitudes (Berger & Mitchell, 1989), while inducing an inverted U-shaped pattern on brand attitudes (e.g., Cacioppo & Petty, 1979; Calder & Sternthal, 1980).

2. Manipulated the choice context. Subjects were required to make their choice either from memory (memory-based choice condition), or with the names of alternative brands externally present (mixed-choice condition). As discussed, we expected accessibility effects to be stronger under the memory-based choice conditions.

3. Chose an existing brand from a well-known product category with many different brands. In order to demonstrate the effects of ad repetition on brand accessibility and attitude, we needed to select a target brand that subjects were aware of, and evaluated fairly positively, but was low on brand accessibility.

We hypothesized that under these conditions, advertising repetition should increase the accessibility of the brand, thereby increasing the likelihood that it will be one of the alternatives that is generated in a memory-based choice situation. Because the brand is initially evaluated fairly positively and initial advertising exposures should increase this evaluation, consideration and choice should initially increase. With additional advertising repetition, evaluations should decline, however, accessibility of the brand and information about the brand, including attitudes, should continue to increase. Depending on the size of the decrease in evaluation and the size of the increase in accessibility, choice may continue to increase, remain constant or decrease. We were less sure what would occur in the mixed-choice condition, however, we felt that the overall effects would be largely alternated.

METHOD

Pretests

A number of pretests were conducted to select a suitable product category and brand. Based on the criteria that were discussed earlier, a brand of candy bar was selected for the study. Pretests were also conducted to determine the shape of the attitude "wear-in—wear-out" curve for the TV advertisement we obtained for the selected brand. These tests indicated that attitudes toward the target brand reached their maximum at two exposures to the ad when embedded in a 30-minute TV program, and then turned down quite dramatically at four exposures. Because we were interested in examining the choice process over the full range of this response curve, the levels of exposure frequency selected were zero, two, and four exposures.

This pretest also indicated that although there was a strong relationship between exposure frequency and recall of the target brand, exposure frequency had little effect on choice. We conjectured that this occurred because the subjects did not have an attitude toward the target brand stored in memory prior to the experiment, and our experimental procedures did not induce them to form an attitude prior to their choosing a brand. Having subjects "consolidate" their thoughts about the target brand after they had seen the ad seemed to solve this problem.

Design

A 2 (memory-based or mixed choice task) by 3 (zero, two, or four ad exposures) full factorial design was employed in this study. The exposure factor was manipulated by varying the number of repetitions of the target ad. Twelve ads were embedded in the TV program, with the target ad appearing zero, two, or four times and filler ads (also repeated zero, two, four times) appearing in the remaining slots.

The choice task factor was manipulated by varying the nature of a lottery gift offer. In the mixed-choice condition subjects were provided with a list of 15 brands of candy bars that included the target brand. The remaining 14 brands were the brands most frequently recalled in pretests. Subjects were asked to choose the 5 candy bars that they would like to receive at the end of the study. In the memory-based condition, by contrast, subjects were given a blank sheet of paper, and asked to list the 5 candy bars they would like to receive.

Subjects

The subjects were 120 undergraduate business students who were randomly assigned to the six experimental conditions. They were recruited from business courses and were paid $8 for their participation.

Procedure

At the start of the experimental session, subjects were told that its purpose was to have them assess the appropriateness of different ads for different types of TV programs. They were told that they would view a representative segment of a TV program that had appeared a few weeks earlier, which contained a number of ads for different types of products. The subjects were asked to think about the appropriateness of the different ads for the program, when they watched the program.

The subjects then viewed a segment of a 30 minute business-news TV program, after which they were given a questionnaire to complete. In keeping with the cover story, the first part of the questionnaire contained a number of questions about the appropriateness of the different ads for the program. Included in these questions, were questions that asked the subjects to list the things they most liked about each advertised brand. This was done to ensure that subjects consolidated their thoughts about the target brand.

The subjects were then told that as an added bonus for participating, several gift baskets (containing one bottle of shampoo, one box of cereal, one tube of toothpaste, three bars of soap, and five candy bars) would be given away by lottery. They were asked to indicate which brands in each category they would like to receive, should their name be drawn. Subjects were allowed to choose more than one bar of the same brand of candy (or soap) if they so desired.

Once subjects had recorded their choices, the experimenter pretended to look at further instructions and said, "Let's see, today we would like some more information on your choice of, umm, candy bars." Then, on a separate sheet of paper, subjects were asked to list the names of all the other brands of candy bars they had seriously considered while they were making their choices. The specific instructions were "Please list the names of all the brands that you thought about but did not choose." Subjects were given 15 seconds to complete the consideration task.

Then, subjects were given another 15 seconds to list any additional brands of candy bars that they could remember. Finally, under guise of another study, subjects were asked to indicate their attitudes toward a number of brands in different product categories. This list included the 15 brands of candy bars. The subjects were then debriefed and paid.

Dependent Measures

Four dependent measures were obtained for each of the 15 brands of candy bars (including the target brand) of interest. The first measure, choice, varied from 0 to 5, and was the number of bars of each brand that subjects indicated they would like to receive if they won the lottery. For the second measure, consideration (0 or 1), a brand was regarded as considered if it was chosen or seriously considered by subjects while making their choice. Similarly, for brand recall (0 or 1), a brand was regarded as generated if it was selected, considered, or recalled. Finally, the fourth measure was the subjects' attitudes toward the brands of candy bars. These were measured on two 9-point, bipolar scales anchored by "very bad—very good," and dislike very much—like very much." The coefficient alpha for these two scales was 0.93, so the two scales were combined to obtain an overall measure of brand attitude.

RESULTS

In this section, we report the effect of ad exposure frequency on attitudes toward the target brand, then on choice, consideration, and recall of the target brand in first the memory- and then the mixed-choice situation. Since most of the previous research examining advertising effects used attitudes as the primary dependent variable, we will also test the effects of advertising repetition and choice situation on these measures after controlling for the effects of attitudes. This will test whether advertising exposure has an effect on recall, consideration, and choice beyond that accounted for by attitudes. Finally, we examine the effect of ad exposure frequency on choice, consideration, and recall of competing brands.

Brand Attitudes

The results of numerous studies indicate that attitudes exhibit an inverted U-shaped pattern with increases in ad repetition (e.g., Cacioppo & Petty, 1979). Given these findings and our pretest results, it was expected that the attitudes in the 2 exposure condition would be more positive than the attitudes in the 0 and 4 exposure conditions.

The choice situation manipulation should not affect attitudes toward the target brand and the results of a two way ANOVA indicates the main effect for choice situation is not significant ($p > 0.3$). Therefore, brand attitude scores were aggregated over this manipulation.

Overall, the effect of the repetition manipulation on brand attitudes partially

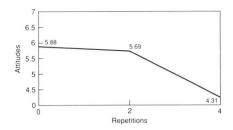

FIG. 3.2. The effect of advertising repetition on the attitude toward the target brand.

confirms our expectations (Fig. 3.2). Whereas four exposures has a very negative reaction to the brand ($p < 0.5$), two exposures has little effect on brand attitudes. Attitudes toward the target brand appear to be very stable between zero and two exposures, then, decline considerably with four exposures.

Memory-Based Choice Situation

Recall and Consideration. It was argued earlier that in order for a brand to be generated as an alternative in a choice situation, it must be accessible. In addition, it must pass some threshold level of acceptability in order to be considered. Consequently, brand accessibility should have a strong and significant impact on the generation stage, and brand attitude should have a strong and significant impact on the consideration stage. In the context of this experiment, support for these propositions would be obtained if the probability of recalling the target brand increases with advertising repetition (zero, two, and four), and the probability that the target brand is considered remains constant from zero to two exposures, and then decreases with four exposures. The probability of the target brand being recalled and considered in the memory-based choice condition is reported in Fig. 3.3 and 3.4, respectively.

These results partially, but not totally, support our expectations. As expected, increases in advertising exposure—from zero to two—result in increases in the probability of the target brand being both recalled and considered and, from two to four exposures, the probability of the target brand being considered decreased dramatically. Contrary to expectations, the probability of the target brand being

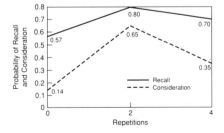

FIG. 3.3. The effect of advertising repetition on the probability of recalling and considering the target brand in memory-based choice.

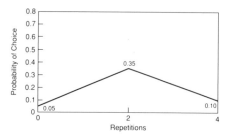

FIG. 3.4. The effect of advertising repetition on the probability of choosing the target brand in memory-based choice.

recalled is relatively stable from two to four exposures. These patterns of results for both recall and considerations are highly significant without controlling for attitudes ($p < 0.01$) and still significant for recall ($p < 0.05$) and marginally significant for consideration ($p < 0.10$) after controlling for attitudes. These results are consistent with our expectations that attitudes have a minor effect on recall, but have an important effect on consideration.

Although the pattern of results for brand recall was unexpected, it is quite consistent with previous findings in the area. First, Craig, Sternthal, and Leavitt (1976) found that high levels of repetition may lead to "wear-out." This appears to occur when individuals reduce the amount of attention paid to additional exposures, so recall ceases to improve. Although we did not expect attentional wear-out to set in as early as two exposures, the pattern of data for brand attitudes, where attitudes did not increase from zero to two exposures, suggests that the ad we used may have stimulated little positive interest in the viewer. (Subsequent testing of this ad in a professional ad-testing environment confirmed our suspicion-the ad received very neutral ratings from the audience.)

Second, it has consistently been found that more preferred brands tend to be recalled earlier in the sequence (e.g., Haley & Case, 1979; Nedungadi & Hutchinson, 1985; Ward & Loken, 1986). Thus, although attitudes may not serve as direct cues to retrieval, preferred brands do enjoy a retrieval advantage. It is thus likely that the extremely low attitudes for the target brand in the four-exposure condition offset the positive influence of repetition/exposure on brand accessibility and brand recall.

These results suggest that both brand accessibility and brand attitudes have some role to play in the brand generation and consideration stages of the choice process. Brand accessibility has a greater effect during brand generation, whereas brand attitude has a greater effect during consideration. In general, these results are consistent with our earlier reasoning.

Choices. If we assume that attitudes alone determined brand choice, we would predict (in line with the attitudinal data) higher choices of the target brand among subjects in the zero- and two-ad exposure conditions than among subjects in the four-advertising exposure condition, with no differences between subjects in the zero- and two-advertising exposure conditions.

However, as was suggested earlier, attitudes alone will not explain brand choice because other factors have an important role to play. In particular, brands that are not sufficiently accessible to be generated and considered are not available to be chosen. Therefore, choice probabilities are expected to be influenced by brand accessibility. In the context of this study, a brand accessibility influence would be suggested by choice probabilities that increase from zero to four advertising exposures.

The proportion of choices of the target brand in the memory-based conditions is given in Fig. 3.4. This proportion increases dramatically from 0.05 in the 0 exposure condition to 0.35 in the 2 exposure condition (as accessibility increases) and then decreases to 0.10 in the 4-exposure condition. These results are marginally significant after controlling for attitudes ($p < 0.10$).

In line with our choice framework, these findings imply that both brand attitudes and brand accessibility play a role in the overall brand choice process. The results suggest that in memory-based choice situations, brand accessibility may be the key determinant of alternative generation and attitudes are important for consideration and brand choice. However, as we demonstrate later, increasing the accessibility of the brand and information about the brand appears to decrease the favorableness of the attitude required for both consideration and choice.

Mixed-Choice Situation

Recall and Consideration.   As shown in Fig. 3.5 the increase from zero to two repetitions resulted in no apparent increase in either the recall or consideration of the target brand, however, from zero to four exposures the probability of recalling and considering the target brand increased. This pattern of results is significantly different from the results obtained in the memory-based condition for recall ($p < .05$), but only marginally significant for consideration ($p < .10$).

These results are particularly surprising for consideration, because the attitude

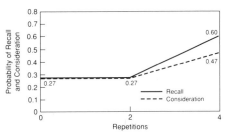

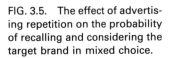

FIG. 3.5.   The effect of advertising repetition on the probability of recalling and considering the target brand in mixed choice.

scores in the four-exposure condition decreased markedly, and because attitudes had such a strong negative effect in the memory-based conditions. Brand accessibility appears to have had an important influence on both brand generation and consideration, particularly at high levels of accessibility in mixed-choice conditions.

This result is particularly interesting given recent findings that brand accessibility (or brand familiarity) may have an important influence on brand recognition (e.g., Alba et al., 1991; Fazio et al., 1989). It appears that subjects, when faced with a "large" list of brands, did not attend to each brand name, but quickly scanned the list looking for brands that were perceptually salient or familiar. Our speculation is that under these circumstances, because all brands were physically present, it took four ad repetitions before the target brand could "stand out" in the list. Thus, four ad repetitions in the mixed condition provided the target brand with the same relative advantage (in perceptual salience or accessibility) that two ad repetitions were able to achieve in the memory-based condition.

Choice.   The probability of choosing the target brand increased gradually from zero to two to four ad exposures (Fig. 3.6). Curiously, these choices reflect almost a total brand accessibility influence, and no influence of attitude in the mixed-choice situation. These results suggest that a tradeoff between brand accessibility and attitudes may be occurring where increases in brand accessibility may compensate for decreases in attitudes or that brand choice may be almost entirely based on recognition.

Attitudes Toward Considered and Chosen Brands

Because a tradeoff between attitude accessibility and attitude valence was clearly found in the mixed-choice condition, we examine if a similar tradeoff occurs in the memory-based condition. For this purpose, we compute the mean attitudes for the target brand and for competing brands when they are considered and not considered across the ad frequency conditions. This analysis indicates that when

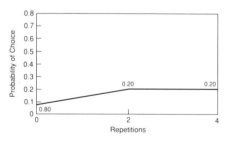

FIG. 3.6.   The effect of advertising repetition on the probability of choosing the target brand in mixed choice.

TABLE 3.1
The Effect of Advertising Repetition on the Attitudes of the Target Brand and Competing Brands
When They are Considered or Not Considered in the Memory-Based Condition

| | | Number of Advertising Repetitions | | | |
		0	2	4	Mean
Target brand	Considered	6.5	6.4	4.6	5.8
	Not considered	5.6	5.3	3.9	4.9
Other brands	Considered	6.4	6.9	7.2	5.8
	Not considered	4.9	5.3	4.4	4.6

considered, the mean attitude for the target brand decreases dramatically between the two and four repetition condition, whereas for the other brands mean attitude remains constant across repetition conditions (Table 3.1). In addition, in the zero and two advertising repetition conditions, the attitudes of the target brand and the competing brands, when they are considered, are about the same, but there is a large difference in these attitudes in the four-repetition condition. Similar effects were found for the chosen and not-chosen brands across the ad frequency conditions. This indicates that by increasing the accessibility of the brand and information about the brand, it is possible to have it considered and chosen over competing brands with more positive attitudes.

Effects on Other Brands

Advertising repetition of the target brand also has interesting effects on the recall, consideration, and selection of competing brands. These effects are almost exactly opposite to the effects on the recall, consideration, and choice of the target brand. For the former two measures, the pattern of results across ad repetitions is significantly different between these brands and the target brand ($p < 0.05$). For instance, as indicated in Table 3.2, in the memory-based condition, the number of competing brands recalled and considered decreases with repetition, whereas the number of competing brands chosen decreases with two repetitions and then increases slightly with four repetitions. Similar effects were found in the mixed-choice condition.

TABLE 3.2
The Effect on Advertising Repetition on the Recall, Consideration, and Selection of Competing
Brands in the Memory-Based Condition

| | | Number of Advertising Repetitions | |
Number of Competing Brands	0	2	4
Recalled	11.66	8.95	8.10
Considered	6.57	5.95	4.75
Chosen	3.52	2.95	3.05

DISCUSSION

In this chapter we presented and discussed a framework for examining the effects of advertising exposure on choice. It was argued that, by focusing on attitudes as the primary dependent variable, previous approaches to understanding advertising effectiveness may have provided us with a limited and possibly erroneous understanding of an ad's effects on brand choice. In addition, previous approaches to understanding brand choice using information boards did not provide an opportunity to examine the effects of advertising because it did not consider the effects of memory. The framework presented here juxtaposes these research streams in order to map the outputs of ad exposure onto the inputs required for the brand choice process. The framework has a number of strengths:

1. It divides the overall choice process into a number of stages or sub-processes, and details the information inputs that are likely to be used at each stage.
2. It separates the influence of advertising exposure into effects on each of the information inputs to choice. Thus, it allows us to examine advertising effects, not only on brand attitudes, but on the accessibility of brand, attribute and attitude information, and on the value of brand attributes and attitudes.
3. It examines the impact of contextual and task factors on the different stages of the choice process, and thus permits an identification of the locus of context effects in different choice situations.
4. By focusing on brand choice, the framework assesses the effectiveness of advertising, not only by its influence on the advertised brand, but by its effect on competing brands.

The framework presented here has a number of implications for practitioners concerned with measuring advertising effectiveness. First, it provides a link between brand accessibility or "top-of-mind awareness" and brand choice, in the advertising context. Although advertisers generally believe that ad-induced top-of-mind awareness is an important indicator of ad effectiveness, there are few theoretical expositions of the links between this variable and choice in an advertising context.

Second, by explicitly separating advertising exposure from choice, and recognizing that these events occur at different points in time, the framework identifies a clear role for memory and the accessibility of brand-related information (see also Keller, Chapter 1 and Baker, Chapter 2 in this volume). Because the accessibility of information will decay over time (Anderson, 1983b), the role of advertising repetition in maintaining accessibility is clearly indicated. Previous approaches to ad effectiveness suggested that advertising's influence on sales came primarily from the formation or change of brand beliefs and attitudes. Once beliefs were formed, it was thought that only a minimal amount of "maintenance" advertising would be necessary to sustain them.

Finally, the framework indicates that advertising for one brand may have important cross effects on recall, consideration, and choice of competing brands. This is in contrast to previous research that has only examined the effect of advertising exposure on the advertised brand.

The results of a preliminary study, intended to test some aspects of our framework, are very encouraging. These results support the use of the overall choice framework to measure advertising effectiveness.

Specifically, our results show that advertising exposure has different patterns of effects on brand recall, consideration, and choice. In order to understand these effects it is necessary to examine the impact of advertising on each stage of the choice process. For instance, in the memory-based condition, attitudes remained constant between zero and two advertising exposures but, choice increased. Presumably this occurred because the increase in ad exposure increased brand accessibility, which, in turn, increased the likelihood that it was considered in the choice process. The data on the proportion of subjects recalling and considering the target brand support this interpretation.

In addition, the effects of advertising repetition differed dramatically between memory-based and mixed-choice conditions. In general, higher levels of repetition were required to produce changes in consideration and choice in the mixed-choice condition. Between zero and two repetitions, brand recall and consideration increased in the memory-based condition, but were relatively flat in the mixed-choice condition. On the other hand, consideration increased between two and four repetitions in the mixed-choice condition, but decreased in the memory-based condition.

These differences of ad repetition and choice task on recall, consideration, and choice were statistically significant even after controlling for the effects of attitudes. Since most of the previous research examining advertising effects used attitudes as the primary dependent variable, these findings indicate that advertising exposure has effect on recall, consideration, and choice beyond those captured by attitude measures. Our framework suggests that these effects may be primarily due to brand accessibility.

The results of the study also confirm that advertising for one brand has an effect on the recall, consideration, and choice of competing brands. This was most evident in the memory-based condition. Here, as the recall, consideration, and choice of the target brand increased between zero and two advertising exposures, the recall, consideration, and choice of competing brands decreased. Between two and four advertising repetitions, recall of the target brand was stable, however, consideration and choice decreased. Correspondingly, recall of competing brands was constant, however, consideration and choice increased.

Finally, there was evidence that increases in the accessibility of the brand and information about the brand compensate for decreases in brand attitude. This seemed to occur in both the memory and mixed conditions. In the memory-based conditions, the mean attitude of the target brand, when it was chosen, was lower in the four-repetition condition, compared to the two repetition condition, and to the mean attitude for competing brands in all conditions. In the mixed-choice condition, choice of the target brand was the same in the two- and four-repetition condition, even though attitudes decreased.

Future Research

The study described in here represents a preliminary attempt to address some of the issues posed by our framework of advertising effects. The framework suggests a number of directions for future research. First, our study examined the impact of advertising repetition on brand accessibility and brand attitude valence. It is important to examine the impact of an ad on all aspects of brand information, including brand, attribute, and attitude accessibility, and attribute and attitude valence. Further, future research should explore the impact of other advertising executions, such as the provision of retrieval cues (e.g., Keller, 1987, 1991; Nedungadi, 1990), or the use of different types of messages on each stage of the choice process.

Second, although the framework discusses the impact of contextual and task factors, such as motivation and opportunity on information use, the study does not address these aspects. A systematic examination of the effects of these contextual factors remains a priority for future research.

Third, more research needs to be directed at understanding the effects of brand accessibility and attitude valence in mixed-choice situations where subjects are exposed to the names of alternative brands in the choice environment, but the remainder of the choice process is memory-based. The results of the study presented here suggest that these processes may be entirely recognition-based with attitudes playing almost no role in the decision process.

Finally, the study identified the likelihood of a tradeoff between the accessibility of the brand and brand information, including attitudes, and attitude valence. Further research needs to systematically explore the possibility of trade-offs between information accessibility and information valence, in general, in controlled experimental settings.

ACKNOWLEDGMENT

We gratefully acknowledge the financial support of the Social Sciences and Humanities Research Council of Canada.

REFERENCES

Alba, J. W., Hutchinson, J. W., & Lynch, J. G. Jr. (1991). Memory and decision making. In T. S. Robertson & H. H. Kassarjian (Eds.), *Handbook of consumer behavior*. Englewood Cliffs, NJ: Prentice-Hall.

Anderson, J. R. (1983a). A spreading activation theory of memory. *Journal of Verbal Learning and Verbal Behavior, 22,* 261–295.

Anderson, J. R. (1983b). *The architecture of cognition.* Cambridge, MA: Harvard University Press.

Baker, W., Hutchinson, J. W., Moore, D., & Nedungadi, P. (1986). Brand familiarity and advertising: Effects on the evoked set and brand preference. In R. J. Lutz (Ed.), *Advances in consumer research* (Vol. 13, pp. 637–642). Provo, UT: Association for Consumer Research.

Baker, W.E., & Lutz, R. J. (1988). The relevance-accessibility model of advertising effectiveness. In S. Heckler & D. M. Stewart (Eds.), *Nonverbal communication in advertising* (pp. 59–84). Lexington, MA: Lexington Books.

Barsalou, L. W. (1983). Ad hoc categories. *Memory and Cognition, 11,* 211–227.

Barsalou, L. W. (1985). Ideals, central tendency, and frequency of instantiations as determinants of graded structure. *Journal of Experimental Psychology: Learning, Memory, and Cognition, 11,* 629–654.

Barsalou, L. W., & Ross, B. H. (1986). The roles of automatic and strategic processing in sensitivity to superordinate and property frequency. *Journal of Experimental Psychology: Learning, Memory, and Cognition, 12,* 116–134.

Baumgardner, M. H., Leippe, M. R., Ronis, D. L., & Greenwald, A. G. (1983). In search of reliable persuasion effects: II. Associative interference and persistence of persuasion in a message-dense environment. *Journal of Personality and Social Psychology, 45,* 524–537.

Berger, I. (1987). *The effect of advertising on attitude accessibility and the attitude behavior relationship,* Unpublished doctoral dissertation, University of Toronto, Toronto, Canada.

Berger, I., & Mitchell, A. A. (1989). The effect of advertising on attitude accessibility, attitude confidence and the attitude-behavior relationship. *Journal of Consumer Research, 7,* 234–248.

Bettman, J. R. (1979). *An information processing theory of consumer choice.* Reading, MA: Addison-Wesley.

Bettman, J. R., Johnson, E. J., & Payne, J. W. (1991). Consumer decision making. In T. S. Robertson & H. H. Kassarjian (Eds.), *Handbook of consumer behavior* (pp. 50–84). New York: Prentice-Hall.

Bettman, J. R., & Park, C. W. (1980). Effects of prior knowledge, experience, and phase of the choice process on consumer decision processes: A protocol analysis. *Journal of Consumer Research, 7,* 234–248.

Biehal, G., & Chakravarti, D. (1983). Information accessibility as a moderator of consumer choice. *Journal of Consumer Research, 10,* 1–14.

Biehal, G., & Chakravarti, D. (1986). Consumers' use of memory and external information on choice: Macro and micro perspectives. *Journal of Consumer Research, 13,* 382–405.

Burke, R. R., & Srull, T. S. (1988). Competitive interference and consumer memory for choice. *Journal of Consumer Research, 15,* 55–68.

Cacioppo, J. T., & Petty, R. E. (1979). Effects of message repetition and position on cognitive response, recall and persuasion. *Journal of Personality and Social Psychology, 37,* 97–109.

Calder, B. J., & Sternthal, B. (1980). Television commercial wearout: An information processing view. *Journal of Marketing Research, 17,* 173–186.

Craig, C. S., Sternthal, B. & Leavitt, C. (1976). Advertising wearout: An experimental analysis. *Journal of Marketing Research, 13,* 365–372.

Crowder, R. G. (1976). *Principles of learning and memory.* Hillsdale, NJ: Lawrence Erlbaum Associates.

Dickson, P. R., & Sawyer, A. G. (1986). *Point-of-purchase behavior and price perceptions of supermarket shoppers* (Working Paper No. 86-102). Cambridge, MA: Marketing Science Institute.

Fazio, R. H. (1986). How do attitudes guide behavior? In R. M. Sorrentino & E. T. Higgins (Eds.), *The handbook of motivation and cognition: Foundations of social behavior* (pp. 204–243). New York: Guilford Press.

Fazio, R. H., Powell, M. C., & Herr, P. M. (1983). Toward a process model of one's attitude upon mere observation of the attitude object. *Journal of Personality and Social Psychology, 44,* 723–735.

Fazio, R. H., Powell, M. C., & Williams, C. (1989). The role of attitude accessibility in the attitude-to-behavior process. *Journal of Consumer Research, 16,* 280–288.

Feldman, J. M., & Lynch, J. G., Jr. (1988). Self-generated validity and other effects of measurement on belief, attitude, intuition and behavior. *Journal of Applied Psychology, 73,* 421–435.

Gardner, M. P. (1983). Advertising effects on attributes recalled and criteria used for brand evaluations. *Journal of Consumer Research, 10,* 310–318.

Gardner, M. P., Mitchell, A. A., & Russo, J. E. (1985). Low involvement strategies for processing advertisements. *Journal of Advertising, 14,* 4–12.

Haley, R. I., & Case, P. B. (1979). Testing thirteen attitude scales for agreement and brand discrimination. *Journal of Marketing, 43,* 20–32.

Hamilton, D., Driscoll, D. M., & Worth, L. T. (1989). Cognitive organization of impressions: Effect of incongruency in complex representations. *Journal of Personality and Social Psychology, 57,* 925–939.

Hastie, R., & Park, B. (1986). The relationship between memory and judgment depends on whether the judgment task is memory-based or on-line. *Psychological Review, 93,* 258–268.

Homer, P. (1990). The mediating role of attitude toward the ad: Some additional evidence. *Journal of Marketing Research, 27,* 78–86.

Hoyer, W. D. (1984). An examination of consumer decision making for a common repeat purchase product. *Journal of Consumer Research, 11,* 822–829.

Humphreys, M. S., Bain, J. D., Pike, R. (1989). Different ways to cue a coherent memory system: A theory for episodic, semantic and procedural tasks. *Psychological Review, 96,* 208–233.

Jacoby, L. L., & Brooks, L. R. (1984). Nonanalytic cognition: Memory, perception, and concept learning. In G. H. Bower (Ed.), *The psychology of learning and motivation* (Vol. 18, pp. 379–421). New York: Academic Press.

Jamieson, D. W., & Zanna, M. P. (1989). Need for structure in attitude formation and expression. In A. R. Pratkanis, S. J. Breckler, & A. G. Greenwald (Eds.), *Attitude structure and function* (pp. 383–406). Hillsdale, NJ: Lawrence Erlbaum Associates.

Keller, K. L. (1987). Memory factors in advertising: The effect of advertising retrieval cues on brand evaluations. *Journal of Consumer Research, 14,* 316–333.

Keller, K. L. (1991). Cue compatibility and framing in advertising. *Journal of Marketing Research, 28,* 42–57.

Kintsch, W., & Young, S. R. (1984). Selective recall of decision-relevant information from texts. *Memory and Cognition, 12,* 112–117.

Lavidge, R. J., & Steiner, G. A. (1961). A model for predictive measurements of advertising effectiveness. *Journal of Marketing, 25,* 59–62.

Lichtenstein, M., & Srull, T. K. (1985). Conceptual and methodological issues in examining the relationship between consumer memory and judgment. In L. F. Alwitt & A. A. Mitchell (Eds.), *Psychological processes and advertising effects: Theory, research and applications* (pp. 113–128). Hillsdale, NJ: Lawrence Erlbaum Associates.

Lingle, J. H., Geva, N., Ostrom, T. M., Leippe, M. R., & Baumgardner, M. H. (1979). Thematic effects of person judgments on impression organization. *Journal of Personality and Social Psychology, 37* (May), 674–687.

Lingle, J. H., Ostrom, T. M. (1979). Retrieval selectivity in memory-based impression judgments. *Journal of Personality and Social Psychology, 37,* 180–194.

Lutz, R. J. (1975). Changing brand attitudes through modification of cognitive structure. *Journal of Consumer Research, 1,* 49–59.

Lynch, J. G., Jr., Marmorstein, H., & Weigold, M. F. (1988). Choices from sets including remembered brands: Use of recalled attributes and prior overall evaluations. *Journal of Consumer Research, 15,* 225–233.

Lynch, J. G. Jr., & Srull, T. K. (1982). Memory and attention factors in consumer choice: Concepts and research methods. *Journal of Consumer Research, 9,* 18–37.

MacInnis, D. J., & Jaworski, B. J. (1989). Information processing from advertisements: Toward an integrative framework. *Journal of Marketing, 53,* 1–23.

MacKenzie, S. B. (1986). The role of attention in mediating the effect of advertising on attribute importance. *Journal of Consumer Research, 13,* 174–195.

MacKenzie, S. B., Lutz, R. J., & Belch, G. E. (1986). The role of attitude toward the ad as a mediator of advertising effectiveness: A test of competing explanations. *Journal of Marketing Research, 23,* 130–143.

Mitchell, A. A. (1986). The effect of verbal and visual components of advertisements on brand attitudes and attitude toward the advertisement. *Journal of Consumer Research, 13,* 12–24.

Mitchell, A. A., & Olson, J. C. (1981). Are product attribute beliefs the only mediator of advertising effects on brand attitude? *Journal of Marketing Research, 18,* 318–332.

Nedungadi, P. (1987). *Formation and use of consideration set: Implications for marketing and research on consumer choice.* Unpublished doctoral dissertation, University of Florida, Gainesville.

Nedungadi, P. (1990). Recall and consumer consideration sets: Influencing choice without altering brand evaluations. *Journal of Consumer Research, 17,* 263–276.

Nedungadi, P., & Hutchinson, J. W. (1985). The prototypicality of brands: Relationships with brand awareness, preference and usage. In E. C. Hirschman & M. B. Holbrook (Eds.), *Advances in consumer research* (Vol. 12, pp. 498–503). Provo, UT: Association for Consumer Research.

Palda, K. (1966). The hypothesis of a hierarchy of effects: A partial evaluation. *Journal of Marketing Research, 3,* 13–26.

Payne, J. (1976). Task complexity and contingent processing in decision making: An information search and protocol analysis. *Organizational Behavior and Human Performance, 16,* 366–387.

Payne, J. (1982). Contingent decision behavior. *Psychological Bulletin, 92,* 382–402.

Petty, R. E., & Cacioppo, J. T. (1986). *The elaboration likelihood model of persuasion: Central and peripheral routes to attitude change.* New York: Springer-Verlag.

Raaijmakers, L. G. W., & Shiffrin, R. M. (1981). Search of associative memory. *Psychological Review, 88* (March), 93–134.

Ratneshwar, S., & Shocker, A. D. (1991). Substitution in use and the role of usage content in product category structures. *Journal of Marketing Research, 28,* 281–295.

Ray, M. L., & Sawyer, A. G. (1971). Repetition in media models: A laboratory technique. *Journal of Marketing Research, 8,* 20–30.

Rosch, E., & Mervis, C. B. (1975). Family resemblances: Studies in the internal structure of categories. *Cognitive Psychology, 7,* 573–605.

Russo, J. E., & Dosher, B. A. (1983). Strategies for multiattribute binary choice. *Journal of Experimental Psychology: Human Learning, Memory and Cognition, 9,* 676–696.

Sanbonmatsu, D. M., & Fazio, R. H. (1990). The role of attitudes in memory based decision making. *Journal of Personality and Social Psychology, 59,* 614–622.

Sawyer, A. G., & Ward, S. (1979). Carry-over effects in advertising. In J. N. Sneth (Ed.), *Research in marketing* (Vol. 2, pp. 259–314). Greenwich, CT: JAI Press.

Srull, T. K. (1981). Person memory: Some tests of associative storage and retrieval models. *Journal of Experimental Psychology: Human Learning, Memory and Cognition, 7,* 440–463.

Srull, T. K., Lichtenstein, M., & Rothbart, M. (1985). Associative storage and retrieval processes in person memory. *Journal of Experimental Psychology: Learning, Memory and Cognition, 11,* 316–345.

Ward, J., & Loken, B. (1986). The quintessential snack food: Measurement of product prototypes. In R. J. Lutz (Ed.), *Advances in consumer research* (Vol. 13, pp. 126–131). Provo, UT: Association for Consumer Research.

Wright, P. (1975). Consumer choice strategies: Simplifying vs. optimizing. *Journal of Marketing Research, 12,* 60–67.

Wright, P., & Barbour, F. (1975). The relevance of decision process models in structuring persuasive messages. *Communications Research, 2,* 246–259.

Wright, P., & Rip, P. D. (1980). Product class advertising effects on first time buyers' decision strategies. *Journal of Consumer Research, 7,* 176–188.

Zanna, M. P., & Fazio, R. H. (1982). The attitude-behavior relation: Moving toward a third generation of research. In M. P. Zanna, E. T. Higgins, & C. P. Herman (Eds.), *Consistency in social behavior: The Ontario symposium* (Vol. 2, pp. 283–301). Hillsdale, NJ: Lawrence Erlbaum Associates.

II

PSYCHOLOGICAL PROCESSES IN PERSUASION

4 The Attitude-to-Behavior Process: Implications for Consumer Behavior

Paul M. Herr
University of Colorado-Boulder

Russell H. Fazio
Indiana University

Within any given product category, consumers typically can choose among a variety of specific brands. Presumably, consumers' attitudes toward each brand (i.e., their summary evaluations) guide or influence this selection process. Indeed, such an assumption appears to be central to much advertising. Although a goal of advertising is often to increase sales, the manner in which this goal is pursued is often via social influence attempts directed at attitudes. Advertising is typically concerned with the formation of positive attitudes toward the specific product—under the assumption that such information or change will prompt corresponding behavior.

Thus, it is important for marketing researchers to arrive at an understanding of the attitude–behavior relation. The purpose of this chapter is to describe a model of the *process* by which attitudes guide behavior and an associated conceptualization of attitudes. The model, which has been proposed by Fazio and his colleagues (Fazio, Chen, McDonel, & Sherman, 1982; Fazio, Powell, & Herr, 1983) and is detailed in Fazio (1986), concerns the various steps involved in the process by which an individual's attitude can influence behavior. Our intent is to summarize the process model (and some of the research that has been conducted to test it) and to discuss its applicability to consumer behavior. In addition, the process model is contrasted with the Ajzen and Fishbein (1980) theory of reasoned action, which enjoys wide acceptance in marketing.

A MODEL OF THE ATTITUDE–BEHAVIOR PROCESS

The process model assumes that behavior is largely a function of an individual's perceptions in the immediate situation in which the attitude object is encountered. According to the model, the critical concern with respect to the attitude-to-behavior process is the extent to which the attitude influences one's definition of the event that is occurring. Thus, in the context of a consumer making a purchase decision, the question becomes "What are the consumer's immediate perceptions of the brand(s) under consideration?"

Does a previously formed summary evaluation of an attitude object bias one's perceptions of the object in the immediate situation? A considerable literature indicates that attitudes are capable of biasing perceptions in this way. As examples, attitudes have been shown to influence individuals' descriptions of ambiguous scenes (e.g., Proshansky, 1943), their perceptions of infractions during a sports event (Hastorf & Cantril, 1954), and their evaluations of empirical evidence relevant to the attitude issues (Lord, Ross, & Lepper, 1979). In addition, attitudes toward a target person are known to influence the manner in which ambiguous behavior on the part of the target person is interpreted and the causal attributions that are made for nonambiguous behaviors (see Darley & Fazio, 1980, for a review of this literature).

The evidence regarding an attitude–perception relation is consistent with what attitude theorists have referred to as the knowledge or object appraisal function of attitudes (Katz, 1960; Smith, Bruner, & White, 1956). One of the major functions thought to be served by attitudes is that of organizing and structuring the multitude of objects that individuals encounter in their social universe. An attitude has been said to provide "a ready aid in 'sizing up' objects and events in the environment" (Smith et al., 1956, p. 41).

This object appraisal function and the related impact that attitudes can have on perceptions when an attitude object is encountered form the crux of the attitude–behavior process model. According to the model, attitudes guide behavior through their mediating impact on perceptions. However, the process model does involve more components than described thus far. This additional complexity is necessitated by the fact that empirical investigations of attitude–behavior consistency indicate that such consistency is sometimes present and sometimes not (see Zanna & Fazio, 1982, for a historical review of this literature). Thus, some factors must prevent the process as outlined thus far from reaching its culmination or from beginning.

Norms constitute such a factor in that they may attenuate the impact of attitude on behavior. According to the process model, behavior is a function of one's definition of the event. Up to this point, we have equated definition of the event with perceptions of the attitude object in the immediate situation. Actually, the attitude object can be considered only one component of the individual's definition of the event. An individual possesses much more in the way of knowledge structures that are stored in memory than the attitude toward the object in question. In particular, the individual's knowledge regarding what behaviors are or are not normatively appropriate for any given situation may be relevant to construal of the event. Norms have been found to exert such a moderating influence on the attitude–behavior relation (e.g., Ajzen & Fishbein, 1973; Schofield, 1975; Warner & DeFleur, 1969).

Within the context of consumer behavior, normative knowledge may sometimes exert a greater impact on individual's definitions than their own attitudes do. This may be particularly true of products that are conspicuous in nature (i.e., visible and identifiable by others; Bourne, 1963). Regardless of one's personal views, one's knowledge regarding the consensual preferences of one's friends, for example, may influence strongly the decision to purchase and serve a particular wine at a dinner party. Thus, normative information regarding appropriate behavior in a given situation may affect one's definition of the situation. This definition of the situation may outweigh one's perceptions of the attitude object itself in the individuals's construal of the event. This may be one reason why attitude–behavior consistency occurs only sometimes.

However, not all situations are normatively prescribed. Even in normatively free situations, considerable variability in attitude–behavior consistency has been observed (for reviews, see Schuman & Johnson, 1976; Zanna, Higgins, & Herman, 1982). The mere fact that many variables in addition to norms (e.g., various qualities of the attitude itself; see Fazio & Zanna, 1981) have been found to moderate the attitude–behavior relation attests to this. The model postulates that a critical step is necessary to initiate the attitude–behavior process. The attitude must be activated from memory upon the individual's encountering the attitude object.[1] Unless the attitude is activated from memory, it cannot produce selective perception of the object in the immediate situation. Indeed, the individual may never view the object in evaluative terms. Or, more likely in the context of consumer behavior, if the individual does consider the object evaluatively, he or she may do so on the basis of whatever features of the situation and the attitude object are sufficiently salient to influence immediate perceptions. This on-the-spot appraisal may not be consistent with any previously stored attitude toward the object.

Thus, the key to the model is attitude accessibility. The attitude must be activated from memory upon the individual's observation of the attitude object if the attitude is to influence perceptions in the immediate situation and in any sense guide subsequent behavior. A schematic summary of the attitude–behavior process model is presented in Fig. 4.1.

Conceptualizing Attitudes and Attitude Accessibility.   Given the importance attached to attitude activation as the initiating step of the attitude–behavior

---

[1]Throughout this chapter, we use the terms *encountering the attitude object* and *observation of the attitude object* in a broad sense. We do not mean to restrict attitude activation to situations involving the physical presence of the attitude object. The terms are intended to refer to the presence of either the physical object or any symbolic representation of the object. The critical issue concerns whether the attitude is activated from memory whenever the memorial representation of the attitude object has been activated through whatever means.

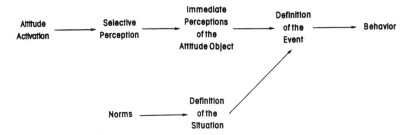

FIG. 4.1. A schematic diagram of the attitude–behavior process model.

process, it is essential to discuss how we conceptualize attitudes and their accessibility from memory within the model. According to the process model, the likelihood of attitude activation upon mere observation of the attitude object depends on the chronic accessibility of attitude. An attitude is viewed as the categorization of an object along an evaluative dimension—a feature that is common to all of the numerous definitions of attitude that have appeared in the literature (see Greenwald, 1968; McGuire, 1969). An attitude, then, is essentially an association between a given object and a given evaluation. This evaluative associate may itself involve "hot" affect (i.e., a strongly emotional response to the attitude object) or a "colder" judgment of the evaluative implications of one's beliefs about the object. In either case, the association between the affect and the object constitutes the attitude.

Unlike some early definitions of attitude (e.g., Allport, 1935; Doob, 1947), this simple definition avoids postulating an attitude–behavior link as part of the very definition. Thus, the extent to which attitude relates to behavior is treated as an empirical, not a definitional, issue. More important, this definition has a useful implication concerning the chronic accessibility of an attitude. The definition implies that the strength of an attitude, like any construct based on associative learning, can vary. That is, the strength of the association between the object and the evaluation can vary. It is this associative strength that is postulated to determine the chronic accessibility of the attitude and, hence, the likelihood that the attitude will be activated upon the individual's encountering the attitude object. Only if it is strongly associated with the object is it likely that the evaluation will be activated spontaneously upon observation of the object.

Empirical tests of the view of attitudes as object-evaluation associations have yielded confirming results. Subjects who had been induced to note and express their attitudes repeatedly, which should have the consequence of strengthening the object-evaluation association, have been found to be capable of responding relatively quickly to direct inquiries about their attitudes (Fazio et al., 1982; Powell & Fazio, 1984). For example, Powell and Fazio manipulated the number of times that an attitude was expressed by varying the number of semantic differential items that were listed relevant to a given attitude issue. In this way, subjects expressed their attitudes zero, one, three, or six times toward a given attitude object. In a subsequent task, subjects were presented with each attitude issue and instructed to make a good/bad judgment about each object as quickly as possible. Response latency was found to relate to the number of previous attitudinal expressions. The greater the number of expressions, the shorter the latency of response to an attitudinal inquiry.

These findings lend credence to the view of attitudes as object-evaluation associations and suggest that attitude accessibility depends on the strength of the object-evaluation association. However, in terms of the attitude–behavior process, the critical issue is whether individuals' attitudes are activated spontaneously from memory upon mere observation of the attitude object. These findings concern accessing one's attitude from memory in response to a direct inquiry. Thus, these findings are not at all informative with respect to the issue of spontaneous activation. Responding quickly to a direct attitudinal inquiry may mean that the stored evaluation was activated spontaneously upon presentation of the attitude issue. Alternatively, it may mean that the evaluation was retrieved efficiently via an effortful process.

The distinction that we wish to draw at this point is between automatic and controlled attitude activation. Automatic versus controlled processes have received considerable theoretical and empirical attention in cognitive psychology (e.g., Schneider & Shiffrin, 1977; Shiffrin & Schneider, 1977). Shiffrin and Dumais (1981) characterized as automatic any process that leads to the activation of some concept of response "whenever a given set of external initiating stimuli are presented, regardless of a subject's attempt to ignore or bypass the distraction" (p. 117). The key feature of such automatic activation is its inescapability. In contrast, a controlled process requires the active attention of the individual. Thus, upon becoming aware of a situational cue implying the importance of considering one's attitude toward an object, the individual might attempt to retrieve a previously stored evaluation of the attitude object or might actively construct such an attitude on the spot. In either case, the process is reflective and effortful in nature.

According to the model, attitudes can be activated automatically and the likelihood of such activation depends on the strength of the object-evaluation association. This hypothesis was confirmed in a recent series of experiments conducted by Fazio, Sanbonmatsu, Powell, and Kardes (1986). These experiments involved a priming procedure that permitted the examination of the hypothesis that the mere presentation of an attitude object toward which an individual possesses a strong evaluative association would automatically activate the evaluation. On each trial, the prime that was presented was the name of an attitude object. Its presentation was followed by the display of a positive or negative evaluative adjective. The subject's task was to press a key as quickly as possible to indicate whether the adjective had a positive or negative connotation.

The latency with which these responses were made was facilitated on trials that involved evaluatively congruent primes (attitude objects) and targets, provided that the attitude object possessed a strong evaluative association for the subject. To provide an example, if a subject had a strong negative association to the object "cockroach," then presentation of cockroach as the prime facilitated the subject's indicating that an evaluative adjective such as "disgusting" had a negative connotation.

Such facilitation was observed only in the case of attitudes characterized by strong object-evaluation associations. In some of the experiments, pre-experimentally strong and weak associations were identified via a measurement procedure. The measurement involved latency of response to a direct attitudinal inquiry—the same measure that had been shown in the research described earlier to reflect the strength of the object-evaluation association. Attitude objects for which the subject was able to respond relatively rapidly when faced with an attitudinal inquiry had served as the strong primes and those for which the subject responded relatively slowly as the weak primes. In an additional experiment, strength of the object-evaluation association was manipulated rather than measured. Attitude objects for which subjects had been induced to express their attitudes repeatedly produced facilitation when the objects later served as primes in the adjective connotation task.

These findings provide corroboration for the hypothesis that the likelihood of automatic activation of an attitude upon mere observation of the attitude object depends on the strength of the object-evaluation association in memory. The existence of facilitation suggests that the subject's attitude toward the object was activated automatically upon its mere presentation as the prime. Subjects were not asked to consider their attitudes toward these primes. Nor was it to the subjects' advantage to do so, for the subjects' major task was simply to respond to the target adjective. Nevertheless, despite this irrelevance of attitudes to the immediate task concerns, exposure to objects for which subjects possessed strong affective associations appears to have prompted activation of the associated evaluation. Thus, the results of these experiments indicate that attitudes can be activated from memory automatically and that the strength of the object-evaluation association determines the likelihood of such automatic activation.

Supporting Evidence.   Some evidence supportive of the process model already has been described. Additional research merits a brief summary. Consistent with the model's assertion regarding attitudes that involve a strong object-evaluation association, experimental work has indicated that this associative strength acts as a determinant of attitude–behavior consistency (Fazio et al., 1982, Experiment 4). Subjects in this experiment were introduced to a set of intellectual puzzles and then indicated how interesting they found each type of puzzle. Under an appropriate ruse, some subjects were asked to copy their original ratings onto two additional forms. Thus, they were induced to note and express these attitudes repeatedly—a procedure that the research described earlier has shown to strengthen the object-evaluation association and, hence, the chronic accessibility of the attitude. When later given the opportunity to play with any of the five types of puzzles in a free-play period, subjects in this repeated expression condition displayed greater attitude–behavior consistency than did subjects who expressed their attitudes only a single time.

In addition, correlational field research has provided support for the model's propositions that attitude accessibility serves as a moderator of both the relation between attitudes and subsequent perceptions of the attitude object and the relation between attitudes and subsequent behavior. In an investigation of the 1984 presidential election, Fazio and Williams (1986) measured attitudes toward Reagan for a large sample of townspeople some 3½ months prior to the election. The accessibility of these attitudes was also assessed, via latency of response to an attitudinal inquiry. (Note that the findings from the earlier described research by Fazio et al., 1986, on automatic activation indicate that latency of response to an attitudinal inquiry provides a reasonable approximation of the likelihood of automatic activation of the attitude upon mere presentation of the attitude object.)

Judgments of the performance of the candidates during the televised debates served as the measure of subsequent perceptions and voting as the measure of behavior. Just as postulated by the model, correlations between attitudes and perceptions and between attitudes and voting behavior were higher among those individuals who were able to respond relatively quickly to the attitudinal inquiry (the high accessibility group) than among those who responded relatively slowly (the low accessibility group). Indeed, within the high accessibility group, attitudes toward Reagan, as measured months before the election by a single scale, accounted for nearly 80% of the variance in voting behavior, compared to 44% within the low accessibility group. The implication is that both the degree to which selective processing of subsequently presented information about the attitude object occurs and the degree to which attitude–behavior consistency occurs depends on the accessibility of the attitude from memory, just as suggested by the model.

A final line of evidence supportive of the proposed process model stems from research concerning the manner of attitude formation—a variable that has been shown to moderate attitude–behavior consistency. In a number of laboratory experiments and field investigations, attitudes formed on the basis of direct behavioral experience with the attitude object have been found to be more predictive of subsequent behavior than attitudes formed via indirect, nonbehavioral experience (see Fazio & Zanna, 1981, for a review of this program of research). The process model explains this finding quite readily. Subsequent research has indicated that attitudes based on direct experience are more chronically accessible from memory than are attitudes formed through indirect experience. For example, attitudes formed toward intellectual puzzles following the opportunity to sample the various puzzle types behaviorally can be expressed more quickly in response to a direct attitudinal inquiry than can attitudes formed after only seeing samples and hearing descriptions of each puzzle type (Fazio et al., 1982, Experiments 1 and 2). That is, one of our standard measures of attitude accessibility, latency of response, reveals a difference between direct and indirect experience attitudes. Furthermore, it has been found that direct experience attitudes are more likely to be evoked spontaneously from memory upon mere observation of the attitude object than indirect experience attitudes (Fazio et al., 1983).

It appears that individuals perceive their own behavior to be a highly valid reflection of their attitude toward a given object. As a result, they form a stronger association between the object and the evaluation implied by their behavior than occurs when only less attitudinally diagnostic indirect experience is available (see Fazio, Herr, & Olney, 1984). This associative strength and the consequent accessibility of the attitude means that attitudes based on direct experience are more likely to guide subsequent behavior than are attitudes based on indirect experience. The manner of attitude formation serves as an illustrative case in point of a general principle offered by the process model. Any variable that affects the chronic accessibility of the attitude will have a corresponding impact on the attitude–behavior relation.

The Attitude–Nonattitude Continuum.   The findings from the research summarized thus far indicate clearly that not all attitudes are equal. Relevant to this idea of attitudes varying in strength is the so-called *attitude–nonattitude* distinction noted by both Hovland (1959) and Converse (1970). The distinction centered on the observation that a person may respond to an item on an attitude survey even though that particular attitude does not really exist in any a priori fashion for the individual. The attitude object may be one the individual has not even considered prior to the administration of the attitude survey. Fazio et al. (1986) suggested that it may be more fruitful to view this attitude–nonattitude dichotomy as a continuum. Our definition of attitudes as object-evaluation associations lends itself nicely to such a conception. These associations can vary in strength, ranging from *not existing at all* (the case of a nonattitude) to a *weak association* that is unlikely to be capable of automatic activation to a *strong association* that can be activated automatically.

This continuum provides an interesting means of conceptualizing the strength of an attitude (see Fazio, 1989). The attitudes of two individuals with identical scores from some attitude measurement instrument may still differ markedly with regard to their strength, that is, their likelihood of activation upon the individual's mere exposure to the object. Upon encountering the attitude object in a given situation, the attitude of one individual may be activated, whereas the attitude of the other may not be. As a result, the two individuals may construe the object quite differently in the immediate situation. Immediate perceptions congruent with the attitude are more likely in the case of the individual whose attitude has been activated. Obviously, given this conceptualization of attitudes and our model of the attitude–behavior process, we would expect the same to be true for consumers' attitudes toward brands. The higher the position of the consumer's attitude along the attitude–nonattitude continuum, the greater the likelihood that the attitude will guide purchase behavior.

GENERALIZING THE MODEL TO ATTITUDES TOWARD PRODUCTS

One of the central tenets of the model is that attitudes can be activated automatically from memory and that the likelihood of such activation depends on the strength of the object-evaluation association. The priming experiments (Fazio et al., 1986) provide support for this hypothesis. Recent research by Sanbonmatsu and Fazio (1986) indicates that the same is true of attitudes toward products. In a replication of the priming experiments described earlier, brand names were presented as the primes. Just as in the previous research, brands toward which the subjects possessed positive attitudes facilitated subjects' responding to positive evaluative adjectives. That is, they were able to indicate the connotation of a positive evaluative adjective relatively quickly when such an adjective was preceded by a positively valued brand name. Likewise, negatively valued brand names facilitated subjects' responding to adjectives that were negative in connotation.

Once again, however, this pattern was observed only for attitudes involving strong object-evaluation associations, as indicated by latency of response to a direct attitudinal inquiry. Only brand names for which the subject was able to respond relatively rapidly when faced with an attitudinal inquiry showed evidence of prompting automatic attitude activation upon their mere presentation during the later adjective connotation task.

A second tenet of the process model is that the accessibility of the attitude from memory acts as a determinant of the extent of the attitude–behavior relation. This too has received confirmation within the domain of attitudes toward products. Fazio, Powell, and Williams (1989) demonstrated the impact of attitude accessibility on actual product choice. At the conclusion of an experimental session in which subjects' response latencies to direct attitudinal inquiries were measured, subjects were allowed to choose 5 of 10 available products as "reimbursement" for participating in the experiment. The available products included such items as candy bars, peanuts, juice, and soda. Product selection was clearly related to subjects' attitudes toward the products. Again, however, additional analyses indicated that the extent of this relation was greater for subjects with highly accessible brand attitudes than for those with less accessible attitudes. These findings suggest that there is no difficulty in generalizing the conclusions that were drawn on the basis of the earlier research concerning automatic attitude activation and choice to the specific domain of products.

Attitudes toward brands can be activated automatically from memory and the likelihood of such activation depends on the strength of the object-evaluation association. Once activated, brand attitudes can in fact influence product choice.

SPONTANEOUS AND DELIBERATIVE PROCESSING

The Ajzen and Fishbein (1980) "theory of reasoned action" has been used considerably by marketers in predicting consumer purchases. It should be clear from the discussion so far that one major departure of the present model from Ajzen and Fishbein's rests in the cognitive work that individuals are presumed to undertake. "Reasoned action" is by definition "effortful" and involves considerable deliberative processing on the part of the individual. This type of processing involves the scrutiny of available information and an analysis of positive and negative features, of costs and benefits. Specific attributes of the attitude object and potential consequences of engaging in a particular course of action are considered and weighed. It is this specific attitude toward the behavior under consideration that is presumed to influence the resulting intention to behave in a particular manner. In contrast, the present model focuses on a much more spontaneous process in which a global attitude toward the object is automatically activated from memory and determines one's appraisal of the object in the immediate situation.

An extensive analysis and comparison of these spontaneous and deliberative processes is provided by Fazio (1990). In addition, Fazio (1990) proposed a model that seeks to integrate the two processes into a more comprehensive framework by identifying the conditions under which each of the two processes is likely to occur. This "MODE" model postulates that both *M*otivation and *O*pportunity are *DE*terminants of which processing mode is likely to occur in a given situation. The model can be viewed as an application of Kruglanski's (1989) general "theory of lay epistemology" to the specific domain of attitude–behavior processes. Kruglanski attempted to delineate the general processes and motivating variables relevant to the acquisition of knowledge. According to his theory, individuals who are motivated to avoid reaching an invalid conclusion due to the perceived costliness of a mistake are said to have "fear of invalidity." The theory suggests that this motivational factor facilitates careful reflection concerning upcoming judgments and decisions. In the context of the MODE model, such fear of invalidity is postulated to motivate persons to undergo the effortful reflection and reasoning involved in a deliberative attitude–behavior process. Without this inducement, individual's behavior may simply follow from their definition of the event. Any impact of attitude on behavior would then depend solely on the strength of the object-evaluation association in memory. The MODE model recognizes, however, that motivation to reflect is insufficient by itself to produce deliberative processing. Because deliberative processing is so effortful, the *opportunity* to take the time required for this process is also necessary.

Thus, the MODE model suggests that individuals reason and deliberate about their future actions in situations characterized by both fear of invalidity and opportunity to reflect. In arriving at their behavioral intention they consider their attitude toward the behavior in question. This attitude is "computed" on the basis of the desirability of the likely consequences of the behavior. The central features of this deliberative process (e.g., construction of an attitude toward the specific behavior under consideration) occur only when the motivation and the opportunity to deliberate exist. Because individuals are motivated to exert cognitive effort by the perceived costliness of the potential behavior, any capacity for automatic activation of the attitude toward the object becomes irrelevant. In situations not characterized by fear of invalidity or that do not permit the individual an opportunity to deliberate, any effect of attitude on behavior will operate only through the spontaneous processing mode. In those cases, individuals will not be motivated to deliberate and construct an attitude toward their behavior. Instead, any effect of attitude will depend on the extent that a strong evaluative association has been formed with the attitude object. Only if a strong association exists will encountering the attitude object result in automatic activation of the attitude from memory. The activated attitude can then color the individual's immediate perceptions in the situation, and, as a consequence, influence behavior. Alternatively, when an evaluative association is too weak to be activated, behavior follows from a definition of the event that is nonattitudinally based. Whatever features of the object and situation that attract attention will determine the individual's immediate perceptions and behavior.

A direct test of the MODE model comes from Sanbonmatsu and Fazio (1990). While instructed to form general evaluations of two department stores, subjects were presented with a series of statements about a variety of departments in each store. One store (Smith's) was described in generally favorable terms, whereas the other store (Brown's) was described in generally unfavorable terms. A global impression of Smith's should be more favorable than of Brown's. This was confirmed by subjects who expressed their attitude toward each store immediately following presentation of the stimuli. However, the information about the camera departments in each store was designed in a manner that was the reverse of these global evaluations. Thus, Brown's camera department was described in more favorable terms than was Smith's camera department. This was done to create a situation in which subjects had created a general attitude toward the store as well as having individual attribute information stored in memory.

At a later point in the experiment, subjects were asked to imagine that they needed to buy a camera from one of the two department stores. A choice of Smith's (the generally better store with the relatively inferior camera department) would be consistent with a relatively effortless process, involving consideration only of the overall attitude toward the store without consideration of any of the attribute information. A choice of Brown's (the generally less desirable store with the better camera department) would be consistent with a deliberative process in which the specific attributes about each camera department were retrieved from memory and considered in forming an attitude toward the act of purchasing a camera at each of the two stores.

Prior to the camera-buying choice task, both motivation and opportunity to deliberate were manipulated. Opportunity was manipulated by telling half the subjects that they would have only 15 seconds to reach a decision about the question to follow. The rest of the subjects were specifically instructed to take as much time as they needed in answering the question. Fear of invalidity was manipulated by informing half the subjects that their decision would be compared with the decisions of other subjects, and that they would have to justify their choice to the experimenter and to the other subjects. These instructions were not given to subjects in the low fear of invalidity condition.

The results corroborated the predictions of the MODE model. The only subjects to engage in the deliberative processing that resulted in choosing Brown's were those who had the motivation and opportunity to do so. That is, subjects who received the high fear of invalidity instructions and were given time to deliberate displayed a significantly greater preference for buying a camera at Brown's than did subjects in any of the other three conditions.

IMPLICATIONS FOR CONSUMER BEHAVIOR

The concept of attitude has long been central in buyer behavior models (cf. Day & Deutscher, 1982; Howard & Sheth, 1969), as a base for market segmentation (Wind, 1978), as a framework for advertising strategy (Boyd, Ray, & Strong, 1972), and in general as a measure of a product's "position" in a consumer's mind. In light of the contributions of the process model to the understanding of attitudes and behavior in general, it seems reasonable to apply the model to marketing, with the goal of increasing our understanding of marketing phenomena. To that end, we examine several areas in which the model may increase our understanding. This discussion is not meant to be exhaustive, but rather suggestive of the model's power in explicating the role and function of attitudes in the marketing domain.

The process model provides several interesting departures from earlier conceptualizations of attitudinal effects on behavior. Specifically, the process model's primary focus is on relatively "small purchases" of a routine nature, rather than on "big ticket" items, for which Ajzen and Fishbein's approach may be more normatively and descriptively appropriate. The purchase of big ticket items is likely to motivate individuals to deliberate about the potential positive and negative consequences of particular brands in a reasoned fashion. The accessibility of previously formed attitudes is less critical in such a context. In contrast, we would suggest that attitude accessibility, and the more spontaneous attitude–behavior process that we have delineated, are critical for products that are unlikely to provoke deliberation. The research conducted to date implies that whether the attitude is activated from memory in response to the product and, if so, what attitude is activated are critical in determining consumer behavior in such cases. The implications of the process model for understanding routine purchases are relatively straightforward and managerially actionable.

Fostering Attitude Accessibility.   Obviously, the marketing manager needs an array of tactics to create attitudes, strengthen weak existing attitudes, or change unfavorable attitudes. However, inducing positive attitudes is not in and of itself sufficient to have much influence on consumer behavior. The general principle offered by the attitude–behavior process model and the research that has been conducted to test it is that attitudes must be accessible from memory in order to influence subsequent perceptions and behavior. Thus, the advertiser cannot be concerned solely with the creation of a positive attitude toward the brand. This new attitude also must involve an object-evaluation association that is sufficiently strong for the attitude to be highly accessible from memory. In other words, if the goal of advertising is to influence purchase behavior, then one needs to be concerned not only with the valence of the resulting attitude but also with its position along the attitude–nonattitude continuum. With this in mind, the remainder of this chapter focuses on actions managers might consider to meet the specific goals of creating positive accessible attitudes, strengthening positive but weak attitudes, and changing negative attitudes.

The research discussed so far suggests means by which consumers' development of accessible attitudes might be promoted. Consider first the research on direct behavioral experience. The findings indicate the relative advantage of direct behavioral experiences over indirect nonbehavioral experience in promoting accessible attitudes that are likely to impact on later behavior. The extension to marketing is quite straightforward in that the findings suggest that promotional strategies that involve product sampling may be particularly effective. In recent studies, both Smith and Swinyard (1983) and Berger and Mitchell (1989) compared the effects of product sampling (direct behavioral experience) versus advertising (indirect experience) on subsequent attitude–behavior consistency. As expected, subjects who sampled the product were significantly more likely to behave consistently with their attitude toward the product than were subjects who were only exposed to advertising about the product.

On the basis of the research discussed earlier, it appears reasonable to presume that the attitudes of persons in the direct experience condition (who sampled the product) were more accessible than were the attitudes of persons in the ad-only condition. Thus, the present framework strongly endorses the use of product trials as a means of instilling accessible attitudes. On the assumption that the brand is indeed good, such direct experience will produce a positive attitude that is relatively likely to impact upon consumer behavior. Of course, if the direct experience produces a negative attitude, the enhanced accessibility characteristic of such behaviorally based attitudes implies that the product will not be used in the future.

Given the emphasis that we have placed on direct experience with the attitude object, it may at first seem that managers are severely limited in their options for fostering positive accessible attitudes about their products. We believe this is not necessarily the case. In fact, anything that strengthens the link between the attitude object and its evaluation increases attitude accessibility. The success of repeated attitudinal expression in enhancing attitude accessibility suggests a general means by which this might be accomplished. We believe that marketers can take advantage of this finding by creating situations in which consumers are induced to note their attitudes about a product frequently. This may be done in any number of ways. Simply seeing the advertisement for a product may be sufficient to activate an attitude for a person who already holds a strong attitude for the advertised product. For a person who has not formed a strong attitude, however, it may be necessary to place cues in the advertising copy that induce an individual to activate a weak attitude, and, as a consequence, strengthen it. These cues may simply involve requests that individuals consider their feelings about the product or product class.

It is also conceivable that something analogous to repeated attitudinal expression might be accomplished within the context of a persuasive message. Many ads appear to rely on an entertaining scene or an endorsement by an attractive celebrity to associate the product with a positive evaluation. Often, this association is explicitly drawn only once at the conclusion of the ad. That is, only once (if at all) is the product directly linked to a positive evaluative statement. In contrast, one can readily imagine a message that asserts the association repeatedly. Exposure to creative, attention-grabbing repetitions of this sort may increase the likelihood that individuals store the desired association between the product and the positive evaluation in memory. As a result, the probability that the evaluation would be activated from memory when the product is encountered may be enhanced. We are not aware of any research concerning persuasive communications that involve such multiple evaluative statements, but this technique may produce a means of instilling positive and relatively accessible attitudes.

Furthermore, Berger and Mitchell (1989) observed a benefit to repeating an entire advertisement multiple times. Although repetitions did not enhance the favorability of individuals' attitudes toward the products, they did increase the likelihood that individuals would behave consistently with those attitudes. Subjects who were exposed to ads four times displayed much more consistency between their attitudes and their brand selection behavior than did subjects who were exposed to the ads a single time and, indeed, displayed just as much consistency as subjects in a direct experience condition who had sampled each brand. Thus, repetitions may serve to enhance the strength of attitudes in terms of their likelihood of influencing actual behavior.

Yet another possible advertising strategy for fostering the development of attitudes that are of sufficient associative strength to influence behavior is suggested by the findings from an experiment conducted by Fazio, Zanna, and Cooper (1978). Subjects were introduced to a set of novel intellectual puzzles by exposure to a videotape of an actor working on examples of each type of puzzle. All subjects were informed that they would be asked to indicate how interesting they found each type of puzzle after viewing the videotape. Half the subjects were instructed to "just listen and watch carefully." In effect, these subjects formed their attitudes via indirect experience with the puzzles. The remaining subjects received a set of instructions intended to promote their empathizing with the videotaped actor. For example, they were told to "imagine how you would feel if you were in her position. Concentrate on how you would react to each type of problem if you were working the examples." In effect, then, these subjects formed attitudes by empathizing with someone engaged in direct behavioral experience with the attitude objects.

The impact of this empathy manipulation on attitude–behavior consistency was examined. After viewing the tape, subjects indicated their attitude toward each puzzle type. They were then given a 15-minute opportunity to work on any of the puzzle types that they wished. Behavior during this "free-play" period was much more correspondent with previously expressed attitudes within the empathy condition than within the control condition. Although attitude accessibility was not assessed in this experiment, the findings imply that the attitudes formed via empathizing with an actor's direct experience are relatively strong and likely to influence behavior.

Much more research concerning the impact of empathy is needed. Nevertheless, the implication is that advertising that induces viewers to imagine how it would feel to use a given product may foster the development of attitudes that are stronger and more accessible from memory than advertising that does not do so. Such an advertising strategy merits investigation as a possible means of instilling accessible attitudes.

The goal of advertising in the cases we are discussing is to create and/or strengthen the attitude sufficiently that it is accessible from memory. The optimal situation would exist if the object-evaluation association were so strong that merely seeing or hearing mention of the product would cause the attitude to be activated automatically. However, this state may be difficult to attain and may occur only after repeated exposure to and experience with the product. In the interim, it may be necessary, or at least desirable, for marketers to attempt to induce consumers to access their attitudes at the point of purchase. Some cue associated with the advertisement might be displayed. This cue could serve to prompt the consumer to access the attitude initially created by the advertisement itself. In other words, instead of relying on the chronic accessibility of the attitude to be sufficient for attitude activation to occur, one might attempt to enhance momentarily the acute accessibility of the attitude in the situation in which the product is encountered.

Recent social psychological research suggests that such cues enhance attitude–behavior consistency. For example, Snyder and Kendzierski (1982) examined the effectiveness of a cue that defined attitudes as relevant to the immediate situation. The experimenters exposed subjects with favorable attitudes toward psychological research to a sign posted on the wall of a waiting room. The notice was a request for volunteers to participate in a psychological experiment. Each subject overheard two confederates conversing about the notice. When one confederate indicated that he did not know whether to volunteer or not, the other responded in one of two ways. In the experimental condition, the reply promoted consideration of one's attitude: "[It's] really a question of how worthwhile you think experiments are." In the control condition, the reply was simply, "Beats me—it's up to you." Although all subjects who heard one of these two exchanges had positive attitudes toward psychological research, significantly more of those in the experimental condition acted in accordance with their attitudes and volunteered than in the control condition.

The experiment illustrates the benefits of employing a cue to prompt attitude activation. A similar strategy might be followed in a consumer context and might be especially valuable in the case of relatively weak attitudes incapable of automatic activation. A point-of-purchase display could be employed to present a cue designed to induce consumers to access previously formed attitudes in a more controlled fashion. The cue, of course, is under the control of the marketer, and should probably be some central feature or theme of the advertisement. For example, if a celebrity has endorsed a product in an advertisement, a point-of-purchase display involving the celebrity may serve to activate the attitude created by the ad itself. That point-of-purchase displays can have profound influence on sales has been demonstrated perhaps most graphically in a Point of Purchase Advertising Institute study in which consumers purchasing snack foods were reported as 600% more likely to buy an item if that item was accompanied by point-of-purchase display in addition to it being advertised (Edel, 1986). When point-of-purchase displays are not feasible or available, the package label itself may serve as a reminder of the attitude, perhaps bearing the likeness of a key feature in the ad, or the tagline associated with the product. The essential notion here is that an appropriately designed point-of-purchase display or package label may help to activate an individual's attitude from memory even though the chronic accessibility of the attitude is such that it is unlikely to be activated without any prompting whatsoever upon mere observation of the product.

Targeting the Ad.   The attitude–behavior process model also offers some interesting suggestions regarding the potential effectiveness of advertising campaigns. The model postulates that the more accessible the attitude is from memory, the greater the extent of selective processing of any information that is presented concerning the attitude object. This postulate is supported by the Fazio and Williams (1986) investigation summarized earlier. Recall that individuals with highly accessible attitudes toward Reagan displayed greater correspondence between those attitudes and their judgments of the performance of the candidates during the televised debates than did individuals whose attitudes were less accessible. Thus, by virtue of their being activated readily and coloring perceptions of subsequent information, initial attitudes characterized by high accessibility are likely to be relatively resistant to change and to persist over time. Consistent with this reasoning, Wood (1982) found that attitude change in response to a persuasive communication is attenuated among individuals who can rapidly retrieve beliefs about the attitude object from memory.

One implication of this reasoning is that advertisers are not likely to be successful in modifying highly accessible negative attitudes toward a product or service. In such a case, advertisers might strive to "re-position" the brand as a new product so as to start with a relatively fresh slate. The marketing manager could attempt to "dissociate" the product from the negative evaluation, perhaps through a combination of advertising and trial with a "new, improved" product. The very nature of a strong attitude, however, makes it difficult to change. After all, it is likely that the attitude was formed through a negative direct behavioral experience (e.g., the car broke down on the expressway) and was further strengthened each time the incident was relived for acquaintances.

There is a second, more hopeful, implication. Because relatively inaccessible attitudes seem to promote less selective processing, individuals who possess attitudes of this sort, as well as those with no initial attitude toward the product, would seem to be more easily swayed by new information about the attitude object. It is for such people, as opposed to those with highly accessible attitudes, that persuasive communications have the best chance to be effective agents of attitude change. Thus, in the context of a marketing campaign, the maximal use of resources might be made by targeting advertisements at individuals whose attitudes are relatively low in accessibility. Especially if marketing research were to reveal that various demographic variables were associated with the accessibility of attitudes toward the given product, such targeting would be possible. Given the costs of advertising, such maximal use of resources is obviously desirable.

The measure of attitude accessibility that was employed in both the Fazio and Williams study and the Fazio, Powell, and Williams study—latency of response to an attitudinal inquiry—appears to provide a feasible means of identifying a target population for whom the marketer's persuasive efforts are likely to pay off. The use of response latencies in connection with attitudes is not new in marketing. LaBarbera and MacLachlan (1979); MacLachlan (1977); and MacLachlan, Czepiel, and LaBarbera (1979) used response latencies to attitudinal inquiries as a measure of the confidence with which the attitude was held, a concept not unrelated to attitudinal strength. The findings of the latter study demonstrated the feasibility of gathering response latency data by telephone (using a voice-operated relay system), the robustness of these response latencies, and the power the measure has in discriminating between answers "based on knowledge" and those answers that were merely guesses. The research that we have discussed indicates that latency of response to an attitudinal inquiry approximates the likelihood that the attitude is capable of automatic activation. Because this variable appears critical to the individual's consideration of new information about the attitude object, the response latency technique may prove useful in identifying segments of the population (those people with relatively inaccessible attitudes) for whom advertising is most likely to have the desired impact.

Constraints Upon Attitude–Behavior Consistency. Even when consumers have accessible, positive attitudes, situations may exist that preclude consistent behavior. Even after the attitude has been activated and the consumer perceives the situation consistently with the attitude, consistent behavior may not follow if the consumer is for some reason unable to behave. For instance, the potential consumer may not have the financial resources to complete a purchase, yet nonetheless hold a favorable accessible attitude about the product. Or, even if the consumer has the wherewithal to purchase the favored brand, the brand may be priced so outrageously high that its cost, rather than its positive qualities, comprises the major perception of the product in the immediate situation. That is, the selective processing fostered by a highly accessible attitude may not be capable of overcoming the reality constraint posed by a seemingly unreasonable price. This may be particularly true in a case in which a competing brand is being extensively discounted. The more accessible the attitude, the more likely that the adverse pricing structure would be overcome. That is, the relative prediction offered by the model of greater consistency among individuals with highly accessible attitudes than among those with less accessible attitudes may still hold true, but the absolute amount of consistency cannot be expected to be great.

Similarly, the selective processing fostered by an accessible attitude and the resulting perceptions of the product in the immediate situation may not be capable of overcoming a normative constraint. As discussed earlier, knowledge about the behaviors that are or are not situationally appropriate (i.e., one's definition of the situation) may attenuate the degree to which those immediate perceptions of the product influence behavior. Even if the immediate perceptions are positive, one is unlikely to purchase the product if it is to be used in a situation for which norms dictate that its use in inappropriate or that the use of some other product is appropriate.

In spite of these, and other potential breaks in the chain of attitude to behavior, the manager with an understanding of the process model is in a better position than one with no such understanding, simply because of the model's focus on how attitudes influence behavior. The "failures" of attitude to influence behavior can be anticipated and remedied by strengthening the attitude, employing cues to make weak attitudes salient at point of purchase, and maintaining managerial awareness of competitors' pricing tactics and advertisers' awareness of relevant normative concerns.

SOME CONCLUDING THOUGHTS

The purpose of this discussion has been to establish the place of the attitude–behavior process model in the arena of consumer behavior research. Regardless of the specific mechanisms potentially involved in attitude formation (Zajonc & Markus, 1982), the degree to which the resulting attitude influences actual consumer behavior is of considerable importance. The process model provides a conceptual framework for considering when and how consumers' attitudes influence their behavior. For an attitude to influence behavior, it must be activated from memory at the time the object is encountered. This activation can be automatic for strong attitudes, or, for weaker attitudes, a consequence of a more controlled process triggered by cues in the environment. Once activated, the attitude is likely to color one's perceptions of the product in the immediate situation, to bias one's interpretation of any information that is presented about the product, and to influence actual behavioral decisions.

In addition to furthering our understanding of the attitude–behavior relation, the process model provides a number of suggestions regarding social influence mechanisms and the effectiveness of advertising. Most generally, the model underscores the point that advertising must be concerned with the development of accessible attitudes for such campaigns to be ultimately effective at the purchase level. The research that has been described offers some suggestions as to how such attitude accessibility might be fostered and about the characteristics of subpopulations for whom advertising is likely to be maximally effective. The challenge for the future may be to arrive at an established array of social influence strategies that are capable not only of affecting the valence of the attitude, but also of enhancing the accessibility of the resulting attitude from memory. Only then will the social influence attempts produce the desired behavior.

REFERENCES

Ajzen, I., & Fishbein, M. (1973). Attitudinal and normative variables as predictors of specific behaviors. *Journal of Personality and Social Psychology, 27,* 41–57.

Ajzen, I., & Fishbein, M. (1980). *Understanding attitudes and predicting social behavior.* Englewood Cliffs, NJ: Prentice-Hall.

Allport, G. W. (1935). Attitudes. In C. Murchison (Ed.), *Handbook of social psychology* (pp. 798–844). Worcester, MA: Clark University Press.

Berger, I. E., & Mitchell, A. A. (1989). The effect of advertising on attitude accessibility, attitude confidence, and the attitude-behavior relationship. *Journal of Consumer Research, 16,* 269–279.

Bourne, F. S. (1963). Different kinds of decision and reference-group influence. In P. Bliss (Ed.), *Marketing and the behavioral sciences* (pp. 247–255). Boston: Allyn & Bacon.

Boyd, H. W., Ray, M. L., & Strong, E. S. (1972). An attitudinal framework for advertising strategy. *Journal of Marketing, 36,* 27–33.

Converse, P. E. (1970). Attitudes and non-attitudes: Continuation of a dialogue. In E. R. Tufte (Ed.), *The quantitative analysis of social problems* (pp. 168–189). Reading, MA: Addison-Wesley.

Darley, J. M., & Fazio, R. H. (1980). Expectancy confirmation processes arising in the social interaction sequence. *American Psychologist, 35,* 867–881.

Day, G. S., & Deutscher, T. (1982). Attitudinal predictions of choices of major appliance brands. *Journal of Marketing Research, 19,* 192–198.

Doob, L. W. (1947). The behavior of attitudes. *Psychological Review, 54,* 135–156.

Edel, R. (1986). Manufactorers create package of ads, incentives, and promotions. *Advertising Age, 57,* 22–26.

Fazio, R. H. (1986). How do attitudes guide behavior? In R. M. Sorrentino & E. T. Higgins (Eds.), *The handbook of motivation and cognition: Foundations of social behavior* (pp. 204–243). New York: Guilford Press.

Fazio, R. H. (1989). On the power and functionality of attitudes: The role of attitude accessibility. In A. R. Pratkanis, S. J. Breckler, & A. G. Greenwald (Eds.), *Attitude structure and function* (pp. 153–179). Hillsdale, NJ: Lawrence Erlbaum Associates.

Fazio, R. H. (1990). Multiple processes by which attitudes guide behavior: The MODE model as an integrative framework. In M. P. Zanna (Ed.), *Advances in experimental social psychology* (Vol. 23, pp. 75–109). New York: Academic Press.

Fazio, R. H., Chen, J., McDonel, E. C., & Sherman, S. J. (1982). Attitude accessibility, attitude–behavior consistency, and the strength of the object-evaluation association. *Journal of Experimental Social Psychology, 18,* 339–357.

Fazio, R. H., Herr, P. M., & Olney, T. J. (1984). Attitude accessibility following a self-perception process. *Journal of Personality and Social Psychology, 47,* 277–286.

Fazio, R. H., Powell, M. C., & Herr, P. M. (1983). Toward a process model of the attitude–behavior relation: Accessing one's attitude upon mere observation of the attitude object. *Journal of Personality and Social Psychology, 44,* 723–735.

Fazio, R. H., Powell, M. C., & Williams, C. J. (1989). The role of attitude accessibility in the attitude-to-behavior process. *Journal of Consumer Research, 16,* 280–288.

Fazio, R. H., Sanbonmatsu, D. M., Powell, M. C., & Kardes, F. R. (1986). On the automatic activation of attitudes. *Journal of Personality and Social Psychology, 50,* 229–238.

Fazio, R. H., & Williams, C. J. (1986). Attitude accessibility as a moderator of the attitude–perception and attitude–behavior relations: An investigation of the 1984 presidential election. *Journal of Personality and Social Psychology, 51,* 505–514.

Fazio, R. H., & Zanna, M. P. (1981). Direct experience and attitude–behavior consistency. In L. Berkowitz (Ed.), *Advances in experimental social psychology* (Vol. 14, pp. 162–202). New York: Academic Press.

Fazio, R. H., Zanna, M. P., & Cooper, J. (1978). Direct experience and attitude-behavior consistency: An information processing analysis. *Personality and Social Psychology Bulletin, 4,* 48–51.

Greenwald, A. G. (1968). On defining attitude and attitude theory. In A. G. Greenwald, T. C. Brock, & T. M. Ostrom (Eds.), *Psychological foundations of attitudes* (pp. 361–388). New York: Academic Press.

Hastorf, A. H., & Cantril, H. (1954). They saw a game: A case study. *Journal of Abnormal and Social Psychology, 49,* 129–134.

Hovland, C. I. (1959). Reconciling conflicting results derived from experimental and survey studies of attitude change. *American Psychologist, 14,* 8–17.

Howard, J. A., & Sheth, J. N. (1969). *The theory of buyer behavior,* New York: Wiley.

Katz, D. (1960). The functional approach to the study of attitudes. *Public Opinion Quarterly, 24,* 163–204.

Kruglanski, A. W. (1989). *Lay epistemics and human knowledge: Cognitive and motivational bases.* New York: Plenum Press.

LaBarbera, P. A., & MacLachlan, J. M. (1979). Response latency in telephone interviews. *Journal of Advertising Research, 19,* 49–55.

Lord, C. G., Ross, L., & Lepper, M. R. (1979). Biased assimilation and attitude polarization: The effects of prior theories on subsequently considered evidence. *Journal of Personality and Social Psychology, 37,* 2098–2109.

MacLachlan, J. M. (1977). *Response latency: A new measure of advertising.* New York: Advertising Research Foundation.

MacLachlan, J. M., Czepiel, J., & LaBarbera, P. (1979). Implementation of response latency measures. *Journal of Marketing Research, 16,* 573–579.

McGuire, W. J. (1969). The nature of attitudes and attitude change. In G. Lindzey & E. Aronson (Eds.), *Handbook of social psychology* (2nd ed., Vol. 3, pp. 136–314). Reading, MA: Addison-Wesley.

Powell, M. C., & Fazio, R. H. (1984). Attitude accessibility as a function of repeated attitudinal expression. *Personality and Social Psychology Bulletin, 10,* 139–148.

Proshansky, H. M. (1943). A projective method for the study of attitudes. *Journal of Abnormal and Social Psychology, 38,* 393–395.

Sanbonmatsu, D. M., & Fazio, R. H. (1986, October). *The automatic activation of attitudes toward products.* Paper presented at the annual meeting of the Association for Consumer Research, Toronto, Canada.

Sanbonmatsu, D. M., & Fazio, R. H. (1990). The role of attitude in memory-based decision making. *Journal of Personality and Social Psychology, 59,* 614–622.

Schofield, J. W. (1975). Effects of norms, public disclosure, and need for approval on volunteering behavior consistent with attitudes. *Journal of Personality and Social Psychology, 31,* 1126–1133.

Schneider, W., & Shiffrin, R. M. (1977). Controlled and automatic human information processing: I. Detection, search, and attention. *Psychological Review, 84,* 1–66.

Schuman, H., & Johnson, M. P. (1976). Attitudes and behavior. *Annual Review of Sociology, 2,* 161–207.

Shiffrin, R., & Dumais, S. T. (1981). The development of automatism. In J. R. Anderson (Ed.), *Cognitive skills and their acquisition* (pp. 111–140). Hillsdale, NJ: Lawrence Erlbaum Associates.

Shiffrin, R., & Schneider, W. (1977). Controlled and automatic human information processing: II. Perceptual learning, automatic attending, and a general theory. *Psychological Review, 84,* 127–190.

Smith, M. B., Bruner, J. S., & White, R. W. (1956). *Opinions and personality.* New York: Wiley.

Smith, R. E., & Swinyard, W. R. (1983). Attitude-behavior consistency: The impact of product trial vs. advertising. *Journal of Marketing Research, 20,* 256–267.

Snyder, M., & Kendzierski, D. (1982). Acting on one's attitude: Procedures for linking attitude and behavior. *Journal of Experimental Social Psychology, 18,* 165–183.

Warner, L. G., & DeFleur, M. L. (1969). Attitude as an interactional concept: Social constraint and social distance as intervening variables between attitudes and action. *American Sociological Review, 34,* 153–169.

Wind, Y. (1978). Issues and advances in segmentation research. *Journal of Marketing Research, 16,* 315–317.

Wood, W. (1982). Retrieval of attitude-relevant information from memory: Effects on susceptibility to persuasion and on intrinsic motivation. *Journal of Personality and Social Psychology, 42,* 798–810.

Zanna, M. P., & Fazio, R. H. (1982). The attitude-behavior relation: Moving toward a third generation of research. In M. P. Zanna, E. T. Higgins, & C. P. Herman, (Eds.), *Consistency in social behavior: The Ontario Symposium* (Vol. 2, pp. 283–301). Hillsdale, NJ: Lawrence Erlbaum Associates.

Zanna, M. P., Higgins, E. T., & Herman, C. P. (Eds.). (1982). *Consistency in social behavior: The Ontario Symposium* (Vol. 2). Hillsdale, NJ: Lawrence Erlbaum Associates.

Zajonc, R. B., & Markus, H. (1982). Affective and cognitive factors in preferences. *Journal of Consumer Research, 9,* 123–131.

5

Message Receptivity: A New Look at the Old Problem of Open- Versus Closed-Mindedness

Mark P. Zanna
University of Waterloo, Ontario

After a period of relative inactivity, social psychologists have, once again, turned their attention to the area of communication and persuasion (cf. Zanna, Olson, & Herman, 1987). In my view, the virtual renaissance of research in this area is due in large part to the "cognitive revolution" in psychology, which has provided new ways of thinking about enduring problems. In the area of communication and persuasion, this "current look" is, perhaps, best exemplified by the creative and influential work of two pairs of researchers: Richard Petty and John Cacioppo, and Shelly Chaiken and Alice Eagly.

Building on cognitive approaches, both from within and without social psychology, these attitude researchers have generated "state-of-the-art" information-processing theories of persuasion. The major, and innovative, distinction that both pairs of theorists have drawn is that information processing in the persuasive communication context can, at times, be relatively thoughtful and detailed and, at other times, relatively superficial. Thus, when motivated and able to do so, recipients in the thoughtful mode will scrutinize a persuasive message and base their final evaluation of it on a thoughtful and rational analysis of the message's content. In contrast, when neither motivated to process the message extensively nor able to do so (and when peripheral cues are salient), recipients in the superficial mode will use peripheral cues to determine the message's validity. Thus, the recipient's attitude can change as a function of either relatively deep or shallow information processing.

In reviewing the research that has tested and largely supported these new formulations of the communication-persuasion process, I have been struck by two related observations. First, based on the research, it would seem to be relatively easy to change an individual's beliefs, and, thus, his or her attitudes.

Second, and related to the first observation, it would seem that the message recipient is assumed, implicitly if not explicitly, to be an "open-minded" information processor. This second observation is not particularly insightful given that Chaiken's Heuristic-Systematic Model (HSM) of Persuasion was "explicitly developed to apply to persuasion settings in which the individual's dominant motivational concern could be assumed to be *the desire to form or to hold valid, accurate attitudes . . .*" (Chaiken, Liberman, & Eagly, 1989, p. 214; see also Chaiken, 1987) and that the first postulate of Petty and Cacioppo's Elaboration Likelihood Model (ELM) of Persuasion is that "people are motivated to hold correct attitudes" (Petty & Cacioppo, 1986, p. 5).[1]

The problem with these observations, at least for me, is that our intuitions and experience, not to mention earlier social psychological research (cf. Hovland, 1959), would tell us that attitude change is not always so easy to produce. Indeed, it is often very difficult to change people's attitudes. Actually, I do not think I am alone in this view.[2] For example, Aronson (1988) noted, in making the transition in his introductory text from the chapter on communication and persuasion to the following chapter on dissonance theory, that compared to opinions and beliefs, attitudes are, in fact, often extremely difficult to change. This reminds me that, in the mid-1970s, I introduced my "dissonance colloquium" by noting that, in the previous 15 years, social psychologists had determined that one of the best ways to change a person's attitude toward some issue was not necessarily to present the person with a persuasive communication, but, instead, to commit the person to a behavior that goes against his or her current beliefs. In any event, recall that the Functional Theories of Attitudes of the 1950s (e.g., Katz, 1960) were formulated, at least in part, to capture the notion that some attitudes are not based on simple (and relatively easy to change) utilitarian beliefs, a view implied by more modern theories such as Fishbein and Ajzen's Theory of Reasoned Action. Recall as well that the social judgment-involvement theory of Muzafer Sherif and his colleagues was explicitly created to explain why "ego-involved" attitudes are highly resistant to change (Sherif & Hovland, 1961). Following Ostrom and Brock's (1968) notion that ego-involved attitudes are those that are perceived to be diagnostic of (or relevant to) important values, Johnson and Eagly (1989) confirmed, in a meta-analytic study, that *value in-*

---

[1]This observation echoes one made by Eagly and Chaiken (1984) in their review of cognitive theories of persuasion in the *Advances in Experimental Social Psychology*. The authors noted that "to the extent that there is an assumption about motivation in these theories, this assumption might be broadly characterized by the statement that message recipients process information in a relatively unbiased manner in order to attain valid opinions that are in line with the relevant facts" (p. 332). Interestingly, Eagly and Chaiken were referring not only to process theories of persuasion such as ELM and HSM, but also to combinatorial theories of persuasion such as Fishbein and Ajzen's Theory of Reasoned Action and Anderson's Information-Integration Theory.

[2]Eagly and Chaiken (1984), in fact, also suggested that "this contemporary focus on information processing and on maximizing the validity of one's opinions implies an openness to information that contrasts sharply with views once popular in the attitude change area" (p. 333).

volvement (their term for *ego involvement,* specifically, "the psychological state that is created by the activation of attitudes that are linked to important values" p. 290), does, indeed, result in less persuasion (or, in other words, induces more resistance to persuasion). It seems, then, that earlier researchers did, implicitly, if not explicitly, encounter "closed-minded" recipients, motivated to defend their strongly held, ego-involved (or value-relevant) attitudes.

Interestingly, the studies reviewed by Johnson and Eagly, which varied value involvement were published long before the current generation of theory and research and tended to utilize social policy issues with which subjects were more knowledgeable and involved (e.g., the morality of the Vietnam War). In contrast, research designed to test current theories of persuasion has tended to employ somewhat more parochial college issues with which subjects are not very knowledgeable and/or involved (e.g., the institution of comprehensive exams for college seniors).

One way, then, to characterize research in the area of communication and persuasion is to suggest that although earlier researchers, interested in changing existing (often value-relevant) attitudes, typically confronted relatively closed-minded recipients motivated to defend their attitudes, more recent, cognitively oriented researchers, interested in the attitude-formation process, typically encountered relatively open-minded recipients, motivated to form valid, accurate attitudes. Whether this characterization turns out to be true or false (or, more appropriately, useful or not), the question remains: Is it relatively easy or hard to change people's attitudes? Or, under what conditions is it more or less difficult to change another's attitude? Actually, the way I would like to frame the question, at least initially, is: When (or under what conditions) will a message recipient be relatively open-minded, and motivated by concerns for validity, and when will he or she be closed-minded, and motivated to defend his or her attitude? For me, this is the critical question now faced by researchers interested in the communication-persuasion process.[3]

ATTEMPTS TO UNDERSTAND BIASED VERSUS UNBIASED INFORMATION PROCESSING IN THE COMMUNICATION-PERSUASION CONTEXT

Theorists, such as Petty and Cacioppo, and Chaiken and Eagly, have recently begun to address the issue of biased versus unbiased information processing in the context of persuasive communications. How, then, is biased information processing (or closed-mindedness) incorporated within ELM and within HSM?

---

[3]Again, this opinion echoes one offered by Eagly and Chaiken (1984), who suspected "that . . . motivational concerns . . . will be increasingly recognized as important issues for persuasion research and theory, as investigators begin to realize that an overemphasis on cognition limits the range of persuasion phenomenon that can be explained" (p. 333).

Biased Processing Within the ELM of Persuasion

First, let us consider the ELM of persuasion. In this model, Petty and Cacioppo (1986) make an initial, important distinction between two qualitatively different routes to persuasion, which they labeled the *central route* and the *peripheral route*. In their second postulate, they formally proposed that "although people want to hold correct attitudes, the amount and nature of issue-relevant elaboration in which they are willing or able to engage to evaluate a message vary with individual and situational factors" (p. 5). Generally speaking, then, Petty and Cacioppo suggested that when an individual's motivation (e.g., personal relevance) and ability (e.g., lack of distraction) to process a persuasive communication is high, issue-relevant elaboration (i.e., "the extent to which a person carefully thinks about issue-relevant information," p. 7) is high. In this situation, Petty and Cacioppo predicted and found that although the actual strength of the arguments presented in the communication does influence persuasion, the presence, on the other hand, of a positive or negative peripheral cue (e.g., a trustworthy vs. an untrustworthy source) does not particularly influence persuasion. Given high elaboration, then, "strong" arguments generally lead to relatively more favorable (rather than unfavorable) thoughts, and, thus, greater attitude change. Conversely, "weak" arguments generally lead to relatively more unfavorable (rather than favorable) thoughts, and, thus, relatively little persuasion (in some cases, even "boomerang" effects).

In contrast, when an individual's motivation and/or ability to process the persuasive communication is low, issue-relevant elaboration is low. In this situation, the quality of the arguments in the communication are predicted and found to have little impact on persuasion, whereas the presence of positive or negative peripheral cues are predicted and found to make a great deal of difference.

Although most of the research conducted by Petty and Cacioppo (and their colleagues) suggests that central-route processing is objective in nature (i.e., high elaboration increases the probability that one will see the validity or the strengths of the cogent arguments and the invalidity or the flaws in the specious arguments), their model does make an important, second-order distinction within the central route. Specifically, Petty and Cacioppo proposed that issue-relevant elaboration can be objective or biased. If objective, individuals will be "appropriately" influenced by argument quality; if biased, individuals will react unfavorably (e.g., formulate counterarguments) to even "strong" communications. Interestingly, then, for Petty and Cacioppo biased elaboration (or closed-mindedness) can occur within the central route of persuasion.

Although Petty and Cacioppo suggested that biased elaboration is a function of both the ability (e.g., having a prior attitude and/or prior knowledge on the issue) and the motivation to defend one's beliefs (e.g., being forewarned of the position of the communication and/or that it is the communicator's intention to persuade), it is not entirely clear, to me at least, precisely what variable(s) are predicted to moderate objective versus biased elaboration. When should "high elaboration" be expected to lead to primarily unfavorable thoughts (e.g., counterarguments) and, thus, to resistance to persuasion?

One interpretation of what Petty and Cacioppo are suggesting (and I must emphasize that this is merely my attempt to understand their model) is that, given the fact that "people are motivated to hold correct attitudes" (Postulate 1, p. 5), then, by default, central-route elaboration will be relatively objective. However, if subjects hold relatively "strong" attitudes (and/or have a great deal of attitude-relevant knowledge), then elaboration can, and, probably will, be biased. Biased elaboration, in this instance, is a consequence of the fact that the communication is processed through the "filter" of the individual's prior attitude and/or attitude structure (cf. Wood, 1982). Thus, given central processing, it would seem that holding a strong attitude may be sufficient for biased processing. Petty and Cacioppo also suggest that central-route elaboration will be biased if, for some reason, individuals become specifically motivated to defend their beliefs (e.g., if they are forewarned that the communicator intends to persuade them). Although this suggestion makes good sense, Petty and Cacioppo do not propose, at least not very generally, the condition(s) under which people will become so motivated.

In summary, although Petty and Cacioppo suggested that biased processing can and does occur within the central route, the theory is not fully developed with respect to exactly what moderates objective versus biased elaboration.

Biased Processing Within the HSM of Persuasion

Next, let us turn to the HSM of persuasion. Again, Chaiken's HSM of Persuasion was "explicitly developed to apply to persuasion settings in which the individual's dominant motivational concern could be assumed to be *the desire to form or to hold valid, accurate attitudes* . . ." (Chaiken et al., 1989, p. 214). Therefore, "the HSM assumes that the primary processing goal of message recipients is to assess the validity of the persuasive messages they encounter" (p. 214). This, as indicated earlier, implies that the HSM of persuasion assumes the message recipient to be relatively open-minded.

But how does this open-minded, validity-seeking recipient go about processing persuasive messages? Like the ELM, the HSM distinguishes between two modes of information processing, in this case, between systematic and heuristic processing.

Systematic processing is thoughtful and rational, whereas heuristic processing occurs when message recipients adopt or reject attitude positions on the basis of simple cues or "heuristics," rather than by analyzing carefully the relevant information. Systematic processing occurs, for example, when recipients of a message scrutinize and objectively analyze the arguments presented in a communication and then adopt a position logically derived from their thoughts. In contrast to this data-driven mode of information processing, heuristic processing is theory-driven. Heuristics are rules or assumptions that we use to simplify the world (e.g., "big things are heavier than little things"). For the most part, these assumptions are valid (although not always true) and reduce the effort we must expend to cope with our environment. In the domain of attitudes, we sometimes use heuristics to evaluate an advocated position, such as "I agree with people I like" (derived from balance theory) and "Long messages are better than short messages." Of course, because these heuristics will occasionally be invalid, we might end up adopting a position that we would have rejected if we had performed a more careful (i.e., systematic) analysis of the relevant information.

When will systematic processing occur? Only when message recipients are motivated and able to do so. And, because people are assumed to prefer modes of information processing requiring less effort (the principle of least effort) and because systematic processing takes more effort, message recipients are less often motivated and able to engage in detailed information processing. Chaiken et al. (1989) formalized the so-called "sufficiency principle" to provide a more explicit theoretical rationale for understanding what moderates the systematic–heuristic distinction. According to the sufficiency principle, "people will exert whatever level of effort is required to attain a sufficient degree of confidence that they have satisfactorily accomplished their processing goals. In validity-seeking persuasion settings, the principle asserts that recipients will invest whatever amount of effort is required to attain a sufficiently confident assessment of the validity of a message's advocated position" (Chaiken et al., 1989, p. 221). Thus, the sufficiency principle, together with the principle of least effort, suggest that a recipient will process heuristically by default (as long as a heuristic cue is primed).

However, if the message recipient's confidence threshold isn't exceeded, the recipient will engage in systematic processing as long as he or she has the ability to do so (and believes that confidence can, in fact, be increased by systematic processing). In this view, then, variables, such as personal relevance, are hypothesized to increase the probability of systematic processing because they increase the confidence threshold, and, therefore, decrease the probability that heuristic processing is likely to provide a sufficient confidence level.

In their chapter, Chaiken, Liberman, and Eagly suggested two ways that biased information processing can occur in the validity-seeking mode. First, they acknowledged (as did Petty and Cacioppo) that strong prior attitudes with an evaluatively biased store of attitude-relevant knowledge can bias systematic processing. Second, they suggested that when arguments are ambiguous (i.e., not clearly strong or weak), heuristic cues, such as, for example, an expert versus nonexpert source, may bias systematic processing. For example, "if a message is delivered by an expert, its arguments may be viewed more positively than if the message is delivered by a non-expert" (p. 228), assuming, of course, that the message content is "ambiguous enough to be *amenable to differential interpretation*" (p. 228).

In the same chapter, Chaiken, Liberman, and Eagly also suggested that individuals will not always be motivated to seek validity. In a major extension of the

HSM of persuasion they proposed, for example, that when individuals are attitudinally committed or when they have a vested interest in an issue, they will be defense-motivated, that is, motivated to form or to defend particular attitude positions. Defense-motivated recipients are assumed to have the processing goal to "confirm the validity of particular attitudinal positions and disconfirm the validity of others" (p. 234). Presumably, they will be most often motivated to defend their own prior attitudes.[4]

Clearly, for Chaiken, Liberman, and Eagly defense-motivated recipients are closed-minded. Interestingly, the authors proposed that processing goal (validity-seeking vs. defense-motivated) and processing mode (heuristic vs. systematic) are orthogonal. Thus, when defense-motivated, heuristic processors use heuristics selectively, picking those heuristics that defend their favored positions (e.g., their prior attitudes). Similarly, when defense-motivated, systematic processors are selective. They pay more attention to, and interpret more positively, information that supports their favored positions or opposes their nonfavored ones than they pay to information that opposes their favored positions or supports their nonfavored ones.

Although this is an interesting and important extension of HSM, Chaiken, Liberman, and Eagly do not, as yet, have a theory about when recipients will be motivated to defend their attitudes. Like Petty and Cacioppo, they simply listed a set of variables (e.g., commitment, vested interest) that should arouse this psychological state in message recipients.[5]

Thus, although both teams of researchers have clearly recognized the need to postulate a closed-minded message recipient, their initial theorizing might be considered a "first pass" at the problem. Let me now make a "second pass," building on the strengths of this theory and research.

A MODEL OF OPEN- VERSUS CLOSED-MINDED MESSAGE RECIPIENTS

I offer a model of the communication-persuasion process that posits two basic psychological states. One state assumes message recipients to be closed-minded. Motivated to defend their prior attitudes, closed-minded recipients counterargue

---

[4]Chaiken et al. (1989) also proposed that recipients are sometimes *impression-motivated;* that is, motivated to express attitudes that will be socially acceptable to potential evaluators. Thus, impression-motivated recipients are assumed to have the processing goal to "assess the social acceptability of alternative attitudinal positions" (p. 235). Discussion of this third motivation is beyond the scope of this chapter.

[5]Although there are similarities in their respective analyses (e.g., prior attitudes can bias processing [although, interestingly, neither refers to Fazio's, 1986, model and his notion of attitude accessibility as an important moderating variable]), there are, as well, interesting differences (e.g., for Petty and Cacioppo bias occurs via the central route; for Chaiken, Liberman, and Eagly both systematic and heuristic processing can be biased).

the communication, derogate the source of the communication and/or simply reaffirm their initial attitudes. The other state assumes message recipients to be open-minded. Motivated to form or hold valid, accurate attitudes, open-minded recipients (consistent with the notions of HSM and ELM) process the message either heuristically or systematically as a function of their motivation and ability to scrutinize the communication.

Given these two psychological states, the big question (for me at least) is what determines whether a recipient will be closed-minded or open-minded. To answer this question, I adopt the approach taken by my colleagues and me in "solving" the dissonance versus self-perception controversy (Fazio, Zanna, & Cooper, 1977; Zanna & Kiesler, 1971). Specifically, I suggest that just as individuals induced to advocate a counterattitudinal position are motivated to defend (i.e., rationalize) their prior behavior, message recipients exposed to a persuasive communication advocating a position that they clearly perceive to be counterattitudinal in nature will be closed-minded and motivated to defend their prior attitudes. On the other hand, just as individuals induced to advocate a position generally consistent with their prior attitudes are open to inferring their attitudes from their own behavior (taking into account the constraints under which it was performed), recipients exposed to a communication advocating a position generally consistent with their prior attitudes are open or predisposed (motivated) to form valid and accurate attitudes.

How, then, are we to know when a communication will be perceived by the recipient to be either inconsistent or generally consistent with his or her attitude? Following our earlier suggestion (cf. Fazio et al., 1977; which, of course, was adapted from the work of Musafer Sherif, cf., Sherif & Hovland, 1961), I propose that recipients will be motivated to defend their attitudes when they clearly perceive the communication to advocate a position within their latitude of rejection. Conversely, when the communication is perceived to advocate a position within their latitude of acceptance (or noncommitment), recipients will be motivated to form valid, accurate attitudes.

But why are recipients expected to be closed-minded when they perceive communications to advocate positions within their latitude of rejection? The first, traditional answer might be that such a communication would threaten one's self-esteem, especially if one were "ego involved" in the attitude issue (i.e., if one's attitude was perceived to be diagnostic of important values).

A second (and not inconsistent) possibility is suggested by the recent theorizing and research of Fazio. Although recipients, who perceive a communication to advocate a position within their latitude of rejection, may be motivated to protect and defend their attitude for self-esteem reasons, they may be aided and abetted in this task by having an activated attitude. Following earlier attitude theorists such as Allport (1935; who argued that "attitudes determine for each individual what he will see and hear . . . ," p. 806) and Smith, Bruner, and White (1956; who proposed that an attitude provides "a ready aid for 'sizing up' objects and events in the environment," p. 41), Fazio (1986, 1990) re-emphasized the notion that attitudes influence our perceptions. In fact, going beyond earlier theorists, Fazio suggested, and provided evidence, that when an attitude object and its evaluation are strongly associated in memory (i.e., when the attitude is highly accessible), the attitude will be spontaneously activated upon mention of the attitude issue and, as a consequence, "the attitude will serve as a 'filter' through which the attitude object will be perceived" (Fazio, 1990, p. 84). For example, in one experiment, subjects' perceptions of candidates in a presidential debate were more attitudinally consistent for those with highly accessible attitudes toward the candidates (Fazio & Williams, 1986). In another experiment, subjects' percep- tions and evaluations of research studies purporting to determine the efficacy of capital punishment as a deterrent of capital crimes were similarly more at- titudinally consistent for those with highly accessible attitudes toward capital punishment (Houston & Fazio, 1989). In Fazio's (1990) words: "the findings indicated that the degree to which an attitude is capable of being activated automatically from memory upon mention of the attitude issue determines the ex- tent to which that attitude biases one's interpretation of the available informa- tion" (p. 86).

Thus, if an attitude is activated, it will bias information processing (cf. also, Petty & Cacioppo, 1986; and Chaiken et al., 1989, who concur, citing the work of Wendy Wood and her colleagues, e.g., Wood, Kallgren, & Preisler, 1985). The question, then, is: Might a communication, which clearly advocates an unacceptable or objectionable position, "activate" the recipient's prior attitude? Activation could come about in three steps. In Step 1, the recipient may recog- nize (perhaps at some low level of awareness) that the communication is objec- tionable (i.e., may recognize there is a basic disagreement). Phenomenologi- cally, the recipient may sense or "feel" a disagreement in his or her "gut" (or to use Cialdini's, 1985, term, *heart of hearts*), experiencing only a "gut feeling" that he or she disagrees with the communication. In Step 2 this gut feeling leads to motivation to determine what makes the communication objectionable. In Step 3 this motivation leads to full activation of the recipient's attitude. Once acti- vated, the attitude biases information processing. Thus, in this view, recipients, motivated to process information in a closed-minded fashion for self-esteem maintenance reasons, are able to do so precisely because they view the world (in this case, the persuasive communication) through the "filter" of their prior attitudes.

Of course, if the attitude is strong to begin with (i.e., in Fazio's terms, if there is a strong "evaluation-object association"), it may be spontaneously activated from memory whether or not the communication advocates a position within the latitude of rejection. However, following Fazio (1990), it will be assumed that the spontaneous activation of the attitude will dissipate quickly or be actively suppressed if the attitude is presumed to be irrelevant to the task at hand. This would be the case when the communication advocates a position within the latitude of acceptance—because recipients are motivated to form a valid, accurate attitude in an "as-open-minded-as-possible" manner. In contrast, when the communication advocates a position within the latitude of rejection, the attitude is relevant to the task at hand and is not likely to dissipate or be actively suppressed. (In a subsequent section on future research directions it is also suggested that an activated attitude may actually increase the probability that a communication is perceived to advocate a position within the latitude of rejection.)

To summarize, then, this model proposes that a message recipient can either be in an open-minded or closed-minded psychological state that is primarily determined by whether he or she perceives the communication to advocate a position within his or her latitude of acceptance or rejection. If the communication is perceived to advocate a position within the latitude of rejection, the perception of disagreement not only threatens the recipient's self-esteem, but activates (or prolongs the activation of) the recipient's attitude. As a consequence, the recipient will be motivated and able to process the information associated with the communication in a biased manner or will simply reaffirm his or her initial attitude.

It should be noted that this model is consistent with my earlier observation that early researchers, in the business of changing existing attitudes, found attitudes relatively difficult to change, whereas on the other hand, more recent, cognitively oriented researchers, who seem to be in the business of attitude formation, have found attitudes relatively easy to influence. Assuming that early researchers tended to use more ego-involving (or value-relevant) issues for which recipients held wide latitudes of rejection, whereas contemporary researchers tend to use less ego-involving issues for which recipients hold narrow latitudes of rejection (cf. Johnson & Eagly, 1989), then, according to the present model, early researchers were more likely to confront closed-minded recipients, whereas contemporary researchers are more likely to encounter open-minded ones.

The present model is also consistent with recent process models of persuasion such as the HSM of persuasion. In fact, when the communication is perceived to advocate a position within the recipient's latitude of acceptance, the present model assumes, just as HSM does, that the recipient is motivated to form or hold valid, accurate attitudes. In this situation, then, the present model assumes that processes, such as those proposed by HSM, characterize attitude change processes. When the communication is perceived to advocate a position within the recipient's latitude of rejection, the present model assumes that the recipient is motivated to defend his or her initial position. In this situation, the present model assumes that processes, such as those proposed by the newly elaborated HSM (Chaiken et al., 1989), characterize resistance to persuasion. The main difference between the present model and HSM, then, is the present model's hypothesis of what determines objective versus biased information processing and, secondarily, the present model's hypothesis that the perception of disagreement activates (or prolongs the activation of) the recipient's attitude (which, in turn, helps mediate biased processing).

Of course, we need to know more about what determines the width of an individual's latitude of rejection and, more importantly, what determines whether an individual perceives a communication to advocate a position within his or her latitude of rejection. But before we turn to future research directions suggested by the model, we need to determine whether the model is generally consistent with and helps organize past research.

IS THE MODEL CONSISTENT WITH PAST RESEARCH?

One might ask whether the model is consistent with past research. Two literatures are relevant. The first includes studies that explicitly manipulate whether the persuasive communication advocates a position within the recipient's latitude of acceptance or rejection. The question here is: Are communications resisted when they are perceived to advocate positions within the latitude of rejection? The second consists of studies concerned more generally with biased information processing and resistance to persuasion. The question here is: Can research on resistance to persuasion be accommodated and, possibly organized, by the present model?

Research on the Position Advocated in the Communication

There is, of course, a large literature on the discrepancy of the communication from the recipient's initial attitude (cf. Brock, 1967). Unfortunately, I could not find a single study with an unconfounded manipulation of position advocated (i.e., a manipulation that presented recipients with identical communications purporting to advocate a position that was either within their latitude of acceptance or their latitude of rejection.)[6]

I was, however, able to locate two early studies (Atkins, Deaux, & Bieri, 1967; Eagly & Telaak, 1972) that employed different messages designed to advocate positions within each latitude. Interestingly, each study clearly demonstrated that recipients are persuaded by messages advocating positions perceived to be within their latitude of acceptance. In contrast, when the messages are perceived by the recipients to advocate positions within their latitude of rejection, no persuasion whatsoever is evidenced. Unfortunately, these early studies did not

---

[6]There are studies (e.g., Brock, 1967) that do hold constant the communication while varying the position advocated. Unfortunately from the present perspective, discrepancy is not coordinated precisely with recipient's latitudes.

include "thought listing" measures of counterarguing and/or source derogation so that it is unclear exactly how resistance to change was mediated.[7]

Research on Resistance to Persuasion

Is past research on resistance to persuasion generally consistent or inconsistent with the model? As mentioned previously, both Petty and Cacioppo (1986) and Chaiken and Eagly (Chaiken et al., 1989) discussed several variables that lead to biased information processing, and, thus, presumably induce resistance to persuasion. First on the lists of both sets of theorists is the notion that prior attitudes or prior knowledge can bias information processing. Indeed, recent work by Wood and her colleagues (Wood, 1982; Wood & Kallgren, 1988; Wood et al., 1985) demonstrated that recipients who are able to retrieve a relatively large number of attitude-relevant beliefs and behaviors from memory are relatively resistant to persuasion. From the perspective of the present model, this makes good sense if one were to assume that those individuals with a relatively large amount of attitude-relevant knowledge are more likely to perceive that the persuasive communication is advocating an objectionable position. This may be true either because such individuals have relatively wide latitudes of rejection, or because their relatively more accessible attitudes allow them to perceive disagreement more clearly and/or to counterargue more easily.[8]

---

[7]It should also be noted that these results are correlational in nature in that whether a communication was considered to be in the recipient's latitude of acceptance or rejection was based on the recipient's judgment, not by experimental manipulation. In both studies, different communications were designed to advocate different positions as rated by independent judges. This experimental strategy creates two problems. First, because the position advocated is not explicitly stated, but ostensibly inferred from the arguments that are presented, it may not be immediately clear to each subject precisely what position is, in fact, being advocated. Second, given that different communications are employed, something other than the position itself could be the critical difference between the communications. In other words, in this procedure, the position advocated is confounded with variables associated with the persuasive communication per se (e.g., the actual arguments employed). Thus, in future studies investigators might be well advised to employ identical communications and manipulate position advocated by explicitly claiming that the communication supports a specific position undeniably within the recipient's latitude of acceptance or rejection. (See section on "How to Manipulate the Position Advocated in the Communication"). An additional procedural problem makes it difficult to interpret Eagly and Telaak's experimental results. After subjects' latitudes were assessed (and before they received their persuasive message), subjects were asked to write a statement, one half to one page in length, for their partners in which they expressed their honest and frank feelings about the attitude issue of birth control. Because such a procedure might have induced subjects to write statements advocating more moderate positions toward birth control, these statements might have, in turn, changed subjects' attitudes and/or their latitudes of acceptance in the anti-birth control direction, especially if, to begin with, subjects held wide latitudes of acceptance. In any event, given this procedure it is not clear whether the experimental design accurately captures the psychological state of the subjects.

[8]Krosnick's (1988a) finding that attitudes people consider to be personally important are less likely to change in the course of everyday life is also consistent if one makes the not unreasonable assumption that important attitudes, typically being more extreme, are associated with wider latitudes of rejection (and/or are more accessible, cf. Krosnick, 1988b).

Both sets of theorists also acknowledge that commitment to a prior attitudinal position induces resistance to persuasion (e.g., Hovland, Campbell, & Brock, 1957; Kiesler, 1971). From the present perspective, commitment, too, might be expected to increase the probability that the communication will be perceived to advocate a disagreeable or objectionable position. Again, this could be true either because commitment increases the width of the recipient's latitude of rejection or, by increasing the accessibility of the recipient's attitude (Fazio, Herr, & Olney, 1984), makes it clearer that a given communication actually does advocate a position within the recipient's latitude of rejection. Chaiken et al. (1989) also suggested that vested interest probably induces defense motivation and, thus, resistance to persuasion. This makes sense for the very same reasons as commitment.

Petty and Cacioppo (1986) suggested that forewarning, both forewarning of the position to be advocated and forewarning of the communicator's intent to persuade, promotes biased information processing and, thus, resistance to persuasion. From the perspective of the present model this, too, makes good sense if one assumes that such forewarning creates the impression of impending disagreement (i.e., creates the belief in the recipient that the communication will advocate a position within his or her latitude of rejection). Inoculation procedures developed by McGuire (1964) and his colleagues can be viewed in much the same manner.

Petty and Cacioppo (1986) also suggested that high levels of message repetition (Cacioppo & Petty, 1979) and horizontal head movements (Wells & Petty, 1980) promote biased information processing. If high levels of message repetition and horizontal head movements make salient the actual disagreement that exists between the recipient's prior attitude and the communication, then these variables, too, can be accommodated by the present model.

Other research has also investigated resistance to persuasion, including the early work of Norman Miller (1965), who found that closed-minded or dogmatic individuals tended to be less persuadable than open-minded or nondogmatic individuals. This finding can be easily accommodated by assuming that dogmatic individuals have large latitudes of rejection (cf. Powell, 1966) and/or are quick to perceive that attitude-discrepant messages advocate positions within their latitudes of rejection. More recently, Wu and Shaffer (1987) found that attitudes based on direct experience with the attitude object were more resistant to persuasion. Assuming that such attitudes are associated with greater latitudes of rejection (cf. Fazio & Zanna, 1978), this finding is also consistent with the present model.

RESEARCH SUGGESTED BY THE MODEL

To be useful, the model has to do more than account for and reorganize past research. It should also suggest fruitful, new avenues of research. I now discuss the directions for future research that the model suggests. First, I describe how the main independent variable proposed by the model, that is, whether a communication is perceived to recommend a position within the recipient's latitude of acceptance or rejection, might be manipulated in an unconfounded manner. Second, I indicate the sorts of dependent variables, besides attitude change (or resistance to persuasion), that would be of interest to examine. Finally, I discuss what strategies the model suggests for overcoming resistance to persuasion.

How to Manipulate the Position Advocated in the Communication

The model suggests that the main independent variable that moderates whether recipients are open- or closed-minded is whether the communication is perceived to advocate a position within the recipient's latitude of acceptance or rejection. To test the model, then, an investigator must manipulate this variable. The question is how best to do so? In the past (e.g., Atkins, Deaux, & Bieri, 1967), investigators have tended to employ different communications judged (by independent observers) to advocate different attitudinal positions that happen to coincide with the recipient's latitude of acceptance or rejection. The main problem with such studies (see footnote 7) is that the position advocated, which is implicit, is confounded with the actual communication and, thus, with variables such as the quality of the arguments, and so on. In future research I recommend explicitly manipulating the position advocated while holding constant the actual communication. That is, I would recommend that the source merely claim that his or her communication advocates either one specific position or another (cf. Brock, 1967). In order to maximize the power of such a manipulation it would be helpful to know in advance which attitudinal positions fall within each recipient's latitude of acceptance and rejection. With this knowledge the experimenter can randomly assign each recipient to a condition in which he or she would receive the identical communication which, from each recipient's perspective, claimed to advocate either the most extreme, yet acceptable, or the least extreme, yet objectionable, position (cf. Fazio et al., 1977).

Dependent Variables Suggested by the Model

In addition to the main dependent variable of attitude change (or resistance to persuasion), the model suggests at least four other dependent variables of interest: width of the latitude of rejection, perception of the position advocated, attitude accessibility, and biased or closed-minded information processing. Each of these variables are discussed here.

The Width of the Latitude of Rejection as a Dependent Variable.   So far we have considered the main independent variable of the model to be whether a communication advocates a position within the recipient's latitude of acceptance or rejection. And indeed it is. However, because closed-mindedness is predicted to be a function of the width of the latitude of rejection (LR), it becomes interesting to determine more systematically what determines this width. Of course, we are already aware of some individual difference correlates. Sherif and his colleagues, for example, first demonstrated that individuals with extreme attitudes often have wider latitudes of rejection (e.g., Sherif & Hovland, 1961). In fact, Sherif, Sherif, and Nebergall (1965) proposed that ego involvement could be indirectly measured by examining the size of the individual's latitude of rejection. And Powell (1966) found that highly dogmatic individuals tend to have wider latitudes of rejection.[9] Finally, Fazio and Zanna (1978) found evidence that attitudes based on direct (as compared to indirect) experience with the attitude object tend to be associated with wider latitudes of rejection.

Future research could explore additional, individual difference correlates and/or antecedents of the width of the LR. Expanding on the work of Wood and her colleagues, it would be interesting to know whether the amount of prior attitude-relevant knowledge, independent of attitude extremity, correlates positively with the width of the LR. Expanding on the work of Fazio and Zanna (1981) on the manner of attitude formation, it would be interesting to know whether attitudes based primarily on affect differ in the width of their LR from attitudes based primarily on cognition (cf. Zanna & Rempel, 1988). More generally, perhaps, it would be interesting to know whether attitudes high in accessibility are associated with wider latitudes of rejection. Following the strategy typically employed by Fazio and his colleagues, one could ask this question correlationally (by measuring subjects' reaction times to enquiries about their attitudes) and experimentally (by manipulating the number of times subjects are induced to express their attitudes). It would, indeed, be interesting to discover that "strong" attitudes (i.e., those attitudes with strong evaluation-attitude object associations) are associated with wider latitudes of rejection (see Fazio et al., 1984, for preliminary correlational evidence).

In addition to individual difference variables, which have been the sort of variables investigated in the past, it would also be interesting to determine whether various situational variables influence the width of the recipient's LR. Possible "candidates" for variables that might be expected to make a difference would include the variables suggested by Petty and Cacioppo (1986) and Chaiken et al. (1989) as those variables that bias information processing. So, for example, does forewarning of the communication's position and/or the communicator's intent to persuade widen the recipient's LR? Does commitment to an

---

[9]A reanalysis of Powell's data, however, suggests that the dogmatism-latitude of rejection relation may be a result of the fact that dogmatism is even more highly related to attitude extremity. Although the correlations between attitude extremity and LR partialling out dogmatism remain significant, the correlations between dogmatism and latitude of rejection partialling out attitude extremity are not reliable.

attitudinal position (and/or having a vested interest in the issue) widen the recipient's LR? And what effect do variables such as high levels of message repetition and horizontal head movements have on the recipient's LR? In general, do variables that induce, in Kruglanski's (1989) terms, a need for closure (e.g., time pressure) widen the recipient's LR, whereas variables that induce a need to avoid closure (e.g., evaluation apprehension) narrow the recipient's LR?

Other variables might also be explored. Interestingly, as long ago as 1968, Norman Miller suggested that "one's latitude of acceptance and rejection for a particular issue may undergo considerable situation variation depending upon the person who presents the counter-persuasive message" (Miller, 1968, p. 280). Miller also suggested that "with each added positive attribute, a communicator broadens a respondent's latitude of acceptance" (p. 295). Do source variables, such as communicator expertise, influence the recipient's LR? If so, under what conditions? These long neglected questions deserve research attention. In general, the model suggests that, if the width of the latitude of rejection is important in determining the psychological state of the message recipient, then more research attention should be paid to determine those variables that are related to its width.[10]

Perception of the Position Advocated as a Dependent Variable. The model proposes that the recipient's perception of the position advocated by the message determines whether the recipient is in an open-minded or closed-minded state. Further, it is unlikely that "real-world" communicators typically will be explicit about the exact position they advocate. Thus, it is also important to determine those variables that, in addition to actual position advocated (as estimated by independent judges) and the explicitness with which the communicator claims a certain position, determine whether or not a communication is perceived to advocate a position within the LR.

Of course, many of the variables that were proposed to influence the width of the LR (e.g., forewarning, commitment and so on) might also influence whether a given communication is perceived to advocate a position within the LR. Most generally, perhaps, it would be interesting to explore the possibility that attitude

---

[10]It should be noted that procedural variations seem to make a difference in the width of the latitude of rejection. Granberg & Steele (1974), for example, found that using four-page instructions (following the original procedure of the Sherifs) versus one-page instructions (following the procedure of most subsequent researchers) makes a difference. In the four-page version subjects are asked on the first page to indicate their most accepted position, on the second page to indicate other acceptable positions, on the third page to indicate their most objectionable position, and, finally, on the fourth page to indicate other unacceptable positions; in the one-page version subjects are asked to make all four responses on the same page. The results indicated that the one-page version of the procedure resulted in wider latitudes of acceptance and rejection and smaller latitudes of noncommitment. Because the one-page version of the procedure may result in overestimating the width of recipients' latitudes of rejection, to be sure of the positions recipients find objectionable it is recommended that future researchers employ the original, four-page procedure.

accessibility influences whether attitude-discrepant communications are perceived to advocate objectionable positions. Based on Fazio's theorizing and research, it would seem reasonable to hypothesize that recipients with highly accessible attitudes on an issue would be more likely to conclude that counterattitudinal communications (i.e., communications rated by independent judges as advocating positions within the recipients' latitudes of rejection) do, in fact, advocate positions within their latitudes of rejection.

Attitude Accessibility as a Dependent Variable.   Although attitude accessibility may very well be associated, as an antecedent variable, with both the width of the recipient's LR and, especially, with the recipient's perception that a counterattitudinal communication advocates a position within his or her LR, the model also proposes that when a communication is clearly objectionable (i.e., clearly advocates a position perceived to be in the recipient's LR), the recipient's attitude will be activated (or prolonged in its activation). Therefore, it would be interesting to determine whether trace measures of attitude accessibility (e.g., reaction time measures), taken during or immediately following the message, indicate that the recipient's attitude has been spontaneously activated.[11]

Closed-Mindedness as a Dependent Variable.   Following the cognitive response theorists such as Petty and Cacioppo (1986), it would be interesting to have recipients "list their thoughts" following the presentation of the persuasive message. Heeding the advice of Chaiken et al. (1989), these thoughts should be coded in accordance with what the model suggests represents biased or closed-minded information processing. Therefore, the thoughts listed by recipients should be coded for counterargumentation and source derogation and, possibly, simple affirmations of the recipient's prior attitudinal position.

However, because it is not entirely clear how recipients will manifest their closed-minded state, researchers should also be cognizant of other possible ways in which recipients might protect their initial attitudes. For instance, they might derogate the communication per se (without necessarily counterarguing the specific points made within the communication) or, as suggested by Chaiken et al. (1989), they might selectively call to mind heuristics that support or defend their initial attitudes. Although evidence for such protective strategies may be ob-

---

[11]It might also be interesting to obtain trace measures of attitude accessibility in the induced compliance context. If a communication perceived to advocate a position within the recipient's latitude of rejection is hypothesized to activate the recipient's attitude, why not hypothesize that a freely performed behavior that implies a position within the actor's latitude of rejection also activates the actor's attitude. If so, this may help to explain why cognitive dissonance is aroused when individuals feel responsible for behaviors which imply positions within their latitude of rejection (Fazio et al., 1977). Further, it would suggest an interesting characterization of cognitive dissonance: To wit, that dissonance is the state that is aroused when two inconsistent cognitions, one having to do with one's attitude, the other having to do with one's behavior, are activated simultaneously.

tained from recipients' thought listings, it would seem prudent to develop additional measures of closed-mindedness as well (e.g., ask recipients to give their [open-ended] impressions of the communication, as well as the communicator, have recipients fill out scales designed to assess various protective strategies, and so on).

Overcoming Resistance to Persuasion

In order to overcome resistance to persuasion, one needs to know what precisely mediates resistance. The present model suggests that when recipients believe that a communication advocates a position within their latitudes of rejection they become defensive. Further, the model suggests that this perception activates (or prolongs the activation of) recipients' prior attitudes, which, in turn, aid recipients in their task of counterarguing the communication and/or derogating its source. If the sort of dependent variables suggested in the preceding section (specifically, perception of whether the communication advocates a position within the LR, attitude accessibility, and counterarguing/source derogation) are all collected in future experiments, investigators can begin to determine more precisely how resistance to persuasion is mediated and whether each of these variables is, in fact, implicated. Assuming for the moment that each of these variables does turn out to be important in mediating resistance to persuasion, what does the model suggest about how to go about overcoming resistance to persuasion (assuming, in addition, a counterattitudinal communication with "strong" arguments)?

One suggestion would be to prevent counterargumentation or source derogation by using information overload techniques such as distraction. Of course, this proposal is hardly new (cf. Osterhouse & Brock, 1970). However, although distraction should reduce counterargumentation, it is not clear that it would entirely prevent recipients from derogating the source or, especially, from merely reaffirming their prior attitudes should they be truly defensive and closed-minded. Nevertheless, distraction is a possible way to overcome resistance to persuasion that could be examined from the perspective of the present model.

A second possible way to overcome resistance to persuasion recently has been suggested by Fazio, who proposed that attitude activation might be "short circuited" or prevented by disguising one's messages. For example, using "mystery ads" recipients might be prevented from discovering what product is being advertised until after they have either formed positive attitudes toward the ad itself or to attributes of what they later discover to be the product advertised (cf. Fazio, Herr, & Powell, 1992). More generally, it might be interesting to determine more precisely how communicators can and do disguise the persuasive intent and, indeed, the topic of their communications.

A third possibility suggested by the model would be to short circuit or prevent recipients from perceiving that the communication advocated a position within their latitudes of rejection. This could be accomplished in two ways. First, one could make sure that the communication, in fact, is designed to advocate a position within the recipient's latitude of acceptance (or noncommitment). Again, such an idea is hardly novel. Miller (1968), in reviewing Sherif's work on social judgment, concluded that "persuasion will succeed when it proceeds by small steps" (p. 301). Second, and possibly more intriguing, one could disguise the position that is being advocated in the communication. Actually, the model would seem to suggest that the best strategy for persuasion is to claim to be advocating the most extreme, yet acceptable, position within the recipient's latitude of acceptance while, at the same time, presenting arguments that could support an even more extreme position within the recipient's latitude of rejection.[12]

SUMMARY AND CONCLUSION

Are message recipients open- or closed-minded? More precisely, under what conditions are message recipients open- versus closed-minded? In this chapter I suggested that these questions should be the major ones now facing researchers interested in the processes of communication and persuasion. I also briefly reviewed how the two most currently influential theories of persuasion, ELM (Petty & Cacioppo, 1986) and HSM (Chaiken, 1987; Chaiken et al., 1989), have begun to address these questions. Finally, building on the strengths of past theory and research, I proposed and discussed a model, which hypothesizes that the critical determinant of the open- versus closed-minded state is whether a communication is perceived to advocate a position within the recipient's latitude of acceptance or rejection.

Hopefully, the chapter will further stimulate thinking and research on the general question of objective versus biased information processing in the persuasive communication context. If it does, it will have met its main purpose. If, in addition, readers find the present model (and the sort of questions that are suggested by it) intriguing enough to capture their research attention, the chapter will have more than met its goal.

ACKNOWLEDGMENTS

A version of this chapter was presented at the Advertising and Consumer Psychology Conference, Toronto, May 19–20, 1989. In addition to the editor and

---

[12]This strategy might be called the "Mark Anthony gambit"—as in "Friends, Romans, countrymen, lend me your ears; I come to bury Caesar, not to praise him," which "loosely" translated, means, "I advocate a position clearly within your LA, not within your LR." Of course, Anthony advocated no such thing!

the participants of the conference, I would like to thank Eugene Borgida, Russell Fazio, James Olson, and Michael Ross for their comments on an earlier draft of the chapter.

REFERENCES

Allport, G. W. (1935). Attitudes. In C. Murchison (Ed.), *Handbook of social psychology* (pp. 798–844). Worcester, MA: Clark University Press.

Aronson, E. (1988). *The social animal* (5th ed.). New York: Freeman.

Atkins, A. L., Deaux, K. K., & Bieri, J. (1967). Latitude of acceptance and attitude change: Empirical evidence for a reformulation. *Journal of Personality and Social Psychology, 6,* 47–54.

Brock, T. C. (1967). Communication discrepancy and intent to persuade as determinants of counterargument production. *Journal of Experimental Social Psychology, 3,* 296–309.

Cacioppo, J. T., & Petty, R. E. (1979). Effects of message repetition and position on cognitive responses, recall, and persuasion. *Journal of Personality and Social Psychology, 37,* 97–109.

Chaiken, S. (1987). The heuristic model of persuasion. In M. P. Zanna, J. M. Olson, & C. P. Herman (Eds.), *Social influence: The Ontario symposium* (Vol. 5, pp. 3–39). Hillsdale, NJ: Lawrence Erlbaum Associates.

Chaiken, S., Liberman, A., & Eagly, A. H. (1989). Heuristic and systematic processing within and beyond the persuasion context. In J. S. Uleman & J. A. Bargh (Eds.), *Unintended thought: Limits of awareness, attention, and control* (pp. 212–252). New York: Guilford Press.

Cialdini, R. (1985). *Influence: Science and practice.* Glenview, IL: Scott-Foresman.

Eagly, A. H., & Chaiken, S. (1984). Cognitive theories of persuasion. In L. Berkowitz (Ed.), *Advances in experimental social psychology* (Vol. 17, pp. 267–359). Orlando, FL: Academic Press.

Eagly, A. H., & Telaak, K. (1972). Width of the latitude of acceptance as a determinant of attitude change. *Journal of Personality and Social Psychology, 23,* 388–397.

Fazio, R. H. (1986). How do attitudes guide behavior? In R. M. Sorrentino & E. T. Higgins (Eds.), *The handbook of motivation and cognition: Foundations of social behavior* (pp. 204–243). New York: Guilford Press.

Fazio, R. H. (1990). Multiple processes by which attitudes guide behavior: The MODE model as an integrative framework. In M. P. Zanna (Ed.), *Advances in experimental social psychology* (Vol. 23, pp. 75–109). San Diego: Academic Press.

Fazio, R. H., Herr, P. M., & Olney, T. J. (1984). Attitude accessibility following a self-inference process. *Journal of Personality and Social Psychology, 47,* 277–286.

Fazio, R. H., Herr, P. M., & Powell, M. C. (1992). On the development and strength of category-brand associations in memory: The case of mystery ads. *Journal of Consumer Psychology, 1,* 1–13.

Fazio, R. H., & Williams, C. J. (1986). Attitude accessibility as a moderator of the attitude-perception and attitude-behavior relations: An investigation of the 1984 presidential election. *Journal of Personality and Social Psychology, 51,* 505–514.

Fazio, R. H., & Zanna, M. P. (1978). Attitudinal qualities affecting the strength of the attitude-behavior relationship. *Journal of Experimental Social Psychology, 14,* 398–408.

Fazio, R. H., & Zanna, M. P. (1981). Direct experience and attitude-behavior consistency. In L. Berkowitz (Ed.), *Advances in experimental social psychology* (Vol. 14, pp. 161–202). New York: Academic Press.

Fazio, R. H., Zanna, M. P., & Cooper, J. (1977). Dissonance and self-perception: An examination of each theory's proper domain of application. *Journal of Experimental Social Psychology, 13,* 464–479.

Granberg, D., & Steele, L. (1974). Procedural considerations in measuring latitudes of acceptance, rejection, and non-commitment. *Social Forces, 52,* 538–542.

Houston, D. A., & Fazio, R. H. (1989). Biased processing as a function of attitude accessibility: Making objective judgments subjectively. *Social Cognition, 7,* 51–66.

Hovland, C. I. (1959). Reconciling conflicting results derived from experimental and survey studies of attitude change. *American Psychologist, 14,* 8–17.

Hovland, C. I., Campbell, E. H., & Brock, T. (1957). The effects of "commitment" on opinion change following communication. In C. I. Hovland (Ed.), *The order of presentation in persuasion* (pp. 23–32). New Haven, CT: Yale University Press.

Johnson, B. T., & Eagly, A. H. (1989). The effects of involvement on persuasion: A meta-analysis. *Psychological Bulletin, 106,* 290–314.

Katz, D. (1960). The functional approach to the study of attitudes. *Public Opinion Quarterly, 24,* 163–204.

Kiesler, C. A. (1971). *The psychology of commitment.* New York: Academic Press.

Krosnick, J. A. (1988a). Attitude importance and attitude change. *Journal of Experimental Social Psychology, 24,* 240–255.

Krosnick, J. A. (1988b). The role of attitude importance in social evaluation: A study of policy preferences, presidential candidate evaluations, and voting behavior. *Journal of Personality and Social Psychology, 55,* 196–210.

Kruglanski, A. W. (1989). *Lay epistemics and human knowledge.* New York: Plenum.

McGuire, W. J. (1964). Inducing resistance to persuasion: Some contemporary approaches. In L. Berkowitz (Ed.), *Advances in experimental social psychology* (Vol. 1, pp. 191–229). New York: Academic Press.

Miller, N. (1965). Involvement and dogmatism as inhibitors of attitude change. *Journal of Experimental Social Psychology, 1,* 121–132.

Miller, N. (1968). Social judgment theory. In C. A. Kiesler, B. E. Collins, & N. Miller (Eds.), *Attitude change: A critical analysis of theoretical approaches* (pp. 238–301). New York: Wiley.

Osterhouse, R. A., & Brock, T. C. (1970). Distraction increases yielding to propaganda by inhibiting counterarguing. *Journal of Personality and Social Psychology, 15,* 344–358.

Ostrom, T. M., & Brock, T. C. (1968). A cognitive model of attitudinal involvement. In R. P. Abelson, E. Aronson, W. J. McGuire, T. M. Newcomb, M. J. Rosenberg, & P. H. Tannenbaum (Eds.), *Theories of cognitive consistency: A sourcebook* (pp. 373–383). Chicago: Rand-McNally.

Petty, R. E., & Cacioppo, J. T. (1986). *Communication and persuasion: Central and peripheral routes to attitude change.* New York: Springer-Verlag.

Powell, F. A. (1966). Latitudes of acceptance and rejection and the belief-disbelief dimension: A correlational comparison. *Journal of Personality and Social Psychology, 4,* 453–456.

Sherif, M., & Hovland, C. I. (1961). *Social judgment.* New Haven, CT: Yale University Press.

Sherif, C. W., Sherif, M., & Nebergall, R. E. (1965). *Attitude and attitude change.* Philadelphia: Saunders.

Smith, M. B., Bruner, J. S., & White, R. W. (1956). *Opinions and personality.* New York: Wiley.

Wells, G. L., & Petty, R. E. (1980). The effects of overt head movements on persuasion: Compatibility and incompatibility of responses. *Basic and Applied Social Psychology, 1,* 219–230.

Wood, W. (1982). Retrieval of attitude-relevant information from memory: Effects on susceptibility to persuasion and on intrinsic motivation, *Journal of Personality and Social Psychology, 42,* 798–810.

Wood, W., & Kallgren, C. A. (1988). Effect of communicator attributes on persuasion: A function of recipients' access to attitude-relevant information in memory. *Personality and Social Psychology Bulletin, 14,* 172–182.

Wood, W., Kallgren, C. A., & Preisler, R. M. (1985). Access to attitude-relevant information in memory as a determinant of persuasion: The role of message attributes. *Journal of Experimental Social Psychology, 21,* 73–85.

Wu, C., & Shaffer, D. R. (1987). Susceptibility to persuasive appeals as a function of source credibility and prior experience with the attitude object. *Journal of Personality and Social Psychology, 52,* 677–688.

Zanna, M. P., & Kiesler, C. A. (1971). Inferring one's beliefs from one's behavior as a function of belief relevance and consistency of behavior. *Psychonomic Science, 24,* 283–285.

Zanna, M. P., Olson, J. M., & Herman, C. P. (Eds.). (1987). *Social influence: The Ontario symposium* (Vol. 5). Hillsdale, NJ: Lawrence Erlbaum Associates.

Zanna, M. P., & Rempel, J. K. (1988). Attitudes: A new look at an old concept. In D. Bar-Tal & A. Kruglanski (Eds.), *The social psychology of knowledge* (pp. 315–334). New York: Cambridge University Press.

6

Consumer Inference: Determinants, Consequences, and Implications for Advertising

Frank R. Kardes
University of Cincinnati, Ohio

Consumers make judgments and decisions about products and services under conditions of uncertainty every day. Only rarely is complete information available for all important features, benefits, and uses of a given product. Several different responses to incomplete information are possible: (a) consumers may simply overlook missing information, (b) they may search for additional information, or (c) if time and energy constraints do not permit extended external search, consumers may attempt to fill gaps in their knowledge by drawing inferences about missing information.

This chapter reviews the conditions that prompt consumers to expand upon advertising claims by drawing elaborative inferences and examines the effects of these inferences on subsequent product-related judgments and decisions. Inferential biases and errors are reviewed and their implications for understanding advertising effects are explored. Before addressing these issues, however, the definition and measurement of inferences is discussed.

INFERENCE MEASUREMENT

An inference is defined as a conclusion that is derived from a given set of information on the basis of a rule that associates the information to the conclusion in a subjectively logical fashion (Hastie, 1983; Kardes, 1988b). Inference formation involves going beyond directly observable events through the use of subjective rules, based on prior knowledge and experience, that enable indi-

163

viduals to expand their current knowledge about these events (Holland, Holyoak, Nisbett, & Thagard, 1986).[1]

A Process-Based Taxonomy of Inferences

A process-based taxonomy of inferences is proposed because the likelihood of inference formation, the content, and the appropriate measurement of inferences are determined by the processes that mediate inference formation. Just as attentional processes can be represented on a continuum ranging from automatic (or effortless) to controlled (or effortful); see Kahneman & Treisman, 1984; Schneider & Shiffrin, 1977; Shiffrin, in press; Shiffrin & Schneider, 1977), so too can inferential processes be represented on a continuum ranging from automatic to controlled. Automatic inferences are elicited by observed information that has extremely strong and obvious implications. For example, if a consumer read a passage stating that "John quenched his thirst," the reader would assume that John drank a refreshing beverage even though this information was not explicitly stated in the text. Little effort is required to reach this conclusion and the likelihood of reaching this conclusion is high.

In contrast, controlled inferences may be emitted in response to observed information that has less obvious implications. For example, if a consumer read that most people prefer Beverage A, the consumer might infer (a) that Beverage A has many desirable qualities (e.g., it's refreshing, it's made of all-natural ingredients, etc.); (b) that the preferences of most people might not correspond to his preferences and, hence, the observed information is irrelevant; or (c) the consumer might infer that the text is misleading (e.g., most people do not prefer Beverage A). A consumer might draw any of these conclusions depending on other available information (e.g., the source of the message) and on what information happens to be readily accessible from memory at the time the message is encountered. Conversely, if a consumer is not motivated or does not have the opportunity to consider the implications of the message, no conclusions may be drawn. Hence, as the amount of effort required to reach a particular conclusion increases, the likelihood of reaching that conclusion decreases.

Although the main purpose of inference formation is to help individuals deal with ambiguity and uncertainty, the manner in which this goal is achieved depends on the amount of effort required to generate inferences. Interpretive inferences tend to require relatively little effort, whereas elaborative inferences

---

[1] Three basic inference processes have been identified: *deduction, induction,* and *abduction* (for a review with marketing implications, see Mick, 1986). Deduction involves applying an abstract rule to a specific case to arrive at a specific conclusion for that case (a "result"). Induction involves examining a specific case and a result and extrapolating a general rule. Abduction involves examining a result and using a rule to infer the case. If the premises are true the conclusion must follow in deduction (rule application), whereas probabilistic conclusions are inferred in induction (rule generation) and in abduction (case identification). This chapter focuses primarily on probabilistic inference.

tend to use up a larger proportion of the limited cognitive capacity available for processing information. Interpretive inferences facilitate the comprehension of ambiguous material by serving a simplification or information-reduction function. Simplification can take one of four forms: (a) a message can be translated into more familiar terms (e.g., "0 to 60 in 7 seconds" can be transformed to "fast"), (b) a set of attributes can be reduced to a single concept (e.g., "fast, efficient, and handles well" can be abstracted to "high performance"), (c) several pieces of attribute information can be integrated into a single global evaluative judgment, or (d) a summary judgment may be formed on the basis of a simple heuristic (Alba & Hutchinson, 1987).

Elaborative inferences aid judgment and decision making under uncertainty by serving a knowledge-extension function (as opposed to a knowledge-reduction function). When only limited information about the attributes, benefits, and uses of a product is available, missing information can be inferred through the use of evaluation-based, similarity-based, correlational, or schema-based rules (Alba & Hutchinson, 1987). Evaluation-based inferences, or halo effects, involve inferring the value of a missing attribute on the basis of an overall evaluation (Beckwith & Lehmann, 1975; Nisbett & Wilson, 1977b). Similarity-based inferences involve reasoning by analogy: If there is a sufficient match between the features of two brands, knowledge pertaining to the more familiar brand can be applied directly to the less familiar brand (Sujan, 1985; Sujan & Dekleva, 1987). Correlational inferences involve using knowledge about one known attribute to make predictions about a subjectively related missing attribute (Ford & Smith, 1987; Gardial & Biehal, 1986; Huber & McCann, 1982; Jaccard & Wood, 1988; Johnson, 1987; Johnson & Levin, 1985; Meyer, 1981; Yamagishi & Hill, 1981, 1983; Zwick, 1988). Finally, schemata provide default values that can be used to fill gaps in knowledge (Abelson, 1981; Hastie, 1981; Taylor & Crocker, 1981; Wyer & Carlston, 1979).[2]

Recognition Confidence

The primary difficulty in assessing inferences is measurement reactivity (Feldman & Lynch, 1988; Kardes, 1988b, 1988c). If subjects exposed to information implying a particular conclusion subsequently received a multiple-choice question containing several possible conclusions, subjects' responses would be difficult to interpret. If subjects endorsed the correct conclusion, it would be impossible to determine if subjects inferred the conclusion while perusing the initial

---

[2]Causal inferences can be subsumed by the four major rules of elaborative inference. For example, Kelley's (1967, 1972a) covariation principle is a special case of the correlational rule, and Kelley's (1972b) causal schemata are schema-based rules. Causal inferences are knowledge expanding because knowledge pertaining to the antecedents of an event enhances one's ability to predict and control that event.

information or if the conclusion became apparent later while reading the multiple-choice alternatives. That is, the measurement procedure itself may prompt inference formation rather than assessing a previously formed inference. In the absence of the reactive measure, inference formation would not have occurred.

One way to overcome this methodological difficulty is to measure intrusions in memory that result from inferential reasoning about explicitly provided information. Any piece of information retrieved from memory must originate from one of two sources: The information may have been actually perceived from the environment, or it may have been inferred on the basis of perceived information. People often experience difficulty in determining whether a given piece of information retrieved from memory was perceived or inferred, and, as a consequence, people often believe that their inferences were perceived rather than inferred (Johnson & Rahe, 1981).

Kardes (1988b) used a recognition-confidence procedure to assess the degree to which subjects believed that their inferences were perceived rather than inferred. Subjects first received a set of product claims in an incidental learning task and later received a surprise recognition task. In the incidental learning phase of the experiment, subjects judged the validity of several product claims of the form "Stresstabs contain B vitamins" and "B vitamins give you energy." Half of the subjects also received the conclusion "Stresstabs give you energy" (explicit conclusion) and half did not (implicit conclusion). Half of the claims pertained to familiar products (e.g., Rolaids, Tylenol) and half did not (e.g., Tolarin, Seratol). Half of the claims were logically related, as in the Stresstabs example, and half were not (e.g., "Seratol helps relieve insomnia," "Intestinal disorders often cause a loss of appetite," "Seratol often causes a loss of appetite").

To minimize pressures to engage in inferential reasoning, 44 claims pertaining to 16 different products were presented. Order of presentation was randomized with the constraint that no two claims pertaining to the same product could be presented consecutively. Moreover, the subjects' task was not related to inference formation and subjects did not expect to receive the recognition-confidence measure of inference formation. This measure consisted of 16 test conclusions to the claims presented earlier. Subjects indicated the degree to which they believed that they had seen or not seen each of these conclusions.

The results indicated that all three independent variables influence recognition confidence (see Table 6.1). In explicit conclusion conditions, recognition confidence was greater for familiar than for unfamiliar products. However, in implicit conclusion conditions, recognition confidence was greater in logically related claim conditions than in logically unrelated claim conditions. If the implications of product claims are sufficiently obvious, consumers automatically infer the conclusions to these claims even when pressures to engage in inferential reasoning are minimized. Hence, inferences that are formed automatically are often confused with explicitly presented information, and, consequently, recognition

TABLE 6.1
Recognition Confidence as a Function of Conclusion Explictness, Familiarity, and the
Relationship Between the Premises and the Conclusion

	Explicit Conclusion		Implicit Conclusion	
	Familiar Products	Unfamiliar Products	Familiar Products	Umfamiliar Products
Logically related	1.67	1.06	-1.93	-1.96
Logically unrelated	1.99	0.65	-2.74	-3.10

Adapted from Kardes (1988b). Higher values reflect greater recognition confidence for conclusions.

confidence provides a useful measure of automatic inferences. However, as the amount of effort required to draw inferences increases, the ability to discriminate between perceived versus inferred information increases (Alba, 1984). Consequently, the utility of the recognition-confidence measure decreases as inferential effort increases. Response latency and protocol analyses are more appropriate for measuring controlled inferences. In contrast, procedures that are useful for assessing controlled inferences cannot be used for tracing less effortful cognitive activities (Ericsson & Simon, 1980; Nisbett & Wilson, 1977a).

Gaze Duration

Gaze duration has been shown to be a useful measure of inference formation in studies of text comprehension (Just & Carpenter, 1980). In a recent study addressing the timing of the formation of simple elaborative inferences (O'Brien, Shank, Myers, & Raynor, 1988), subjects read passages containing either an explicit (e.g., popcorn) or an implicit (e.g., snack) antecedent and an anaphor (e.g., "he asked her what she was preparing"). Moreover, the context of the passage either strongly (e.g., "She got out the salt, heated the oil, and melted the butter") or weakly ("She searched the pantry for something she and he liked to eat") supported instantiation of the target concept (popcorn). When the context strongly implied the target concept, gaze durations on an anaphor did not differ as a function of antecedent explicitness. However, when the context was less informative, gaze duration was longer in implicit than in explicit antecedent conditions. This suggests that inference formation occurred while processing the anaphor rather than previously. Hence, if the inferential implications are sufficiently strong, contextual information can prompt consumers to generate on-line elaborative inferences. If the inferential implications are weak, inference formation is withheld until the anaphor is encountered, at which time interpretive inferences are required for comprehension.

Response Latency and Protocol Analysis

One of the more important concepts in memory research is the distinction between retrieval versus computational processes (Collins & Quillian, 1969). The distinction has been drawn in theories of semantic memory (Collins & Loftus, 1975), episodic memory (Tulving, 1985), text comprehension (Just & Carpenter, 1980), intelligence (Sternberg, 1985), and consumer memory and judgment (Beattie & Mitchell, 1985; Lichtenstein & Srull, 1985). Retrieval processes involve the direct retrieval of information from memory, whereas computational processes involve figuring out or computing an answer to a problem. For example, consider the retrieval question "What was O'Henry's real name?" If one knows the answer, one can retrieve it directly from memory (Porter). If one does not know the answer, there is no way to figure it out. In contrast, consider the computational question "How many states border the Atlantic Ocean?" It is unlikely that one can directly retrieve the answer from memory, but the answer could be figured out from common knowledge (14).

Camp, Lachman, and Lachman (1980) constructed 30 retrieval questions and 30 computational questions to investigate question-answering strategies. Half of the questions from each set were employed in a protocol task and the remaining questions were used in a response latency task. All subjects participated in both tasks (order of participation had no effects). In the protocol task, subjects verbalized how they arrived at each answer and two judges rated the protocols for the degree to which retrieval versus computational processes were used. In the response latency task, each question was paired with one answer, to which subjects responded either "true" or "false" as quickly as possible. The results revealed that (a) subjects were more likely to use a retrieval process for retrieval questions than for computational questions, and (b) response latencies were faster for retrieval questions than for computational questions. Hence, the protocol and response latency data provide converging evidence for the existence of retrieval and computational processes. Moreover, the experiment demonstrates that the two processes can be reliably manipulated and measured.

INFERENCE AND PERSUASION

Many prominent advertising researchers agree that inference plays an important role in persuasion (e.g., Batra & Ray, 1986; Chattopadhyay & Alba, 1988; Mitchell & Olson, 1981; Petty, Cacioppo, & Schumann, 1983). In fact, in his classic chapter that introduced the cognitive response approach to persuasion, Greenwald (1968) argued that recipients' inferences have a greater impact on persuasion than the message that provided the impetus for these inferences.

Advertisers also seem to recognize the significance of inferences in persuasion. For example, Burger King recently aired a commercial in which a young employee stated: "People prefer their hamburgers at home flame-broiled. Now if McDonald's and Wendy's fry their hamburgers and Burger King flame-broils theirs, where do you think people should go for a hamburger?" No answer to this question was provided. Instead, the advertiser decided to let consumers draw their own conclusions (for other examples of ads using implicit conclusions, see Sawyer, 1988).

Can conclusion omission be an effective persuasion technique? Early studies suggest that explicit conclusions are more persuasive (Fine, 1957; Hovland & Mandell, 1952), but recent evidence indicates that implicit conclusions are effective under some circumstances (Kardes, 1988c; Sawyer, 1988). Conclusion omission is not likely to be effective when consumers are unlikely to draw inferences about missing conclusions, and they clearly do not form inferences all the time (Lim, Olshavsky, & Kim, 1988). Only when the likelihood of inference formation is high can conclusion omission be effective. The critical question, then, is when do consumers naturally and spontaneously form inferences?

Motivation and Inference

Consumers generate inferences only when these inferences are likely to be useful for solving a particular problem or achieving a certain goal. Of course many different goals are possible, and the informational content of an inference and the confidence with which an inference is held depends on which goal is most salient at the time of inference formation (Kruglanski, 1980; Kruglanski & Freund, 1983).

Attitudinal and inferential judgments can serve a knowledge, ego-defensive, value-expressive, and/or a utilitarian function (Katz, 1960; Smith, Bruner, & White, 1956). The knowledge function involves the goal of forming accurate judgments about an object or issue. Such judgments enable consumers to organize, relate, and ascribe meaning to a rather complex universe of objects. However, consumers are not always motivated to form valid judgments. Smokers are less convinced about the link between smoking and cancer than nonsmokers, and optimistic or "wishful" thinking has been observed in beliefs about financial, professional, interpersonal, health-related, and crime-related matters (Kunda, 1987). Such optimism is driven by ego-defensive motives. Value-expressive (self-presentational) concerns arise when consumers are motivated to associate themselves with favorably evaluated concepts and disassociate themselves from unfavorably evaluated concepts. Finally, judgments may serve a utilitarian function. Strong situational inducements (i.e., rewards and punishments) can prompt people to form expedient judgments to meet time constraints or to please others.

Knowledge-related, ego-defensive, value-expressive, and utilitarian goals are activated by various situational and personal cues that influence issue involvement, ego-defensive involvement, identity involvement, and outcome involvement, respectively. For example, Leippe and Elkin (1987) manipulated issue involvement by varying the personal relevance of an issue and manipulated identity involvement by varying whether or not subjects anticipated discussing their views with others after reading about the issue. The results indicated that argument quality had a very strong impact on persuasion in the high issue-involvement condition, a moderately strong effect when both issue- and identity-involvement was high, and no effect in the high identity-involvement condition. This pattern occurred on both public and private attitudinal measures. Hence, different motives lead consumers to focus on different pieces of information and to form different attitudes on the basis of this information. However, in addition to influencing what information is processed, goals can influence how that information is processed (Kruglanski, 1989).

Finally, it should be emphasized that motivation is only part of the picture. Consumers can be motivated to diligently consider the implications of advertising claims and yet fail to draw inferences on the basis of these claims if distractions (Petty, Wells, & Brock, 1976), time constraints (Moore, Hausknecht, & Thamodaran, 1986), or high levels of physiological arousal (Sanbonmatsu & Kardes, 1988) inhibit their ability to elaborate on the claims.

Effects of Inferences on Subsequent Judgments

Kardes (1988c) conducted an experiment designed to investigate the antecedents and consequences of spontaneous inference formation. A mock ad about a fictional compact disc player was developed and issue involvement was manipulated by varying the boldface header within the ad. The highly involving header was designed to stimulate thinking about the text, whereas the uninvolving header was unprovocative. Furthermore, the text of the ad contained three sets of arguments implying three conclusions about the benefits of the advertised brand. These three conclusions were either presented (explicit conclusions) or omitted (implicit conclusions) from the text.

The effects of issue involvement and conclusion omission on the primary dependent measures are presented in Table 6.2. A response-latency procedure, similar to the Camp et al. (1980) procedure discussed earlier, was employed. As Table 6.2 indicates, when conclusions were presented explicitly, subjects responded relatively quickly to inquiries about the conclusions. In contrast, when conclusions were omitted and issue involvement was low, subjects responded relatively slowly to inferential inquiries. This pattern suggests that explicit-conclusion subjects retrieved the answers directly from memory, whereas control subjects were forced to compute answers, on the spot, after exposure to the inference measures. The critical comparisons, however, involve the implicit conclusion-high issue involvement cell. Subjects in this cell responded as quickly as explicit-conclusion subjects and more quickly than control subjects. Hence, the issue involvement manipulation was effective in prompting spontaneous inference formation when conclusions were omitted.

TABLE 6.2
Conclusion Latency, Attitude Favorability, and Evaluation Latency as a Function of Conclusion
Explicitness and Issue Involvement

Dependent Measure	Explicit Conclusion		Implicit Conclusion	
	High Issue Involvement	Low Issue Involvement	High Issue Involvement	Low Issue Involvement
Conclusion latency	4,520	4,413	4,503	4,722
Attitude favorability	5.54	5.21	5.65	4.88
Evaluation latency	2,734	2,431	2,063	2,459

Adapted from Kardes (1988c). The conclusion and evaluation latency means (in msec) are adjusted for a covariate designed to control for individual differences in overall response speed. Higher attitude means indicate more favorable attitudes.

The effects of spontaneous inference formation on brand attitudes were also investigated. Two aspects of brand attitudes were examined, their contents (favorability) and their strength (accessibility). As Table 6.1 indicates, more favorable attitudes were formed when explicit conclusions were provided than when conclusions were omitted and issue involvement was low (replicating Hovland & Mandell, 1952). However, the most favorable attitudes tended to be formed when conclusions were omitted and issue involvement was high. Thus, the effectiveness of conclusion omission as a persuasion technique is contingent upon the likelihood of spontaneous inference formation.

The key advantage of conclusion omission, however, lies in its effect on brand attitude accessibility. The accessibility of an attitude from memory depends on the strength of the association between an object and an individual's evaluation of the object. Experimental manipulations of the strength of the object-evaluation association have shown that increasing the strength of the association increases the speed with which individuals can respond to attitudinal inquiries (Fazio, Chen, McDonel, & Sherman, 1982; Fazio, Powell, & Herr, 1983; Fazio, Sanbonmatsu, Powell, & Kardes, 1986), and, consequently, evaluation latencies provide a useful measure of attitude accessibility. Moreover, highly accessible attitudes are automatically activated from memory whenever the attitude object is encountered (Fazio et al., 1986) and exert a strong impact on subsequent overt behavior (Fazio, 1986, 1990; Fazio & Williams, 1986). Because the ultimate goal of persuasion is to influence overt behavior, identifying the determinants of attitude accessibility is of critical importance.

Two such determinants have been investigated in previous experiments, direct experience with the attitude object and repeated attitude activation (for a review, see Fazio, 1986). A third determinant is implied by the data shown in Table 6.2. As Table 6.2 indicates, highly accessible attitudes are formed when conclusions are omitted and when recipients are sufficiently motivated to infer their own conclusions.[3] Attitudes formed on the basis of self-generated inferences are more accessible than attitudes formed on the basis of a less effortful process. Because relatively little effort is likely to be expended when explicit conclusions are provided or when issue involvement is low, relatively inaccessible attitudes are formed under these conditions.

Managerial Implications

When recipients are not sufficiently motivated to process message arguments effortfully, more favorable attitudes are formed when conclusions are presented explicitly. In contrast, when spontaneous formation is likely, equally favorable but more accessible attitudes are formed when conclusions are omitted. Although it may be difficult to induce spontaneous inference formation in some situations, efforts to design ads that prompt consumers to form favorable and accessible attitudes can obviously lead to great rewards.

A few additional points about this experiment should be noted. First, issue involvement was manipulated within the ad, which is more useful to managers than manipulations performed through experimental instructions. The study also examined inferences about benefits to the user rather than missing attributes because benefits should be more proximal to brand choice. Furthermore, attitude favorability and accessibility was investigated. This focus is important because only accessible attitudes exert a strong influence on perceptions and behavior (Fazio, 1986). Moreover, many variables that have been found to moderate the relationship between attitudes and behavior (e.g., self-monitoring; see Snyder, 1982) may do so, at least in part, because they are correlated with attitude accessibility (Kardes, Sanbonmatsu, Voss, & Fazio, 1986). Hence, the attitude accessibility construct may provide a theoretical integration of a rather lengthy and disorganized list of moderator variables. Finally, a clearer understanding of the antecedents of attitude accessibility is crucial for bridging the days, weeks, or months that are likely to pass between ad exposure and brand choice (Baker & Lutz, 1988).

The present study also suggests a new approach for influencing consumers, an approach I refer to as *indirect persuasion*. This approach is potentially useful for a number of reasons. First and foremost, it is important to recognize that consumers are not passive processors of information. When consumers are exposed

---

[3]Half of the subjects participated in the evaluation latency task first and half participated in the conclusion latency task first. Evaluation latencies for subjects in evaluation latency first conditions are presented in Table 6.1. When conclusion latencies were measured first, all subjects were required to think about the inferential implications of the message arguments and the predicted interaction was suppressed. Hence, two different manipulations, high issue involvement and direct questioning, prompted subjects to engage in a relatively effortful attitude formation process, and relatively accessible attitudes were formed as a result of this effortful process.

to advertising information, they know that the advertiser is trying to influence them and this knowledge affects how they process the information. Specifically, they are more likely to counterargue if they know that an influence attempt is being made and these counterarguments may serve as an innoculation that may help protect them from further influence attempts (Cialdini & Petty, 1981). Moreover, if the advertiser's intent to persuade is too transparent, psychological reactance may be aroused and a "boomerang" effect might occur (Clee & Wicklund, 1980). For example, if an advertiser is too forceful in his or her instructions to buy Brand A, consumers may become irritated and buy Brand B.

Subtle, indirect approaches, however, avoid these problems. Further, it might be possible to influence a chain of inferences, where one inference implies another inference that implies another, and so on. When inference processes are better understood, it might become possible to influence the string of inferences that are likely to be generated, thereby leading consumers "down the garden path." Hence, indirect persuasion offers several important advantages over more commonly employed approaches:

1. counterarguing is minimized;
2. psychological reactance is avoided;
3. self-persuasion is encouraged;
4. self-generated inferences about the attributes, benefits, and uses of a product are more memorable than information that was simply read from a text (Moore, Reardon, & Durso, 1986; Tyler, Hertel, McCallum, & Ellis, 1979);
5. inferences are often held with greater confidence, relative to information that was simply read (Levin, Johnson, & Chapman, 1988);
6. attitudes formed on the basis of self-generated inferences are more accessible than attitudes formed through a less effortful process; and
7. accessible attitudes exert a strong influence on overt behavior and are resistant to counterpersuasion (Fazio, 1986).

INFERENTIAL BIASES

When consumers are required to judge a person (e.g., a salesperson, a spokesperson in an ad), a product, or an event, they search their immediate surroundings (external search) and memory (internal search) for judgment-relevant information. A systematic and exhaustive search is unlikely, however, because only a limited amount of cognitive capacity is available for processing information (Bettman, 1979; Kahneman, 1973). A number of predictable inferential biases are likely because information-processing constraints on attention and memory often force consumers to focus on a relatively small set of information. When only a small set of information is considered, important information is likely to be overlooked. A list of attention and memory biases is provided in Table 6.3.

However, inferential biases do not occur only during internal and external search. After information has been gathered, consumers do not always use this information in a normatively appropriate manner. As Table 6.3 indicates, relevant information is sometimes not weighed heavily enough (see the list of biases that result from the underutilization of information in Table 6.3) and irrelevant information is sometimes weighed much too heavily (see the list of biases that result from the overutilization of information in Table 6.3). These biases have a number of interesting and important implications for managerial decision making (e.g., Cox & Summers, 1987; Lee, Acito, & Day, 1987) and for advertising. Some of these biases and their advertising implications are discussed here.

Attention and Memory Biases in Advertising

A list of selective attention and selective memory biases are presented in Table 6.3. These phenomena can be further subdivided into four general categories: context effects, salience and vividness effects, prior knowledge effects, and accessibility effects. The remaining effects are special cases of these four categories.

Context Effects.   Advertising researchers have long been interested in how consumers integrate specific attribute information into an overall evaluation of a product. It is well known that when product attribute information is presented sequentially, either the first few attributes (primacy) or the last few (recency) tend to have a disproportionately large impact on overall evaluations. When product attribute information is presented simultaneously, judgments of some attributes tend to be displaced toward a reference point (assimilation), whereas judgments of other attributes tend to be displaced away from the reference point (contrast). Jones and Goethals (1972) maintained that context effects observed when information is presented sequentially (i.e., primacy and recency effects) are mediated by the same psychological processes that underlie context effects found when information is presented simultaneously (i.e., assimilation and contrast effects). When people are motivated to form an on-line impression of a product, an impression is formed on the basis of the first few attributes and judgments of subsequent attributes tend to be assimilated toward the first impression. As a consequence, insufficient adjustments to an initial impression are made as additional information is encountered.

On the other hand, when people withhold judgment until all of the evidence has been accumulated (Lichtenstein & Srull, 1985, 1987), or when attribute information is processed in a "piecemeal" (Sujan, 1985) or "nonbrand" (Beattie & Mitchell, 1985) fashion, recency or contrast effects should occur, at least under some circumstances. Considerable controversy remains regarding the prev-

TABLE 6.3
Inferential Biases

Attention and Memory Biases

1. Context effects (Anderson, 1981, 1982; Higgins & Stangor, 1988; Jones & Goethals, 1972; Kardes & Herr, 1990; Kardes et al., 1989)

2. Salience and vividness effects (Kisielius & Sternthal, 1984, 1986; Taylor & Fiske, 1978; Taylor & Thompson, 1982)

3. Accessibility effects (Fazio, 1986; Herr, 1989; Higgins et al., 1985; Wyer & Srull, 1986)

4. Explanation, imagination, and simulation effects (Hoch, 1984, 1985; Sherman & Corty, 1984)

5. Biased assimiliation and hypothesis confirmation (Deighton, 1984; Hoch & Ha, 1986; Houston & Fazio, in press; Lee, Acito, & Day, 1987; Lord, Ross, & Lepper, 1979)

6. Illusory correlation (Bettman, John, & Scott, 1986; John et al., 1986; Sanbonmatsu et al., 1987; Sanbonmatsu et al., 1987)

7. Attributional biases (i.e., misattribution, hedonic relevance, personalism, and self-serving biases; for a review, see Ross & Fletcher, 1985)

8. Logical biases (i.e., affirmation of the consequent and denial of the antecedent; for a review, see Evans, 1982, Wyer, 1977)

9. The false consensus effect (Hoch, 1987, 1988, Marks & Miller, 1987)

10. The hindsight effect (Fischhoff & Beyth, 1975; Hoch & Loewenstein, 1989)

11. The pseudodiagnosticity effect (Fischhoff & Beyth-Marom, 1983)

12. The feature-positive effect (Fazio, Sherman, & Herr, 1982; Kardes et al., 1990)

13. The initial judgment effect (Kardes, 1986; Kardes & Strahle, 1986)

14. The direction-of-comparison effect (Houston et al., 1989; Sanbonmatsu et al., 1989)

Underutilization of Relevant Information

1. Overreliance on cognitive heuristics (Kahneman, Slovic, & Tversky, 1982; Nisbett & Ross, 1980; Sherman & Corty, 1894; Tversky & Kahneman, 1974)

2. The base rate fallacy (Kahneman et al., 1982; Kardes, 1988a; Lynch & Ofir, 1989; Ofir & Lynch, 1984)

3. The gambler's fallacy (Kahneman et al., 1982)

4. The conjunction fallacy (Leddo, Abelson, & Gross, 1984; Tversky & Kahneman, 1983)

5. Anchoring and adjustment (Einhorn & Hogarth, 1985; Kahneman et al., 1982)

6. Nonregressive judgment (Cox & Summers, 1987; Schaffner, 1985)

7. Insensitivity to the reliability and validity of information and overconfidence (Hogarth, 1987; Kahneman et al., 1982)

Overutilization of Irrelevant Information

1. Correspondence bias (Gilbert & Jones, 1986; Gilbert & Krull, 1988)

2. Using irrelevant analogies (Gilovich, 1981; Read, 1983, 1984)

3. The perseverance effect (Ross, Lepper, & Hubbard, 1975)

4. The dilution effect (Nisbett et al., 1981)

5. Premature cognitive commitment (Chanowitz & Langer, 1981)

alence of assimilation versus contrast effects. Some argue that spontaneous, on-line information processing is not easily disrupted (Hastie & Park, 1986), where-as others maintain that surprise/contrast effects are common (Einhorn & Hogarth, 1987). Hence, it is unclear whether advertisers should put their best foot forward or save the best for last.

Salience and Vividness Effects.   Because consumers are often unable to at-tend to all available information, it is important to determine what information will be focused on. What makes a particular piece of information attention-drawing? Some types of information are inherently attention-drawing or vivid. For example, it has been argued that visual information is more vivid than verbal information (Mitchell, 1986; Mitchell & Olson, 1981). Vivid information is concrete, image-provoking, and tends to elicit strong emotional feelings (Nisbett & Ross, 1980). Salient information, on the other hand, is attention-drawing because of the particular context in which it is perceived (Taylor & Thompson, 1982). For example, novel advertising executions tend to really stick out from the background provided by typical, everyday ads. Both salient and vivid informa-tion are weighed heavily in judgment. However, information that is salient in one situation may not be attention-drawing in other situations. Vivid information, on the other hand, is attention-drawing across situations.

Effects of Prior Knowledge.   Knowledgeable consumers often form expecta-tions, hypotheses, and implicit "theories" that are remarkably resistant to contra-dictory evidence. For example, most consumers believe that there is a strong positive relationship between price and quality. This belief leads them to pay special attention to belief-consistent information and to discount or ignore incon-sistent information. Furthermore, ambiguous evidence is interpreted as consis-tent with the belief. As a consequence, the belief that guided the differential processing of consistent, inconsistent, and ambiguous information receives strong support and confidence in the belief increases. Theory-based information processing can account for several inferential biases including (a) explanation, imagination, and simulation effects; (b) illusory correlation, and (c) biased as-similation and hypothesis confirmation.

Clearly, preconceptions can bias the way people interpret events. At the same time, however, it is also clear that prior knowledge can be extremely valuable. Beliefs and theories lend structure to experience and facilitate the comprehension and retention of information about a product or topic (Alba & Hutchinson, 1987; Mick, 1988). Prior knowledge is likely to have many other beneficial effects on inference as well. Consider the results of an experiment conducted recently by Kardes, Sanbonmatsu, and Herr (1990). In this study, subjects differing in knowledgeability were exposed to a fabricated description of a bicycle. Informa-tion about two important attributes (frame strength and weight) was intentionally omitted from the description. In "prompt" conditions, subjects were warned that no information was provided about the strength of the frame or the weight of the bicycle, whereas in no-prompt conditions, no such warning was delivered. This manipulation had a strong impact on the brand attitudes of subjects who were moderately knowledgeable about bicycles. In no-prompt conditions, these subjects were likely to overlook the missing features and form very favorable brand attitudes. In prompt conditions, however, the warning created uncertainty about the product and much less favorable attitudes were formed.

By contrast, highly knowledgeable subjects spontaneously detected the absence of the missing attributes and did not need the prompt to alert them to the fact that relevant information was missing. As a consequence, equally unfavorable attitudes were formed across prompt conditions. The prompt manipulation also failed to influence the attitudes of unknowledgeable subjects, presumably because they failed to recognize the significance of the missing features. The pattern of results on subjects' attitude-confidence ratings support this interpretation of data. High confidence ratings were expressed by low knowledge subjects and low confidence ratings were provided by high knowledge subjects, regardless of whether or not the prompt was offered. Moderately knowledgeable subjects, on the other hand, were more confident in no-prompt than in prompt conditions. Hence, this study demonstrates that the feature positive effect, or the tendency to overlook nonoccurrences, decreases as knowledge increases. This finding suggests an important prerequisite for inference formation: One must first notice that important information is missing before one bothers to draw inferences about this information. Because knowledgeable consumers are more likely to detect the absence of information, they should also be more likely to draw inferences.

Accessibility Effects.   Many different types of information are stored in memory, including attitudes (evaluative judgments), beliefs (nonevaluative judgments), schemata (organized sets of interrelated attitudes and/or beliefs), and categories (lists of shared features). Information differs in terms of the readiness with which it can be retrieved from long-term memory. Accessibility, or the readiness or ease with which information can be retrieved from memory, depends on (a) recency of activation (recently considered information is easier to retrieve), (b) frequency of activation (frequently considered information is easier to retrieve), and (c) elaboration. Several variables influence the extent to which consumers elaborate on information: Salient (contextually distinctive) and vivid (inherently attention-drawing) information is likely to be elaborated upon, and various situational cues can induce consumers to explain the causes of an event, to imagine the consequences of an event, or to think about the interrelationships between events. Elaborative processing increases the number of propositions associated with a given piece of information. Later, during a recall task, if an individual is unable to directly retrieve the target piece of information, he or she may be able to retrieve related propositions that can then be used to infer the target piece of information.[4]

Although elaborative processing can indirectly influence the likelihood with which information can be retrieved, frequency and recency of activation can directly affect the likelihood of retrieval. For example, Srull and Wyer (1979, 1980) used a priming paradigm to manipulate frequency and recency of activation. Priming, or category activation by unobtrusive exposure to category exemplars, was manipulated by asking subjects to work on an intellectual puzzle that involved the use of words related to a given trait category, such as the category "kind." In an ostensibly unrelated second experiment, subjects read a description of a target person that was ambiguous, with respect to the primed category. More favorable impressions of the target person were formed as frequency (i.e., the number of exemplars used during the priming procedure) and recency (i.e., how soon subjects were exposed to the target stimulus after priming) increased. Hence, information that is readily accessible from memory influences the interpretation of ambiguous stimuli.

Fazio et al. (1986) employed a similar priming procedure to show that highly accessible attitudes are spontaneously activated whenever an individual encounters the attitude object. In the first phase of this experiment, subjects were asked to express their attitudes toward a wide variety of attitude objects (e.g., coffee, vodka, cake) by pressing a button labeled "good" or a button labeled "bad" when the word appeared on a monitor (both speed and accuracy were emphasized). Latency of response was recorded automatically by a microprocessor. Attitude objects eliciting fast-positive, fast-negative, slow-positive, and slow-negative responses were identified for each subject and these objects served as primes in the second phase of the study. In the second phase, an unambiguous target adjective (e.g., appealing, repulsive) followed each prime that was presented on the monitor. Subjects were instructed to press either the "good" or the "bad" button in response to the target adjective. When fast-positive or fast-negative objects served as primes, latency of response was faster for evaluatively congruent than for incongruent target adjectives (a facilitation effect). However, when slow-positive or slow-negative objects served as primes, no facilitation was found. Hence, highly accessible attitudes are spontaneously activated whenever the attitude object is observed, even when attitude activation is irrelevant to the task at hand. As a consequence of this spontaneous activation, a priming facilitation effect occurs. Inaccessible attitudes, on the other hand, are not activated spontaneously and do not influence response latencies to related stimuli.

---

[4]According to Anderson (1983), elaborative processing can enhance recall either directly (through a direct retrieval process using one out of many pathways) or indirectly (through a computational process). However, Walker (1986) found no evidence for the multiple-pathway hypothesis. In fact, when inferential reconstruction was prevented, elaboration actually *decreased* recall performance.

The results of this study have important implications for understanding the effects of repetitive advertising. If exposure to an attitude object elicits spontaneous attitude activation, then multiple exposures (e.g., high ad repetition) should lead to frequent activation. Because accessibility increases as frequency of activation increases, repetitive advertising should increase brand attitude accessibility and brand choice (Fazio, 1986). Note, however, that this sequence of events should not occur for consumers with relatively inaccessible attitudes toward the brand because these consumers are unlikely to activate their attitudes from memory when they are exposed to the ad. Indirect evidence for these predictions is provided by studies showing that repetitive advertising has a stronger impact on the choice probabilities of high as opposed to low brand loyal consumers (Raj, 1982; Tellis, 1988). Hence, instead of promoting brand switching, repetitive advertising seems to influence choice by making already accessible attitudes even more accessible.

Biases Due to the Underutilization of Relevant Information

The average consumer is exposed to over 300 ads every day (Britt, Adams & Miller, 1972). On top of this, the consumer receives a great deal of product-related information from friends, salespeople, point-of-purchase displays, product packages, coupons, and so forth. Rather than performing a systematic and exhaustive analysis on all available information, the consumer is often forced to use heuristics or short cuts to simplify judgment and decision making. Although heuristics frequently lead to reasonable judgments and decisions, there is always a possibility that an important piece of information may be overlooked.

The most heavily researched heuristics are Tversky and Kahneman's (1974) representativeness and availability heuristics. The representativeness heuristic is used to make judgments about category membership based on similarity (if it looks like a duck and quacks like a duck, then it is a duck) and the availability heuristic is used to make predictions based on the ease with which instances come to mind (frequently occurring events are accessible and are likely to reoccur). However, focusing on only a few features can lead to erroneous categorizations and relying too heavily on memory can lead to incorrect predictions.

People also tend to rely on a few surface cues (peripheral processing; Petty & Cacioppo, 1986) and heuristics (heuristic processing; Chaiken, 1987) in advertising. For example, heuristics like "length implies strength," "people agree with people they like," "arguments based on expert opinions are valid" can be used to quickly infer the accuracy of persuasive communications without carefully construing the implications of each argument presented. Of course, carefully processing the arguments should lead to a more accurate assessment of their validity. However, effort does not guarantee accuracy.

Biases Due to Overutilization of Irrelevant Information

Consumers are likely to focus on a small sample of information ("underprocessing") when motivation is low and/or when time pressures are high. On the other hand, consumers are likely to perform a more systematic and exhaustive analysis when misjudgment is likely to lead to serious consequences and when time constraints permit such an analysis (Kruglanski, 1989). However, if too much cognitive effort is devoted to an information-processing task, "overprocessing" biases can result (Gilbert & Krull, 1988). For example, when people observe a target person perform a given trait-related behavior when strong situational pressures to exhibit the trait are present, observers tend to draw extreme dispositional inferences about the actor (correspondence bias). However, when distracting tasks force observers to allocate less cognitive effort toward interpreting the actor's behavior, less extreme dispostional inferences are formed. These inferences are more accurate because behaviors performed under strong situational constraints are fairly uninformative about the actor's underlying dispositions (only freely chosen behaviors are highly informative). Hence, people tend to read too much into uninformative information. More accurate inferences are formed when irrelevant information is not presented or when distractions reduce the amount of cognitive capacity available for processing irrelevant information.

The correspondence bias may also play an important role in advertising. For example, most consumers realize that famous spokepersons have been well compensated for their endorsements. Moreover, most consumers know that advertisers provide scripts telling endorsers exactly what to say. Nevertheless, strong dispositional inferences about the preferences of spokepersons are likely to be inferred. This may especially be true when the ad is simple and little effort is required to process the claims.

Another type of overprocessing bias is the tendency to use irrelevant prior knowledge when reasoning by analogy. For example, Gilovich (1981) found that sportswriters and coaches (i.e., individuals who are knowledgeable about sports) rated a player more favorably when irrelevant information about the player's hometown (e.g., he's from the same town as Gene Upshaw) was present as opposed to absent. In a third experiment, Gilovich asked undergraduates enrolled in a political science course on World War II and Vietnam to consider a hypothetical situation in which an aggressive, totalitarian country (Country A) was threatening a small, democratic, neighbor (Country B). Additional information containing irrelevant parallels to either World War II or Vietnam was presented. For example, the description containing irrelevant parallels to World War II stated that a conference would be held in the Winston Churchill Hall; the impending invasion was referred to as a Blitzkrieg invasion; and in an emergency, U.S. troops could be flown in via troop transports. The description containing irrelevant parallels to Vietnam stated that a conference would be held in the Dean Rusk Hall; the impending invasion was referred to as Quickstrike invasion; and in an emergency, U.S. troops could be flown in via Chinook helicopters. Although the descriptions were equivalent in meaning (only names were manipulated), subjects favored U.S. involvement more in the World War II condition than in the Vietnam condition.

Similar irrelevant analogies are often drawn in advertising. For example, a car ad may state that Brand A has more leg room than a Cadillac, more head room than a BMW, a sharper turning radius than a Mercedes, and so on, implying that Brand A is superior to several well-known brands. Gilovich's data imply that these irrelevant analogies are likely to influence brand evaluations.

What happens when irrelevant information later becomes relevant? Chanowitz and Langer (1981) addressed this interesting question by manipulating the perceived relevance of information provided about a novel, perceptual task. They found that initially irrelevant information is accepted at face value. Later, when the information becomes relevant, it has a stronger influence on task performance, relative to information that had been perceived as relevant from the beginning. Although this study was conducted in a clinical psychological setting, it could have important implications for advertising. Consumers are often exposed to ads for products they do not use, and consequently, the ad claims are likely to be accepted uncritically (without counterargumentation). Later, if they become users, they may purchase a brand they already know a lot about even if better alternatives are available.

Where is the Bias?

One of the biggest controversies in the inference literature is whether or not biases really exist. At one extreme, Tversky and Kahneman (1974) argued that people often rely too extensively on simplifying heuristics, and, consequently, important information is underutilized and non-normative judgments are formed. At the other extreme, Cohen (1981) argued that experimenters—not experimental subjects—are biased because they often focus on the wrong norms (e.g., Bayesian as opposed to Pascalian principles). Kruglanski (1980; Kruglanski & Freund, 1983) maintained that any piece of information has multiple implications and when people have different information-processing goals, they focus on different implications and form different inferences. Hence, subjects and experimenters can interpret the same information differently and both interpretations can be valid, given their respective information-processing goals.

Throughout this chapter, I have argued for a process-based perspective on consumer inference and judgment. Consistent with this perspective, I suggest that people are biased when they overlook or underutilize information they should not overlook or underutilize (i.e., relevant information). Furthermore, bias occurs when they use information that they would have been better off without (i.e., irrelevant information). By focusing on the process rather than the outcome of inferential reasoning, one avoids the confusion caused by situations in which a biased process leads to a valid inference (heuristics often lead to remarkably accurate inferences; the dilution effect is another good example of a biased process leading to a reasonable judgment) or by situations in which carefully reasoned thought leads to an inappropriate inference (reasoning by analogy can be a powerful tool unless the wrong analogy is chosen). It is critical to separate the process from the outcome of inferential judgment.

CONCLUSION

Inference processes clearly play an important role in advertising. Early work on message-related inferences (i.e., cognitive responses) has changed the way we view the effects of advertising on brand attitude favorability. More recent work on product-related, gap-filling inferences and on inferential biases offers new insights regarding the effects of advertising on other dimensions besides attitude favorability. Going beyond attitude favorability should lead to some important new perspectives on the effects of advertising.

Advertising Claims as Hypotheses

Research on biased assimilation and hypothesis confirmation (e.g., Lord, Ross, & Lepper, 1979) has led to the development of a new model of advertising that emphasizes the role of advertising in influencing the way subsequent evidence is interpreted (Deighton, 1984). Consumers often use advertising information to form tentatively held hypotheses or expectations about a product. Subsequently encountered information (e.g., *Consumer Reports* data, product trial) tends to be assimilated toward consumers' expectations, especially when this information is ambiguous (Hoch & Ha, 1986). As a consequence of this biased assimilation, consumers tend to find support for their hypotheses everywhere, and these confirmed hypotheses are likely to be held with a high degree of confidence.

Overcoming Competitive Advertising Inference

Recent research has shown that recall for information conveyed in a target ad is inhibited by exposure to the ads of competitors (Aaker, Stayman, & Hagerty, 1986; Burke & Srull, 1988; Keller, 1987). Hence, it is not surprising that low levels of ad recall are found in today's highly competitive, message-dense, cluttered, mass media environment (Franz, 1986; Webb & Ray, 1979). To overcome this adverse situation, one has to design ads that promote the development of strong, accessible brand attitudes. One way to accomplish this is to create thought-provoking ads that are likely to elicit spontaneous inference formation and to omit conclusions so that consumers can infer their own conclusions (Kardes, 1988c). If the ad is for an established brand, it would be desirable to prompt loyal consumers to spontaneously activate their attitudes repeatedly within each ad exposure and across repeated exposures because attitude accessibility increases with frequency of activation (Fazio et al., 1986).

The Fazio et al. (1986) study suggests that it may be possible to take advantage of competitive advertising. If a consumer has an extremely accessible attitude toward a given brand, the attitude should be activated spontaneously whenever the consumer is exposed to the brand (in any form), and may be activated spontaneously whenever the consumer is exposed to stimuli strongly associated with the target brand. Thus, if a competitor's offering is strongly associated with the target brand, the consumer may activate his or her attitude toward the target brand whenever he or she is exposed to an ad for the competitor's brand. If so, the competitor's ads would increase the strength of the consumer's attitude toward the target brand. Hence, an ostensibly undesirable event (i.e., competitive advertising) may actually have desirable effects, under some circumstances.

Underprocessing and Overprocessing in Advertising

It has been well established that low issue involvement, time constraints, and distractions decrease the likelihood of message elaboration (Petty & Cacioppo, 1986). When elaboration likelihood is low, consumers are strongly influenced by peripheral cues (Petty & Cacioppo, 1986) and heuristics (Chaiken, 1987) that simplify judgment and decision making by reducing the amount of information required for processing (underprocessing).

In an intriguing study, Gilbert and Krull (1988) demonstrated that people can also process too much information (overprocessing). While holding the information presented constant, Gilbert and Krull manipulated the amount of cognitive capacity available for processing this information and found that people are more likely to process irrelevant information as capacity increases. When this is the case, the correspondence bias (Gilbert & Jones, 1986; Gilbert & Krull, 1988), irrelevant analogies (Gilovich, 1981; Read, 1983, 1984), and nondiagnostic information (Nisbett, Zukler, & Lemley, 1981) are likely to influence brand attitudes formed on the basis of advertising claims.

Minimizing Counterargumentation in Advertising

Premature Cognitive Commitment. Chanowitz and Langer (1981) demonstrated that the incidental learning of irrelevant information can have important consequences if the irrelevant information later becomes relevant. Consumers are constantly exposed to ads for products that they do not use and much of this information is likely to be learned incidentally. Most importantly, consumers are unlikely to counterargue and the information should be accepted at face value. Later, if a need arises for the product, brands processed without counterargumentation should have an advantage over brands processed with counterarguments.

Indirect Persuasion. Conclusion omission is an effective persuasion technique when consumers are sufficiently motivated and have the opportunity to infer their own conclusions. Although spontaneous inference processes are unlikely to occur for some people (e.g., cognitive misers), for some products (e.g., convenience goods), and under some circumstances (e.g., the presence of distractions), advertisers are not completely at the mercy of the environment. It is possible to create ads that increase the likelihood of spontaneous inference generation. Highlighting the personal relevance of the message, using rhetorical questions, using novel ad appeals and executions, and stressing the aversive consequences that could ensue if an inferior brand is selected should incite more effortful and extensive information processing. Once spontaneous inference formation has been induced, consumers are likely to form highly accessible attitudes that exert a strong influence on brand choice and are resistant to counterpersuasion. Further, because highly accessible attitudes are activated spontaneously whenever individuals are exposed to the target brand, repetitive advertising should increase brand attitude accessibility and increase the advantages conferred through indirect persuasion.

In conclusion, this chapter has addressed several issues pertaining to the measurement of inferences, the factors that prompt consumers to spontaneously form inferences, and the effects of inferences on judgment and persuasion. The focus on inference processes has lead to a broader view of persuasion and to the development of a number of new perspectives on the effects of advertising. Persuasion involves much more than simply changing the direction and/or the extremity of attitudinal judgments. Going beyond the information given and going beyond attitude favorability should continue to challenge advertising researchers and should lead to interesting and important new discoveries.

ACKNOWLEDGMENTS

The author wishes to thank Joe Alba, David Mick, and Andy Mitchell for their helpful comments on an earlier version of this chapter.

REFERENCES

Aaker, D. A., Stayman, D. M., & Hagerty, M. R. (1986). Warmth in advertising: Measurement, impact, and sequence effects. *Journal of Consumer Research, 12,* 365–381.

Abelson, R. P. (1981). Psychological status of the script concept. *American Psychologist, 36,* 715–729.

Alba, J. W. (1984). The nature of inference representation. *American Journal of Psychology, 97,* 215–233.

Alba, J. W., & Hutchinson, J. W. (1987). Dimensions of consumer expertise. *Journal of Consumer Research, 13,* 411–454.

Anderson, J. R. (1983). *The architecture of cognition.* Cambridge, MA: Harvard University Press.

Anderson, N. H. (1981). *Foundations of information integration theory.* New York: Academic Press.

Anderson, N. H. (1982). *Methods of information integration theory.* New York: Academic Press.

Baker, W. E., & Lutz, R. J. (1988). The relevance-accessibility model of advertising effectiveness. In S. Hecker & D. W. Stewart (Eds.), *Nonverbal communication in advertising* (pp. 59–84). Lexington, MA: Lexington.

Batra, R., & Ray, M. L. (1986). Affective responses mediating acceptance of advertising. *Journal of Consumer Research, 13,* 234–249.

Beattie, A. E., & Mitchell, A. A. (1985). The relationship between advertising recall and persuasion: An experimental investigation. In L. F. Alwitt & A. A. Mitchell (Eds.), *Psychological processes and advertising effects: Theory research, and application* (pp. 129–155). Hillsdale, NJ: Lawrence Erlbaum Associates.

Beckwith, N. E., & Lehmann, D. R. (1975). The importance of halo effects in multi-attribute attitude models. *Journal of Marketing Research, 12,* 265–275.

Bettman, J. R. (1979). *An information processing theory of consumer choice.* Reading, MA: Addison-Wesley.

Bettman, J. R., John, D. R., & Scott, C. A. (1986). Covariation assessment by consumers. *Journal of Consumer Research, 13,* 316–326.

Britt, S. H., Adams, S. C., & Miller, A. S. (1972). How many advertising exposures per day? *Journal of Advertising Research, 12,* 3–9.

Burke, R. R., & Srull, T. K. (1988). Competitive interference and consumer memory for advertising. *Journal of Consumer Research, 15,* 55–68.

Camp, C. J., Lachman, J. L., & Lachman, R. (1980). Evidence for direct-access and inferential retrieval in question-answering. *Journal of Verbal Learning and Verbal Behavior, 19,* 583–596.

Chaiken, S. (1987). The heuristic model of persuasion. In M. P. Zanna, J. M. Olson, & C. P. Herman (Eds.), *Social influence: The Ontario symposium* (Vol. 5, pp. 3–39). Hillsdale, NJ: Lawrence Erlbaum Associates.

Chanowitz, B., & Langer, E. J. (1981). Premature cognitive commitment. *Journal of Personality and Social Psychology, 41,* 1051–1063.

Chattopadhyay, A., & Alba, J. W. (1988). The situational importance of recall and inference in consumer decision making. *Journal of Consumer Research, 15,* 1–12.

Cialdini, R. B., & Petty, R. E. (1981). Anticipatory opinion effects. In R. E. Petty, T. C. Brock, & T. M. Ostrom (Eds.), *Cognitive responses in persuasion* (pp. 217–235). Hillsdale, NJ: Lawrence Erlbaum Associates.

Clee, M. A., & Wicklund, R. A. (1980). Consumer behavior and psychological reactance. *Journal of Consumer Research, 6,* 389–405.

Cohen, L. J. (1981). Can human irrationality be experimentally demonstrated? *Behavioral and Brain Sciences, 4,* 317–331.

Collins, A. M., & Loftus, E. F. (1975). A spreading activation theory of semantic processing. *Psychological Review, 82,* 407–428.

Collins, A. M., & Quillian, M. R. (1969). retrieval time from semantic memory. *Journal of Verbal Learning and Verbal Behavior, 8,* 240–247.

Cox, A. D., & Summers, J. O. (1987). Heuristics and biases in the intuitive projection of retail sales. *Journal of Marketing Research, 24,* 190–207.

Deighton, J. (1984). The interaction of advertising and evidence. *Journal of Consumer Research, 11,* 763–770.

Einhorn, H. J., & Hogarth, R. M. (1985). Ambiguity and uncertainty in probabilistic inference. *Psychological Review, 92,* 433–461.

Einhorn, H. J., & Hogarth, R. M. (1987). *Adaptation and inertia in belief updating: The contrast-inertia model.* Unpublished manuscript, University of Chicago, Chicago.

Ericsson, K. A., & Simon, H. A. (1980). Verbal reports as data. *Psychological Review, 87,* 215–251.

Evans, J. St. B. T. (1982). *The psychology of deductive reasoning.* London: Routledge & Kegan Paul.

Fazio, R. H. (1986). How do attitudes guide behavior? In R. M. Sorrentino & E. T. Higgins (Eds.), *Handbook of motivation and cognition: Foundations of social behavior* (pp. 204–243). New York: Guilford Press.

Fazio, R. H. (1990). Multiple processes by which attitudes guide behavior: The MODE model as an integrative framework. In M. P. Zanna (Ed.), *Advances in experimental social psychology* (vol. 23, pp. 75–109). New York: Academic Press.

Fazio, R. H., Chen, J., McDonel, E. C., & Sherman, S. J. (1982). Attitude accessibility, attitude-behavior consistency, and the strength of the object-evaluation association. *Journal of Experimental Social Psychology, 18,* 339–357.

Fazio, R. H., Powell, M. C., & Herr, P. M. (1983). Toward a process model of the attitude-behavior relation: Accessing one's attitude upon mere observation of the attitude object. *Journal of Personality and Social Psychology, 44,* 723–735.

Fazio, R. H., Sanbonmatsu, D. M., Powell, M. C., & Kardes, F. R. (1986). On the automatic activation of attitudes. *Journal of Personality and Social Psychology, 50,* 229–238.

Fazio, R. H., Sherman, S. J., & Herr, P. M. (1982). The feature-positive effect in the self-perception process: Does not doing matter as much as doing? *Journal of Personality and Social Psychology, 42,* 404–411.

Fazio, R. H., & Williams, C. J. (1986). Attitude accessibility as a moderator of the attitude-perception and attitude-behavior relations. *Journal of Personality and Social Psychology, 51,* 505–514.

Feldman, J. M., & Lynch, J. G. (1988). Self-generated validity and other effects of measurement on belief, attitude, intention, and behavior. *Journal of Applied Psychology, 73,* 421–435.

Fine, B. J. (1957). Conclusion-drawing, communicator credibility, and anxiety as factors in opinion change. *Journal of Abnormal and Social Psychology, 54,* 369–374.

Fischhoff, B., & Beyth, R. (1975). "I knew it would happen"—Remembered probabilities of once future things. *Organizational Behavior and Human Performance, 13,* 1–16.

Fischhoff, B., & Beyth-Marom, R. (1983). Hypothesis evaluation from a Bayesian perspective. *Psychological Review, 90,* 239–260.

Ford, G. T., & Smith, R. A. (1987). Inferential beliefs in consumer evaluations: An assessment of alternative processing strategies. *Journal of Consumer Research, 14,* 363–371.

Franz, J. (1986). $39 Billion for what? Ads remembered as "forgettable" in 1985. *Advertising Age, 57,* 4.

Gardial, S., & Biehal, G. (1986). Measuring consumers' inferential processing in choice. In M. Wallendorf & P. Anderson (Eds.), *Advances in consumer research* (Vol. 14, pp. 101–105). Provo, UT: Association for Consumer Research.

Gilbert, D. T., & Jones, E. E. (1986). Perceiver-induced constraint: Interpretations of self-generated reality. *Journal of Personality and Social Psychology, 50,* 269–280.

Gilbert, D. T., & Krull, D. S. (1988). Seeing less and knowing more: The benefits of perceptual ignorance. *Journal of Personality and Social Psychology, 54,* 193–202.

Gilovich, T. (1981). Seeing the past in the present: The effect of associations to familiar events on judgments and decisions. *Journal of Personality and Social Psychology, 40,* 797–808.

Greenwald, A. G. (1968). Cognitive learning, cognitive response to persuasion, and attitude change. In A. G. Greenwald, T. C. Brock, & T. M. Ostrom (Eds.), *Psychological foundations of attitudes* (pp. 147–170). New York: Academic Press.

Hastie, R. (1981). Schematic principles in human memory. In E. T. Higgins, C. P. Herman, & M. P. Zanna (Eds.), *Social cognition: The Ontario symposium* (Vol. 1, pp. 39–88). Hillsdale, NJ: Lawrence Erlbaum Associates.

Hastie, R. (1983). Social inference. In M. R. Rosenzweig & L. W. Porter (Eds.), *Annual review of psychology* (Vol. 34, pp. 511–542). Palo Alto, CA: Annual Reviews.

Hastie, R., & Park, B. (1986). The relationship between memory and judgment depends on whether the judgment task is memory-based or on-line. *Psychological Review, 93,* 258–268.

Herr, P. M. (1989). Priming price: Prior knowledge and context effects. *Journal of Consumer Research, 16,* 67–75.

Higgins, E. T., Bargh, J. A., & Lombardi, W. (1985). The nature of priming effects on categorization. *Journal of Experimental Psychology: Learning, Memory, and Cognition, 11,* 59–69.

Higgins, E. T., & Stangor, C. (1988). "A change-of-standard" perspective on the relations among context, judgment, and memory. *Journal of Personality and Social Psychology, 54,* 181–192.

Hoch, S. J. (1984). Availability and interference in predictive judgment. *Journal of Experimental Psychology: Learning, Memory, and Cognition, 10,* 649–662.

Hoch, S. J. (1985). Counterfactual reasoning and accuracy in predicting personal events. *Journal of Experimental Psychology: Learning, Memory, and Cognition, 11,* 719–731.

Hoch, S. J. (1987). Perceived consensus and predictive accuracy: The pros and cons of projection. *Journal of Personality and Social Psychology, 53,* 221–234.

Hoch, S. J. (1988). Who do we know: Predicting the interests and opinions of the American consumer. *Journal of Consumer Research, 15,* 315-324.

Hoch, S. J., & Ha, Y. (1986). Consumer learning: Advertising and the ambiguity of product experience. *Journal of Consumer Research, 13,* 221–233.

Hoch, S. J., & Loewenstein, G. F. (1989). Outcome feedback: Hindsight *and* information. *Journal of Experimental Psychology: Learning, Memory, and Cognition, 15,* 605–619.

Hogarth, R. (1987). *Judgment and choice: The psychology of decision.* New York: Wiley.

Holland, J. H., Holyoak, K. J., Nisbett, R. E., & Thagard, P. R. (1986). *Induction: Processes of inference, learning, and discovery.* Cambridge, MA: MIT Press.

Houston, D. A., & Fazio, R. H. (in press). Biased processing as a function of attitude accessibility: Making objective judgments subjectively. *Social Cognition.*

Houston, D. A., Sherman, S. J., & Baker, S. M. (1989). The influence of unique features and direction of comparison on preferences. *Journal of Experimental Social Psychology, 25,* 121-141.

Hovland, C. I., & Mandell, W. (1952). An experimental comparison of conclusion-drawing by the communicator and by the audience. *Journal of Abnormal and Social Psychology, 47,* 581–588.

Huber, J., & McCann, J. (1982). The impact of inferential beliefs on product evaluations. *Journal of Marketing Research, 19,* 324–333.

Jaccard, J., & Wood, G. (1988). The effects of incomplete information on the formation of attitudes toward behavioral alternatives. *Journal of Personality and Social Psychology, 54,* 580–591.

John, D. R., Scott, C. A., & Bettman, J. R. (1986). Sampling data for covariation assessment: The effect of prior beliefs on search patterns. *Journal of Consumer Research, 13,* 38–47.

Johnson, M. K., & Rahe, C. L. (1981). Reality monitoring. *Psychological Review, 88,* 67–85.

Johnson, R. D. (1987). Making judgments when information is missing: Inferences, biases, and framing effects. *Acta Psychologica, 66,* 69–82.

Johnson, R. D., & Levin, I. P. (1985). More than meets the eye: The effect of missing information on purchase evaluations. *Journal of Consumer Research, 12,* 169-177.

Jones, E. E., & Goethals, G. R. (1972). Order effects in impression formation: Attribution context and the nature of the entity. In E. E. Jones, D. E. Kanouse, H. H. Kelley, R. E. Nisbett, S. Valins, & B. Weiner (Eds.), *Attribution: Perceiving the causes of behavior* (pp. 27–46). Morristown, NJ: General Learning Press.

Just, M. A., & Carpenter, P. A. (1980). A theory of reading: From eye fixations to comprehension. *Psychological Review, 87,* 329–354.

Kahneman, D. (1973). *Attention and effort.* Englewood Cliffs, NJ: Prentice-Hall.

Kahneman, D., Slovic, P., & Tversky, A. (Eds.). (1982). *Judgment under uncertainty: Heuristics and biases.* New York: Cambridge University Press.

Kahneman, D., & Treisman, A. (1984). Changing views of attention and automaticity. In R. Parasuraman & R. Davies (Eds.), *Varieties of attention* (pp. 29–61). New York: Academic Press.

Kardes, F. R. (1986). Effects of initial product judgments on subsequent memory-based judgments. *Journal of Consumer Research, 13,* 1–11.

Kardes, F. R. (1988a). Base rate information, causal inference, and preference. In M. J. Houston (Ed.), *Advances in consumer research* (Vol. 15, pp. 96–100). Provo, UT: Association for Consumer Research.

Kardes, F. R. (1988b). A nonreactive measure of inferential beliefs. *Psychology & Marketing, 5,* 273–286.

Kardes, F. R. (1988c). Spontaneous inference processes in advertising: The effects of conclusion omission and involvement on persuasion. *Journal of Consumer Research, 15,* 225–233.

Kardes, F. R., & Herr, P. M. (1990). Order effects in consumer judgment, choice, and memory: The role of initial processing goals. In G. J. Gorn, R. Pollay, & M. E. Goldberg (Eds.), *Advances in Consumer Research* (Vol. 17, pp. 541–546). Provo, UT: Association for Consumer Research.

Kardes, F. R., Herr, P. M., & Marlino, D. (1989). Some new light on substitution and attraction effects. In T. K. Srull (Ed.), *Advances in consumer research* (Vol. 16), pp. 203–208). Provo, UT: Association for Consumer Research.

Kardes, F. R., Sanbonmatsu, D. M., & Herr, P. M. 1990). Consumer expertise and the feature-positive effect: Implications for judgment and inference. In G. J. Gorn, R. Pollay, & M. E. Goldberg (Eds.), *Advances in consumer research* (Vol. 17, pp. 351–354). Provo, UT: Association for Consumer Research.

Kardes, F. R., Sanbonmatsu, D. M., Voss, R. T., & Fazio, R. H. (1986). Self-monitoring and attitude accessibility. *Personality and Social Psychology Bulletin, 12,* 468–474.

Kardes, F. R., & Strahle, W. M. (1986). Positivity and negativity effects in inferences about products. In R. J. Lutz (Ed.), *Advances in consumer research* (Vol. 13, pp. 23–26). Provo, UT: Association for Consumer Research.

Katz, D. (1960). The functional approach to the study of attitudes. *Public Opinion Quarterly, 24,* 163–204.

Keller, K. L. (1987). Memory in advertising: The effect of advertising memory cues on brand evaluations. *Journal of Consumer Research, 14,* 316–333.

Kelley, H. H. (1967). Attribution theory in social psychology. In D. Levine (Ed.), *Nebraska symposium on motivation* (pp. 192–238). Lincoln, NE: University of Nebraska Press.

Kelley, H. H. (1972a). Attribution in social interaction. In E. E. Jones, D. E. Kanouse, H. H. Kelley, R. E. Nisbett, S. Valins, & B. Weiner (Eds.), *Attribution: Perceiving the causes of behavior* (pp. 1–26). Morristown, NJ: General Learning Press.

Kelley, H. H. (1972b). Causal schemata and the attribution process. In E. E. Jones, D. E. Kanouse, H. H. Kelley, R. E. Nisbett, S. Valins, & B. Weiner (Eds.), *Attribution: Perceiving the causes of behavior* (pp. 151-174). Morristown, NJ: General Learning Press.

Kisielius, J., & Sternthal, B. (1984). Detecting and explaining vividness effects in attitudinal judgments. *Journal of Marketing Research, 21,* 54-64.

Kisielius, J., & Sternthal, B. (1986). Examining the vividness controversy: An availability-valence interpretation. *Journal of Consumer Research, 12,* 418–431.

Kruglanski, A. W. (1980). Lay epistemo-logic—process and contents: Another look at attribution theory. *Psychological Review, 87,* 70–87.

Kruglanski, A. W. (1989). *Lay epistemics and human knowledge: Cognitive and motivational bases.* New York: Plenum Press.

Kruglanski, A. W., & Freund, T. (1983). The freezing and unfreezing of lay-inferences: Effects on impressional primacy, ethnic stereotyping, and numerical anchoring. *Journal of Experimental Social Psychology, 19,* 448–468.

Kunda, Z. (1987). Motivated inference: Self-serving generation and evaluation of causal theories. *Journal of Personality and Social Psychology, 53,* 636-647.

Leddo, J., Abelson, R. P., & Gross, P. H. (1984). Conjunctive explanations: When two reasons are better than one. *Journal of Personality and Social Psychology, 47,* 933-943.

Lee, H., Acito, F., & Day, R. L. (1987). Evaluation and use of marketing research by decision makers: A behavioral simulation. *Journal of Marketing Research, 24,* 187–196.

Leippe, M. R., & Elkin, R. A. (1987). When motives clash: Issue involvement and response involvement as determinants of persuasion. *Journal of Personality and Social Psychology, 52,* 269–278.

Levin, I. P., Johnson, R. D., & Chapman, D. P. (1988). Confidence in judgments based on incomplete information: An investigation using both hypothetical and real gambles. *Journal of Behavioral Decision Making, 1,* 29–41.

Lichtenstein, M., & Srull, T. K. (1985). Conceptual and methodological issues in examining the relationship between consumer memory and judgment. In L. F. Alwitt & A. A. Mitchell (Eds.), *Psychological processes and advertising effects: Theory, research, and application* (pp. 113–128). Hillsdale, NJ: Lawrence Erlbaum Associates.

Lichtenstein, M., & Srull, T. K. (1987). Processing objectives as a determinant of the relationship between recall and judgment. *Journal of Experimental Social Psychology, 23,* 93–118.

Lim, J., Olshavsky, R. W., & Kim, J. (1988). The impact of inferences on product evaluations: Replication and extension. *Journal of Marketing Research, 25,* 308–316.

Lord, C. G., Ross, L., & Lepper, M. R. (1979). Biased assimilation and attitude polarization: The effects of prior theories on subsequently considered evidence. *Journal of Personality and Social Psychology, 37,* 2098–2109.

Lynch, J. G., & Ofir, C. (1989). Effects of cue consistency and value on base-rate utilization. *Journal of Personality and Social Psychology, 56,* 170–181.

Marks, G., & Miller, N. (1987). Ten years of research on the false-consensus effect: An empirical and theoretical review. *Psychological Bulletin, 102,* 72–90.

Meyer, R. J. (1981). A model of multiattribute judgments under uncertainty and informational constraints. *Journal of Marketing Research, 18,* 428–441.

Mick, D. G. (1986). Consumer research and semiotics: Exploring the morphology of signs, symbols, and significance. *Journal of Consumer Research, 13,* 196-213.

Mick, D. G. (1988). *A critical review of the comprehension construct in marketing communications research.* Unpublished manuscript, University of Florida, Gainesville.

Mitchell, A. A. (1986). The effect of verbal and visual components of advertisements on brand attitudes and attitude toward the ad. *Journal of Consumer Research, 13,* 12–24.

Mitchell, A. A., & Olson, J. C. (1981). Are product attribute beliefs the only mediator of advertising effects on brand attitude? *Journal of Marketing Research, 28,* 318–332.

Moore, D. J., Reardon, R., & Durso, F. T. (1986). The generation effect in advertising appeals. In R. J. Lutz (Ed.), *Advances in consumer research* (Vol. 13, pp. 117–120). Provo, UT: Association for Consumer Research.

Moore, D. L., Hausknecht, D., & Thamodaran, K. (1986). Time compression, response opportunity, and persuasion. *Journal of Consumer Research, 13,* 85–99.

Nisbett, R. E., & Ross, L. (1980). *Human inference: Strategies and shortcomings of social judgment.* Englewood Cliffs, NJ: Prentice-Hall.

Nisbett, R. E., & Wilson, T. D. (1977a). Telling more than we can know: Verbal reports on mental processes. *Psychological Review, 84,* 231–259.

Nisbett, R. E., & Wilson, T. D. (1977b). The halo effect: Evidence for unconscious alteration of judgments. *Journal of Personality and Social Psychology, 35,* 250–256.

Nisbett, R. E., Zukler, H., & Lemley, R. E. (1981). The dilution effect: Nondiagnostic information weakens the implications of diagnostic information. *Cognitive Psychology, 13,* 248–277.

O'Brien, E. J., Shank, D. M., Myers, J. L., & Rayner, K. (1988). Elaborative inferences during reading: Do they occur on-line? *Journal of Experimental Psychology: Learning, Memory, and Cognition, 14,* 410–420.

Ofir, C., & Lynch, J. G. (1984). Context effects on judgment under uncertainty. *Journal of Consumer Research, 11,* 668–679.

Petty, R. E., & Cacioppo, J. T. (1986). The elaboration likelihood model of persuasion. In L. Berkowitz (Ed.), *Advances in experimental social psychology* (Vol. 19, pp. 123–205). New York: Academic Press.

Petty, R. E., Cacioppo, J. T., & Schumann, D. (1983). Central and peripheral routes to advertising effectiveness: The moderating role of involvement. *Journal of Consumer Research, 10,* 135–146.

Petty, R. E., Wells, G. L., & Brock, T. C. (1976). Distraction can enhance or reduce yielding to propaganda: Thought disruption versus effort justification. *Journal of Personality and Social Psychology, 34,* 874–884.

Raj, S. P. (1982). The effects of advertising on high and low loyalty consumer segments. *Journal of Consumer Research, 9,* 77–89.

Read, S. J. (1983). Once is enough: Causal reasoning from a single instance. *Journal of Personality and Social Psychology, 45,* 323–334.

Read, S. J. (1984). Analogical reasoning in social judgment: The importance of causal theories. *Journal of Personality and Social Psychology, 46,* 14–25.

Ross, L., Lepper, M. R., & Hubbard, M. (1975). Perseverance in self-perception and social perception: Biased attributional processes in the debriefing paradigm. *Journal of Personality and Social Psychology, 32,* 880–892.

Ross, M., & Fletcher, G. J. O. (1985). Attribution and social perception. In G. Lindzey & E. Aronson (Eds.), *Handbook of social psychology* (pp. 73–122). Reading, MA: Addison-Wesley.

Sanbonmatsu, D. M., & Kardes, F. R. (1988). The effects of physiological arousal on information processing and persuasion. *Journal of Consumer Research, 15,* 379–385.

Sanbonmatsu, D. M., Kardes, F. R., & Gibson, B. D. (1989). The impact of initial processing goals on memory-based brand comparisons. In T. K. Srull (Ed.), *Advances in consumer research* (Vol. 16, 429–432). Provo, UT: Association for Consumer Research.

Sanbonmatsu, D. M., Shavitt, S., Sherman, S. J., & Roskos-Ewoldson, D. R. (1987). Illusory correlation in the perception of performance by self or a salient other. *Journal of Experimental Social Psychology, 23,* 518–543.

Sanbonmatsu, D. M., Sherman, S. J., & Hamilton, D. L. (1987). Illusory correlation in the perception of individuals and groups. *Social Cognition, 5,* 1–25.

Sawyer, A. G. (1988). Can there be effective advertising without explicit conclusions? Decide for yourself. In S. Hecker & D. W. Stewart (Eds.), *Nonverbal communication in advertising* (pp. 159–184). Lexington, MA: Lexington.

Schaffner, P. E. (1985). Specious learning about reward and punishment. *Journal of Personality and Social Psychology, 48,* 1377–1386.

Schneider, W., & Shiffrin, R. M. (1977). Controlled and automatic human information processing: I. Detection, search, and attention. *Psychological Review, 84,* 1–66.

Sherman, S. J., & Corty, E. (1984). Cognitive heuristics. In R. S. Wyer & T. K. Srull (Eds.), *Handbook of social cognition* (Vol. 2, pp. 189–286). Hillsdale, NJ: Lawrence Erlbaum Associates.

Shiffrin, R. M. (in press). Attention. In R. C. Atkinson, R. J. Herrnstein, G. Lindzey, & R. D. Luce (Eds.), *Stevens' handbook of experimental psychology.* New York: Wiley.

Shiffrin, R. M., & Schneider, W. (1977). Controlled and automatic human information processing: II. Perceptual learning, automatic attending, and a general theory. *Psychological Review, 84,* 127–190.

Smith, M. B., Bruner, J. S., & White, R. W. (1956). *Opinions and personality.* New York: Wiley.

Snyder, M. (1982). When believing means doing: Creating links between attitudes and behavior. In M. P. Zanna, E. T. Higgins, & C. P. Herman (Eds.), *Consistency in social behavior: The Ontario symposium* (Vol. 2, pp. 105–130). Hillsdale, NJ: Lawrence Erlbaum Associates.

Srull, T. K., & Wyer, R. S. (1979). The role of category accessibility in the interpretation of information about persons: Some determinants and implications. *Journal of Personality and Social Psychology, 37,* 1660–1672.

Srull, T. K., & Wyer, R. S. (1980). ategory accessibility and social perception: Some implications for the study of person memory and interpersonal judgments. *Journal of Personality and Social Psychology, 38,* 841–856.

Sternberg, R. J. (1985). *Beyond IQ.* New York: Cambridge University Press.

Sujan, M. (1985). Consumer knowledge: Effects on evaluation processes mediating consumer judgments. *Journal of Consumer Research, 12,* 31–46.

Sujan, M., & Dekleva, C. (1987). Product categorization and inference making: Some implications for comparative advertising. *Journal of Consumer Research, 14,* 372–378.

Taylor, S. E., & Crocker, J. (1981). Schematic bases of social information processing. In E. T. Higgins, C. P. Herman, & M. P. Zanna (Eds.), *Social cognition: The Ontario symposium* (Vol. 1, pp. 89–134). Hillsdale, NJ: Lawrence Erlbaum Associates.

Taylor, S. E., & Fiske, S. (1978). Salience, attention, and attribution: Top of the head phenomena. In L. Berkowitz (Ed.), *Advances in experimental social psychology* (Vol. 11, pp. 249–288). New York: Academic Press.

Taylor, S. E., & Thompson, S. C. (1982). Stalking the elusive "vividness" effect. *Psychological Review, 89,* 155–181.

Tellis, G. J. (1988). Advertising exposure, loyalty, and brand choice: A two-stage model of choice. *Journal of Marketing Research, 25,* 134–144.

Tulving, E. (1985). How many memory systems are there? *American Psychologist, 40,* 385–398.

Tversky, A., & Kahneman, D. (1974). Judgment under uncertainty: Heuristics and biases. *Science, 185,* 1124–1131.

Tversky, A., & Kahneman, D. (1983). Extensional versus intuitive reasoning: The conjunction fallacy in probability judgment. *Psychological Review, 90,* 293–315.

Tyler, S. W., Hertel, P. T., McCallum, M. C., & Ellis, H. C. (1979). Cognitive effort and memory. *Journal of Experimental Psychology: Human Learning and Memory, 5,* 607–617.

Walker, N. (1986). Direct retrieval from elaborated memory traces. *Memory & Cognition, 14,* 321-328.

Webb, P. H., & Ray, M. L. (1979). Effects of TV clutter. *Journal of Advertising Research, 19,* 7–12.

Wyer, R. S. (1977). The role of logical and nonlogical factors in making inferences about category membership. *Journal of Experimental Social Psychology, 13,* 577–595.

Wyer, R. S., & Carlston, D. E. (1979). *Social cognition, inference, and attribution.* Hillsdale, NJ: Lawrence Erlbaum Associates.

Wyer, R. S., & Srull, T. K. (1986). Human cognition in its social context. *Psychological Review, 93,* 322–359.

Yamagishi, T., & Hill, C. T. (1981). Adding versus averaging models revisited: A test of a path-analytic integration model. *Journal of Personality and Social Psychology, 41,* 13–25.

Yamagishi, T., & Hill, C. T. (1983). Initial impression versus missing information as explanations of the set-size effect. *Journal of Personality and Social Psychology, 44,* 942–951.

Zwick, R. (1988). *Same- and other-brands information sources in the formation of inferential beliefs about partially described multiattribute products.* Unpublished manuscript, Pennsylvania State University, University Park.

III BEHAVIORAL MODELS OF ADVERTISING EFFECTS

7 Advertising Interactions: A Route to Understanding Brand Equity

Julie A. Edell
Duke University, Durham, North Carolina

For years, advertising researchers and practitioners have been asking, "How does advertising work?" Most of what has been learned in addressing this question relates to how consumers interact with a specific advertisement. The impact of that one advertisement is usually measured immediately or very shortly after the subject views it once. This allows consumer's ad processing activities to be examined and the impact of these activities on brand attitudes to be isolated. In this chapter, I briefly review the knowledge development in this ad exposure–brand attitude relationship. I then suggest ways to extend knowledge about this relationship to more dynamic advertising situations. These situations include the use of multiple advertising executions, and the interaction of advertising executions and other forms of marketing communications (e.g., packaging, sales messages). The purpose of this chapter is to formulate and discuss ways to apply what we have learned about how an individual advertising execution is processed in order to begin to study how advertising can create and sustain brand equity.

The brand equity concept is currently receiving a great deal of attention. Farquhar (1989) defined brand equity "as the 'added value' with which a given brand endows a product" (p. 25). (cf. Jones, 1986; Leuthesser, 1988). He goes on to state that "the brand can have added value to the firm, the trade or the consumer" (p. 25). I am considering brand equity from the consumer's perspective, rather than from the firm's or trade's perspective. For a brand to have positive brand equity or value to the consumer, the difference between the consumer's evaluation of a branded product and an unbranded product with the same attributes must be positive. Brands may also have negative equity (i.e., the difference between the evaluation of a branded product and an unbranded product with the same attributes is negative), but as used here, brand equity will be limited to positive equity.

In addition to having a positive evaluation, the consumer can quickly retrieve associations from memory for brands with equity (Edell & Burke, 1986; Farquhar, 1989). These highly accessible associations may be to the overall evaluation or attitude about the brand (e.g., "Mercedes is the best automobile"). Or the accessible association may be to an attitude component: cognitive ("Ivory is very pure"), affective ("Betty Crocker can 'bake someone happy' "), or behavioral ("Cheer is the detergent I always buy") (Rosenberg & Hovland, 1960). The accessibility of any item from the brand's memory trace will be influenced by the frequency, the consistency, and the time that has elapsed since the item was last retrieved.

The impact of advertising, as previously mentioned, has often focused on changes in the consumer's brand attitude. In order to extend our thinking from examining advertising's impact on brand attitude to its impact on brand equity, it is important to distinguish between these two concepts. *Brand attitude* is a summary or overall evaluation and is commonly measured as the sum or average of multiple evaluation scales (*good–bad, dislike very much–like very much*) regarding the product being advertised. After an initial exposure to an ad, a consumer might be asked to report his or her brand attitude. If after seeing the ad a second time, the valence of the brand attitude has not changed, the exposure is said to have had no effect on brand attitude. Although the second exposure may not have changed the valence of the attitude, it may have changed the consumer's memory structure for that brand by changing the accessibility of that attitude, the willingness of the consumer to make inferences about other aspects of the brand, or the ability of the brand attitude to withstand competitive attack. If aspects of the memory structure for the brand have changed, then the brand equity has changed and the advertising has had an effect. To capture advertising's effect on brand equity, changes in the memory structure for the brand will need to be assessed.

DEVELOPMENT OF ADVERTISING KNOWLEDGE

It is important to assess the progress of the field before extending this knowledge to more dynamic advertising situations. In this section, I briefly review the development of the ad exposure–brand attitude relationship. Early research in advertising was primarily macro in its approach. Researchers examined the effect of varied levels of advertising spending on sales volume (Montgomery & Silk, 1972; Palda, 1964). The goal was to identify the aggregate relationship between advertising and sales. The consumer was considered only in aggregate terms in these early models, not as an individual who would influence the success or failure of the advertising spending.

Research in advertising paralleled the early econometric work and adopted the stimulus–response framework popular in behavioral psychology. In this research, the advertisement itself was the focus of the inquiry. Examples of the topics that were investigated are: size of the ad (Starch, 1966; Twedt, 1952); color versus black-and-white ads (Gardner & Cohen, 1966; Twedt, 1952); headline structure (Caples, 1947); and pictures (Starch, 1966). Again, the consumer was not explicitly considered in this research stream. However, recognition of the advertisement by the consumer was the key dependent variable in the majority of these studies.

The introduction of the consumer into the models of advertising research grew out of the research of the Yale Communications Research Program, under the direction of Carl I. Hovland, studying the effectiveness of persuasive communications. The researchers viewed their task as "the investigation of 'who' says 'what' to 'whom' with 'what effect' " (Fishbein & Ajzen, 1975, pp. 451–452). The Yale Program investigated characteristics of the source (e.g., expertise, likability), the message (e.g., type of appeal, one-sided vs. two-sided arguments), and audience characteristics. Audience characteristics such as sex differences (Janis & Field, 1959; Silverman, Ford, & Morgani, 1966); education (Hovland, Lunsdaine, & Sheffield, 1949) and personality traits such as anxiety (Janis & Feshbach, 1953) and self-esteem (Janis, 1954; Silverman, Ford, & Morgani, 1966) were explored to explain the differential effects of persuasive communication. Here, attitude change toward the position advocated in the communication was the primary variable of interest. The research using audience characteristics frequently had inconsistent findings; this led researchers to turn their attention to examining mediators of the brand attitude formation process.

Multiattribute models of the consumers' brand attitude formation process were used in the advertising literature to explore why ads had differential effects on different individuals. Fishbein's (1967) formulation of the attitude formation process was that individual's cognitive structure (beliefs and evaluative aspects about the salient attributes of the attitude object) differed, causing different attitudes. Lutz (1975) showed consumers' brand attitudes could be changed with an ad by either changing the belief strength of an attribute of the brand or by changing the evaluation of that attribute. Cognitive structure was just the first of the mediational processes explored by advertising researchers.

Greenwald (1968) found that the content of a persuasive communication frequently could not be recalled even though an attitude change persisted. This led him to hypothesize that a recipient's own thoughts (cognitive responses) about the message were more important in persuasion than the message content. Cognitive responses were also shown to mediate acceptance of advertising (Wright, 1973). Wright used a coding scheme that categorized thoughts into three types: counter-arguments, source derogations, and support arguments. His work showed that receivers of advertising relied heavily on these evaluative, mental responses to the ad, rather than the content of the ad itself, in forming brand attitudes. Olson, Toy, and Dover (1978) and Lutz and Swasy (1977) showed the value of combining the cognitive structure and cognitive response approaches to better understand the intervening cognitive activities between ad exposure and attitude formation or change.

Mitchell and Olson (1981) added attitude toward the advertisement as an additional mediator between ad exposure and attitude toward the brand. They showed that consumers' brand attitudes are influenced by both their assessment of salient beliefs about product attributes and their evaluation of the ad itself. This led researchers to begin to consider other mediators that were more affective in nature and to focus, not only on the message of the ad, but the importance of the ad structure.

Batra and Ray (1986), using a thought elicitation approach, showed that feelings experienced by consumers during an ad mediated the attitude toward the ad. Burke and Edell (1989) extended this finding by showing that feelings experienced during an ad mediate, not only attitude toward the ad, but also the beliefs that are formed about the brand's attributes and the attitude toward the brand.

Thus, advertising researchers have developed a detailed model of how feelings and thoughts mediate the formation and change of beliefs about the brand's attributes, and attitudes toward the ad and the brand in response to seeing a particular advertising execution. A current conceptualization is depicted in the Fig. 7.1. Exposure to an advertising execution may generate a combination of feelings and thoughts about the ad and the brand. These feelings and thoughts experienced at exposure have the potential to influence the beliefs that one forms about the brand and the attitude one has about the ad. The brand attitude is influenced by these thoughts and feelings and by the beliefs and attitude toward the ad.

It appears that the field has now developed a good understanding of how consumers process a particular advertising execution and the impact of that processing on memory and evaluations of the ad and the brand. Our theory develop-

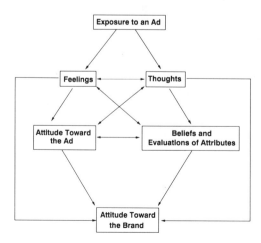

FIG. 7.1. Model of ad exposure-brand attitude formation process.

ment about a particular ad execution may be far enough advanced that we can profitably apply our learning to larger units of advertising than a single exposure to a particular execution within a single medium. As a result of processing a particular ad execution in a particular medium, the consumer will establish in memory a trace of that ad. The memory trace may include (a) elements of the ad (the scenes, the actors, the claims, etc.), (b) the thoughts and feelings experienced while processing the ad, (c) the beliefs and evaluations of the brand's attributes, (d) the attitude toward the ad, and (e) the attitude toward the brand. The memory trace from one exposure to a TV ad execution may be activated and impact subsequent exposures to that same TV execution, to similar executions in other media, to other executions for the same brand, and to other marketing communications.

ADVERTISING INTERACTIONS

The processing of one execution might be expected to impact the processing of other executions for the same brand. Most brands do not air just a single ad execution. Rather, there is an ad campaign that is made up of multiple executions, all working together to accomplish a specific goal or objective. International Business Machines (IBM), for example, had a corporate umbrella campaign that they introduced with nine television executions. The executions within this ad campaign all had a very similar structure. The executions each used a doubly truncated TV picture, a stark, colorless background, a close-up of a person with a problem, use of a freeze frame, and the superimposing of the words "The Solution." A campaign such as this, using structural similarity among executions, raises a number of questions about the nature of consumer's processing. Is each ad execution evaluated independently? Is the memory trace of a previously seen execution activated at exposure to the next execution and updated, forming a composite memory trace? Does a campaign that uses executional similarities strengthen the common elements of the consumer's ad trace? Does it strengthen the accessibility of some components of the memory structure at the expense of other components? These questions are all ways of inquiring about how such a campaign might impact the brand equity of IBM by changing the consumer's memory structure and the accessibility of elements within it.

In addition to the corporate campaign, IBM also aired executions from specific product campaigns. In a number of these executions, it was not the executional elements that were similar to the corporate campaign, but the message, "IBM is the solution." When executions have very different executional styles but similar messages, the processing of one execution may still influence the processing of subsequent executions. However, the *nature* of that processing is expected to be different. Greater processing involvement may be required to have the memory traces of the various executions integrated. Even greater cognitive effort may be required for consumers to relate executions when they do not share either executional or message similarities. A campaign such as this, using a similar message for a variety of a company's products, also raises interesting issues about brand equity. Can the equity that one brand (or the corporation) has, be shared with other brands made by the same manufacturer? Can this be done with the structure of the campaign, rather than by extending the brand name?

Another kind of advertising interaction that may impact brand equity is the interaction of an ad execution or campaign and other marketing communications. An example of this type of interaction was demonstrated by Keller (1987). He found that the package can be used as a communication vehicle to facilitate the recall of ad information. Use of packages to facilitate the retrieval of ad reactions may increase the brand's equity, both by strengthening the positive elements of the ad memory trace, and by making the attitude highly accessible at the most opportune time for purchase to occur.

A third type of advertising interaction that may influence the consumer's memory structure for a brand is the interaction between executions in different media. It is common practice to use multiple media to deliver an ad campaign. The IBM corporate campaign that I mentioned previously had print executions as well as the television executions. The print executions were similar to the TV executions, both in style (cropped borders, stark background, close-up of spokesperson with a problem, use of bold print for "The Solution") and in message. Similarly, some advertisers use the audio track of a TV execution as a radio execution in another form of media interaction. I will use the coordinated television–radio media campaign as an illustration of the kinds of differences one obtains in the memory structure.

COORDINATED MEDIA CAMPAIGNS

A coordinated media campaign is an ad campaign that includes executions in at least two different media and the executions share some common executional elements. For example, a coordinated TV–radio campaign might be one where the radio ad contains the audio track from the TV ad. This form of the coordinated TV–radio strategy has been suggested by several sources (e.g., Gay, 1985; Runyon, 1984; Sternthal & Craig, 1984). It is implicitly assumed that when consumers are exposed to a TV ad and later hear the audio on the radio, the audio track serves as a retrieval cue to the video and to the ad reactions that consumers stored in memory during the TV ad exposure. With "radio replay," the advertiser hopes, through cued imagery retrieval, to receive the benefits of another TV exposure at a much lower cost. An individual level, information-processing perspective will be used to examine a coordinated TV-radio ad campaign. This perspective is an example of how one might address advertising interactions and it shows the impact of changes in the memory structure that, in the long run, have the potential to change the brand's equity.

Information Processing Issues

To adequately explain consumer response to a coordinated TV–radio campaign with an information processing model of advertising, the following processes must be addressed: (a) the encoding of the initial execution (that may be either the radio or TV version); (b) retrieval of some or all of this stored ad trace; and (c) subsequent encoding of the same or different media execution. These processes are discussed in more detail in the following sections.

Encoding at Initial Exposure

This section examines how the ad elements (e.g., spoken words, music, voices, written words, scenes) influence the consumer's processing of an ad. The elements may affect processing by: (a) directly evoking cognitive or affective reactions or by (b) indirectly influencing the processing of and reactions to other elements (Edell, 1988). For example, a viewer of a TV commercial containing music may really like the song (a direct, positive, affective reaction) and the music may distract her from processing the text of the audio track (an indirect effect).

The content, number, and relationship of the ad elements differs between a TV ad and its radio counterpart. The TV version has more elements to be processed. These additional elements may provide more information to the viewer, but their presence may mean that more overall effort or capacity is required for the ad to be processed completely. Thus, it is unclear whether consumers will extract more or less information and meaning from a TV ad as compared to its radio counterpart.

A number of studies have examined the relationship of audio and video or pictorial and verbal elements within an ad. Some studies have shown that multiple elements facilitate learning (Kisielius & Sternthal, 1984; see Taylor & Thompson, 1982 for a review), while others have shown an interference effect (Bither & Wright, 1973; Warshaw, 1978). A facilitating effect is consistent with research on learning a target message in a thematic context (Bransford & Johnson, 1973). This research suggests that recognizing the meaning of information in one mode may facilitate the interpretation of meaning in another mode. Young and Bellezza's (1982) work on encoding variability also suggests that seeing the same information conveyed in slightly different ways increases its memorability.

Interference effects in processing are consistent with research on selective attention (Broadbent, 1958; Duncan, 1980) that demonstrated that it takes time to switch from processing visual to verbal inputs (e.g., 50msec to 1.5 seconds).

Researchers also found that concurrent distractors can inhibit cognitive activity and critical thinking (e.g., Festinger & Maccoby, 1964; Petty, Wells, & Brock, 1976).

What factors determine the extent of facilitation or distraction from multiple elements? Wright (1980) suggested that distraction from concurrently displayed elements depends on the nature of the elements themselves—their postponability, interest value, and the absolute information load. However, little empirical research has actually been conducted on the processing implications of the elements used in TV versus radio ads. And the existing empirical research on the difference between audio and audio–visual messages has not produced conclusive findings. For example, Jacoby, Hoyer, and Zimmer (1983) suggested that an audio presentation could facilitate message comprehension relative to an audio–visual presentation (because of the lack of visual distractors in the audio-only presentation), but noted that other unrelated visual stimuli in the environment may also distract from an audio presentation, impeding message comprehension. Their experiment found no differences between miscomprehension of material in the two media. Chaiken and Eagly (1976) did not find any differences in counterarguing between an audio and an audio–video message. Conversely, Liu and Stout (1987) found that TV ads elicited more counterarguments than radio ads using the corresponding audio track.

The relationship among the elements may also affect the extent of processing distraction (Edell & Staelin, 1983; K. A. Lutz & R. L. Lutz, 1977). Bither and Wright (1973) found, for subjects with moderate levels of self-confidence, that unrelated video, because of its greater distracting effects, resulted in greater acceptance of the audio message than did video that was "completely congruent" with the audio. Warshaw (1978) demonstrated that there are also distracting effects of related audio and video. In Warshaw's study, audio alone resulted in greater recall of audio information than audio presented with related video. The review of the modality research suggests that the effects of an ad in different media will be impacted by the content, number, and relationship of the components of the ad.

A typical advertising study concerned with media differences might end here. In studying how advertising interactions influence the memory structure and brand equity, however, understanding initial encoding differences is just the starting point. The goal now is to explore how this differential encoding will affect the nature of the processing of subsequent ad executions that may be in either the same or different media.

Retrieval Effects

Processing intensity and focus at the time of ad encoding determine what is stored in the ad memory trace (Hutchinson & Moore, 1984). The ad memory trace may include many different elements (e.g., brand name, product category, brand claims, ad execution elements, brand attitude, affective reactions to the ad, cognitive reactions). If a viewer attends and reacts primarily to a particular executional element of an ad, then the ad memory trace is likely to include that element and the viewer's reactions to it. At a subsequent exposure to this execution, the memory trace is likely to be activated, influencing the nature of the processing at this exposure. Thus, the type and organization of the information that is initially stored in the ad memory trace and the nature of the cues that one has available at subsequent exposure will impact what information (if any) is retrieved from memory when the ad is seen again (Lynch & Srull, 1982; Tulving & Thomson, 1973).

The assertion here is that the activated memory trace will affect the processing done during subsequent exposures to the ad. That is, when a person is exposed to an ad for a second time, the ad may serve as a retrieval cue for the initial ad trace. Keller (1987) showed that using components of a print ad as retrieval cues at the point of purchase can improve access to the ad trace. The relationship between the activated memory trace and the second ad exposure (the cue) will impact the allocation of processing resources between the memory trace and the current stimulus. A person may completely ignore the incoming ad and concentrate solely on the stored ad trace, ignore the memory trace and focus all processing on the incoming ad, or allocate some processing effort to both the trace and the stimulus (Norman & Bobrow, 1975). The allocation of processing effort is examined for the case where the second exposure to the ad is in the same medium and for the case where mixed media are used.

Same medium.   In the case where the second exposure to an ad execution is in the same medium as the first exposure, the second exposure provides an exact "copy cue" of the first exposure. Because the incoming stimulus and the ad elements of the ad memory trace are very likely to be quite similar, few processing differences should result from allocating processing resources to the ad trace rather than to the current stimulus. Thus, whether one actually recalls the ad and his or her cognitive and affective reactions to the first exposure or reprocesses the ad at the second exposure and generates reactions again, the resulting memory structure should be quite similar.

The results of a study by Edell and Keller (1989) showed support for this speculation. Subjects being exposed to the same ad twice, either on TV or on the radio, have about the same number of thoughts and a similar number of evaluative thoughts during the second exposure as do subjects seeing the ad only once in that medium. These similarities in processing result in similar attitudes toward the ad, attitudes toward the brand, and purchase intentions. Even though the attitudes of these groups are the same, the memory structures are different. Subjects seeing the TV ad twice were more likely to correctly recall the brand name and recalled more video elements of the ad than subjects seeing the TV ad only once. Similarly, subjects hearing the radio ad twice were more likely to correctly recall the brand name and recalled more audio elements of the ad than subjects hearing the radio ad only once. These data show that even when there is no change in the valence of the attitudes, there has been a change in the memory structure. These changes in the memory structure have made particular elements more accessible and, if positively evaluated, increased the brand's equity.

Mixed media: TV-Radio sequence.   When the second exposure to the ad is the radio version, composed of the audio track from a previously seen television execution, it may serve as a retrieval cue for elements stored in the ad trace from the previous TV exposure. Because the radio ad is an incomplete cue (rather than an exact copy cue), the processing effort required to retrieve the rest of the previously stored ad trace may be so great that the recipient does no processing of the currently playing radio ad.

Contrasting those subjects seeing the TV ad twice (TV–TV) with those subjects seeing the TV ad followed by the radio (TV–R), one finds that during the second exposure, TV–R subjects have fewer total thoughts, fewer brand and ad-evaluative thoughts, but more neutral ad thoughts, and more thoughts and reactions about the video (Edell & Keller, 1989). It appears from these data that when hearing the radio execution after viewing the TV execution, TV–R subjects appear to "replay" the TV video in their mind. This video replay seems to restrict subjects from evaluating the currently playing ad or thinking about their evaluative reaction from their first exposure to the ad.

The recall data (Edell & Keller, 1989) show that the memory structure for the TV–R subjects is similar to that of the subjects seeing the TV ad only once (TV), rather than like that of subjects seeing the TV ad twice (TV–TV). The TV subjects recalled 4.35 video elements, whereas the TV–R subjects recalled 4.32 video elements. The TV–TV subjects recalled 4.75 video elements. The replaying of the video elements stored in memory may have made these elements more accessible, but did not increase the number of video elements able to be recalled. Over longer delays, one would expect the TV–R subjects to have access to more video elements than would TV subjects.

Mixed media: Radio-TV sequence.   In the Radio-TV sequence, the TV execution is an enhanced memory cue. The audio track is an exact copy cue of the radio ad heard previously, but the video track is completely new. When a person hears a radio ad without prior exposure to the TV ad, he or she may visualize what is being described in the audio (Childers & Houston, 1984; MacInnis & Price, 1987). The individual's self-generated visualization from the radio ad may be more personally relevant than those contained in the video. These self-generated images may be quite different from the actual video of the TV ad. Thus, during the TV exposure, a person may find the video incongruent with the self-generated images stored in memory from the initial radio exposure. With an enhanced cue, then, people are likely to divide their processing activities between retrieving the stored ad trace and resolving these incongruencies and processing the on-going TV ad.

An examination of the results of Edell and Keller (1989) showed some support for the hypothesis of reduced processing of the current stimulus during exposure to the TV ad for subjects in the Radio–TV condition (R–TV). Compared with subjects in the TV–TV condition, R–TV subjects had fewer total thoughts, fewer evaluative thoughts, and fewer ad-evaluative thoughts. The memory structure, as reflected in the recall data, also shows somewhat of a different pattern when compared with TV–TV subjects. For R-TV subjects, the number of items recalled from the video is less, and the number of items recalled from the audio is greater.

Summary

These data indicate that changes in memory structures from exposure to advertising can take different forms. Subsequent exposures to an ad change both the components of the ad memory trace and the accessibility of these components. Elements may be added to the ad trace or existing elements of the trace may be strengthened; brand equity may be changed by both of these processes. The addition of more elements to the memory structure is more likely to impact brand equity by changing the valence of the brand attitude, whereas activating existing elements may impact brand equity by increasing the accessibility of components of the memory structure.

In the preceding sections, an individual-level information processing perspective has been the basis for examining coordinated media interactions. Clearly, the radio-TV interaction illustrated here is a relatively simple form of advertising interaction and examines only how the processing of one ad execution would affect the processing of a related execution. Yet, even in this simplified situation, there is evidence that the memory structure for a brand influences subsequent processing, reinforcing some elements of the memory structure and changing the accessibility of others. In these ways, over time and multiple exposures and experiences with a brand, the brand's equity is established in the consumer's mind. To understand how a brand comes to have meaning beyond its physical attributes, it is essential to understand the interrelationship among the structural properties of the ad executions and the content and linkages among elements of the ad memory trace. Specifying these relationships will be necessary in studying other forms of advertising interactions.

CONCLUSIONS

The purpose of this chapter is to provide a motivation and framework for researching advertising interactions. Each ad execution a consumer encounters does not stand alone. Rather, consumers' processing of one execution creates a memory trace that has the potential to impact all future brand experiences. In order to understand the role of advertising in creating and enhancing brand equity, a more complete picture of the memory structure is required. This will require more dynamic research studies and more precise specification and measurement of the structure of the ad-memory trace. The result will be, I believe, a much more complete answer to that perennial question, "How does advertising work?"

REFERENCES

Batra, R., & Ray, M. L. (1986). Situational effects of advertising repetition: The moderating influence of motivation, ability, and opportunity to respond. *Journal of Consumer Research, 12,* 432–445.

Bither, S. W., & Wright, P. L. (1973). The self-confidence—advertising relationship: A function of situational distraction. *Journal of Marketing Research, 10,* 146–152.

Bransford, J. D., & Johnson, M. K. (1983). Consideration of Some Problems of Comprehension. In W. G. Chase (Ed.), *Visual Information Processing.* New York: Academic Press.

Broadbent, D. E. (1958). *Perception and communication.* London: Pergamon Press.

Burke, M. C., & Edell, J. A. (1989). Ad-based emotions, affect, and cognition. *Journal of Marketing Research, 26,* 69–83.

Caples, J. (1947). *Tested advertising methods* (rev. ed.). New York: Harper & Row.

Chaiken, S., & Eagly, A. H. (1976). Communication modality as a determinant of message persuasiveness and message comprehensibility. *Journal of Personality and Social Psychology, 34,* 605–614.

Childers, T. L., & Houston, M. (1984). Conditions for a picture superiority effect on consumer memory. *Journal of Consumer Research, 11,* 643–655.

Duncan, J. (1980). The locus of interference in the perception of simultaneous stimuli. *Psychological Review, 87,* 272–300.

Edell, J. A. (1988). Nonverbal effects in ads: A review and synthesis. In S. Hecker and D. W. Stewart (Eds), *Nonverbal Communication in Advertising* (pp. 11–27). Lexington, MA: Lexington.

Edell, J. A., & Burke, M. C. (1986). The relative impact of prior brand attitude and attitude toward the ad on brand attitude after ad exposure. In J. Olson & K. Sentis (Eds), *Advertising and Consumer Psychology (Vol. 3,* pp. 93–107). New York: Praeger.

Edell, J. A., & Staelin, R. (1983). The information processing of pictures in print advertisements. *Journal of Consumer Research, 10,* 45–60.

Edell, J. A., & Keller, K. L. (1989). The information processing of coordinated media campaigns. *Journal of Marketing Research, 26,* 149–163.

Farquhar, P. H. (1989, September). Managing brand equity. *Marketing Research,* pp. 24–33.

Festinger, L., & Maccoby, N. (1964). On resistance to persuasive communication. *Journal of Abnormal and Social Psychology, 68,* 359–366.

Fishbein, M. (Ed.). (1967). A consideration of beliefs and their role in attitude measurement. In *Readings in Attitude Theory and Measurement* (pp. 257–266). New York: Wiley.

Fishbein, M., & Ajzen, I. (1975). *Belief, attitude, intention, and behavior: An introduction to theory and research.* Reading, MA: Addison-Wesley.

Gardner, D., & Cohen, J. (1966). ROP color and its effect on newspaper advertising. *Journal of Marketing Research, 3,* 365–371.

Gay, V. (1985, January 24). Image transfer: Radio ads making aural history. *Advertising Age,* pp. 1, 45.

Greenwald, A. G. (1968). Cognitive learning, cognitive response to persuasion, and attitude change. In A. G. Greenwald, T. C. Brock, & T. W. Ostrom (Eds.), *Psychological Foundations of Attitudes* (pp. 147–170). New York: Academic Press.

Hovland, C. I., Lunsdaine, A. A. & Sheffield, F. D. (1949). *Experiments on mass communications.* New Haven, CN: Yale University Press.

Hutchinson, J. W., & Moore, D. L. (1984). Issues surrounding the examination of delay effects of advertising. In Thomas C. Kinnear (Ed), *Advances in Consumer Research* (Vol. 11, pp. 650–655). Provo, UT: Association for Consumer Research.

Jacoby, J., Hoyer, W. D., & Zimmer, M. R. (1983). To read, view, or listen? A cross-media comparison of comprehension. In J. H. Leigh & C. R. Martin, Jr. (Eds.), *Current Issues and Research in Advertising* (pp. 201–218). Ann Arbor, MI: University of Michigan.

Janis, I. L. (1954). Personality correlates of susceptibility to persuasion. *Journal of Personality, 22,* 504–518.

Janis, I. L., & Feshbach, S. (1953). Effects of fear-arousing communications. *Journal of Abnormal Social Psychology, 48,* 78–92.

Janis, I. L., & Field, P. B. (1959). Sex differences and personality factors related to persuasibility. In C. I. Hovland & I. L. Janis (Eds.), *Personality and Persuasibility* (pp. 55–68). New Haven, CT: Yale University Press.

Jones, J. P. (1986). *What's in a name? Advertising and the concept of brands.* Lexington, MA: Lexington Books.

Keller, K. L. (1987). Memory factors in advertising: The effect of advertising retrieval cues on brand evaluations. *Journal of Consumer Research, 14,* 316–333.

Kisielius, J., & Sternthal, B. (1984). Detecting and explaining vividness effects in attitudinal judgments. *Journal of Marketing Research, 21,* 54–64.

Leuthesser, L. (Ed.) (1988). Defining, measuring, and managing brand equity: A conference summary (Rep. No. 88–104). Cambridge, MA: Marketing Science Institute.

Liu, S. S., & Stout, P. A. (1987). Effects of message modality and appeal on advertising acceptance. *Psychology and Marketing, 4,* 167–187.

Lutz, K. A., & Lutz, R. J. (1977). The effects of interactive imagery and learning: Application to advertising. *Journal of Applied Psychology, 62,* 493–498.

Lutz, R. J. (1975). Changing brand attitudes through modification of cognitive structure. *Journal of Consumer Behavior, 1,* 49–59.

Lutz, R. J., & Swasy, J. L. (1977). Integrating cognitive structure and cognitive response approaches to monitoring communication effects. In W. Perreault, Jr. (Ed.), *Advances in Consumer Research* (Vol. 4, pp. 363–371). Atlanta, GA: Association for Consumer Research.

Lynch, J. G., Jr., & Srull, T. K. (1982). Memory and attentional factors in consumer choice: Concepts and research methods. *Journal of Consumer Research, 9,* 18–36.

MacInnis, D. J., & Price, L. L. (1987). The role of imagery in information processing: Review and extensions. *Journal of Consumer Research, 13,* 473–491.

Mitchell, A. A., & Olson, J. C. (1981). Are product attribute beliefs the only mediator of advertising effects on brand attitudes? *Journal of Marketing Research, 18,* 318–322.

Montgomery, D. B., & Silk, A. J. (1972). Estimating dynamic effects of market communications expenditures. *Management Science,* Vol. 18, No. 10, 485–501.

Norman, D. A., & Bobrow, D. G. (1975). On data-limited and resource-limited processes. *Cognitive Psychologist, 7,* 44–64.

Olson, J. C., Toy, D. R., & Dover, P. A. (1978). Mediating effects of cognitive responses to advertising on cognitive structure. In H. Keith Hunt (Ed.), *Advances in Consumer Research* (Vol. 5 pp. 72–78). Ann Arbor, MI: Association for Consumer Research.

Palda, K. S. (1964). *The measurement of cumulative advertising effect.* Englewood Cliffs, NJ: Prentice-Hall.

Petty, R. E., Wells, G. L., & Brock, T. C. (1976). Distraction can enhance or reduce yielding to propaganda: Thought disruption versus effort justification. *Journal of Personality and Social Psychology, 34,* 874–884.

Rosenberg, M. J., & Hovland, C. I. (1960). Cognitive, affective, and behavioral components of attitudes. In C. I. Hovland & M. J. Russell (Eds.), *Attitude organization and change* (pp. 1–14). New Haven, CT: Yale University Press.

Runyon, K. E. (1984). *Advertising and the practice of marketing.* Columbus, OH: Merrill.

Silverman, I., Ford, L. H., & Morgani, J. B. (1966). Interrelated effects of social desirability, sex, self-esteem, and complexity of argument on persuasibility. *Journal of Personality, 34,* 555–568.

Starch, D. (1966). How does the shape of ads affect readership? *Media/Scope, 10,* 83–85.

Sternthal, B., & Craig, C. S. (1984). *Consumer behavior: An information processing perspective.* Englewood Cliffs, NJ: Prentice-Hall.

Taylor, S. E., & Thompson, S. C. (1982). Stalking the elusive "vividness" effect. *Psychological Review, 89,* 155–181.

Tulving, E., & Thomson, D. M. (1973). Encoding specificity and retrieval processes in episodic memory. *Psychological Review, 80,* 352-373.

Twedt, D. W. (1952). A multiple factor analysis of advertising readership. *Journal of Advertising Research, 26,* 207–215.

Warshaw, P. R. (1978). Application of selective attention theory to advertising displays. *Journal of Applied Psychology, 63,* (2), 373–376.

Wright, P. L. (1973). The cognitive processes mediating acceptance to advertising. *Journal of Marketing Research, 10,* 53–62.

Wright, P. L. (1980). Message-evoked thoughts: Persuasion research using thought verbalizations. *Journal of Consumer Research, 7,* 151–175.

Young, D. R., & Bellezza, F. S. (1982). Encoding variability, memory organization, and the repetition effect. *Journal of Experimental Psychology: Learning, Memory, and Cognition, 8,* 545–559.

8 Attitude Toward the Advertisement Effects Over Time and in Attitude Change Situations

Andrew A. Mitchell
University of Toronto

An individual's evaluation of an advertisement, as measured by their attitude toward the advertisement A_{ad}, has been found to be an important mediator of the effects of an advertisement on brand attitude (e.g., Mitchell & Olson, 1981). Recently, there has been considerable research directed at understanding the antecedents of attitude toward the ad (e.g., Mackenzie & Lutz, 1989) and the relationship between attitude toward the ad and brand attitudes (e.g., Homer, 1990). To date, however, most of the studies have examined advertising effects under attitude formation conditions and have examined the relationship between the mediators of attitude formation and change shortly after exposure to the advertisement (for exceptions, see Moore & Hutchinson, 1985; Burke & Edell, 1986). This limits the generalizability of the results in two ways. First, because brand attitudes are measured immediately after exposure to the advertisement, it is possible that the effect of A_{ad} on brand attitudes may be relatively minor or may even disappear entirely shortly after subjects leave the laboratory environment. Alternatively, the relationship between the individual's attitude toward the advertisement (A_{ad}) and brand attitudes may change over time due to memory factors (cf. Moore & Hutchinson, 1985).

Second, the role of these mediators, particularly A_{ad}, may differ between attitude formation and attitude change situations. For instance, if A_{ad} effects are relatively stable over time, an important issue is whether the effects of A_{ad} from exposure to an initial advertisement for a brand remain after a change in attitudes. Assume, for instance, that a consumer has formed an attitude toward a new brand of toothpaste. If this attitude was formed in an advertising context, then a portion of this attitude should be due to A_{ad} (cf. Lutz, 1985). Assume further that the consumer now receives new information about this brand of toothpaste, which results in a change in the consumer's attitude toward the brand. The issue here is whether the new attitude will still be, at least partially, based on the original A_{ad}.

These two issues will be examined in this chapter. First, however, research examining the effect of A_{ad} on brand attitudes is reviewed. Next, a number of alternative models of attitude change that include and exclude A_{ad} effects from attitude formation are developed. Finally, the results of a study are presented designed to examine these issues.

THEORETICAL FRAMEWORK

Attitude Toward the Advertisement Effects

Recent research indicates that brand attitudes formed within an advertising context are based on two individual level components (e.g., Batra & Ray, 1985; Gardner, 1985; Moore & Hutchinson, 1983, 1985; Park & Young, 1986). The first component is attitude toward the advertisement (A_{ad}); the second is the cognitive reaction induced by the information about the advertised brand contained in the ad. This component is typically measured by cognitive responses (e.g., Greenwald, 1968) or the beliefs formed or changed about the brand (e.g., Fishbein & Ajzen, 1975). Different elements of an advertisement may affect each of these two components. For instance, the visual elements of an advertisement may affect both A_{ad} and the beliefs associated with the brand (cf. Mitchell, 1986).

A number of studies indicate that the processing strategy used during exposure to the advertisement may affect the impact of these two components on brand attitudes (e.g., Gardner, 1985; Lutz, MacKenzie, & Belch, 1983; Park and Young, 1986). The general finding is that when individuals process the information from the advertisement with the goal of evaluating the advertised brand (e.g., a brand evaluation set), both A_{ad} and the predicted attitude from the product attribute beliefs will affect attitude formation.[1] When individuals process information from an advertisement to achieve some other goal (e.g., a nonbrand evaluation set), only A_{ad} seems to have an effect on brand attitudes regardless of whether brand attitudes are measured before or after beliefs.

In some situations, attitude A_{ad} may have an effect on cognitive reactions to the same advertisements. MacKenzie, Lutz and Belch (1986) tested a number of alternative models of the relationship between the different mediators, brand attitudes, and purchase intentions. The model that provided the best fit to the data was the Dual Mediation Model. In this model, the attitude toward the ad has an affect on both brand attitudes and the cognitive responses generated about the

---

[1]These effects, however, seem to occur only when brand attitudes are measured after beliefs are measured. Only A_{ad} seems to have an effect when brand attitudes are measured before beliefs (cf. Mitchell, 1986).

brand. When this occurs, A_{ad} has both a direct effect on brand attitudes and an indirect effect, which operates through the cognitive component. Homer (1990) tested the same models with data from an experiment where subjects were given either a brand or an advertising processing set. The results indicated that the Dual Mediation Model provided the best explanation for both processing sets.

As mentioned previously, most of these studies examined these relationships using measures obtained immediately after exposure to the advertisements. One exception is a study by Moore and Hutchinson (1985), which examined the effects of A_{ad} and brand familiarity on brand attitudes after both 2- and 7-day delays. The results indicated that A_{ad} had an effect on brand attitudes only when the advertisement was recalled, whereas brand familiarity had an effect on brand attitudes regardless of whether or not the advertisement was recalled. Later in this chapter, however, we argue that these results were dependent on the processing strategy used by the subjects during exposure to the advertisements.

Attitude Change Models

Another issue is whether A_{ad} from attitude formation has an effect on brand attitudes after the attitudes have changed. In order to examine this, a number of alternative models of high involvement attitude change processes are developed, which will be tested in the reported study. A more general model would include low-involvement processes and the possibility that the individual may not accept the new information (e.g., may counterargue against it).

The previous discussion of attitude toward the advertisement effects suggests that after exposure to an advertisement for a new brand, three conceptual elements may exist in memory. First, there should be a knowledge structure containing beliefs about the brand. Second, there may be a memory trace of the advertisement that was seen and, possibly, an attitude toward that advertisement. Finally, there may also be an overall attitude toward the brand (A_o) and an attitude toward purchasing and using the brand (A_{act}). In order to understand *how* attitudes change when individuals are exposed to new information about the brand, we have to understand how these three conceptual elements, which may exist at the time of exposure to new information, interact with the new information to cause the resulting attitude change. As a first step in obtaining a conceptual understanding of this interaction, a brief review of attitude change processes in Fishbein's Attitude Theory will be presented.

According to Fishbein's Attitude Theory, in order to form or change attitudes about an object, one or more of the primary or salient beliefs about the object or the evaluations of one or more of these beliefs must first be formed or changed (Fishbein & Ajzen, 1975). Because the study reported here uses only the former method to form or change attitudes, this discussion will focus on the two ways that beliefs can be formed or changed with a message. First, the message may provide information about characteristics of the brand, which directly result in the forming or changing of primary beliefs.

Alternatively, the message may present information about characteristics of the brand, which may result in the forming or changing of nonsalient beliefs; this, in turn, may result in the forming or changing of primary beliefs. Consequently, according to Fishbein's Attitude Theory, some primary or salient beliefs should have been formed when the attitude was formed. If an advertisement does not contain any information that directly relates to the primary or salient beliefs, inferences should have been made to form these beliefs.

This discussion suggests that in most attitude change situations, individuals already have a number of salient or primary beliefs about the attitude object. Consequently, when new information about important characteristics of the brand is provided, it will probably cause changes in a number of these primary beliefs if the new information is actively processed and accepted by the individual. When this occurs, individuals should first restructure their knowledge about the brand by adjusting their previous brand beliefs. This is similar to what Rumelhart and Norman (1978) referred to as the restructuring mode of learning. After this restructuring has occurred, individuals should recompute their attitudes based on the restructured knowledge. This conceptual model of the attitude change process underlies most of the previous research examining attitude change in consumer behavior (e.g., Lutz, 1975).

The five proposed models of attitude change fall into two classes. The first class of models are based on this restructuring process and contain four different models. The second class of models are based on an anchor and adjustment process, where the anchor is a previously formed attitude. The following models come from the first class.

Belief Restructuring Model. Under this model, individuals integrate the newly acquired information with their previously formed beliefs to form a new set of beliefs about the brand. These new beliefs are then retrieved and used to form a new attitude according to Fishbein's Attitude Theory (Fig. 8.1). With this model, the previously formed A_{ad} does *not* have an effect on the new brand attitude, unless A_{ad} had an effect on the original beliefs that were formed. This latter effect is indicated by a dotted arrow.

Belief Restructuring Model with Direct A_{ad} Effects. This model is similar to the first, but the attitude toward the initial advertisement (A_{ad}) also has a direct effect on the new brand attitude. This direct effect may occur if the advertisement is linked to the brand in memory or if the advertisement is retrieved from memory when attitudes are recomputed. If A_{ad} has an effect on the original beliefs, it also has an indirect effect on brand attitudes. This indirect effect is indicated in Fig. 8.1 by the dotted arrow.

Belief Accretion Model. With this model, the newly acquired information does not cause individuals to change their previously formed beliefs. The new

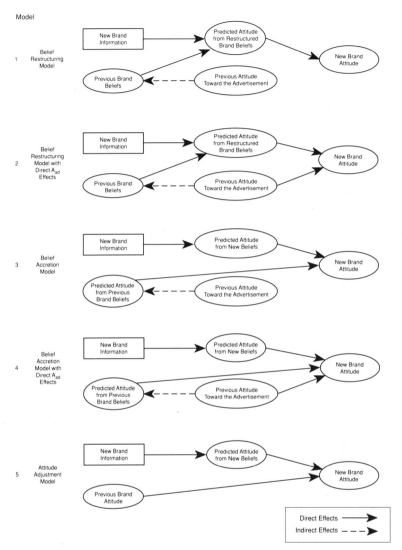

FIG. 8.1.   Alternative models of attitude change.

information causes the formation of new beliefs, which are simply added to the previous knowledge structure for the brand. This is similar to what Rumelhart and Norman (1978) referred to as the accretion mode of learning. After adding this new information to the knowledge structure, all the salient beliefs are retrieved and attitudes are recomputed according to Fishbein's Attitude Theory. Consequently, to form a new attitude, individuals use the predicted attitude from both the previous brand beliefs and the new beliefs they just acquired. With this model, the new information does *not* affect the previous beliefs formed about the brand. Also A_{ad} does *not* have an effect on the new brand attitude, unless A_{ad} had an effect on the original beliefs that were formed. This latter effect is also indicated in Fig. 8.1 with a dotted arrow.

Belief Accretion Model With Direct A_{ad} Effects.   This model is similar to the third, only the A_{ad} from the initial advertisement also has a direct effect on the new brand attitude. Again, this may occur if the advertisement is linked to the brand in memory or if the advertisement is retrieved from memory when attitudes are computed. In addition, if A_{ad} has an effect on the original beliefs, then it also has an indirect effect on brand attitudes as indicated by the dotted arrow.

The next model comes from the second class of models.

Attitude Adjustment Model.   This model assumes that individuals store their previously formed brand attitude (cf. Lichtenstein & Srull, 1985; Lingle & Ostrom, 1979) and when exposed to new information about a brand, simply adjust their old attitude with the new information that is acquired. If the old attitude is still influenced by the A_{ad} from attitude formation, then A_{ad} will have an effect on the new brand attitude. As mentioned before, this model is based on the anchor-and-adjust principle that has been found in a number of different judgment tasks (e.g., Anderson, 1981a; Einhorn and Hogarth, 1985). Here, the old attitude is the "anchor" that is adjusted with the new information acquired.

In summary, with first and third models, individuals use their brand beliefs formed or changed after exposure to the new information to form a new attitude toward the brand. In the first model, the new information changes the previous beliefs that were formed. In contrast, with the third model, this information does not change the previous beliefs.

The second and fourth models are the same as the first and third models, respectively, except that the A_{ad} from the initial advertisement has a direct effect on the new brand attitude. Finally, the fifth model is quite different from the other four in that subjects adjust their old attitude with the new information acquired.

The questions concerning the stability of brand attitudes based on A_{ad} and whether the A_{ad} component from attitude formation has an effect on the new brand attitudes that are formed after the acquisition of new information provide a better theoretical understanding of the A_{ad} construct and its theoretical and practical importance. If, for instance, A_{ad} effects decay rapidly over time, are highly dependent on the recall of the advertisement, or disappear when individuals acquire new information about the attitude object or brand, they still would have theoretical importance, but may have somewhat less practical importance.

RESEARCH STRATEGY

The purpose of this study is to examine A_{ad} effects over time and in an attitude change situation. These issues will be examined by first creating brand attitudes that are strongly influenced by A_{ad}. This is accomplished by constructing advertisements that contain valenced photographs and copy that provides relatively neutral information about the advertised brand along moderately salient attributes. As suggested by Fishbein's Attitude Theory, if only information along moderately salient attributes is provided in an advertisement when attitudes are formed, subjects should make inferences about how the brands perform along the highly salient attributes. When making these inferences, previous research indicates that individuals tend to use average values (e.g., Meyer, 1981). Consequently, the overall attitudes based on these inferences and the neutral information that is presented in the advertisement should be relatively neutral. Because previous research indicates that the use of valenced photographs in advertisements has a strong effect on both A_{ad} and brand attitudes (Mitchell, 1986), the resulting attitudes should be based primarily on A_{ad}. Two weeks after exposure to these initial advertisements, highly positive information about the brands along highly salient attributes will be presented.

If subjects make inferences about how the brands perform along the highly salient attributes, then the presentation of new information along these same salient attributes should cause the subjects to change their beliefs along these attributes. Consequently, prior theory suggests the new information should cause subjects to change their highly salient beliefs about the brands and then compute a new attitude based on these readjusted salient beliefs. The critical issue, then, is whether subjects use the A_{ad} from attitude formation in forming this new attitude.

In order to examine these two research issues, correlational methods are required. Although the use of experimentation is generally preferred over the use of correlational methods, the complexity of the issues preclude this approach. For instance, in order to examine whether A_{ad} effects decay over time, we need to determine whether A_{ad} has a significant effect on brand attitudes after controlling for the predicted attitude from product attribute beliefs. Because both attitudes and beliefs will generally decay over a significant period of time (Cook & Flay, 1977), correlational methods are required to determine whether the decay is due to A_{ad} effects or the decay of product attribute beliefs.

Correlational methods are also required to examine whether A_{ad} still has an effect on brand attitudes after the acquisition of new information about the brand. As discussed earlier, there are a number of alternative models that may underlie the attitude change process and it would be difficult to design a study that would allow for the selection of one model over another. The use of this methodology to examine this issue, however, creates problems in deciding which model is most appropriate for a particular data set. If the alternative models are nested, direct statistical tests can be used to discriminate between models. If the models are not nested, other criteria such as the amount of variance explained by the different models, must be used.[2] The use of this latter criterion, however, is valid only if one model explains considerably more variance than the others. If there are only small differences in the amount of variance explained across models, these differences may be due simply to random error (cf., Anderson, 1981b).

Because correlational methods are used to examine these issues, hypothetical brands from different product categories were used in the advertisements to minimize the confusion subjects may experience when attempting to retrieve brand attitudes and beliefs in the delay conditions. Pretests indicated that the decay of the brand attitudes formed from the advertisements used in this study were similar for the four products.

METHOD

Design

The design used in this study contains four conditions (Table 8.1). Subjects in Condition 1 saw four advertisements, one for each of four different products. Measures of brand attitudes, beliefs, and A_{ad} were taken immediately after exposure. Subjects in Condition 2 saw the same advertisements; however, the same measures were taken two weeks later. In Condition 3, subjects saw the same four advertisements and 2 weeks later were provided with new information about the brands. Measures of brand attitudes, beliefs, and A_{ad} were taken after these subjects received the new information. Finally, subjects in Condition 4 also received the new information 2 weeks later; however, measures of brand attitudes and beliefs were taken both before and after the presentation of the new informa-

---

[2]The use of this latter criterion to discriminate between alternative models of decision making has been criticized by Birnbaum (1973, 1974). His criticism was directed at their use in situations where subjects are asked to make judgments on a series of stimuli that vary along a number of attributes; and regression models are used to predict the judgments, using the attribute values of the stimuli as the independent variables. Birnbaum noted that in this situation, there were three psychological processes operating between the stimuli and the judgment. These were the converting of the stimulus values to subjective values, the integration of the subjective values to form an impression, and the overt judgment based on the impression. Although researchers using this methodology were primarily interested in determining the form of the integration function, Birnbaum pointed out that their use of regression to determine this confounded the first two psychological processes so the use of correlations as a measure of fit would be essentially worthless. However, in the study reported here, the regression models are estimated on subjective values, so this same problem does not exist. The use of regression analysis in this study does assume that there is a linear relationship between the impression and the reported attitudes; however, this does not seem to be a particularly severe assumption.

TABLE 8.1
Experimental Design

Condition	Immediate		Delay		
1	Exposure to advertisements	Measures			
2	Exposure to advertisements		Measures		
3	Exposure to advertisements			Exposure to new Information	Measures
4	Exposure to advertisements		Partial measures	Exposure to new information	Measures

tion. Conditions 2 and 3, then, can be viewed as controls for the before and after measures taken in Condition 4 (Table 8.1).

Subjects

The subjects were 78 junior and senior undergraduates of both sexes recruited from business courses at an eastern university. During the recruitment process, interested subjects gave their phone numbers and times when it would be convenient for them to participate in the study. They were then contacted by telephone and randomly assigned to conditions.

In order to disguise the delay portion of the experiment, the subjects were asked to participate in two different experiments. After participating in the first part of the experiment, they were told that they would be contacted in a couple of weeks for the second experiment. Depending on the condition, the two parts of the experiment lasted between 1 and 2 hours. The subjects were paid either $4 or $6, depending on the experimental conditions.

Stimuli

The products were selected using two criteria. First, the products should be ones that undergraduate students had purchased and used. Second, the products should have a relatively small number of highly salient attributes. Based on these criteria, the following products were selected: toothpaste, facial tissue, deodorant, and a ball point pen.

The advertisements contained a photograph and approximately 30 words of copy that presented attribute information for two moderately salient attributes for each product (Table 8.2). The salience of the attributes for each product class

TABLE 8.2
Attributes on Which Information was Provided

	Products	
	Toothpaste	Ball Point Pen
Information in advertisement (moderately salient)	Keeps breath fresher longer Whitens your teeth	Long lasting ink supply Special shape/easy to grip
New Information (highly salient)	Prevents cavities Taste	Smooth ink flow Fine writing line Never skips or blotches
	Deodorant	Facial Tissues
Information in advertisement (moderately salient)	All day protection Stick and spray form	Less likely to tear Comes in many colors
New information (highly salient)	Dries quickly Protects longer Scent	Softer More absorbent

were determined through pretests. The photographs were also selected through pretests to insure that they varied with respect to their valence to increase the amount of variance on brand attitudes and A_{ad} across products. Slides were made of each of the advertisements.

The new information about the products described consumer or laboratory tests conducted by an independent research company. This format was used to insure that the subjects would accept the new information and not counterargue against it. These tests demonstrated that the products outperformed competing products on two highly salient attributes. This new information about the test results contained between 80 and 90 words and was placed on overheads (Table 8.2) to emphasize that the messages were not advertisements.

Procedure

The subjects participated in groups of three to five in all the conditions. After being seated, the subjects were told that they were going to see advertisements for four new products that were not currently available on the market. They were told to evaluate each of the advertised products and decide whether or not they would be interested in purchasing the product while they looked at the advertisements. In other words, they were instructed to execute a brand processing strategy (e.g., Mitchell, 1983).

They were then shown the slides of the four advertisements projected on the screen. Because Krugman (1972) argued that the first exposure to an advertisement results in an orienting response and the acquisition of information occurs primarily on the second exposure, the advertisements were shown to the subjects twice. For the first exposure, each advertisement was displayed on the screen for 5 seconds, and for the second exposure the advertisement was displayed on the screen for 1 minute. While the advertisements were shown the second time, the subjects were reminded to think about each advertised product, evaluate it, and decide whether or not they would be interested in purchasing the product.

In Condition 1, the subjects were then given a short filler task to clear short-term memory after viewing the advertisements. This task required them to read a passage and circle the misspelled words. After this task, they filled out a short questionnaire (Questionnaire 1) to obtain a measure of their overall attitude (A_o) and their attitudes toward purchasing and using each of the advertised products (A_{act}).

After completing the first questionnaire, the subjects were instructed to turn it over. They were then given a second questionnaire (Questionnaire 2). The purpose of this questionnaire was to measure the actual beliefs associated with each brand in memory. In order to accomplish this, the subjects were asked to write down everything that came to mind when they thought about each of the advertised products. A separate page was provided for each product in the questionnaire.

The experimenter then drew a 7-point scale anchored by the words *very likely, very unlikely* on a blackboard. The subjects were asked to go through each of the statements they had written down and, for each statement that was a product attribute, write down the appropriate number on the left-hand side of the statement that indicated how likely they thought it was that the advertised product possessed that attribute. The experimenter defined a product attribute statement as "any statement that describes how the product looks, how it performs, or a particular feature of the product" and gave the subjects examples of product attributes. Subjects were encouraged to ask the experimenter about any statement if they were unsure whether it was a product attribute or not.

After the subjects had completed this task for each product, the experimenter drew a 7-point scale anchored by the words *good–bad* on the blackboard. The subjects were then asked to indicate how good or bad they thought it was that a product from that product category contained that attribute by writing the appropriate number on the right hand side of the statement.

After completing this task, the subjects were asked to turn over the questionnaire and were given a third questionnaire (Questionnaire 3) to obtain measures of A_{ad}, beliefs associated with each product (b_i) and the evaluation of each belief (e_i). In this questionnaire, the beliefs and evaluations were measured on scales for specific attributes associated with each product. When this questionnaire was completed, the subjects were asked to turn the questionnaire over and write down their thoughts as to the purpose of the experiment.

In the remaining conditions (2, 3 and 4), the subjects were given a short, open-ended questionnaire (Questionnaire 4) after exposure to the advertisements and were asked to write a few sentences that expressed their general opinions about and their interest in purchasing the advertised brands.[3] This was done to insure that subjects had formed an impression of each of the advertised products. Previous studies of attitude change processes have been criticized because there was some question as to whether subjects had formed an initial attitude (e.g., Carnegie-Mellon Marketing Seminar, 1978). The subjects were then dismissed and reminded that they would be contacted in a couple of weeks for the second experiment.

In Condition 2, the subjects returned to the laboratory two weeks later and were given the same instructions, filler task, and questionnaires (Questionnaires 1, 2 and 3) the subjects in the first conditions received after viewing the advertisements.

In Condition 3, the subjects returned to the laboratory two weeks later and were told that they were going to receive new information about the advertised products they had seen two weeks earlier. They were told that the new information was from an independent research company that had conducted consumer and laboratory tests of the performance of the new products. After being shown this information on an overhead projector, the subjects were given the same instructions, filler task, and set of questionnaires (Questionnaires 1, 2 and 3).

Finally, in Condition 4, the subjects were first given the short attitude questionnaire (Questionnaire 1) and the questionnaire (Questionnaire 2) that asked for the concepts associated with each of the advertised brands. They were then shown the new information and given the same instructions, filler task, and the complete set of questionnaires (Questionnaires 1, 2 and 3).

Dependent Measures

The dependent measures included measures of cognitive structure based on Fishbein's Attitude Theory. Overall brand attitudes (A_o) were measured by the mean of three 7-point scales anchored by the words: *good–bad; dislike very much–like very much;* and *pleasant-unpleasant.* The mean of three 7-point scales anchored by: *good–bad; foolish–wise; beneficial–harmful,* were used to measure attitude toward purchasing and using the brand (A_{act}). Both of these attitude measures had coefficient alpha values of between .86 and .95, in all the conditions. Finally, behavioral intentions (BI) were measured with a 7-point scale anchored by the phrases *not at all likely to buy* and *very likely to buy.*

The modification of the Fishbein model used by Mitchell and Olson (1981) was used to obtain a prediction of attitudes from the product attribute beliefs.

---

[3]Scales were not used in this questionnaire to obtain measures of brand attitudes, attitudes toward the act of purchasing, and using the brand or purchase intentions to avoid test–retest problems.

With this modification, measures of different levels of each product attribute are obtained. The belief strength (b_i) for each attribute level was measured using a 7-point scale anchored by the words *very unlikely* and *very likely*. The evaluation of each attribute level (e_i) was measured on a 7-point scale anchored by the adjectives *good-bad*. Pretests were used to determine the salient beliefs for each product and the levels for each attribute.

Two different measures of predicted attitudes were developed, based on the elicited beliefs. One of these measures was based on the summation of the evaluations of the product attributes associated with the advertised products (SE), whereas the second was the sum of the product of the belief strength and evaluations (PA). These measures were developed using the elicited beliefs from the questions asking the respondents to write down everything that came to mind when they thought about the advertised brand. These written statements were first screened by a research assistant using the definition of product attributes given to the subjects, so only product attitude statements were used for these measures.

Finally, following Mitchell and Olson (1981), attitude toward the advertisement (A_{ad}) was measured by the mean of four 5-point scales anchored by the words: *good–bad; like–dislike; irritating–nonirritating;* and *interesting–uninteresting*. The coefficient alpha for this measure was between .88 and .92 in all conditions.

RESULTS

The results are presented in two sections. In the first section, the effect of the 2-week delay is examined by comparing the effects of the first two conditions. In the second section, alternative models of the attitude change process are examined. First, however, we examine whether the subjects guessed the purpose of the experiment.

Demand Characteristics

An examination of the statements written by the subjects mentioning what they believed to be the purpose of the experiment indicates that none of the subjects guessed the true purpose of the study. Almost all of the subjects repeated the cover story given by the experimenter.

Immediate and Delayed Conditions

Brand Attitudes.   In order to determine if there are significant differences in brand attitudes between the immediate and delay conditions, a two-way repeated measure ANOVA is estimated. The results indicate a significant difference

($p < 0.05$) between the immediate and delay conditions (Conditions 1 and 2) for the brand attitude measure (A_o), but not for the attitude toward purchasing and using the brand (A_{act}) ($p > 0.4$). The interaction between the immediate and delay conditions and the different products is not significant for either measure ($p > 0.7$), indicating no product differences between the immediate and delay conditions. Overall, the mean brand attitude (A_o) across products decreased from 4.04 in the immediate condition to 3.73 in the delay condition.

Attitude Toward the Advertisement.   A similar analysis is used for the A_{ad} measure. The results indicate that neither the main effect between the immediate and delay conditions nor the interaction between these conditions and the different products is significant ($p > 0.15$). Across products, the mean A_{ad} is 2.92 in the immediate condition and 2.77 in the delay condition. This indicates that even though subjects in the delay condition had to recall and evaluate the advertisements they saw 2 weeks earlier, this delay had little effect on the resulting evaluations.

Prediction of Direct A_{ad} Effects.   In order to determine if A_{ad} has a direct effect on brand attitudes in the delay condition, regression models are estimated for each condition and each attitude measure. These models also include the two measures of the cognitive component to control for its effects. These measures are the predicted attitude score from the structured scales ($\Sigma\Sigma b_i e_i$) and the summed evaluation score from the elicited beliefs (SE).[4]

The estimated models are presented in Table 8.3. In the immediate condition, A_{ad} always has the strongest effect on the different attitude measures as indicated by the size of the beta weight and the t-statistics. In the equation with the brand attitude measure (A_o) as the dependent variable, the coefficient for the predicted attitude from the structured scales ($\Sigma\Sigma b_i e_i$) is not significantly different than zero. Similar results were found in a previous study (Mitchell, 1986).

The same pattern of results holds, in general, for the delay condition. The only difference is that the predicted score from the structured scales ($\Sigma\Sigma b_i e_i$) also has a significant effect on the brand attitude measure (A_o). Again, A_{ad} has the strongest effect as indicated by the size of the beta weights and t-statistics.[5]

Note that the amount of variance explained by the regression models *decreases* by 35% between the immediate and delay conditions when brand attitude (A_o) is the dependent variable. However, when attitude toward purchasing and

---

[4]The models were estimated with both the SE and PA measures of predicted attitudes from the elicited beliefs. There were virtually no differences in the resulting models, so only the models with the SE variable are reported. The models were also estimated with dummy variables for three of the four brands. Again, there were no differences in the resulting models, however, as expected, the R^2 values increased slightly.

[5]The simple correlations between A_{ad} and $\Sigma\Sigma b_i e_i$ was 0.30, and between A_{ad} and SE was 0.43, which indicates that multicollinearity could not account for these results.

TABLE 8.3
Prediction of Attitudes

	Beta Weights (t- Statistics)			
Immediate	$\Sigma\Sigma b_j e_j$	A_{ad}	SE	R^2
A_o	0.103 (1.28)	0.777[a] (10.48)	-0.003 (0.105)	0.78
A_{act}	0.093 (0.98)	0.725[a] (7.28)	0.050 (0.59)	0.67
Delayed				
A_o	0.208[c] (2.33)	0.593[a] (6.24)	0.040 (0.45)	0.51
A_{act}	0.137[c] (1.67)	0.647[a] (8.02)	0.161 (1.97)	0.62

Note. Superscripts indicate significance levels as indicated below.
$a_p < 0.001$.
$c_p < 0.05$.

using the brand (A_{act}) is the dependent variable, the amount of explained variance decreases by only 7% between these conditions.[6] An interpretation of this finding will be given later in the discussion section.

Prediction of Total A_{ad} Effects.   As mentioned previously, MacKenzie, Lutz and Belch (1986) found evidence that A_{ad} may also affect the cognitive component in attitude formation. If it does, then A_{ad} also has an indirect effect on brand attitudes, which operates through the cognitive component. To determine if this occurred in this study, regression analysis was used to estimate the effect of A_{ad} on the two measures of the cognitive component. In the immediate condition, A_{ad} has a highly significant effect ($p < 0.001$) on the predicted attitude from the structured scales ($\Sigma\Sigma b_i e_i$), but not on SE ($p > 0.20$).

In the delay condition, A_{ad} has a significant effect on both measures of the cognitive component ($p < 0.001$). The amount of variance explained in the predicted attitude from the structured scales ($\Sigma\Sigma b_i e_i$) declines from 0.43 in the

---

[6]The product moment correlation between Brand Attitudes (A_o) and both the predicted attitude from the structured scales ($\Sigma\Sigma b_i e_i$) and attitude toward the advertisement (A_{ad}) decreased by approximately the same amount between the immediate and delayed conditions. These declines in correlations could be due to a reduction in the reliability of the measures in the delay condition. However, an examination of the coefficient alpha measure of reliability indicated that this explanation is not valid. This measure declined slightly for the brand attitude measure (from 0.94 to 0.91), increased slightly for the attitude toward the act of purchasing and using the brand measure (from 0.90 to 0.92), and stayed the same for the attitude toward the advertisement measure (0.90).

immediate condition to 0.13 in the delay condition, whereas the amount of variance explained in the predicted attitude from the summed evaluation of the elicited beliefs (SE) increases from 0.02 to 0.14. This suggests that the effect of A_{ad} on these two measures of cognitive structure may vary over time.

If it is assumed that the common variance between the cognitive component and A_{ad} is caused by A_{ad}, as assumed by MacKenzie, Lutz and Belch (1986), the total effect of A_{ad} on brand attitudes can also be estimated. These total effects are estimated by first removing the effect of A_{ad} from both $\Sigma\Sigma b_i e_i$ and SE and using these residuals along with A_{ad} as independent variables in the regression models to predict brand attitudes. In effect, this procedure allocates the common variance between A_{ad} and the cognitive component to A_{ad} in predicting brand attitudes.

This, of course, increases the beta weights and t-statistics for A_{ad} in all four equations. For instance, in the immediate condition, the estimated beta weights are 0.84 and 0.81 and the t-statistics are 13.49 and 11.75 in the regression equation used to predict A_o and A_{act}, respectively. Also, as expected, the beta weights and t-statistics for the residuals of the two measures of the cognitive component are reduced in all four equations with two exceptions. These exceptions occur for the beta weights and t-statistics for the residuals of the predicted attitude from the structured scales in the two regression models in the delay condition.

Finally, because this analysis only affects the allocation of the common variance between A_{ad} and the cognitive component, the amount of variance explained by the models in the immediate and delay conditions is virtually the same as the variance explained in the previous analysis of the direct effects.

Summary. These results indicate that brand attitudes based on A_{ad} effects were fairly stable over the 2-week period and the effect of A_{ad} on brand attitudes is not transitory. The regression analyses indicates that A_{ad} still had the strongest effect on attitudes after a 2-week delay. In addition, there is a relatively large decrease in the amount of variance explained by the regression models over the 2-week period for the brand attitude (A_o) measures, and a small decrease for the attitude toward purchasing and using the brand (A_{act}) measures.

Although there are similarities between these results and the results of the Moore and Hutchinson (1985) study, there are also differences. One of the most important difference is that the amount of variance explained by the regression models predicting brand attitudes (A_o) increased slightly over time in the Moore and Hutchinson study, but decreases dramatically in this study. These different results most likely occurred for two reasons. First, in the Moore and Hutchinson study, subjects were asked to evaluate the advertisements during exposure—an advertising processing set, whereas in the present study, they were instructed to execute a brand processing set. When executing the former set, subjects do not form or alter their brand attitudes during exposure to the advertisement and only do so later when asked to report their attitudes (cf. Hastie & Park, 1986; Lichtenstein & Srull, 1985). Second, in the Moore and Hutchinson study, only data for unfamiliar brands were analyzed, so the subjects probably had not formed attitudes toward these brands before participating in the study.

` The finding that A_{ad} only had an effect on brand attitudes if the advertisement could be recalled provides further support for the claim that subjects did not form or alter their attitudes during exposure to the advertisement. When asked to report their attitudes later, subjects had to recall the advertisement before A_{ad} could have an effect on brand attitudes. Similar effects were reported by Beattie and Mitchell (1985) who found that recall of an advertisement affected brand attitudes under a nonbrand processing strategy, but not under a brand processing strategy.

In the Moore and Hutchinson study, the amount of variance explained in brand attitude remained relatively constant over time because subjects had to retrieve the relevant information from memory to report their attitudes. In the study reported here, however, subjects formed their attitudes toward the advertised brands while they were exposed to the advertisements. Two weeks later, when asked to report their attitudes, they simply retrieve them from memory. They no longer had to access their evaluation of the advertisement (A_{ad}) and information about the brand stored in memory. Consequently, the correlation between these elements and brand attitudes decreases over time.[7] Further evidence supporting this view will be presented in the next section.

Attitude Change Processes

In this section, the second issue will be examined—whether the A_{ad} from attitude formation still has an effect on brand attitudes after they have been changed by the presentation of new information about the brands. In order to examine this, a number of regression models, based on the alternative models of attitude change discussed earlier will be estimated using the data from Condition 4, where all the measures on the variables used in the models were taken in the delay condition. First, however, we need to determine that the new information that was presented changed attitudes and that the measurement of attitudes and beliefs before exposure to the new information in Condition 4 did not bias the results.

---

[7]Still to be explained is why the measure of Brand Familiarity had a significant effect on Brand Attitudes whether or not the advertisement was recalled. This probably occurred because only data for unfamiliar brands was analyzed in the study. Consequently, exposure to an advertisement for the brand even under nonbrand processing conditions probably increased Brand Familiarity since some learning about the brand (e.g., membership in a particular product category) should occur even if the advertisement was not recalled.

Attitude Change Manipulation Check.   In order to assess whether the presentation of new information caused changes in brand attitudes and beliefs, measures of these constructs are compared before (Condition 2) and after the presentation of the new information (Condition 4).

Repeated measures analysis of variance (ANOVA) indicated highly significant differences on both attitude measures between Conditions 2 and 4 ($p < 0.001$). Across products, the brand attitudes (A_o) increase from 3.73 to 5.25, whereas attitudes toward the act of purchasing and using the brand (A_{act}) increase from 3.85 to 5.20.

In addition, there are significant differences on 23 of the 63 belief strength measures (b_i) for all four product categories between the two conditions. Eighteen or 78% of the belief strength differences are on attributes on which new information was presented to the subjects. The other five differences are on the "cost" or "economical to use" attribute. In each case, the new information caused subjects to believe that the new product would be more expensive suggesting that subjects made a price–quality inference. These results indicate that subjects readjusted their beliefs about the salient attributes after being exposed to the new information. It also indicates that the subjects were very involved in the task. For the 63 different belief evaluations (e_i), only one was significantly different between these two conditions—an event most likely due to chance.

There are also large differences in the summed evaluations of the elicited beliefs (SE) which increase from -0.461 to 5.763 and in the predicted attitude from the structured scales ($\Sigma\Sigma b_i e_i$), which increase from 9.289 to 27.924. Both differences are highly significant at the 0.001 level. In summary, then, the provision of new information resulted in significantly different brand attitudes and beliefs.

Control for Test-Retest Bias.   In order to test each of the hypothesized models of attitude change, it was necessary to have measures of brand attitudes for each subject, both before and after the presentation of the new information. However, the use of before-and-after attitude measures raises the possibility of testing bias. To determine if this occurred, both the before-and-after attitude measures from Condition 4 are tested against the appropriate control. More specifically, the before measures from Condition 4 are compared to the measures from Condition 2, which did not receive the new information, and the after measures from Condition 4 are compared to the measures from Condition 3 where no measures were taken before the subjects received the new information.

Separate repeated measures analysis of variance indicated that attitudes were not significantly different between the appropriate control for either the before measures (Condition 2 vs. Condition 4) or the after measures (Condition 3 vs. Condition 4). In fact, the attitudinal measures were very similar for these comparisons. For instance, the mean of the A_o measure over products for Conditions

3 and 4 are 5.25 and 5.24, respectively. For A_{act}, the means for Condition 3 and Condition 4 are 5.39 and 5.22, respectively. In addition, the Condition by Product interactions are not significant ($p > 0.05$).[8]

The belief strength scores (b_i) and the belief evaluation scores (e_i) are also compared after the presentation of new information in Conditions 3 and 4. Only four of the 63 belief strength scores (6%) are significantly different at the 0.05 level—an event very likely due to chance. None of the belief evaluation scores are significantly different. Consequently, the use of before-and-after attitudinal measures did not seem to produce any detectable bias.

Alternative Attitude Change Models

Earlier, five different models of the attitude change process were discussed. In this section, regression analysis is used to examine the validity of these alternative models.

First, however, the five different models and their corresponding regression models will be briefly reviewed.

Belief Restructuring Model. With this model, individuals integrate the new information with their previously formed beliefs to form a new set of beliefs. These new beliefs are then used to form a new attitude. In this model, the attitude toward the original advertisement is not used in forming a new attitude. The regression analysis representing this model contains only the predicted attitude from the elicited beliefs (SE) measured after the presentation of the new information as an independent variable.

Belief Restructuring Model with Direct A_{ad} Effects. Here the attitude toward the original advertisement (A_{ad}) also has a direct effect on the new brand attitude. The regression analysis representing this model contains the predicted attitude from the elicited beliefs (SE) and A_{ad} as independent variables. Note that these two models are nested.

Belief Accretion Model. With this model, individuals use the prediction of attitudes based on the previously formed beliefs and the prediction of attitudes based on the beliefs formed from the new information to compute their new attitudes. The difference between the Belief Restructuring Model and the Belief Accretion Model is that the new information changes the previously formed beliefs with the former model, but not with the latter model. The regression analysis for the Belief Accretion Model has only two independent variables, the

---

[8]This test can detect medium size attitudinal differences with a power value of .93 (Cohen, 1977).

prediction of attitudes based on the previously formed beliefs (Old SE) and the predicted attitude based on the beliefs formed from the new information (New SE)[9] as independent variables.

Belief Accretion Model with Direct A_{ad} Effects.   This model is the same as the third, only the attitude toward the original advertisement (A_{ad}) is also used in forming the new attitude. Consequently, the regression analysis for this model is the same as for the previous model except that it also includes A_{ad} as an independent variable. Note again that third and fourth models are nested.

Attitude Adjustment Model.   Here individuals use their old attitude and simply add the incremental predicted attitude from the new information that is acquired. The regression analysis representing this model includes a measure of their previous attitude (Old A_o or Old A_{act}) and the predicted attitude from the beliefs formed from the new information (New SE) as independent variables. Note that if the subjects simply used the elements that determined their Old Attitude (A_{ad}, Old SE, and Old $\Sigma\Sigma b_i e_i$), then one of the other models, the Belief Restructuring or Belief Accretion Models with or without Direct A_{ad} Effects, would provide a better prediction of the new attitude.

The previous analysis of the effect of A_{ad} on brand attitudes in the immediate and delay conditions found that A_{ad} had an effect on the original beliefs that were formed. This indicates that A_{ad} has both a direct and an indirect effect on brand attitudes. As before, both the direct and indirect effects can be assessed by first removing the effect of A_{ad} on the two measures of the predicted attitude from the original beliefs that were formed and, then, using these residuals in the regression models.

Estimation of Direct A_{ad} Effects.   The estimated regression coefficients for the five different models, which examine only the direct effect of A_{ad}, are presented in Table 8.4, along with the estimated coefficients for a sixth model.[10] This latter model is identical to Model 5, only the old attitudinal measures are switched. For instance, if attitude toward the act of purchasing and using the brand (A_{act}) is the dependent variable, the previous brand attitude (Old A_o) is used as an independent variable. This model is estimated because the amount of

---

[9]The new SE measure was calculated for each subject by subtracting the SE measured obtained before exposure to the new information (Old SE) from the SE measure obtained after exposure to the new information.

[10]Since there were four data points for each subject, the observations were not strictly independent. One way to control for this is to add dummy variables for three of the four brands. The reestimated models with these dummy variables had virtually the same coefficients as the previously estimated models.

TABLE 8.4
Estimation of Models Representing Alternative Attitude Change Processes

Beta Weights (t-statistics)

Model	Dependent Variables	A_{ad}	SE	Old A_o	Old A_{act}	Old SE	New SE	Adjusted R^2
1 Belief Restructuring Model	A_o		0.282[b] (2.60)					0.07
	A_{act}		0.422[a] (4.11)					0.17
2 Belief Restructuring Model with Direct A_{ad} Effects	A_o	0.292[b] (2.79)	0.255[c] (2.44)					0.14
	A_{act}	0.256[b] (2.57)	0.397[a] (3.99)					0.22
3 Belief Accretion Model	A_o					0.350[c] (2.27)	0.479[b] (3.11)	0.11
	A_{act}					0.374[b] (2.62)	0.570[a] (3.99)	0.18
4 Belief Accretion Model with Direct A_{ad} Effects	A_o	0.433[a] (3.27)				0.146 (0.93)	0.530[b] (3.68)	0.23
	A_{act}	0.408[a] (3.34)				0.181 (1.25)	0.618[a] (4.64)	0.30
5 Attitude Adjustment Model	A_o			0.873[a] (17.29)			0.197[a] (3.74)	0.83
	A_{act}				0.473[a] (4.54)		0.411[a] (3.95)	0.32
6 Attitude Adjustment Model	A_o			0.738[a] (11.27)			0.335[b] (2.97)	0.25
	A_{act}				0.474[a] (4.20)		0.283[a] (4.15)	0.70

Note. Superscripts indicate significance levels as indicated below. [a] $p < 0.001$; [b] $p < 0.01$; [c] $p < 0.05$.

229

variance in A_{act} explained by the other models is considerably less than that explained in A_o.[11]

The estimated coefficients for all the models are, as theory predicts, all positive and, with one exception, significantly different than zero. The exception is the coefficient for Old SE in the Belief Accretion Model with Direct A_{ad} Effects (Model 4). Since the coefficient for this variable is significant for the Belief Accretion Model (Model 3), this seems to occur because A_{ad} and Old SE are highly related ($r = 0.51$).

An examination of the adjusted R^2 measures for the different models indicates that Attitude Adjustment Model explains almost three times as much variance in A_o as the other models. This indicates that in forming a new attitude, subjects simply adjusted their old attitude with the predicted attitude from the new information acquired. We can be quite confident that attitudes changed according to this process, because if subjects would have simply used the elements that originally determined their old attitude (A_{ad}, Old SE and Old $\Sigma\Sigma b_i e_i$), then either the Belief Restructuring or Belief Accretion Models, with or without Direct A_{ad} Effects, should have provided a better prediction of the new attitude.

It might be argued, however, that this occurred because this model contains a lagged measure of the dependent variable, which in most situations increases the amount of variance explained. An examination of the results for attitude toward purchasing and using the brand (A_{act}), however, indicates that this alternative explanation is not valid.

The results for attitude toward purchasing and using the brand (A_{act}) indicates that the regression results for the sixth model, which contains the original brand attitude measure (Old A_o) as an independent variable explains over twice the variance as all the other models with A_{act} as the dependent variable.

These results have two implications. First, they indicate that including a lagged measure of the dependent variable does not automatically inflate the percentage of the variance explained. The use of the Old A_{act} measure to predict A_{act} after the acquisition of the new information in the fifth model results in an adjusted R^2 that is comparable to those of the other models tested. This indicates that the superiority of the fifth model for the A_o measure is not simply due to the inclusion of the lagged measure of the dependent variable. Second, these results suggest that the reported attitude toward purchasing and using the brand (A_{act}) after the acquisition of the new information is based on the previous brand attitude (Old A_o) and the prediction of attitudes from the new information acquired. This model explained twice as much of the variance in A_{act} as the other hypothesized models.

---

[11]One reason why the models may have explained more variance for A_o than for A_{act} is that the formed measure may be more reliable. Although the coefficient alpha measure of reliability was slightly larger for A_o than A_{act} (0.91 vs. 0.86), these differences do not seem to be great enough to cause such large differences in the amount of variance explained in the two variables.

Estimation of Total A_{ad} Effects. In order to estimate both the direct and indirect effects of A_{ad} on brand attitudes, the first four models were reestimated using the residuals of the predicted attitudes from the summed evaluations from the elicited beliefs that were formed from exposure to the first advertisement (Old SE Residuals), after removing the effect of A_{ad}. As expected, A_{ad} had a highly significant effect on Old SE ($p < 0.001$). Because these original beliefs did not affect the brand attitudes after the acquisition of new information in the fifth and sixth models, these models were not reestimated.

The results of these reestimated models are presented in Table 8.5. For the first and third models, the amount of variance explained by these reestimated models decreases in comparison to the previous models. For the first model, the Belief Restructuring Model, the adjusted R^2 measures decrease by around 30% when A_o is the dependent variable and 12% when A_{act} is the dependent variable. For the Belief Accretion Model the adjusted R^2 measures decreases by 50%. This means that the indirect effect of A_{ad} on brand attitudes explains a smaller portion of the variance in brand attitudes in the Belief Restructuring Model than in the Belief Accretion Model. These results are consistent with the view that the A_{ad} for the initial advertisement only affected the previously formed beliefs. The simple correlation between A_{ad} and the predicted attitude from the belief formed from the new information was -0.39.

Finally, it should be noted that the amount of variance explained between the analysis of the direct A_{ad} effects and the total A_{ad} effects for Belief Restructuring and the Belief Accretion Models with Direct A_{ad} Effects (Model 2 and Model 4) remains the same. With these two models, the analysis of the direct and total effects, only affects the allocation of the common variance between A_{ad} and the cognitive component.

Test of Whether A_{ad} Effects are Contained in the Old Brand Attitude. In order to determine whether the effect of A_{ad} is contained in the previous brand attitude (Old A_o) measure in fifth and sixth models, the Attitude Adjustment Models, these two models were reestimated with the addition of A_{ad} as an independent variable. If the effect of A_{ad} is contained in the previous brand attitude measure (Old A_o), the inclusion of A_{ad} in the model should not significantly increase the amount of variance explained. This was confirmed. The F test for both equations indicated that the addition of A_{ad} in the models did not significantly increase the amount of variance explained ($p > 0.5$).

Summary. The results of the regression analysis indicates that the attitude change process for both brand attitudes (A_o) and attitudes toward purchasing and using the brand (A_{act}) in this study, was similar. For both attitude measures, subjects apparently adjusted their previous brand attitude (Old A_o) with the beliefs formed from the new information. In addition, the results indicate that the old brand attitude measure (Old A_o) contained the effect of A_{ad} from the first advertisement.

TABLE 8.5

Estimation of Both Direct and Indirect A_{ad} Effects on Brand Attitudes After the Acquisition of new Information

Model	Dependent Variables	Beta Weights (t-statistics)							Adjusted R^2
		A_{ad}	Se Residuals	Old A_o	Old A_{act}	Old Se Residuals	New SE		
1 Belief Restructuring Model	A_o		0.254^c (2.32)						0.05
	A_{act}		0.395^c (3.81)						0.15
2 Belief Restructuring Model with Direct A_{ad} Effects	A_o	0.316^b (3.03)	0.254^c (2.44)						0.14
	A_{act}	0.277^b (2.95)	0.395^a (3.99)						0.22
3 Belief Accretion Model	A_o					0.000 (0.01)	0.452^b (3.21)		0.05
	A_{act}					0.083 (0.64)	0.478^a (4.05)		0.09
4 Belief Accretion Model with Direct A_{ad}	A_o	0.492^a (4.16)				0.115 (0.91)	0.505^a (3.68)		0.22
	A_{act}	0.498^a (4.52)				0.198 (1.69)	0.644^a (5.03)		0.30

Note. Superscripts indicate significance levels as indicated below.

[a] $p < 0.001$.
[b] $p < 0.01$.
[c] $p < 0.05$.

DISCUSSION

Stability of Brand Attitudes

The results of this study indicate that brand attitudes based on A_{ad} effects are not transitory, but remain relatively stable over a two week time period. Both brand attitude (A_o) and attitude toward the act of purchasing and using the brand (A_{act}) declined over the 2-week period; however, the differences in attitudes between the immediate and delay conditions were significantly different only for A_o. The results of the regression analysis in the delayed condition indicated that A_{ad} still had both a strong direct and indirect effect on both attitude measures. Consequently, the component of attitudes due to A_{ad} remained after the 2-week time period.

It should be noted, however, that these effects occurred when subjects executed a brand processing strategy during exposure to the initial advertisement. If subjects had executed a nonbrand processing strategy, as apparently occurred in the Moore and Hutchinson (1985) study, they would not have formed an attitude toward the advertised brands. In order to form this attitude at some later point in time, they would need to retrieve whatever information they had about the brand and their recall of the advertisement. The results of the Moore and Hutchinson study indicate that A_{ad} will have an effect on brand attitudes after 1 week, if the advertisement can be recalled.

Attitude Change Processes

It was originally expected that subjects would integrate the new information that they had acquired into their previously formed knowledge structure for the brand and then form a new attitude. This did not seem to occur. The use of regression analyses to estimate the different models indicated that the subjects adjusted their previous brand attitude (Old A_o) with the predicted attitude from the beliefs formed from the new information to form a new brand attitude (A_o). The amount of variance explained by this model was almost three times greater than the amount of variance explained by all the other hypothesized models.

In forming a new attitude toward purchasing and using the brand (A_{act}), however, subjects used their previous brand attitude (Old A_o) and the beliefs formed from the new information to form this attitude. The regression model that represented this process explained twice as much variance as the other hypothesized models. This suggests that in this study, the attitude toward purchasing and using a brand (A_{act}) was not stored, but was, instead, computed from the old-brand attitudes (Old A_o) and the new beliefs that were formed. If the old A_{act} was stored in memory, it should have been used to compute the new A_{act}.

Although the anchor and adjust principle that underlies this model has been found in a number of judgment tasks (e.g., Anderson, 1981a; Einhorn &

233

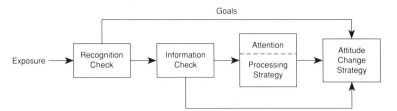

FIG. 8.2. Cognitive checking mechanisms in attitude change situations.

Hogarth, 1985), its application here may be somewhat dependent on the experimental situation used in this study. Subjects may have recalled the information from the initial advertisement and, upon realizing that the new information concerned different attributes of the products, executed an attitude adjustment strategy. Alternatively, subjects may not have made inferences about how the products performed along the highly salient attributes from the information presented in the initial advertisement. Consequently, they may have compared the presented information to the information stored in memory and, upon realizing that it was different, executed an attitude adjustment strategy.

In either case, these results suggest that when individuals are exposed to messages about known objects and have a goal of evaluating the object, they may cognitively execute some type of checking task before processing the information. A proposed model of what may occur when consumers are exposed to an advertisement for a known brand and have a brand evaluation goal is shown in Fig. 8.2. In the model, it is hypothesized that consumers first make a recognition check to determine if the advertisement has been seen before. If it has, consumers may adjust the amount of attention devoted to the advertisement or the goals to be achieved while exposed to the advertisement, based on what they remember about the ad. For instance, if a consumer remembers that she didn't understand part of the advertisement, she may focus on trying to understand this part of the advertisement. Alternatively, a consumer may recognize the advertisement, decide that there is nothing more to learn from the ad, and remember that it was very entertaining. Under these conditions, she may decide to view the advertisement for its entertainment value.

If the advertisement is new, then consumers may check to determine if new information is provided in the message. The outcome of this check may determine the type of attitude change strategy that is executed. For instance, as indicated in the reported study, if the information is new, believable, and does not cause changes in other beliefs about the product, consumers may simply adjust their old attitude with the predicted attitude from the new beliefs that are formed. Alternatively, if the information is new, believable, but causes changes in other beliefs about the product, consumers may compute a new attitude toward the brand, using all the salient beliefs about the brand and, possibly, the evaluation of recalled advertisements for the brand.

In order to obtain a better understanding of this checking task and the extent to which individuals use the adjustment strategy identified here, future research should be directed at testing the alternative models of attitude change in situations where there is overlap in the information presented initially and in the attitude change situation.

Attitudes as Mental Elements.   The results of this study and other studies in both consumer behavior (e.g., Beattie & Mitchell, 1985; Lichtenstein & Srull, 1985; Srull, 1986) and social cognition (Hastie & Park, 1986; Higgins & Lurie, 1983; Higgins & McCann, 1984; Lingle, Dukerich, & Ostrom, 1984; Lingle & Ostrom, 1979) suggest that overall attitudes (A_o), once formed, exist as mental elements in memory.

The results of this study indicate that the previous brand attitude existed in memory, and, when provided new information about the attitude object, subjects adjusted this attitude, forming a new attitude, with the predicted attitude from the beliefs that were formed from the new information. In addition, a relatively large reduction was found in the amount of variance explained in A_o by the regression models between the immediate and delay conditions. These results suggest that over time, the linkages between brand attitudes (A_o), and both beliefs and A_{ad} seems to weaken, resulting in a reduction in the correlation between these elements.

For the attitude toward purchasing and using the brand (A_{act}), however, the results suggests that subjects did not store this attitude in memory and then retrieve it later when asked to do so. Instead, subjects seemed to have used the previous brand attitude (Old A_o) to compute A_{act}. This occurred even though subjects were requested to make this judgment while they were exposed to the advertisements. Theoretically, forming different attitudes toward a number of different behaviors and storing these in memory may be very inefficient. It would be more efficient to simply store overall attitude and then compute an attitude toward a particular behavior as required.[12]

The finding that attitudes toward purchasing and using the brand (A_{act}) are computed from brand attitudes (A_o), provides additional support for the importance of the A_{ad} construct. Most studies (e.g., Mitchell, 1986; Mitchell & Olson, 1981), have found stronger A_{ad} effects on overall brand attitudes (A_o) than on attitudes toward purchasing and using the brand (A_{act}). However, if A_{act} in future time periods is computed from A_o, as found in this study, A_{ad} may have a stronger effect on purchase behavior than previously thought.

---

[12]In situations, however, where individuals make a number of repeat purchases of a particular brand, the attitude toward this behavior may be stored in memory.

SUMMARY

The results of the study reported here demonstrate the importance of A_{ad} effects. The results indicate that these effects are not transitory—they still have a strong effect on attitudes over time. Attitudes based on these effects are also relatively stable. Although the attitudes became less favorable over time, this change is not due to any particular component. In fact, over time both the set of associations (e.g., product attribute beliefs) and A_{ad} that originally affected its formation become disassociated from it.

In this study, when subjects were presented with new information about the attitude objects, they seemed to adjust their old brand attitude (Old A_o) with the new information that was presented to form a new brand attitude (A_o) and attitude toward purchasing and using the brand (A_{act}). Consequently, the effect of the A_{ad} from the initial advertisement had an effect on both the new brand attitudes and attitude toward purchasing and using the brand after the initial attitudes were changed with the beliefs formed from the new information.

ACKNOWLEDGMENTS

The author would like to thank Kevin Keller, Deborah MacInnis, and Prakash Nedungadi for their comments on an earlier version of this paper.

REFERENCES

Anderson, N. H. (1981a). *Foundations of information integrating theory.* New York: Academic Press.

Anderson, N. H. (1981b). Integration theory applied to cognitive responses and attitudes. In R. E. Petty, T. M. Ostrom, & T. C. Bruck (Eds.), *Cognitive responses in persuasion* (pp. 361–398). Hillsdale, NJ: Lawrence Erlbaum Associates.

Batra, R., & Ray, M. L. (1985). How advertising works at contact. In L. Alwitt & A. A. Mitchell (Eds.), *Psychological processes and advertising effects* (pp. 13–44). Hillsdale, NJ: Lawrence Erlbaum Associates.

Beattie, A. E., & Mitchell, A. A. (1984). Advertising recall and persuasion. In L. Alwitt & A. A. Mitchell (Eds.), *Psychological processes and advertising effects* (pp. 129–156). Hillsdale, NJ: Lawrence Erlbaum Associates.

Birnbaum, M. H. (1973). The devil rides again: Correlation as an index of fit. *Psychological Bulletin, 79*, 239–292.

Birnbaum, M. H. (1974). Reply to the devil's advocates: Don't confound model testing and measurement. *Psychological Bulletin, 81*, 854–859.

Burke, M. C., & Edell, J. A. (1986). Ad reactions over time: Capturing change in the real world. *Journal of Consumer Research, 13*, 56–65.

Burke, M. C., & Edell, J. A. (1989). The impact of feelings on ad-based affect and cognition. *Journal of Marketing Research, 26*, 69–83.

Carnegie-Mellon Marketing Seminar (1978). Attitude change or attitude formation? An unanswered question. *Journal of Consumer Research, 4*, 271–275.

Cohen, J. (1977). *Statistical power analysis for the behavioral sciences.* New York: Academic Press.

Cook, T. D., & Flay, B. R. (1978). The persistence of experimentally induced attitude change. In L. Berkowitz (Ed.), *Advances in experimental social psychology* (pp. 1–57). New York: Academic Press.

Einhorn, H. J., & Hogarth, R. M. (1985). Ambiguity and uncertainty in probabalistic inference. *Psychological Review, 92,* 433–461.

Fishbein, M., & Ajzen, I. (1975). *Belief, attitude, intention and behavior: An introduction to theory and research.* Reading, M.A.: Addison-Wesley.

Gardner, M. (1985). Does attitude toward the advertisement affect brand attitude under a brand evaluation set? *Journal of Marketing Research, 22,* 192–198.

Greenwald, A. G. (1968). Cognitive learning, cognitive response to persuasion, and attitude change. In A. G. Greenwald, T. C. Brock, & Thomas M. Ostrom (Eds.), *Psychological foundations of attitudes* (pp. 147–170). New York: Academic Press.

Hastie, R., & Park, B. (1986). The relationship between memory and judgment depends on whether the judgment task is memory based or on line. *Psychological Review, 93,* 258–268.

Higgins, E. T., & Lurie, L. (1983). Context, categorization and recall: The change of standard effect. *Cognitive Psychology, 15,* 525–547.

Higgins, E. T., & McCann, C. D. (1984). Social encoding and subsequent attitudes, impressions, and memory: "Context driven" and motivational aspects of processing. *Journal of Personality and Social Psychology, 47,* 26-39.

Homer, P. (1990). The mediating role of attitude toward the ad: Some additional evidence. *Journal of Marketing Research, 27,* 76–86.

Johns, G. (1981). Difference score measures of organizational behavior variables: A critique. *Organizational Behavior and Human Performance, 27,* 443-463.

Krugman, H. E. (1972). Why three exposures may be enough. *Journal of Advertising Research, 12,* 11–14.

Lichtenstein, M., & Srull, T. K. (1985). Conceptual and methodological issues in examining the relationship between consumer memory and judgment. In L. Alwitt & A. A. Mitchell (Eds.), *Psychological processes and advertising effects: Theory, research and applications* (pp. 113–128). Hillsdale, NJ: Lawrence Erlbaum Associates.

Lingle, J. H., & Ostrom, T. M. (1979). Retrieval selectivity in memory-based impression judgments. *Journal of Personality and Social Psychology 37,* 180–194.

Lingle, J. H., Dukerich, J. M., & Ostrom, T. M. (1984). Accessing information in memory-based impression judgments: ˉIncongruity versus negativity in retrieval selectivity. *Journal of Personality and Social Psychology, 44,* 262-272.

Lutz, R. J. (1975). Changing brand attitudes through modification of cognitive structure. *Journal of Consumer Research, 1,* 49–59.

Lutz, R. J. (1985). Affective and cognitive antecedents of attitude toward the ad: A conceptual framework. In L. Alwitt & A. A. Mitchell (Eds.), *Psychological processes and advertising effects: Theory, research and applications* (pp. 45–63). Hillsdale, NJ: Lawrence Erlbaum Associates.

Lutz, R. J., Mackenzie, S. B., & Belch, B. E. (1983). Attitude toward the ad as a mediator of advertising effectiveness: Determinants and consequences. In R. P. Bagozzie & A. M. Tybout (Eds.), *Advances in consumer research* (Vol. 10, pp. 532–539). Ann Arbor, MI: Association for Consumer Research.

MacKenzie, S. B., & Lutz, R. J. (1989). An empirical examination of the structural antecedents of attitude toward the ad in an advertising pretesting context. *Journal of Marketing, 53,* 48–65.

MacKenzie, S. B., Lutz, R. J., & Belch, G. E. (1986). The role of attitude toward the ad as mediator of advertising effectiveness: A test of competing explanations. *Journal of Marketing Research, 23,* 130–143.

Meyer, R. J. (1981). A model of multiattribute judgments under attribute uncertainty and information constraint. *Journal of Marketing Research, 18,* 428–441.

Mitchell, A. A. (1983). Cognitive processes initiated by exposure to advertising. In R. Harris (Ed.), *Information Processing Research in Advertising* (pp. 13–42). Hillsdale, NJ: Lawrence Erlbaum Associates.

Mitchell, A. A. (1986). The effect of verbal and visual components in advertisements on brand attitudes and attitude toward the advertisement. *Journal of Consumer Research, 13,* 12–24.

Mitchell, A. A., & Olson, J. C. (1981). Are product attribute beliefs the only mediator of advertising effects on brand attitudes. *Journal of Marketing Research, 18,* 318–332.

Moore, D. L., & Hutchinson, J. W. (1983). The effects of ad affect on advertising effectiveness. In R. P. Bagozzi & A. M. Tybout (Eds.), *Advances in consumer research* (Vol. 10, pp. 526–531). Ann Arbor, MI: Association for Consumer Research.

Moore, D. L., & Hutchinson, J. W. (1985). The influence of affective reactions to advertising: Direct and indirect mechanisms of attitude change. In L. Alwitt & A. A. Mitchell (Eds.), *Psychological processes and advertising effects: Theory, research and application* (pp. 65–87). Hillsdale, NJ: Lawrence Erlbaum Associates.

Park, C. W., & Young, S. M. (1986). Consumer response to television commercials: The impact of involvement and background music on brand attitude formation. *Journal of Marketing Research, 22,* 11–24.

Rumelhart, D. E., & Norman, D. A. (1978). Accretion, tuning and restructuring: Three modes of learning. In J. W. Cotton & R. Klatzky (Eds.), *Semantic factors in cognition*. Hillsdale, NJ: Lawrence Erlbaum Associates.

Srull, T. K. (1986). A model of consumer memory and judgment. In R. J. Lutz (Ed.), *Advances in Consumer Research* (Vol. 13, pp. 643–647). Provo, UT: Association for Consumer Research.

The Influence of Positive Affect on Cognitive Organization: Some Implications for Consumer Decision Making in Response to Advertising

Alice M. Isen
Cornell University, Ithaca, NY

The focus of this volume is on considering the influence of advertising on judgment, decision making, and behavior that occur at the time of purchase and product use. The emphasis is on looking at effects on behavior rather than on attitudes or recall of the ad, and on processes that occur at some time after exposure to the ad rather than on immediate or short-term effects. This contrasts in two ways with much of the advertising research to date, which has tended to focus on ad recall and attitudes or evaluations, most frequently at the time of the ad or shortly thereafter. Thus, as suggested recently also by Alba, Hutchinson, and Lynch (1991), there is a sense that it would be useful to supplement the important work that has been done on the influence of advertising on recall and attitudes, with information regarding ways in which advertising might influence actual decision making and behaviors relevant to product purchase and use. Such a focus requires understanding of the factors and processes that influence, not only judgment or evaluation, but also decision making itself. Further, because these decisions and behaviors often occur long after the advertising experience itself, it is also necessary to consider some aspects of the processes that may lead advertising's effects to be sustained in time.

This chapter, then, focuses on some of the ways in which positive affect can influence the impact that advertising has on decisions and choices. In particular, the chapter considers the influence of affect on cognitive organization and the ways in which this influence can have an impact on thoughts about products and brands, and can play a role in resultant decision making. Second, it considers ways in which these organizational changes as well as the information learned from advertisements that influence affect may be maintained over time in order to have an influence on later decisions. These topics have received little direct investigation; the goal in this chapter will be to suggest some possibilities and to stimulate thinking about them.

AFFECT AND COGNITIVE ORGANIZATION

A growing body of literature indicates that positive affect can result in different ways of seeing or experiencing stimuli, different ways of organizing the stimuli or thinking about them, and different associates to the stimuli. This kind of effect of feelings would imply that affect might also influence the processing of advertising, the generation of associates to ads and products, and the decisions that are made regarding purchase and use of such products.

First, several studies suggest that positive affect tends to increase the range of people's associations to cognitive material, to change the perceived relatedness among cognitions, and to facilitate creativity and a more integrated and flexible thinking style. To illustrate, in one series of studies, people in whom positive affect had been induced gave more unusual and more diverse first-associates to neutral stimulus words in a word-association task (Isen, Johnson, Mertz, & Robinson, 1985). For instance, to the stimulus word "house," the most common associate of which is "home," people in positive-affect conditions tended, significantly more than control subjects, to respond with related but uncommon words such as "residence" or "apartment." In addition, the responses of the positive-affect group were significantly more diverse than the responses of the controls. The unusual responses of people in the positive-affect conditions suggest that their associations to the target words were more far-ranging and their thoughts more flexible.

In another series of studies, positive affect was seen to influence the way in which neutral material was categorized. Subjects in whom positive affect had been induced tended to categorize a wider range of neutral stimuli together, as measured by either a rating task or a sorting task (Isen & Daubman, 1984). In the rating task, similar to that used by Rosch (1975), to study prototypicality, for instance, people were asked to rate on a scale from 1 to 10 the degree to which they felt an item was a member of a category. Those in whom positive affect had been induced rated nontypical exemplars (i.e., words like "purse," "cane," and "ring" in the category *clothing*) as better members of the category than did people in a control condition. In a sorting task, in which subjects were asked to sort the stimuli into groupings of items that went together, people in whom positive affect had been induced made larger groupings (indicating that more items could go together) relative to control subjects (Isen & Daubman, 1984). More recently, though, it has also been found that, if given multiple trials and asked how many *different* ways the items could be organized, positive-affect subjects sorted stimuli into more different groupings than did control subjects (Isen, 1987, p. 234). A similar flexibility in grouping items in broader or narrower categories, depending on the task assigned, has been found by Murray, Sujan, Hirt, and Sujan (1990). Thus, persons who are feeling happy seem more cognitively flexible and more able to make associations and see different, multiple relations (similarities *or* differences) among stimuli than do persons in a neutral state.

A recent study extended this work on affect's influence on categorization to the domain of person-categorization (Isen, Neidenthal, & Cantor, 1992). In that study, subjects were asked to rate the degree to which nonprototypic exemplars of positive or negative person categories (for example, "bartender" as a member of the category *nurturant people,* or "genius" as a member of the category *unstable people*) fit as members of the category. People in whom positive affect had been induced, relative to controls, indicated a better fit for the weakly related members of the *positive* categories, but not for those of the *negative* person categories. Thus, they rated "bartender" as a better exemplar of the category *nurturant people* than did controls, but did *not* rate "genius" as a better exemplar of the category *unstable people* than did controls. Presumably, they could see more positive aspects of the relatively neutral exemplar, "bartender," more ways in which it could fit into the positive category of nurturant people; but nothing in their affective state prompted seeing the person type "genius" as better fitting a negative category.

This interaction between affect and category valence also indicates that the effects of positive feelings on categorization are not best attributed to response bias, or simple carelessness, or dropping of criteria for categorization. This is because the interaction indicates that the influence of positive affect occurs with one category (*positive* person types), but not with the other (*negative* person types). In contrast, if positive affect gave rise to only response bias, the ratings of all of the person types would be influenced similarly; likewise, if positive affect resulted in reduced capacity or unsystematic processing, the ratings of all person types should be equally likely to be influenced.

Following from this stream of research showing that positive affect can influence categorization, another study investigated whether positive affect might influence the perceived acceptability of unusual or innovative products as members of a product class (Isen & Stayman, 1992). Subjects in different affect conditions (positive vs. control) were given descriptions of cameras differing in congruence with the *instamatic camera* category. Results indicated that positive-affect subjects who were knowledgeable about cameras rated a product with an unusual feature as more similar to, or fitting better with, the instamatic category than did comparable control-affect subjects. These subjects also evaluated the unusual product more positively than did controls and showed evidence of more elaborated processing when evaluating the incongruent product. These differences between the affect and control conditions were not found when a congruent product description was used (they were not expected, because in that condition, it was expected that all subjects would find the description congruent with the category). That is, people in whom positive affect had been induced found an unusual product more acceptable as a member of the instamatic camera category; in addition, they liked the unusual (but not the typical) exemplar better, and had more thoughts about it (but not about the congruent one) than did control subjects.

Again, the interactions between affect and incongruence in determining evaluation and rated membership in the category indicate that the influence of affect is not attributable simply to a response bias and is not the result of faulty or careless processing or a lack of cognitive capacity. This is because the effects occur systematically with one type of product but not with the other. If response bias or carelessness were the cause of the effects, the ratings of all products, not just the unusual, should be equally likely to be influenced. Moreover, the significantly *increased* number of relevant thoughts on the part of the positive-affect subjects thinking about the unusual product, but, again, not about the usual, corresponds to an abundance of capacity and also speaks against an interpretation in terms of these alternative accounts.

Similarly, Kahn and Isen (in press), in a series of studies on the influence of positive affect on variety seeking (to be discussed), found that people in whom positive affect had been induced considered nontypical items of a food category more acceptable as members of the category, included those.items in their choice sets, and switched among the items in the set more than did control subjects.

All of these results imply that positive affect promotes a cognitive organization that is different from the usual one, and that it may promote more flexible processing as well. One reflection of this is that positive affect can facilitate creativity or the solution of problems that require innovative thinking or putting ideas together in unaccustomed ways. Several studies, for example, have indicated that under conditions of positive affect, induced by receipt of a small bag of candy, by watching 5 minutes of a comedy film, or by focusing on statements expressing happiness, people perform better on tasks usually considered to require creativity, such as Duncker's (1945) candle task and M. T. Mednick, S. A. Mednick, & E. V. Mednick's (1964) Remote Associates Test (Isen, Daubman, & Nowicki, 1987).

In the candle task, the subject is presented with the common objects of a box of tacks, a candle, and a book of matches, and is asked to attach the candle to the wall (a cork board) in such a way that it can be lit and will burn without dropping wax on the table or floor beneath. (This problem can be solved if the box containing the tacks is emptied, tacked to the wall, and used as a platform for the candle, almost like a "candleholder.")

The second task used to examine the influence of positive affect on creative problem solving or cognitive flexibility was based on the Mednicks' Remote Associates Test (Mednick et al., 1964). This test, in its full form, was designed as an individual-difference measure of creativity, in accord with S. A. Mednick's (1962) theory that creativity involves the combination of elements that are remotely associated. In it, subjects are presented with three words and a blank line, and they are asked to provide, in the blank, a word that relates to each of the three words given in the item. An example of a Remote Associates Test item is the following:

MOWER   ATOMIC   FOREIGN   _____

(In this example, "power" would be the correct answer.) Items were pretested for difficulty and seven of moderate difficulty were used.

A more recent set of follow-up studies (Isen & Berg, 1991) explored these effects further by (a) broadening the range of affect inductions, and (b) examining the effects of these states on routine tasks as well as creative tasks. It was not expected that positive affect would improve performance on routine tasks, but rather that its effect would be specific to the creative task. This is because it is hypothesized that positive affect facilitates specific cognitive processes rather than, for example, simply raising people's level of general motivation. These studies indicated that positive affect, again induced by means of receipt of a small bag of candy or induced by subjects' concentrating on statements expressing positive feelings, resulted in improved performance on the Remote Associates Test items, but did not improve performance on the routine task (finding the letter "a" every time it appeared in a page of randomly generated letters).

Thus, there was no support for the idea that the apparent effect of positive feelings on creativity might be only an effect on general motivation. Rather, it appears to facilitate creative responding in particular. (It might also be noted that, in contrast with the effects of these positive-affect inductions, negative affect, induced by music designed to create tension, or induced by concentrating on statements designed to arouse anger or worry, had no effect on performance on that test.)

Another study extended these results to a different creative task, a logic problem (representing something like scientific creativity). Again, positive affect, induced by a small gift or by reading statements, facilitated performance on the logical reasoning task, but had no effect on performance on a routine task (this time, long-division problems). Again, treatments designed to induce negative affects had no influence on performance on the logical reasoning task (Isen, & Berg, 1991).

These findings all suggest that positive affect is associated with greater cognitive flexibility and broader or more interrelated cognitive structures. This might imply that positive affect would influence decision making; and indeed several interesting effects on decision processes have been observed.

For example, in a complex decision task that involved choice of a car for purchase from among six hypothetical alternatives, differing along each of nine dimensions, subjects in whom positive affect had been induced (by report of success on an unrelated task) were more efficient in reaching a decision than were control subjects (Isen & Means, 1983). The cars chosen by the two groups did not differ on average, but the subjects in the positive-affect group reached a decision in about half the time taken by the control group. Protocol analyses indicated that they engaged in significantly less rechecking of information already considered and tended significantly more than control subjects to eliminate unimportant dimensions of the material.

In a decision-making study using a medical decision problem, results were conceptually compatible with those just mentioned, but slightly different in detail (Isen, Rosenzweig, & Young, 1991). In that study, the subjects were medical students who had completed their third year of medical training and had finished either a pediatrics or an internal-medicine rotation. Participants were asked to identify the one of six patients most likely to have lung cancer. Subjects were told that each patient had a solitary pulmonary nodule, and the subject was to make his choice on the basis of data from any or all of nine different dimensions (e.g., chest x-ray, cough, smoking history, weight loss, etc.). The materials were in the same format as has been described for the car-choice problem.

In this study, as in the car-choice problem, people in whom positive feelings had been induced by report of success on an unrelated task performed more efficiently: They reached a decision about the cancer diagnosis earlier. However, in this case, they did not stop working earlier, in terms of total time spent working with the materials. They continued working with the materials even after solving the assigned problem, and were significantly more likely to go beyond the task and attempt to diagnose the remaining cases as well. In addition, positive-affect subjects were significantly more likely to integrate dimensions in reasoning about the problem, and their protocols showed significantly less evidence of confusion than did those of controls. Thus, people in whom positive affect had been induced were both more efficient and more thorough. Moreover, the results of this study suggest that this may apply to experts reasoning in their domain of expertise.

The findings of the car-choice and medical-diagnosis studies suggest that, under conditions of positive affect, people tend to integrate material for decision making. This allows them to work faster and either finish earlier (as in the case of the car-choice task) or to turn attention to other important tasks within the materials (as in the medical-diagnosis task).

Another point illustrated by these studies is that people in whom positive affect has been induced have a different experience with stimuli and may think about them differently from the way others do. They seem better able to see potential ways of relating and integrating material, they appear to have more different associates to it in memory, and they are capable of categorizing it differently. This may be the reason that they can appear both more efficient *and* more thorough.

One question that arises is how these effects might occur. A topic relevant to this discussion is the asymmetry between happiness and sadness in influence on memory (see Isen, 1984, 1985, 1989). Studies on affect and memory tend to suggest that people who have undergone positive-affect inductions show better recall of positive material (compared with other material and with other people), but that people who have undergone negative-affect (especially sadness) inductions do not usually show improved recall of negative material. They have occasionally been found to show impaired recall of the positive, but this may involve another process.

This asymmetry suggests that negative and positive material may be asymmetrically accessed or stored in memory, and this difference may play a role in the divergent effects of these states on cognitive flexibility. That is, the structures of negative and positive material in mind may differ—in size, in internal consistency or variety, and/or in interrelatedness with other material. Evidence suggests that the positive may be large, broad, and well interconnected. The negative structures, in contrast, may be smaller, more specific, and less well interconnected with other material (Isen, 1990). This possibility is currently under investigation.

In any case, compatibly with the affect-and-memory-findings, one possible source of the increased cognitive flexibility observed as a function of positive affect may be the increased accessibility that positive affect affords to positive material. Positive material is known to be diverse and extensive (cf. Isen, 1987). Thus, when people feel good, they have ready access to a broad range of ideas, and this may promote creativity and integration of seemingly diverse material, as ideas not usually considered in the same context are more likely to come to mind simultaneously. It is also possible, on this basis, that people who are feeling happy may engage in more cognitive elaboration and multiple encoding of stimuli and ideas, and may notice more features of stimuli. In fact data reported above regarding elaboration of thoughts about novel products support this suggestion (Isen & Stayman, 1992).

Given that positive affect promotes more interest in, and liking for, relatively unusual products and other stimuli, and given that it leads to greater cognitive elaboration and multiple encoding of stimuli, one might expect more variety seeking among people in whom positive affect has been induced, as they seek to enjoy and experience the positive features of the items that they anticipate. However, one might also expect this phenomenon to be limited to products about which there is no unpleasantness or danger (or, at least, about which unpleasantness or danger is not salient). This is because, if the most salient features of items are negative, there is no reason to expect positive-affect subjects to anticipate more pleasure in using them. (Positive affect has been found to cue positive material and to influence judgments of neutral material, but not to result in distortion of negative material or ignoring of negative features; Isen et al., 1985; Isen & Shalker, 1982; Isen, Shalker, Clark, & Karp, 1978; Isen & Simmonds, 1978; Schiffenbauer, 1974.)

This reasoning, together with data showing that potential negative outcomes loom especially large for people in positive-affect states (e.g., Isen & Geva, 1987; Isen, Nygren & Ashby, 1988), suggest that positive affect should stimulate increased variety seeking, but only where the products involve no apparent danger or unpleasantness. Both of these expectations have been upheld in a series of studies investigating the influence of positive affect on variety seeking in product categories of different levels of unpleasantness (Kahn & Isen, in press). Results of these studies indicate that, relative to controls, people in the positive-affect conditions showed greater variety seeking in three food categories—crackers, soup, and junk food—but not when the potential for unpleasant taste was introduced by, for example, having the items be low-salt varieties. As noted earlier, these subjects also were more likely than controls to categorize non-typical items as belonging to the product category, and they engaged in more variety seeking than controls in conditions in which the items were from such an extended category.

In addition, people in whom positive affect had been induced showed more diverse thought about the products in the extended-brand condition and where there was little uncertainty about the quality of the product (but not where potential negative aspects of the product were salient). This indicates, like the thought-listing results of the study by Isen and Stayman (1992) and the word-association, creative problem-solving, and decision-making findings (Isen et al., 1985; Isen et al., 1987; Isen et al., 1991; previously described), that under conditions of positive affect, people think more, or have more different thoughts, but only relevant to material in which they are interested or about which they want to think.

Another factor that may influence how people respond to ads and think about products may be the perceived riskiness of the product or situation depicted in the ad (see Isen, 1989, for fuller discussion of this topic). This may bear some relationship to the variety–seeking findings, although risk taking and variety seeking are not the same thing. (In variety seeking among safe and enjoyable products, there is no risk.) Several studies indicate that people who are feeling happy are especially sensitive to the possibility of loss (Isen et al., 1988), and in situations of meaningful, real risk, they are risk-avoidant compared with controls (Isen & Patrick, 1983; Isen & Geva, 1987). However, it should also be noted that, in situations of negligible or hypothetical risk, those in whom positive affect has been induced express greater willingness to take a risk. Thus, perceived risk interacts with affect to influence amount of caution or risk taking that people exhibit. These findings suggest that, perhaps in consumer decision making, as has been found in other types of decision making situations, the perceived risk inherent or depicted in a situation may well influence other aspects of the cognitive contexts of ads and products, and in this way also influence people's responses and choices. Further, these results indicate that any such effect may interact with affect. (See Isen, 1989, for discussion.)

In summary, these findings suggest that positive affect may influence cognitive organization (the patterns of relatedness perceived among stimuli and ideas) and, by implication, the inferences that people may make from material presented and the things they notice or think about in conjunction with various stimuli, including both ads and products. The implication is that affect can influence the evaluation of products, not only through influencing the perceptions of the attributes of the product, but also by influencing the way the product is categorized and thought about, and the associations that may be drawn between the product and other material. Such effects are likely to influence many factors related to perception of the product.

For example, the extent of perceived congruity or incongruity between a specific product advertised and a product category, and the way in which this incongruity is advertised or highlighted, may lead to increased recall of unusual attributes. This, in turn, may make the product seem more interesting (as occurred, for example, with the unique features of the camera in the study reported by Isen & Stayman, 1992), and it may prompt more variety seeking, as was found in the studies by Kahn and Isen (in press).

Affect has been shown to influence the acceptability or attractiveness of unusual things and thus it can interact with unusualness or innovation to influence the acceptance of new products. It may also influence the range of perceived appropriate usage occasions of certain types of products (see Isen, 1989, for fuller discussion of this topic). Thus, affect may influence the settings in which the product would seem to be appropriate and, in turn, the cues that may bring the product to mind.

A consideration of the material presented thus far suggests several promising lines of investigation regarding ways in which people may think differently about products and brands when they are feeling good, and ways in which this might influence their processing of advertising as well as their subsequent decisions.

First, under conditions of positive affect, people may think more innovatively about products: They may see features of products or brands that they don't normally see, and they may entertain more uses for products (see Isen, 1989, for a discussion of this topic). This may be especially significant for some classes of products that suppliers may feel have been underutilized or utilized in a too-limited context (as exemplified by, for example, the recent orange juice campaign of "it's not just for breakfast anymore"), or for products with divergent possible applications (e.g., baking soda). The research discussed thus far, indicating that positive affect facilitates thinking about neutral material in new or expanded ways, suggests that these efforts might be most effective among consumers who are feeling good.

Second, people's associations to products and/or brands may be expanded under conditions of positive affect, and they may be likely to think about these products and/or brands in more different ways. Not only may they see additional possible uses of (or occasions for using) products, when feeling happy, but they may make connections among products and/or brands that they might not make at other times. The literature suggests that this would seem especially likely for products with potential for positive affect or for maintaining positive affect. Thus, people in whom positive feelings have been induced may relate relatively neutral products or brands, but not negative ones, to more highly valued products or brands (see Isen, 1989, for discussion).

Some recent research has begun to examine these questions of whether people have more diverse associations to different types of products and whether they see more potential uses for products when positive affect has been induced (Isen & Ford, 1989). It is first necessary to identify positive, negative, and neutral product classes because the earlier work on affect and word association indicated that the effect was observed most clearly on neutral words: Positive words had a broader pool of associates than the others, regardless of the affect state induced in the study, and associations to negative words were not influenced by the affect treatment (Isen et al., 1985). The situation may be the same for products. As noted above, this suggests that neutral items with positive-affect *potential* (rather than already strongly positive products) are the ones that will be the most likely to be influenced.

Third, research is being undertaken to examine whether positive affect enhances the degree of association among product types and brands, especially that between neutral and positively regarded classes. If this is true, producers might try to use induction of positive affect to help elevate the status of a moderately valued item with upward potential, by association with a high-prestige product. Note that this does not refer to a process strictly like classical conditioning or recall of a specific brand-attribute belief; rather, it denotes a change in categorization or classification, a change in the way in which the product is thought about. It should be kept in mind that this process may not apply to negative material. Thus, something else may have to be tried if one is attempting to elevate the status or regard of a negatively viewed product or a brand with an image problem (see Isen, 1989, for discussion).

Fourth, from the research presented, it seems likely that people who are feeling happy may have expanded and elaborated views of themselves (a positive category), in a positive direction (see Isen, 1987 and Isen et al., 1992, for discussion). Therefore, they may see more things as potentially self-relevant, and they may be more open to image-enhancing and image-maintaining products than people under more neutral conditions. Additionally, a person in whom positive-affect has been induced may be capable of seeing a broader range of products and brands as potentially contributing to image enhancement. However, this may be a complex process because it may be that, under conditions of positive affect, personal image maintenance takes on other forms or dimensions completely (that is, it may be that one does not use products as much to serve this function). Thus, several studies are under way investigating the influence of positive affect on self-concept, self-relevance, ways of viewing oneself, the tendency to use products to establish, maintain, and enhance identities, and the range of products and activities that can serve these functions.

Related research suggests that positive affect can also enhance the variety of associates to specific items or messages. For example, Isen et al. (1985) found that the positive valence of the stimulus (in this case, words), as well as the affective state of the subject, led to more diverse and more unusual first associates to common words. Thus, carrying this effect into the domain of products and advertisements, one might expect that the product category itself, and/or the affect elicited during an advertisement, might influence the associates that would be active when the person processed information about the product being advertised. This might have important effects on how the product would be conceptualized and encoded. Most advertising research that relates to affect emphasizes the influence of a positive affect state on the accessibility of congruent versus incongruent material in memory, rather than on the extensiveness of the information that comes to mind, or on the variety of ways in which the ad or product is conceptualized and encoded. Consideration of the latter topic might lead to research on the influence of affect on the range of associations to ads and/or to products. This seems an interesting and important area for investigation.

Another topic that would seem a promising one for research involves the area of risk perception and affect. The research on the influence of affect on risk preference suggests that positive affect may influence the kinds of attributes that may be salient or important to viewers, and thus may influence viewers' responses to ads and products that involve risk or uncertainty. A related factor may be that positive affect appears to give rise to a goal to maintain the good feelings. This line of work suggests that relatively specific attribute knowledge, such as the attribute's potential for risk reduction or affect maintenance, may moderate any more general influence of affect on attribute beliefs.

AFFECT AND DECISION MAKING

The second focus of this chapter, compatibly with that of the volume, is on how affect may play a role in determining whether material learned in ads, for example, is sustained in memory, kept available and rendered accessible at the time of making a decision regarding product purchase or use. There are several points to consider and several ways in which positive affect may play a role in these processes.

Affect's Influence on Memory

One way in which affect at time of advertising might influence retention of learned material might be through relatively direct influences on memory. Positive affect at time of attempted recall is known to influence memory, but it is not clear how positive affect at one point in time, say at time of seeing an ad, may contribute to later recall of that material when in a neutral (or different) affective state, say at time of purchasing a product. One interesting question is whether affect experienced at the time of exposure to an ad may somehow be accessed later, at the time of a decision, induced again, and in that way influence the decision, even at the remote time.

Certainly we can all think of instances of reminding of this kind. Further, there is evidence suggesting that advertising-related cues can be influential at later decision times (Keller, this volume), that affect in advertising can influence attitude toward the brand independently of brand attributes (e.g., Mitchell, 1986; Mitchell & Olson, 1981), that under some circumstances a brand advertised in a positive-affect context may later cue affect (Stayman & Batra, 1991), and that feelings can be directly related to brand cognition (Burke & Edell, 1989; Edell & Moore, 1990; See also Mitchell, 1988, and Shimp's discussion of classical conditioning, 1991). In order to understand the types of cues at decision time that might be most effective in prompting recall of feelings or recall of material learned at the time of an affective state earlier, a brief review of the literature on affect and memory may be helpful here.

Accessibility.   Much research has been done on the influence of affect on memory. An influence of positive feelings at time of retrieval has been obtained by a number of researchers (e.g., Isen et al., 1978; Teasdale & Fogarty, 1979; Teasdale & Russell, 1983). This work indicates that positive affect can serve as a retrieval cue to increase the accessibility of congruent material in memory. That is, positive affect results in improved recall of positive material; this suggests that material is encoded and stored in terms of the feelings it induces. Sadness typically has not been as effective as positive feelings as a retrieval cue or as an encoding device (see Isen, 1987, for a more detailed review of this work).

In terms of an effect of feelings at the time of encoding (learning) material for memorization, Bower and his colleagues have discussed what they term *mood-congruent learning* (Bower, Gilligan, & Monteiro, 1981). These studies found that material learned in a feeling state that was congruent with the meaning of the material (e.g., positive words when feeling happy) was better recalled than material learned in an incompatible feeling state. Again reflecting the asymmetry between negative and positive feelings in this effect, results are more equivocal regarding sadness than happiness. For example, Bower and his colleagues report symmetrical effects of negative and positive feelings, but some other authors do not (e.g., Nasby & Yando, 1982). It is possible that Bower's finding may be related to the mood induction and instructions that his group uses—hypnosis and instructions to maintain the mood at its induced level of intensity. (See Isen, 1984, 1987, 1989, for consideration of this and related issues.)

A third type of effect that was initially identified in the literature on affect and memory was state-dependent learning based on affect (Bower, 1981). In state-dependent learning, which was originally observed in the animal-learning literature and pertains to drug-induced physiological states, memory for material (any material, regardless of its content) learned in a given state was thought to be improved if the attempted recall took place under conditions of the same physiological state. Initially, Bower (1981) reported such an effect for hypnotically induced positive or negative mood; but subsequent attempts to replicate this finding have failed, and Bower has retracted it (Bower & Mayer, 1985). For these reasons, the effects of normal affect on memory seem related to the content of the material to be recalled; affect's influence on memory is not just a matter of state-to-state matching, with this match automatically cuing anything that happened to be present at both times.

Thus, state-dependent learning based on affect has not been reliably observed and, therefore, cannot be suggested as a major mechanism for sustaining affect's influence, over time. That is, simply re-creating an affective state at some later time (say, time of purchase) should not be expected to cue everything that was learned under a similar affective state (say, during an affect-inducing ad). The problem would be rather simply solved if this were the case (although it would also introduce new problems, such as how to limit the amount cued). But the situation does not appear to be that simple.

On the other hand, positive affect has been found to cue positive material in memory. This suggests that an affective state at time of decision or purchase will cue material that was encoded in terms of positive affect (i.e., material with a positive meaning for the person). Furthermore, because the body of research on affect and memory, as well as the work on memory more generally (e.g., Tulving & Thompson, 1973), indicates that material is most often encoded and stored in terms of its meaning, and therefore is also best cued by its meaning (not just its matching state at time of learning), this work suggests that positive affect at time of a decision may be an especially good cue for material related, in its content, to both the positive affect and the decision to be made. Thus, a positive-affect ad may have an effect that is sustained over time, but especially if the positive affect is appropriate to the content or meaning of the ad, product, and the decision that needs to be made later.

Finally, then, if there is concern that the cue (say affect) at the decision point provide preferential access to certain material (i.e., cue your ad and/or product but not a competitor's ad for a similar product or a different brand), then one will need to make the material distinctive, as well, or especially closely linked to the cuing stimulus in the context of the choice. (See Isen, 1989, and Wells, 1989, for discussion of the problem of possibly cuing a whole class of products, rather than a specific brand, with a positive-affect ad.)

These ideas are compatible with work reported by Calder & Gruder (1989) regarding the influence of theme-congruent affective advertising, as well as with the work of Feldman & Lynch (1988; Lynch, Marmorstein & Weigold, 1988). This point suggests that, for information in memory to be used at the time of making a decision, it must be both relatively accessible (in comparison to other information which might be used for the decision), as well as relatively distinctive or diagnostic in helping to make the decision (again, in comparison to other potentially relevant material).

This brief review of the affect and memory literature, then, suggests that an influence of affect at the time of exposure to material can be sustained in memory and be influential at the time of decision making if the message content is properly cued in terms of meaning, by both content and affect, at the time of the decision. Further research is needed to investigate the parameters of this possibility.

Availability: The Role of Rehearsal.   One means by which learned material is retained and remains available in memory (for later access, if the conditions at retrieval are appropriate) is through repetition or rehearsal. Similarly, material that is used is retained better. Because material associated with positive affect is more pleasant, it can be expected to be more likely to be rehearsed, repeated, and thought about. Consequently, such material's chances of being retained are increased. Thus, positive affect's influence may be sustained in time because people are more likely to think about the ads and products that promote that feeling, and they may rehearse those thoughts, associate them with other things, and remember them. As a result, a positive-affect ad may have a greater influence on subsequent thinking and decision making.

It might be added, parenthetically, in this context, that the apparent effectiveness of some unpleasant ads may derive from the repetition that they employ, rather than from their negative affect. It has been suggested that these commercials, such as Wisk's old "ring-around-the-collar" ads, may be successful, not because of their negative-affect component, but in spite of it. It may be other factors such as repetition that increase their memorability (see Isen, 1989, for discussion).

The Role of Changes in Cognitive Organization and Elaboration

Further, however, the material described in this chapter regarding the impact of positive affect on cognitive organization and on elaboration suggests other ways in which affect's influence may be effective over time. Several points might be considered.

Context.   First, because positive affect has been found to influence the perceived degree of interrelatedness of cognitive material (e.g., Isen & Daubman, 1984; Isen, et al., 1992; Murray, Sujan, Hirt, & Sujan, 1990), the range of associates to a given neutral stimulus (Isen et al., 1985), and the amount of information that is integrated in response to a specific task (Isen et al., 1991), it may be that positive affect at the time of making a decision will change the pattern of material accessible from memory. Moreover, positive affect's influence on the perceived relatedness of cognitive material may influence the perceived relevance, or diagnosticity, of material for particular decisions: Through the influence of positive affect, a broader range of material may seem relevant and diagnostic for a given decision. Thus, the context for the decision may be altered. However, more work is needed to determine the dimensions and types of stimuli to which this will apply. Moreover, it should be noted that this point still does not address the question of how these changed or alternative organizations of material, if induced at time of advertising, are maintained over time and able, later, to be reactivated or, by some other means, have influence.

A second important area of research in the impact of affect on choice has been to understand how memory may influence the choice set and, in turn, how changes in choice set, or this aspect of context, influence a decision (Nedungadi, 1990). A growing body of evidence indicates that the range and nature of items present in the choice set at the time a decision is being made may play an important, and sometimes unexpected, role in the choice made, influencing items by contrast comparison, by implication, and by changing the range of perceived options (e.g., Glazer, Kahn, & Moore, 1991; Isen, 1990b; Kahn, 1990; Simonson, 1990).

Two ways in which affect may influence the choice set are the following: First, because affect influences elaboration and perceived relatedness, it may well influence the choice set seen as relevant to some decisions. Second, because affect can influence the extensiveness of perceived product categories, it is likely that, within a category, the range of alternatives that comes to mind (and thus is used in the decision) is likely to be influenced by affect. But, again, this refers to affect present at the time of making the decision, not at the time of exposure to the material (for example, an ad). The question still remains as to how the expanded choice set at time of seeing the ad would be carried over to the time of decision making, if the affect itself is not reinstated at that time. This will be addressed now.

Encoding Devices.   One important key to understanding how the effects of feelings on cognitive organization are sustained over time, or have influence later on, lies in the encoding-specificity principle (Tulving & Thompson, 1973). That principle holds that the process of memory is an active one and that for any cue (including affect) to increase accessibility of material at the time of attempted retrieval, the material to be retrieved must have been encoded in memory, and stored, in terms of that cue. Then the cue relevant to the way in which the material is organized and stored must be present (in a form that allows it to be recognized as relevant to the material) at the time that recall is attempted. These effects are not thought to occur simply as a function of the cues being present at both time of encoding and time of retrieval, as would be true for a simple state-dependent-learning effect; rather, the process is thought to be an active one, and the cue must have been used actively by the person as a way of organizing the material. One implication is that positive affect, which has been found to be an effective retrieval cue, is a category in which material related to it is organized and stored in memory.

But the important aspect of the encoding-specificity principle, from the standpoint of the discussion of how affect's influence may be sustained over time, is that it indicates that a retrieval cue can only be effective if the material was originally encoded in terms of that concept. Thus, whatever encourages multiple ways of encoding material, as affect does, will result in increased chances of that material being recalled later (even if affect itself is not present later). That is, material that is encoded in more different ways has a larger range of cues that are effective in cuing it, a larger number of ways of being accessed later; and it is therefore more likely to be recalled.

Given the work described regarding the influence of affect on cognitive organization, elaboration, and associated thoughts, one important means by which positive affect at time of encoding may influence later processing and decisions is by influencing the diversity of the ways in which the learned material is encoded. The effects of positive affect on cognitive organization suggest that material learned and thought about during a positive feeling state will be more broadly and elaborately encoded: It will be thought about in more ways, and it will have more associates. This means that, later, that material will be cueable by more different retrieval cues. This, in turn, means that at time of retrieval, even if positive affect is not induced again, this material will be more likely to be recalled because it is more likely that the person will encounter a cue that is an effective retrieval cue for the material.

Thus, a positive-affect ad for a neutral product will enhance the ad's and the product's likelihood of being recalled, in a more diverse set of circumstances, and by a wider range of cues, later. In effect, then, material that is learned during a positive affective state may be functionally more memorable—at least it may be expected to be recalled in a broader range of circumstances, in response to a more diverse set of cues. This, then, would suggest that positive affect at the time of viewing an advertisement may have an impact on choices and decisions later, not because it "carries over" to the second situation, but because it enriches the material learned and thus renders it more accessible by a greater number of cues later. (Presumably, of course, something that is more likely to be recalled can also be considered to be more likely to be influential in the decision process.)

Research is needed, however, to determine the parameters of this kind of effect. Is there a way to predict, for example, just what cues, or what range of cues, or what topics of cues, will become more effective (i.e., the range and types of ways in which the material is elaborated when the person is in the affective state)? One might hypothesize that at least one effective dimension may be the positive-affect dimension. But there may be others as well. One other that has already been identified, for example, is social material. A recent study suggests that positive affect is an effective cue for social material that is neutral in affective tone (See Isen, 1990a). Thus, delineating the parameters of the elaboration that results from positive affect seems a promising direction for research.

In sum, there is reason to believe that positive affect at time of advertising may exert an influence on memory later, at time of product choice, even if the person is not in an affective state at that time. This can occur either through the positive affect giving rise to more elaborated encoding of, or ways of thinking about, the ad-related material, and thus enabling more potential retrieval cues; or because material experienced during positive affect may be more likely to be rehearsed and repeated, and therefore remains more available for later access under the appropriate cuing circumstances. Moreover, it seems likely that these two processes would interact and reinforce one another: Items that are multiply encoded would be likely to be cued relatively frequently in the interim between the ad and the later product decision; every time that happened the material would be repeated or rehearsed again and would become more likely to be remembered. Further, if the material is pleasant, the person may linger over the thought and rehearse it additionally.

CONCLUSION

This chapter has considered ways in which affective states of ad viewers and consumers can influence the way they think about products and brands and thus influence the impact of advertising on behaviors and decisions that take place at another time. We have seen three broad classes of ways in which positive affect can influence decision-making:

1. through the way the material is categorized and thought about (both more positively and more flexibly)
2. through a process that can be both more efficient and more thorough, perhaps something like "chunking" in the cognitive literature; and
3. through motives that the positive state engenders (which include maintenance of the positive state; avoidance of real danger; increasing of safe, enjoyable stimulation; and promotion of helpfulness and social responsibility, to name only a few; see Isen, 1987, for fuller review).

The focus here has been on the influence of positive affect on cognitive organization and implications of this cognitive effect for decision making. Some consideration has been given to ways in which the cognitive impact of affect generated at one point in time can be sustained and influential at later times, when decisions relevant to purchase or use are being made. Processes that have been discussed include:

1. rehearsal and availability; and
2. elaboration, multiple encoding, and enhanced accessibility.

Nonetheless, this chapter has only scratched the surface of these topics. First, more needs to be known about affect's influence on cognitive organization and elaboration. Second, it would be interesting to integrate the findings regarding the influence of affect on cognitive organization with those on the more-often-studied topics of the influence of affect on evaluation and attribute beliefs. If these effects interact or summate in some way, it would be important to know about that. Third, the question of the conditions that enhance or disrupt the maintenance of advertising's effects over time has not been directly addressed. I have offered, here, some suggestions regarding general principles that are important considerations to keep in mind. However, the range of situations in which affect's (or advertising's) influence might be sustained and the conditions under which this might be most likely to occur need to be addressed specifically in order to advance our understanding of the lasting effects of advertising.

REFERENCES

Alba, J. W., Hutchinson, J. W., & Lynch, Jr., J. G., (1991). Memory and decision making. In T. S. Robertson & H. H. Kassarjian (Eds.), *Handbook of Consumer Theory and Research* (pp. 1–49). Englewood Cliffs, NJ: Prentice-Hall.

Bower, G. H. (1981). Mood and memory. *American Psychologist, 36,* 129–148.

Bower, G. H., & Mayer, D. (1985). Failure to replicate mood dependent retrieval. *Bulletin of the Psychonomic Society, 23,* 39–42.

Bower, G. H., Gilligan, S. G., & Monteiro, K. P. (1981). Selectivity of learning caused by affective states. *Journal of Experimental Psychology: General, 110,* 451-473.

Burke, M. C., & Edell, J. A. (1989). The impact of feelings on ad-based affect and cognition. *Journal of Marketing Research, 26,* 69–83.

Calder, B. J., & Gruder, C. L. (1989). Emotional advertising appeals. In P. Cafferata & A. M. Tybout (Eds.), *Cognitive and Affective Responses to Advertising* (pp. 277–286). Lexington, MA: Lexington Books.

Duncker, K. (1945). On problem-solving. *Psychological Monographs, 58,* (Whole No. 5).

Edell, J. A., & Moore, M. C. (1990, October). The effect of feelings on attitude toward the ad and brand beliefs. Paper presented at the Conference of the Association for Consumer Research, New York.

Feldman, J. M., & Lynch, J. G. (1988). Self-generated validity and other effects of measurement on belief, attitude, attention and behavior. *Journal of Applied Psychology, 73,* 421–435.

Glazer, R., Kahn, B. E., & Moore, W. L. (1991). The influence of external constraints on brand choice: The lone alternative effect. *Journal of Consumer Research, 18,* 119–127.

Isen, A. M. (1984). Toward understanding the role of affect in cognition. In R. Wyer & T. Srull (Eds.), *Handbook of Social Cognition* (pp. 179–236). Hillsdale, NJ: Lawrence Erlbaum Associates.

Isen, A. M. (1985). The asymmetry of happiness and sadness in effects on memory in normal college students. *Journal of Experimental Psychology: General, 114,* 388–391.

Isen, A. M. (1987). Positive affect, cognitive processes, and social behavior. In L. Berkowitz (Ed.), *Advances in Experimental Social Psychology* (Vol. 20, pp. 203–253). New York: Academic Press.

Isen, A. M. (1989). Some ways in which affect influences cognitive processes: Implications for advertising and consumer behavior. In P. Cafferata & A. M. Tybout (Eds.), *Cognitive and Affective Responses to Advertising* (pp. 91–118). Lexington, MA: Lexington Books.

Isen, A. M. (1990a). The influence of positive and negative affect on cognitive organization: Some implications for development. In N. Stein, B. Leventhal, & T. Trabasso (Eds.), *Psychological and Biological Approaches to Emotion* (pp. 75-94). Hillsdale, NJ: Lawrence Erlbaum Associates.

Isen, A. M. (1990b, May). *Positive affect as a factor influencing choice-set in decision making.* Paper presented at the Banff Symposium. Banff, Alberta, Canada.

Isen, A. M., & Berg, J. W., (1991). *The influence of affect on a creative vs. a routine task.* Unpublished manuscript, Cornell University, Ithaca, NY.

Isen, A. M., and Daubman, K. A. (1984). The influence of affect on categorization. *Journal of Personality and Social Psychology, 47,* 1206–1217.

Isen, A. M., Daubman, K. A., & Nowicki, G. P. (1987). Positive affect facilitates creative problem solving. *Journal of Personality and Social Psychology, 52,* 1122–1131.

Isen, A. M., & Ford, C. (1989). *The influence of positive affect on perceived uses of products.* Unpublished manuscript, Cornell University, Ithaca, NY.

Isen, A. M., & Geva, N. (1987). The influence of positive affect on acceptable level of risk: The person with a large canoe has a large worry. *Organizational Behavior and Human Decision Processes, 39,* 145–154.

Isen, A. M., Johnson, M. M. S., Mertz, E., & Robinson, G. F. (1985). The influence of positive affect on the unusualness of word associations. *Journal of Personality and Social Psychology, 48,* 1413-1426.

Isen, A. M., & Means, B. (1983). The influence of positive affect on decision-making strategy. *Social Cognition, 2,* 18–31.

Isen, A. M., Niedenthal, P., & Cantor, N. (1992). An influence of positive affect on social categorization. *Motivation and Emotion, 16,* 65–78.

Isen, A. M., Nygren, T. E., & Ashby, F. G. (1988). The influence of positive affect on the subjective utility of gains and losses: It is just not worth the risk. *Journal of Personality and Social Psychology, 55,* 710–717.

Isen, A.M., & Patrick, R. (1983). The effect of positive feelings on risk-taking: When the chips are down. *Organizational Behavior and Human Performance, 31,* 194–202.

Isen, A. M., Rosenzweig, A. S., & Young, M. J. (1991). The influence of positive affect on clinical problem solving. *Medical Decision Making, 11* (3), 221–227.

Isen, A. M., & Shalker, T. E. (1982). Do you 'accentuate the positive, eliminate the negative' when you are in a good mood? *Social Psychology Quarterly, 45,* 58–63.

Isen, A. M., Shalker, T., Clark, M. S., & Karp, L. (1978). Affect, accessibility of material and behavior: A cognitive loop? *Journal of Personality and Social Psychology, 36,* 1–12.

Isen, A. M., & Simmonds, S. F. (1978). The effect of feeling good on a helping task that is incompatible with good mood. *Social Psychology Quarterly, 41,* 345–349.

Isen, A. M., & Stayman, D. M. (1992). *The influences of positive affect on categorization of, and liking for, novel material.* Unpublished manuscript. Cornell University, Ithaca, NY.

Kahn (1990, May). *Constrained choice: The lone alternative effect.* Paper presented at the Banff Symposium. Banff, Alberta, Canada.

Kahn, B., & Isen, A. M. (in press). The influence of positive affect on variety-seeking among safe, enjoyable products. *Journal of Consumer Research.*

Keller, K. L. (1991). "Cue compatibility and framing in advertising. *Journal of Marketing Research, 28,* 42–57.

Lynch, J. G., Marmorstein, H., & Weigold, M. F. (1988). Choices from sets including remembered brands: Use of recalled attributes and prior overall evaluation. *Journal of Consumer Research, 15,* 169–184.

Mednick, S. A. (1962). The associative basis of the creative process. *Psychological Review, 69,* 220–232.

Mednick, M.T ., Mednick, S. A., & Mednick, E. V. (1964). Incubation of creative performance and specific associative priming. *Journal of Abnormal and Social Psychology, 69,*84–88.

Mitchell, A. A. (1986). The effect of verbal and visual components of advertising on brand attitudes and attitude toward the advertisement. *Journal of Consumer Research, 13,* 12–24.

Mitchell, A. A. (1988). Current perspectives and issues concerning the explanation of 'feeling' advertising effects. In S. Hecker & D. W. Stewart (Eds.), *Nonverbal Communications in Advertising* (pp. 127–143). Lexington, MA: Lexington Books.

Mitchell, A. A., & Olson, J. C. (1981). Are product attribute beliefs the only mediator of advertising effects on brand attitude? *Journal of Marketing Research, 18,* 318–322.

Murray, N., Sujan, H., Hirt, E. R., & Sujan, M. (1990). The influence of mood on categorization: A cognitive flexibility interpretation. *Journal of Personality and Social Psychology, 59,* 411–425.

Nasby, W., & Yando, R. (1982). Selective encoding and retrieval of affectively valent information. *Journal of Personality and Social Psychology, 43,* 1244–1255.

Nedungadi, P. (1990). Recall and consumer consideration sets: Influencing choice without altering brand evaluations. *Journal of Consumer Research, 17,* 263–276.

Rosch, E. (1975). Cognitive representations of semantic categories. *Journal of Experimental Psychology: General, 104*(3), 192–233.

Schiffenbauer, A. (1974). Effects of observer's emotional state on judgments of the emotional state of others. *Journal of Personality and Social Psychology, 30*(1), 31–36.

Shimp, T. A. (1991). Neo-Pavlovian conditioning and its implications for consumer theory and research. In T. S. Robertson & H. H. Kassarjian (Eds.), *Handbook of consumer behavior* (pp. 162–187). Englewood Cliffs, NJ: Prentice Hall.

Simonson, I. (1990). The effect of purchase quantity and timing on variety-seeking behavior. *Journal of Marketing Research, 27,* 150–162.

Stayman, D. M., & Batra, R. (1991). The encoding and retrieval of ad affect in memory. *Journal of Marketing Research, 28,* 232–239.

Teasdale, J. D., & Fogarty, S. J. (1979). Differential effects of induced mood on retrieval of pleasant and unpleasant events from episodic memory. *Journal of Abnormal Psychology, 88,* 248–257.

Teasdale, J. D., Russell, M. L. (1983). Differential aspects of induced mood on the recall of positive, negative, and neutral words. *British Journal of Clinical Psychology, 22,* 163–171.

Tulving, E., & Thompson, D. M. (1973). Encoding specificity and retrieval processes in episodic memory. *Psychological Review, 80,* 352–373.

Wells, W. D. (1989). Lectures and dramas. In P. Cafferata & A. M. Tybout (Eds.), *Cognitive and Affective Responses to Advertising* (pp. 13–20). Lexington, MA: Lexington Books.

IV MEASURING ADVERTISING EFFECTIVENESS

10 Teaching Emotion With Drama Advertising

John Deighton
Stephen J. Hoch
University of Chicago

Advertising research has long recognized that some advertisements are more blunt than others. Some make claims so explicitly that audiences have no trouble, recognizing and playing back the communicator's "main idea." In others, there is much less agreement about what the communicator is trying to say about the product, and to infer a claim requires a considerable feat of interpretation. We know that Merit cigarette advertising wants us to believe that Merit has less tar, but what does Marlboro's cowboy advertising want us to believe?

Advertising researchers have used a number of terms to reflect these manifest differences in subtlety:

- *thinking* versus *feeling* commercials (Vaughn, 1980)
- *factual* versus *evaluative* claims (Holbrook, 1978)
- *objective* versus *subjective* content (Edell & Staelin, 1983)
- *informational* versus *transformational* goals (Puto & Wells, 1984)
- arguments versus *dramas* (Deighton, Romer, & McQueen, 1989; Wells, 1988)
- *instrumental* versus *expressive* appeals (Holbrook & Hirschman, 1982).

There is a fair degree of consensus on the process by which the blunter forms of advertising work, derived from a long tradition of social psychological research on response to messages in the form of arguments (Hovland, Janis, & Kelley, 1953; Petty & Caccioppo, 1986). But for the subtler forms, stories and appeals to emotion, there is little agreement on how and when persuasion occurs (Calder & Gruder, 1988).

There is, consequently, little objective basis for telling a good subtle communication from a bad one. Diagnostic tests like recall or the registration of advertising claims seem not to work for non arguments (Zielski, 1982). The standard cognitive response categories are derived from theories of persuasion by argument. Although in principle measures like changes in attitude toward the brand might capture the persuasive effects of these more subtle advertising forms, in practice they are often not sensitive or timely enough to be of much use to creative directors or management. Our aim in this chapter is to suggest ways to measure the effectiveness of nonargument advertising, by identifying mediating processes similar to the cognitive responses that mediate acceptance of arguments. To make our case, we present our view of how advertising might work when it is not blunt.

We contend there are two sources of subtlety—two reasons why an audience might have difficulty reporting what the ad is "trying to say." First, the ad may make a claim about the way consumers should feel, not what they should believe. Feeling claims are harder to replay than belief claims because most of us are more skilled at using language to convey facts rather than sentiments. Second, the execution may show, rather than tell, what it claims, taking the form of a story or drama. These two sources of subtlety necessitate a new approach to testing comprehension of feeling claims in story formats. We present a framework, based on theories of narrative comprehension, to determine whether a story's audience has comprehended a feeling claim transmitted in story form. We illustrate the method with some preliminary data.

We are not proposing that either subtlety or bluntness is consistently the better advertising choice. When advertisers choose subtle over blunt executions they may reduce resistance to the persuasion process, but they lose control of message content. Blunt claims are very clear but may lack credibility and meet with a more vigilant audience—the audience may hear what is said but not believe it. Subtle claims are less clear, but also encounter less critical attitudes; they tend to be experiential rather than educational in the way they teach (Hoch & Deighton, 1989).

WHAT DOES IT MEAN TO PERSUADE
WITHOUT ARGUMENT?

When General Motors runs advertising that baldly states "We build excitement," they use argument to make a claim about feeling. We know whether the audience has received the claim because the audience can replay it to us in the precise words the commercial used to make it. Coca Cola's famous "Mean Joe Green" commercial, showing a confrontation between a small boy and the football star, makes no argument. It merely tells a story.

Why would an advertiser choose to influence consumer learning using drama rather than argument? Why would one choose the rather onerous task of "showing" rather than just coming straight out and "telling" the point of the message? Why not be blunt rather than taking the more risky route of being subtle? We consider two reasons to use drama. (a) Drama advertising has some of the advantages of first-hand experiential, as opposed to educational, learning; (b) Drama advertising may be able to convey messages concerning feelings and emotions that cannot be delivered effectively and credibly by argument.

Two Learning Modes

Consumers learn in two different ways: through education and from experience (Hoch & Deighton, 1989). Education attempts to transfer knowledge through description; information is conveyed indirectly through verbal description, depiction, or argument. Experience provides knowledge firsthand, through acquaintance (Russell, 1948). Learning from experience is more interactive; its constructive nature means that, not only does the stimulus act on the subject, as in education, but the subject also acts on the stimulus.

Descriptive methods are blunt—information is efficiently transferred, and message content is easily controlled by the advertiser. Descriptive methods, however, also serve to forewarn the audience of persuasive intent, so source credibility and believability are low, especially when speaking to an audience that is not very motivated or involved. Methods relying on acquaintance, on the other hand, are more subtle. Information is usually more vivid and concrete and so more easily remembered. Motivation is often higher, as consumers get a sense of pride from feeling in control and "getting it." The intent to persuade is less salient, so counterarguing is lower; but at the same time, the advertiser sacrifices control over the content of learning. It is not that consumers will learn nothing through acquaintance, but because the information is not conveyed explicitly, it is more likely that consumers may idiosyncratically learn the "wrong" thing.

In discussing how to influence what consumers learn from experience, Hoch and Deighton (1989) identified a number of channel (retail and distribution) and promotional tactics available to the marketer. But what can advertisers do to gain the advantages of learning from experience (higher source credibility, better memory, and greater involvement) while still relying on descriptive methods? We believe that drama advertising—advertising that presents a vicarious experience in the form of a story—provides a possible vehicle.

The Argument-Drama Distinction

Wells (1988) argued that there are two ways of making a claim, by arguing for it (a lecture) and by depicting it (a drama). He asserted that dramas work in quite different ways than lectures, and the distinction can be understood metaphorically by the distance between the viewer and the action. A drama draws the viewer into the events it portrays. The viewer becomes involved in the concerns and feelings of the characters, and samples their emotions. When a drama is successful, the audience is said to become "lost in" the story. Arguments or lectures, on the other hand, hold the viewer at arm's length. It offers ideas for the audience to think about, and to which the audience may yield if it chooses.

Deighton, Romer, and McQueen (1989) proposed that argument and drama are seldom encountered as pure forms in advertising. They proposed a scale for measuring form on which argument and drama are end points. Movement along the scale is marked by changes in three attributes: plot, character, and narrativity.

At one extreme of the scale, advertising in argument form is discourse without plot and character, presented by a narrator. The first step away from argument occurs when the plot is introduced. There are three stages to plot: a stable state of affairs, some frustration of intentions that induces a crisis, and finally, redress (see Bruner, 1986). Although plot often involves human intentions, commercials sometimes "star" products, not humans (Durgee, 1988). When a detergent fights a stain, or one diaper competes with another to retain water, the events enact a plot. We use the term *demonstration* to refer to a commercial with plot but no human character.

Character marks the next transition. *Characters* are protagonists who act within the context of a plot, as distinct from narrators who address the audience. Character serves to make human values salient (Scholes, 1981), so that characters placed in conjunction with products are a resource by which advertising can express value claims.

The final step in transforming an argument into a drama involves removing the narrator, who stands as interpreter between events and the audience. This step changes telling into showing (Booth, 1961), where character and visual action are the only available devices for carrying the story. Drama's power derives from its ability to simply portray what argument would have to find words to say. Narration draws attention to the fact that events have been selected from a larger set of events that have already happened (Scholes, 1981) and are being reported to the audience for a reason—to highlight important from unimportant details. Although a narrator can underscore an event's meaning by explaining its relevance to a claim, he or she does so at the cost of signaling persuasive intent. In a drama, things are not so obviously selected and ordered: They seem to simply unfold (White, 1981) of their own accord, and the audience can make of them what they please.

In the place of a narrator, drama depends on verisimilitude to build an empathic bond between its audience and the concerns of its characters. Often the audience does not even realize that a claim has been made. On the positive side, nothing intrudes between the audience and the immediacy of the experience. On the negative side, there is no interpreter to underscore the point. There is a higher probability that the audience will miss the intended point. If it fails to create verisimilitude, the drama is no more than an argument, depending on its ability to persuade and overcome counterargument.

The drama scale can be summarized as follows. Three attributes define argument: It is plotless, characterless, and narrated. Its indicative mood can be quite explicit about what consumers should believe and why. At the other extreme, drama is defined by plot, character, and the absence of a narrator. Its subjunctive (indirect) mood gives up the ability to make explicit claims in exchange for the power of empathy. In between are mixed forms: narrated drama, (e.g., the slice-of-life with commentary), or dramatized argument (e.g., when protagonists debate the merits of a product). It is also possible to show character without plot, creating a tableau in which very little develops. The drama scale is constructed as follows:

ARGUMENT	Narrated	No character	No plot
DEMONSTRATION	Narrated	No character	Plot
STORY	Narrated	Character	Plot
DRAMA	Unnarrated	Character	Plot

Deighton, Romer, and McQueen (1990) showed that the route to successful persuasion for a particular execution depends critically on the extent of dramatization present. For argumentative advertising, counterarguing and belief are crucial; emotions and feelings are inconsequential. For more dramatic advertising, feeling and verisimilitude are the crucial mediators for achieving success.

Comprehension Through Construction

Cognitive response theory describes *persuasion* as self-persuasion, because it is thoughts generated in response to arguments that persuade, and not the argument itself (Greenwald, 1968). Similarly, we contend that it is the story each audience member constructs in response to the drama shown that determines what they learn from the drama. The literal text and the intentions of the copywriter in telling the story are incidental.

Drama's path to persuasion is, however, longer and more difficult than argument's path. Argument directly elicits the counterarguments and support arguments that determine beliefs. Drama leaves more work for the audience to do. Drama ads intend more than they can actually say; but for the ads to do so, the audience must engage in "production." The ads present mainly setting and action; it is up to the audience to infer or recognize the existence of character, goals, attempts to satisfy goals, and obstacles to doing so. In effect, the audience must construct a virtual text, drawing on knowledge of human motivation and emotion, mapping it onto the events of the story.

A virtual text is necessary because the meaning of drama is open to interpretation. According to Bruner (1986), this openness is precisely the characteristic that makes drama persuasive. Drama compels the audience to draw inferences if the audience wants to get the point of the story. Drawing on Iser (1978), Bruner (1986) observes that plot and character recruit the imagination to "perform" the meaning of the drama; the aim of authors is "not to evoke a standard reaction but to recruit whatever is most appropriate and emotionally lively in the reader's repertory" (p. 35).

A good drama, then, is subjectively relevant to each audience member in the sense that he or she can translate the events of the story from action on a physical plane to action on a personally meaningful psychological plane. The ad must relate to the audience member's concerns and capacities for empathy and feeling. If it does, and if it goes on to show the product as prop, setting, or in some other sense ancillary to the mood, feeling, or emotional expression that it displays, then it is not only a good drama but also persuasive advertising for the product.

WHAT DOES IT MEAN TO CLAIM A FEELING?

Most discussions of *emotion* in the consumer research literature treat it as a response (Aaker, Stayman, & Hagerty, 1986; Edell & Burke, 1987; Holbrook & Batra, 1988; and particularly Holbrook, O'Shaughnessy, & Bell, 1990). This work conceives of an innate and finite set of emotional potentialities, for example the eight emotion categories of Plutchik (1980), which are evoked in the respondent by environmental cues. For these authors, it would not be correct to speak of advertising as "claiming" an emotion for a product. Rather, advertising presents a cue that "elicits" the emotion and associates it with the product. It is an implication of this view that an ad is persuasive only if it causes its audience to manifest some of the physiological correlates of emotion.

Our view of the nature of emotion is different, and so our criterion for persuasion is different. This view is influenced by social constructionist theory, which treats emotions less as innate capacities and more as learned social roles (Averill, 1983; Harre, 1986; Sarbin, 1988) or cognitive labels (Schacter & Singer, 1962).

Sarbin (1986), for example, takes the view that emotional expressions are rhetorical acts, undertaken by actors to persuade relevant audiences of the legitimacy of their self-concept or identity claims. An actor who expresses an emotion is, in this view, responding (either calculatedly or spontaneously) to an identity threat or taking advantage of an opportunity for identity definition. *Anger,* for example, is a display intended to defuse a threat to the self-concept. It can be defensive, as when it is a response to an insult; or it can be assertive, as when, for example, one takes offense at an action taken against a group to which one wants to claim affiliation. *Shame* is a defensive display, intended to maintain others' respect in the face of behavior inconsistent with the self-schema. *Joy* is the expression of happiness that has the effect of asserting a link between the actor's identity and some identity-enhancing environmental event.

Emotion is therefore a communicative act, and audiences are able to interpret the intention and meaning of emotion displays because the actions follow well-known scripts. These scripts are learned at the level of culture or subculture, disseminated by a variety of story-like forms: myths, legends, folktales, parables, proverbs, morality plays and religious narratives, as well as story advertising.

The Product as Prop.   In our view, advertising that tells a story is simply another medium for teaching and perpetuating emotion scripts. The main difference between drama advertising and other discourse that teaches emotion displays is that advertising aims to implicate products or services as props in emotion scripts. So, for example, advertising links soft drinks to the script for adolescent high spirits, cigarettes to machismo, and deodorants to self-confidence. AT&T teaches us that if we want to lay claim to the role of warm friend or loyal family member, the telephone can be instrumental.

In the social constructionist view, in order to claim an emotion, it is not necessary for advertising to evoke the emotion at all. Rather, it must teach "how to have" the emotion, a process in which the learner could conceivably be quite dispassionate. We recognize the legitimacy of the attitude toward the ad construct, and, in fact, although drama may often lead to a more positive attitude toward the ad A_{ad}, we contend that it is not necessary. All that advertising must do is show the product as a plausible accomplice in an emotion script, which the target audience will want to remember and use some time in the future because the script makes an attractive identity claim or offers a useful identity defense.

So, for example, AT&T's "Reach Out and Touch Someone" advertising does not have to arouse warm emotions in the viewing audience while they watch it. And it does not have to associate warm feelings with AT&T itself: a positive attitude toward the service is quite unnecessary. What the ad *must* do is teach us that a particular self-concept, such as *good neighbor* or *warm friend,* which is already intrinsically desirable, can be ours with a little help from the telephone.

MEASURING TRANSMISSION OF A CLAIM OF FEELING BY DRAMA

To summarize our view, when advertising "claims" a feeling by dramatization, it tells a story that causes members of the audience to respond by constructing a virtual story. The virtual action occurs at least in part on the psychological plane, and depicts an emotion script useful to the audience's self-concept. The advertised product is implicated in the script in some necessary way.

Following this view, there are four questions that must be answered before an audience can be said to have accepted a feeling claim for a product:

1. *Was a story comprehended?* First the audience must have seen that the chain of actions depicted in the discourse hangs together to make a story. The critical point is to recognize the dynamic dimension: to see forces at work in the story that induce change, not a static tableau.

2. *Did the virtual story report human feelings?* The audience must see some of the action unfolding on the psychological plane, so that the concrete events of the story can be interpreted as emotion displays.

3. *Was the product implicated in those feelings?* The audience must comprehend that the product has a determining role in the emotion display, ideally a role that no other product or brand could fill.

4. *Did the display of feelings have some relevance to the audience's self-concept?* As with claims of fact, there is a difference between receiving a claim and yielding to it. Step 1 through Step 3 establish that the claim has been received, but this step is necessary for persuasion.

To illustrate and explore this conception of advertising, we have chosen four ads as case studies. Each was shown to seven to nine respondents, who were then asked to tell us the story of the commercial as if they were telling the story to entertain us, and assuming we had not seen the commercial. The oral stories were recorded and used to try to answer the four questions just posed.

This study is preliminary, and we do not suggest that, even if our respondents were representative, we would have a basis for deciding objectively which of these four commercials would perform best in the marketplace. Our aim is only to illustrate the criteria we think are important.

Case 1: McDonald's "New Kid"

This commercial tells the story of a retired man who takes a job at McDonald's. The story is narrated, but the narration provides very little clue as to the communicative intent. Here is the text of the narration, which is sung:

> First day at work, wanna be on time,
> Got to make a good impression.
> What if they think it's a little late
> To start a new profession?
> You've got what it takes, you know it's true:
> Bet you'll show them a trick or two . . .

There is no explicit claim in the narration or the dialogue. The first verse narrates what we see on the screen. The elderly man sets off on an attempt to reenter the job market after his retirement. He is a little apprehensive, but musters the resolve to brush off an invitation from his friends to go fishing. In a flash forward we see that two teenage girls who work at the store are expecting a new kid. "I hope he's cute," one says, suggesting the old man has good reason to be apprehensive. The song makes no attempt to narrate the resolution of the plot. Midway through the second verse the song is abandoned in favor of dialogue, and we see the old man triumphantly negotiating a complicated order. He receives admiring glances from the young girls, and returns home to tell his wife, "I don't know how they ever got along without me."

There is no closing narrative to draw a conclusion here. Consequently, the commercial might support many claims: it offers evidence consistent with the idea that McDonald's is a good citizen because it employs older people, that older people should consider working at McDonald's, that customers should be tolerant of older people behind the counter, or just that McDonald's is a place where happy experiences happen. Perhaps some or all of these claims are intended simultaneously. There is an openness of meaning in this drama that would not be possible in argument.

To find the virtual text of this commercial, we showed it to seven subjects and asked them to tell us the story as they saw it. We produced a written transcript of each subject's story, and divided the transcript into units. A unit was defined as an element of the transcript containing a single idea. We looked for units of the following kind:

Setting	A statement describing the context within which the action unfolds.
Goal	An inference about the intentions of an actor.
Expectation	An inference about the expectations of an actor.
Action	A statement describing action, recognizing that the action contradicts an expectation.
Violation	A statement describing action, recognizing that the action contradicts an expectation.
Outcome	A statement describing action, interpreting the action as a resolution of tensions in the plot.
Evaluation	A statement expressing a subjective response to the story.

The shortest story divided into four units, and the longest into eleven. At this point we disregarded the particular wording of a unit, and looked for repetition of the same general idea in units from the stories of different subjects. We identified twelve distinct ideas from across the stories of the seven subjects, although no one story contained all twelve. Three of the stories appear in Table 1, mapped into the twelve units. The union of the subjects' story units constituted the commercial's virtual text.

The virtual text of the "New Kid" commercial, as we inferred it, is as follows. The labels attached to each unit are our own summary of the unit's theme. The number of subjects who expressed the idea is given on the right in parentheses.

1. Setting 1   Old man is introduced   (7)
2. Goal   He decides to work at McDonald's   (7)

TABLE 10.1
McDonald's: New Kid Unit

	Transcript of Respondent		
	Respondent 1	*Respondent 2*	*Respondent 3*
1	Okay there is this old man	There is this old gentlemen	The old man
2	and he is retired and he decided to go back to work at McDonald's	on his way to his first day of work at McDonald's	gets a job at McDonald's
3		his wife wishes him good luck	
4		he runs into his friends. They want to go fishing.	all of his buddies are away from home which is weird.
5		but he says no I am going to work. Goes to work.	
6	and there are a lot of younger people there and they think at first that it will be another kid who is coming to work	before he gets to work the girls are chatting about who the new employee is going to be and they think it is going to be some cute guy, well they were hoping	The people at McDonald's are expecting one thing
7	and so they are a little bit surprised when he comes in	and they see this older gentleman	but they get the old man
8			
9	he does a really good job and all the people who come to his register like him	You see the gentleman serving the customers. He is serving them breakfast items, something like Egg McMuffin and also orange juice	who kicks ass
10	but as soon as they see him they realize that they are going to like him. And when it's over one of the girls asked him if he has worked there before		and they ah I don't know they love him
11	and then he goes back and he really enjoyed his day at work	and then he returns from his first day of work and his wife said "How did it go?"	and he goes back home to his loving wife and he is so happy
12			and it's nice; I don't know, it's very flowery.

Read down a column to read the transcript of an individual subject.
Read across a row to read how three subjects expressed one unit of the virtual text.

3.	Setting 2	His wife wishes him good luck	(3)
4.	Action	His friends ask him to go fishing	(3)
5.	Outcome 1	He says "no"	(3)
6.	Expectation 1	Workers are expecting a new kid	(6)
7.	Violation 1	Old man arrives	(5)

8.	Expectation 2	Workers think he will be slow	(2)
9.	Violation 2	He performs well	(7)
10.	Outcome 2	Workers admire him	(4)
11.	Outcome 3	He returns home in pride	(7)
12.	Evaluation	(Various)	(2)

The individual stories can be mapped against the four questions identified earlier.

1. *Was a story comprehended?* None of our subjects failed to construct a story. The least common denominator of these stories was made up of Units 1, 2, 9 and 11. That is not much of a story, but it does unfold (see the next case for one that does not) and is coherent.

2. *Did it report human feelings?* These stories take place almost entirely on the psychological dimension. The units deal with intention, surprise, resolve, and other feeling states. Transcript #3 in Table 1 was a conspicuous exception in that it does not use any feeling terms.

3. *Was the brand implicated in the feelings?* McDonald's role in this drama is as setting. It is sufficient for the drama, but hardly necessary. At best it could be said that "this is the sort of thing that happens at McDonald's." The link between emotion and product is not as strong as in 'Recital' (analyzed as Case 4).

4. *Were the feelings relevant to the audience's self-concept?* We did not explicitly measure whether the drama had self-concept relevance. The commercial offered several possible loci for empathy. The ostensible hero is the old man, and the most obvious emotion displays are his, but there is also opportunity to identify with the workers and their displays of generous acceptance, or with the customers showing pleasure at his efficiency.

Case 2: Pepsi Cola "Wedding"

This commercial, like the previous one, is narrated by a song, but here the song "tells" the claim quite directly:

No other taste attracts so much attention.
Diet Pepsi you've got to be the most refreshingest invention.
See that smile, see that look,
Diet Pepsi is all it took.
Diet Pepsi, have I mentioned?
You've got to be the most refreshingest invention.
No other taste attracts so much attention.

The commercial depicts a rather somber wedding party. Two small children take a Diet Pepsi from a tray and hand it to a stern-faced old man. He pops it open, spraying himself in the face, and grins. Pepsi is offered all around, glasses are filled, the children kiss and the camera pans to various laughing faces.

TABLE 10.2
Diet Pepsi: Wedding

		Transcript of Respondent	
	Respondent 1	Respondent 2	Respondent 3
1	It looked like an outdoor wedding	A wedding	It's at a wedding.
2		Stuffy people there and everyone is being real stuffy	First thing you see is a lady—may be somebody's mother. Looks like a bitch, like she is in a bad mood and then you see these cute little kids. Then there's an old man--you're not sure if he's stern or not but then you see he's actually a nice, funny old man
3		(kids) play around with some Diet Pepsi	and he opens up a Diet Pepsi and it sprays all over his face,
4	A bunch of people having a good time and laughing--fooling around--they were all drinking Diet Pepsi--	and these kids cheer them up.	so everyone starts laughing and then the music picks up—even the bitch lady becomes a nice lady and smiles and I think you get a glimpse of the bride and groom
5			and then you notice that the wedding is over and everyone is tired and smiling.
6	I guess the point they were trying to get across was trying to equate good times with drinking Diet Pepsi.		

Read down a column to read the transcript of an individual subject.
Read across a row to read how three subjects expressed one unit of the virtual text.

To establish the virtual text, we followed the same procedure as before. This time five units were obtained when we parsed the seven stories (see Table 10.2 for three of the stories). The units were:

1.	Setting	A wedding is in progress	(7)
2.	Expectation	The event is going to be stuffy	(4)
3.	Action	Kids introduce Pepsi into the party	(5)
4.	Violation	The party livens up	(5)

| 5. | Outcome | At the end, everyone is tired, happy | (1) |
| 6. | Evaluation | (Various negative). | (3) |

Again we use the virtual text to address the four questions related to dramatized claims of feelings.

1. *Was a story comprehended?* Two of the seven respondents saw no story. Nothing unfolded over time. (For example see Transcript #1 in Table 2.) They missed the expectation/action/violation sequence in the action, and saw only a tableau depicting people having a good time at a party where Diet Pepsi was being served. They did not notice that Diet Pepsi changed the mood of the party. This is the only one of the commercials we studied in which any of the subjects failed to identify a story. We speculate that, for these two respondents, this was not a drama commercial at all. It was processed as an argument: a telling (admittedly in pictures) but not a showing. It kept its audience at arms length, detached and judgmental, not drawn in to an empathic concern for the characters by a plot. The processing, we surmise, contained more counterargument than imaginative elaboration. And in fact, in the Deighton, Romer, and McQueen (1990) study, "Wedding" was found to encourage counterarguing.

2. *Did it report human feelings?* Like "New Kid," the units of the virtual story are mainly descriptions of feelings, not physical action. On this criterion, the commercial was successful. That is not to say it was persuasive. We have argued that description of feelings is necessary, but not sufficient, for persuasion.

3. *Was the brand implicated in the feelings?* Pepsi is a "prop" in the display of feeling. It is, however, a weak prop. It is even less necessary to the action than McDonald's was in the previous commercial. No distinctive facet of the meaning of Pepsi makes it indispensible: Any carbonated beverage could have sprayed in the old man's face.

4. *Were the feelings relevant to the audience's self-concept?* The only data we have on this question are three stories which conclude with remarks about the implausibility of the story they are telling. One reason this may be so is that the stories lack a strong character on which to focus empathy. The story has to do with change in mood of a collective entity, the wedding party. It is difficult for the audience to identify with the concerns of this heterogeneous group, even if those feelings had been plausible.

Case 3: Diet Pepsi "Apartment 10G"

This commercial opens with a young man (Michael J. Fox) returning to his apartment. There is a knock on the door and an attractive woman says, "Hi. I just moved in next door and I was wondering, could I borrow a Diet Pepsi?" He backs off from her toward the kitchen and, out of sight, leaps jubilantly into the air. In the kitchen, he finds his Diet Pepsi is empty. He heads for the window, down the fire escape, and across the street to a vending machine. A chorus sings in the background:

> Heading up to heaven,
> Heading up to heaven.
> Chasing down a dream,
> Tuning up my engine,
> Tensions scream.
> Night's really dark,
> Danger's burning bright,
> I'm out on the edge.
> Chasing down a dream tonight,
> I'm on the edge tonight.

Approaching the vending machine, his path is blocked by a motorcycle gang. He hesitates, but the face of the girl and the words, "Can I have a Diet Pepsi?" are recalled. He returns with the Pepsi and climbs the fire escape, to find his window has closed. The scene shifts to the waiting girl. She hears the sound of breaking glass. She asks, "Are you OK in there?" He enters, wet and bleeding. "Here's your Diet Pepsi." Another knock is heard on the door. "That must be my room-mate, Danny." "Danny?" A second attractive woman enters. "Hi, I'm Danielle. Do you have another Diet Pepsi?" Mixed emotions cross the young man's face and he replies, "Sure." The slogan "Diet Pepsi. Choice of a New Generation" appears on the screen.

Three of our subjects' virtual texts appear in Table 10.3. The following struc-ture emerges as the basic unitization of the tests:

1.	Setting	Young man appears	(6)
2.	Action	Beautiful woman knocks on the door	(7)
3.	Response	He shows delight	(1)
4.	Goal	Woman wants a Diet Pepsi	(7)
5.	Outcome 1	There is none in the apartment	(5)
6.	Outcome 2	He goes to lengths to get one	(7)
7.	Response	He wants to please her	(2)
8.	Outcome 3	He returns successful	(5)
9.	Outcome 4	She appreciates it	(2)
10.	Outcome 5	Her roommate wants another	(6)

1. *Was a story comprehended?* It is unlikely that anyone could view this commercial and fail to encode a story. Despite the absence of narration, there is a strong dependence structure among the Units (2, 4, 6) that every respondent reported.

TABLE 10.3
Diet Pepsi: "Apartment 10G"

	Transcript of Respondent	
Respondent 1	*Respondent 2*	*Respondent 3*
1	A guy is living in an apartment	There is the story this guy
2		thinks his dream has come true
3 The story goes a new neighbor comes in	his roommate—his neighbor comes over	because this beautiful woman comes and knocks on his door
4	to borrow a Diet Pepsi	to go get Coke, no Diet Pepsi
5 Michael J. Fox looks in the fridge,		
6 goes out the window jumps over cars through a bike gang	so he runs around and nearly kills himself trying to get one,	and he ends up having to go to all extremes
7	obviously to impress her	to please her
8 gets a Diet Pepsi, comes back	and then he comes back and gets one	
9	and the two hit it off pretty well, I guess, because he get her a Diet Pepsi.	
10 The other roommate comes in, asks for another Diet Pepsi.		And then at the end another one comes in he's like, "Oh my God I've got to do it again."

Read down a column to read the transcript of an individual subject.
Read across a row to read how three subjects expressed one unit of the virtual text.

2. *Did it report human feelings?* This commercial differs from the previous two in that the action in the virtual text takes place almost entirely on the physical plane. Most of the respondents, and most of the units, dealt more with what happened to the actors than with their intentions or felt responses. Although the urgency associated with the young man's efforts to find a Diet Pepsi for the young woman (6) was recognized clearly by all respondents, the units most concerned with psychological states (3,7,9) were used by no more than two respondents. It may be that the intensity of the activity overwhelmed issues of motivation in the viewers' minds. We speculate that texts of this kind indicate that, for these subjects, the commercial has held attention but has not made an intelligible claim of feeling. It is may be that the commercial makes a dramatized

claim of fact (for example, Pepsi is the choice of a new generation because young singles are using it to get to meet their neighbors).

3. *Was the product implicated in the feeling?* Even among those respondents who gave evidence of recognizing feelings in the commercial, the role of Pepsi in a feeling claim is no more necessary here than in "Wedding."

4. *Were these feelings relevant to the audience's self-concept?* The commercial offers both a hero and heroine as possible targets for empathy, but because there is no clear feeling claim, this asset is not exploited.

Case 4: McDonald's "Recital"

This commercial is set in a school auditorium filled with parents and children. A young girl in audience turns to her father and says, "I don't want to do this." He encourages her by promising a trip to McDonald's when her recital is over. She reluctantly goes to the piano.

(Speaks)	I'll be glad when I'm done.
	I'll be glad when I'm done.
	I'll be . . . (looks at audience) Think McDonald's.

(Sings)	How I wish I were already there
to tune	Instead of here
of *Fur*	Playing this song.
Elise)	Oh I would have a big chocolate shake
	A cheeseburger
	And also . . . whoops! . . . and also fries.
	And I would eat
	My fries myself
	And not give any
	To my dumb brother
	Hands off, they're mine all mine.
	Oh Boy! my recital's almost done
	It wasn't bad
	I'm still alive
	And now I can have my chocolate shake
	My cheeseburger
	And also . . . whoops! . . . and also fries.

(Plays McDonald's theme tune on piano, leaves stage to applause.)

Three of the subjects virtual stories appear in Table 10.4. The following structure captures the basic unitization of the stories:

1.	Setting	Little girl at recital	(7)
2.	Expectation	She is nervous	(4)
3.	Action	Father offers McDonald's as incentive	(7)

TABLE 10.4
McDonald's "Recital"

	Transcript of Respondent		
	Respondent 1	*Respondent 2*	*Respondent 3*
1	This McDonald's ad was about a little girl. They were at a recital in front of a large audience		Picture a little girl who has to give a piano recital. She's only about 7 or 8 years old,
2	and in order to coax her along		and petrified of performing.
3	her father says that if she does her job that they'll go to McDonald's.	Well, first the parents of the girl bribed her into playing the piano by saying she could go to McDonald's.	To give her courage, her father tells her that when she's done they can all go to McDonald's as a treat.
4	She gets up there and sits down, does her recital,		So she climbs the stage, sees the crowd, freezes.
5	and while she's doing it she thinks of this song in her mind and plays it along and sings	To get the song over with the girl sang a song about McDonald's,	But she tells herself finally, "Think McDonald's." And as she plays, she composes a little song in her head to match the piece she's playing,
6	and while she's thinking there are little shots of her with chocolate shake and stuff	about how she just can't wait till she gets there,	and the words are all about how she's gong to eat all her favorite food at McDonald's after this
7	and there's this whole thing with her brohter where she's going to get fries and not give any to her brother		(and not share with her brother).
8	and when she makes a mistake she says "Oops!" and then it's all over and she says it wasn't that bad.		This gets her through the recital (in spite of a few mistakes).
9	Just before she's going to leave she plays the little theme song of McDonald's and everyone's surprised and they all clap.	then at the end she plays the McDonald's theme tune.	However, thinking about McDonald's causes her to get a little mixed up and play the McDonald's theme at the end. But everyone applauds anyway, and all is well.

<u>Read down a column</u> to read the transcript of an individual subject.
<u>Read across a row</u> to read how three subjects expressed one unit of the virtual text.

4.	Violation	She goes ahead with the recital	(3)
5.	Response 1	She sings about McDonalds	(7)
6.	Response 2	Describing her anticipation	(6)
7.	Response 3	And her plan to exclude her brother	(4)
8.	Outcome 1	The recital ends with few errors	(7)
9.	Response 4	She tags the McDonald's theme tune on	(4)

1. *Was the story comprehended?* None of the subjects failed to construct a story. At a minimum, the story was of nervousness overcome by the bribe of a visit to McDonald's, leading to a successful performance.

2. *Did it report feelings?* As with "New Kid," the virtual stories are re-counted almost exclusively on the psychological plane. Physical action is less intrusive here than in "Apartment 10G," perhaps because there are fewer dis-crete events to catch the attention. Consequently, even the shortest virtual story (#2 in Table 10.4) is told as a story of feelings.

3. *Was the product implicated?* We contend that McDonald's is a crucial prop in all of the virtual stories. None of the other commercials implicate the product so effectively in the story plots. It is the imputed attributes of McDonald's that make it effective as a bribe and a worthy subject for the child's song.

4. *Were the feelings relevant to the audience's self-concept?* The virtual stories seem to have two possible empathic foci. Most subjects adopted the perspective of the child, so that McDonald's became a prop (rather than a setting) in the enactment of hedonic gratification. A meal at McDonald's is seen as a way to reward oneself for a job well done. Other subjects, however, took the perspec-tive of the father. For these subjects, the meal is an incentive or bribe to get the child to comply with the parents' wishes. Subject 1 (Table 10.4), for example, reports that the food is used "to coax her along."

Summary of the Four Cases

These analyses permit one to make some speculative inferences about the path to persuasion that each of the four commercials seems to be using, and the like-lihood that each is doing a good job of following that path. "Apartment 10G," although it is unquestionably dramatic in form, seems not to make a "feeling" claim. We suggest that it is using drama mainly to get and hold attention. The claim ("Pepsi is the choice of a new generation") is a claim of fact, not feeling. The events of the drama are essentially arguments in support of that claim. A conventional ad test, such as comprehension and registration of copy points, should be effective in measuring whether the ad is persuasive or not.

We speculate that conventional testing would give misleading results for the other three ads. They are dramatizations of feeling claims, following the em-pathic path to persuasion. "Wedding" is the ad least likely to follow that path successfully; it loses some of its viewers at the first stage (comprehension that there *is* a story), and seems to lose the others by failing to show that the feeling is caused by a determinant attribute of the brand. "Wedding" fails to present an emotion script that the audience would want to employ. "New Kid" and "Re-cital" follow the dramatization path successfully. Both are comprehended as stories on the psychological plane, both implicate the product in the display of emotion, and both seem to present emotion displays that are quite relevant to the self-concepts of significant groups of consumers.

CONCLUSIONS

We have dealt with drama, a type of advertising execution that plays an important role in the creative portfolios of advertisers. We began by contending that most of the diagnostics currently available for assessing advertising effectiveness are appropriate only to argument-based appeals. These techniques give poor measures of the subtler effects of dramas that claim feelings. Drama and argument accomplish different goals in different ways.

In our effort to understand how drama-based advertising might work, we have intentionally adopted a narrow view. We have attempted to push as far as possible a social constructionist perspective on emotion and have adapted techniques of narrative analysis to the virtual stories that the audience plays back. Within this system we posit four steps necessary to the acceptance of a feeling claim for a product:

1. *Was a story comprehended?*
2. *Did the virtual story report human feelings?*
3. *Was the product implicated in those feelings?*
4. *Did the display of feelings have relevance to the audience's self-concept?*

Drama has a variety of attributes that contribute to persuasion. The teaching of emotional scripts is only one of these ways. Because drama is more experiential than educational, there is less forewarning of persuasive intent, so that perceptual defenses are lower and counterarguing less. Consequently, an argument successfully embedded in a drama may be more persuasive. Dramas may also be better able to hold an audience's attention. Michael J. Fox's "Apartment 10G" commercial contains repeated visual and verbal references to the goal object, a can of Diet Pepsi. Keeping the brand in mind for the duration of an entertaining 90-second commercial may be much more important than whether the audience has received a feeling claim that implicates the brand. Drama can also work by creating more positive attitudes toward the ad and advertiser. The transfer of drama-aroused positive feelings to the product could work at a conditioning level. Finally, drama could work in a more cognitive manner, showing how to use the product to experience the intended benefits, whether physical or emotional.

In evaluating drama-based advertising, it is important to do so in relation to the communication goals of the advertiser. This requires specialized diagnostics. Our attempt to apply narrative analysis to the virtual stories constructed by the audience represents a preliminary effort to evaluate how well a drama has communicated an emotional script.

REFERENCES

Aaker, D. A., Stayman, D. M., & Hagerty, M. R. (1986). Warmth in advertising: Measurement, impact, and sequence effects. *Journal of Consumer Research, 12,* 365–381.

Averill, J. (1983). *Anger and aggression.* New York: Springer-Verlag.

Booth, W. C. (1961). *The rhetoric of fiction.* Chicago: University of Chicago Press.

Bruner, J. (1986). *Actual minds, possible worlds.* Cambridge, MA: Harvard University Press.

Calder, B. J., & Gruder, C. L. (1988). Emotional advertising appeals. In R. A. Peterson, W. D. Hoyer, & W. R. Wilson (Eds.), *The role of affect in consumer behavior: Emerging theories and applications* (pp. 277–285). Lexington, MA: D. C. Heath & Co.

Deighton, J., Romer, D., & McQueen, J. (1989). Using drama to persuade. *Journal of Consumer Research.*

Durgee, J. F. (1988). Product drama. *Journal of Advertising Research, 1,* 42–49.

Edell, J. A., & Burke, M. C. (1987). The power of feelings in understanding advertising effects. *Journal of Consumer Research, 14,* 421–433.

Edell, J. A., & Staelin, R. (1983). The information processing of pictures in print advertising. *Journal of Consumer Research, 10,* 45–61.

Greenwald, A. G. (1968). Cognitive learning, cognitive response to persuasion, and attitude change. In A. G. Greenwald, T. C. Brock & T. M. Ostrom (Eds.), *Psychological foundations of attitudes* (pp. 147–170). New York: Academic Press.

Harre, R. (1986). An outline of the social constructionist viewpoint. In R. Harre (Ed.), *The social construction of emotions* (pp. 2–14). Oxford, England: Basil Blackwell Ltd.

Hoch, S. J., & Deighton, J. (1989). Managing what consumers learn from experience. *Journal of Marketing, 53,* 1–20.

Holbrook, M. B. (1978). Beyond attitude structure: Toward the informational determinants of attitude. *Journal of Marketing Research, 15,* 546–556.

Holbrook, M. B., & Batra, R. (1987). Assessing the role of emotions as mediators of consumer response to advertising. *Journal of Consumer Research, 14,* 404–420.

Holbrook, M. B., & Hirschman, E. C. (1982). The experiential aspects of consumption: Consumer fantasies, feelings and fun. *Journal of Consumer Research, 9,* 132–140.

Holbrook, M. B., O'Shaughnessy, J., & Bell S. (1990). Actions and reactions in the consumption experience: The complementary roles of reasons and emotions in consumer behavior. In E. C. Hirschman (Ed.), *Research in Consumer Behavior* (Vol. 4, pp. 131–163).

Hovland, C., Janis, I., & Kelley, H. H. (1953). *Communication and persuasion.* New Haven: Yale University Press.

Iser, W. (1978). *The art of reading.* Baltimore, MD: Johns Hopkins University Press.

Petty, R. E., & Caccioppo, J. T. (1986). The elaboration-Likelihood Model of Persuasion. In Leonard Berkowitz, Ed.), *Advances in Experimental Social Psychology* (pp. 123–205). New York: Academic Press.

Plutchik, R. (1980). *Emotion: A psychoevolutionary synthesis.* New York: Harper & Row.

Puto, C. P., & Wells, W. D. (1984). Informational and transformational advertising: The differential effects of time. In Thomas C. Kinnear (Ed.), *Advances in consumer research* (Vol. 11, pp. 638–643). Provo, UT: Association for Consumer Research.

Russell, B. (1948). *Human knowledge: Its scope and limits.* London: George Allen and Unwin Ltd.

Sarbin, T. R. (1988). Emotion and act: Roles and rhetoric. In R. Harre (Ed.), *The Social Construction of Emotions* (pp. 83–97). Oxford: Basil Blackwell Ltd.

Schachter, S., & Singer J. E. (1962). Cognitive, social, and physiological determinants of emotional state. *Psychological Review, 69,* 379–399.

Scholes, R. (1981). Language, narrative and anti-narrative. In W. J. T. Mitchell (Ed.), *On narrative* (pp. 200–208). Chicago: University of Chicago Press.

Vaughn, R. (1980). How advertising works: A planning model. *Journal of Advertising Research, 20,* 27–36.

Wells, W. D. (1988). Lectures and dramas. In P. Cafferata & A. Tybout (Eds.), *Cognitive and Affective Responses to Advertising* (pp. 13–20). Lexington, MA: D. C. Heath.

White, H. (1981). The value of narrativity in the representation of reality. In W. J. T. Mitchell (Ed.), *On Narrative* (pp. 1–24). Chicago: University of Chicago Press.

Zielski, H. A. (1982). Does day-after recall penalize 'Feeling' Ads? *Journal of Advertising Research, 22,* 19–23.

11

A Structural Model of Advertising Effects

Charles E. Gengler
Thomas J. Reynolds
The University of Texas, Dallas

In a general sense, scientific research can be described as the process of articulating and answering questions about phenomena. In the study of advertising, *econometric studies* can, at best, tell us *if* something has happened through evaluation of sales response models. *Positioning studies* typically address the issue of *what* happened in terms of brand perceptions by the consumer. However, in designing and choosing copy to promote a particular brand, important and difficult questions that surface are *how* and *why* does advertising work. If we were gifted with knowledge of these particulars, copy evaluation would be a relatively simple matter. Several decades of work in copy research has explored various methods of assessing advertising effectiveness and understanding the underlying variables theorized to contribute to advertising effectiveness. Measures and theories have abounded, many of which have received acceptance in industry without proven validity (Ostlund, Clancy, & Sapra, 1980).

The key element spurring the diverse and often nonconvergent research streams in advertising is lack of a unified direction. The Positioning Advertising Copy Testing (PACT) committee on copytesting standards observed this in their recommendations, proposing that a system should ". . . provide measurements which are relevant to the objectives of advertising . . ." (1982, p. 10). The important phrase of this principle is "objectives of advertising." It is generally accepted that a major goal of advertising is to differentiate the product. Creating strategy for advertising, then, is devising a blueprint for accomplishing this goal. More specifically, Reynolds and Gutman (1984) stated, ". . . the advertising function may be equated, at least in part, to the creation and management of product imagery; that is, the set of meanings and associations that serve to differentiate a product or service from its competition . . ." (p. 27).

In this chapter, we advocate an alternative proposed by Reynolds and Rochon (in press) to conventional copy-testing approaches. We propose that advertising should be assessed according to the particular differentiation or positioning strategy it communicates; and, at a higher level, strategic advertising messages can be evaluated across different executions to understand the effectiveness of a given strategy.

Addressing this issue, we find that the use of the term *strategy* is broadly applied across current advertising literature, yet rarely, if ever, defined. Here, advertising strategy is defined as the specification of the manner by which the brand will be meaningfully differentiated by the target consumer. To operationalize this concept, we implement descriptions of strategic meaning in terms of the means–end categorization paradigm (Gutman, 1982). Both individual strategic concepts and the interrelationships or connections between concepts are measured to assess the effectiveness of the communication in delivering the desired strategic message.

BACKGROUND

Advertising research is a junction of several academic fields, the most obvious of which being general communication theory. Beyond this broad perspective offered by communication, researchers and strategists must consider the actual psychological meanings communicated by the advertising message and the relevance of those meanings to the consumer. Furthermore, researchers must consider advertising from a mass-persuasion perspective; the sociological/social psychological aspects of generalizing meaning and relevance across large groups of individuals is also of importance. In this chapter, we address the problem from these three perspectives simultaneously. We first review the communication aspects specifically relevant to the advertising development process. The concept of *meaning* is then discussed and developed in terms relevant to the advertising domain. A means–end perspective (Gutman, 1982) is discussed as a methodology for describing personal relevance of the meanings communicated, and these concepts are then related to current cognitive theories of associative memory.

The Communications Perspective

A popular model for communications is presented by Shannon and Weaver (1949). The model consists of six elements: an information source, a transmitter, the channel, a receiver, a destination, and noise (see Fig. 11.1). Their model is generalized to portray all communication processes, whether person-to-person or machine-to-machine. Advertising can be viewed as a special case of this model (see Fig. 11.2). We can operationalize the source of the communication as an

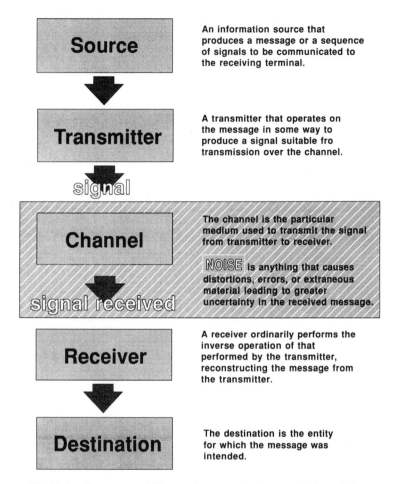

FIG. 11.1. Shannon and Weavers' communication model (1949). Reproduced by permission of the University of Illinois Press.

advertiser who produces a particular positioning message to be established. An advertising agency (or in-house creative staff) must take the *image* concept established by the advertiser and transform it into a message suitable for the advertising medium involved. This act of generating advertising copy plays the transmitter role in Shannon and Weaver's (1949) model. An advertising medium can take on many forms, such as television, radio, or print. The consumer must act as both receiver and destination. Consumers find meaning in advertising messages through the individual internal translations (or decodings) of the message. The goal of communication, then, is to achieve a desired end-state in the destination; the personal relevance to the consumer of the meaning, which is ac-

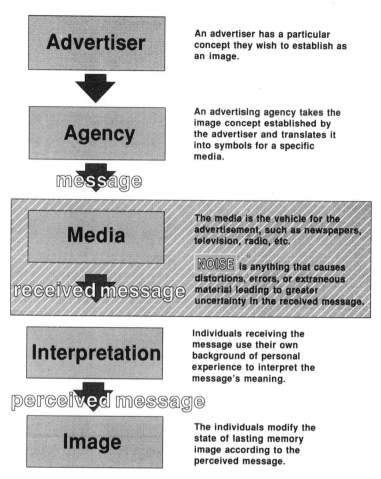

FIG. 11.2.   A macro model of advertising communication. Reproduced by permission of the University of Illinois Press.

tually decoded, determines whether product-evaluative components of memory are altered to achieve this desired end state.

In essence, the selection of a message by an advertiser is dependent upon the anticipated effect on the consumer evaluation process. Furthermore, the encoding of a message by advertising professionals is dependent upon the anticipated decoding. Therefore, the personal relevance and personal meaning derived from advertising exposure are of paramount interest.

Meaning in Advertising

The topic of meaning in advertising has been discussed in detail by Friedmann and Zimmer (1988). Meaning is categorized into three types: lexical meaning, philosophical meaning, and psychological meaning. *Lexical meaning* pertains to the relationship between words and referents. *Philosophical meaning* focuses on rational concept–referent relationships. *Psychological meaning* is the individuals subjective perception and affective reaction to stimuli. Psychological meaning is the dominant area in which consumer researchers concentrate (Friedmann, 1986).

Of particular bearing on the subject of meaning is the study of *semiotics,* the study of linguistic symbols and the ways in which they function to give meaning. This field was pioneered by de Sassure (1959). Sassure presented the argument that language should be studied not only in terms of the meanings of the individual parts; not diachronically, but in terms of the relationships between parts, and synchronically, in terms of the synergistic adequacy of a given interpretation within situational constraints.

Sassure defined two ways in which communicated signals can be classified. The first method is that of the paradigm. A *paradigm* is the set or group from which the particular sign is chosen. For example, in English an individual may choose from a vocabulary set of size descriptors to discuss an object, such as big, enormous, small, tiny, or infinitesimal. For this domain of study, the set of symbolic options to communicate a particular type of information can be considered a paradigm. The second way in which signs can be classified is by the message into which they are combined, or syntagmaticly. A *syntagm* is the particular message into which signs are combined. The sign's meaning is determined by its relationship to other signs in the syntagm.

Mick (1986) thoroughly reviewed applications of semiotic theory to marketing. We consider all of the content of a given advertisement to be a syntagm. Many different paradigms have been used to describe the various components of the advertisement, yet these paradigms have led us to diachronic rather than synchronic analyses. The meaning of any of these components is derived from the relational structure with other elements of the syntagm. This point is illustrated in dramatic fashion by the following quote from the distinguished communications researchers, McLuhan and Nevitt (1974), ". . . Nothing has meaning alone. A single note in isolation is not music. The meaning of a word is not what it says, not merely its definition, but what it does as a figure in its context or ground. . ." (p. 29).

Personal Relevance: A Means–End Perspective

Although specific meanings may be communicated successfully, the issue of personal relevance of these meanings to bear on product evaluation and motivational structure remains. In 1949, Cartwright published results of research on several years advertising and sales of war bond issues during World War II. He proposed a structural network of pathways to goals that provide a motivational structure within individuals, and stated, ". . . A given action will be accepted as a path to a goal only if the connections 'fit' the persons larger cognitive structure . . ." (p. 262).

A similar concept is presented in the means–end perspective (Gutman, 1982), which provides a theoretical basis to explain brand differentiation through cognitive categorization processes. Categorization processes are theorized to be strongly related to consumer evaluation processes (Cohen & Basu, 1987). Put simply, the *means–end perspective* posits that the categorization process pertinent to product differentiation for advertising is based on the particular way in which individuals find products personally relevant.

The theory is based on the personal values orientation for motivation of human behavior. Following a similar perspective, Rosenberg (1956) showed a significant relationship between the degree and type of value associated with objects and affect generated for the objects. Rokeach (1973) extended this viewpoint through research across social groups, establishing that a set of socially influenced, shared personal values can serve to characterize the motivational forces of individuals. Under this perspective, personal relevance is theorized to be determined by the amount of satisfaction/negation of these values for an individual.

From the means–end viewpoint, the physical attributes of a product are relevant to the degree that they contribute to satisfaction of the personal values for an individual. This is described as a means–end chaining process (Gutman, 1982; Gutman & Reynolds, 1979) from physical attributes of a product/service to the consequence or functional benefits derived from the attributes to the higher level values stimulated by these consequences. This relational viewpoint of information processing is supported from observations made by Maslow (1963) in psychoanalytic research, who observed a "vectorial quality" in which the dynamic characteristics of facts are the links between knowledge of the physical world and one's personal values.

An in-depth survey technique known as *laddering* has been devised for collecting and analyzing consumer perspectives within a market (Gutman & Reynolds, 1979; Olson & Reynolds, 1983; Reynolds & Gutman, 1984; Reynolds & Gutman, 1988). In this process, one-on-one interviews are conducted, during which the basis upon which an individual makes differentiations between products is elicited. The roots of the differentiation, in terms of personal relevance, are then extracted through a series of probing questions to determine not only *what* is the relevant point of differentiation, but *why* is this differentiation personally important to the subject. After a number of individuals have been surveyed, results are aggregated to form an understanding of the various perceptual positionings within the market.

The means–end perspective has been proposed as a paradigm for describing advertising strategy, termed *Means-End Conceptualization of the Components of Advertising Strategy,* or MECCAS (Olson & Reynolds, 1983; Reynolds & Gutman, 1984; Reynolds & Craddock, 1988). The MECCAS model proposes five categories of conceptual information communicated in an advertisement: Message Elements, Consumer Benefits, Leverage Points, Personal Values, and the

Executional Framework. *Message Elements* are the specific attributes of the physical product that are communicated. *Consumer Benefits* are the major positive consequences of product attributes derived by the consumer. *Leverage Points* are the instrumental values, or personal traits, between consequences of product usage and terminal values related to the self. Driving forces are the terminal values that relate directly to the individual's self. And lastly, *Executional Frameworks* are the general, tactical characteristics of the communication as a vehicle for delivering the means–end chain, such as humor, fear, or irritation.

Reynolds and Trivedi (1989) examined the relationship of the individual MECCAS levels to product affect generated by an advertisement and found significant relationships. The major limitation of this work is that only bivariate relationships are considered, and structural considerations of the entire communication are not considered. The simple relationships of individual concepts to affect can only provide partial understanding of a communication. The structural interrelationships, or syntagmatic properties of communication are the key to meaning received, and relevance derived, from messages. In terms of semiotics, each of the individual MECCAS levels can be considered a paradigm for a certain conceptual type of information, at a different level of abstraction. The syntagm in this case is the complete chain of MECCAS levels and their perceived relationships linking product to self.

The Cognitive Perspective

The means–end conceptualization can be related to the growing attention received by associative theories of memory in recent cognitive psychological literature. The most common representation of knowledge structures currently is that of a network of interrelated concepts. In attempting to represent linguistic/semantic concepts, Quillian (1969) proposed the concept of spreading activation. The concept has been revised (Collins & Loftus, 1975) and provides a fundamental basis for the more prevalent current theories of general cognition (Anderson 1983; McClelland & Rumelhart, 1986).

The connections or associations between concepts in a network compose a unique portion of knowledge representation. Spreading activation theory implies that activation of a specific node of knowledge will cause activation, to some degree, of nodes connected/associated to that node. In turn, these nodes will cause further activation of others, ad infinitum, until the level of activation has been diluted below a threshold level where no further activation is possible. Connectionist, or Neural based theories presented by McClelland and Rumelhart (1986) carry the activation concept further to the point where actual nodes of concepts do not exist, but all of knowledge is contained in the complex pattern of connections/associations that are made. Although the connectionist models have appealing qualities in their physiological representations of cognition, the symbolic approach can be viewed as a higher level implementation of connectionist models and is far more tractable for our uses (Fodor & Pylyshyn, 1988).

Bearing this research stream in mind, we propose that a successful communication is the creation/strengthening of connections or associations between concepts within the recipient's symbolic memory. Measurement of concepts communicated alone does not ensure that the desired knowledge *structure* has been created/strengthened in the recipient of the message. Anderson (1983) presented the concept of production systems as specialized structural systems for traversing through a network of complex associations according to a specific purpose. For instance, the set of dormant associations and connections we have connected with the concept of a 1969 Buick are not all activated/accessed simultaneously, with equal strength, in different situations. When one is considering the purchase of a used car, a certain set of associations and meanings for a 1969 Buick will be activated in memory by the associated production system. On the other hand, when one is a pedestrian crossing the street and sees a 1969 Buick approaching at a high velocity, it is very unlikely that considerations of fuel economy or trade-in value will be activated in memory.

It has been proposed that product evaluation can be viewed as a special type of production system within cognition (Smith, Mitchell, & Meyer, 1982). We propose that the product evaluation production system can be operationalized through the means–end perspective. Activation of the terminal values is what gives products personal relevance and thus serves as the basis for subsequent evaluation and choice. The degree to which we can formulate a system of connections/associations between the properties of the product and the self (via the value system) is proposed to correspond to consideration and evaluation of the product. Of interest, then, is the study of the structural relations between product and self being communicated; in other words, the study of syntagmatic structures of product involvement. Furthermore, we are interested in analyzing the degree to which these associative relationships affect brand evaluation.

From a larger perspective, each of the set of pathways of connections from product to self can be viewed as a specific strategic positioning message. Therefore, assessment of a strategic communication involves three basic issues: the degree of communication of the specific MECCAS levels; the degree to which these levels were communicated to be interrelated, both to the individual and to the product; and the relationship of these measures to brand evaluation.

METHOD

Data Collection

Questionnaire administration was performed via one of the new generation of personal computer based interactive interviewing systems, STRATA$_{(TM)}$. This system integrates a personal computer and a video cassette recorder so that ads being assessed and questions directed to the subjects can be shown alternately on the same color monitor. The personal computer allows flexibility in questionnaire administration, while at the same time reducing the amount of interviewer bias that can be introduced. Responses are given verbally by subjects and entered into the computer by interview administrators.

STRATA$_{(TM)}$ is designed to assess the strategic communication effects of the advertising through implementation of the MECCAS model discussed earlier. Before any interviews are begun, the system is set up by entering all of the study specific demographic profiles and the product category specific MECCAS elements at each respective level that are applicable to the study.

During the actual interview, the software first requests demographic information and confirms that the subject falls within the a priori specified target market. After subject demographic verification, subjects are shown two of the advertisements being analyzed. At this point, questions are asked to measure the affective responses inspired by the communication. Both affect toward the advertisement and affect toward the brand measures are collected. This study is only concerned with the brand measures. Two statements designed to measure positive brand affect generated by the ad were displayed one at a time. Subjects were asked to rate the degree to which they agree with each of the two statements. The statements are shown in Table 11.1. The ratings were combined into an aggregate measure of brand affect. This measure demonstrated a Cronbach's alpha coefficient of .70. Mean scores for product affect generated by each ad are shown in Table 11.2.

The next phase of the questionnaire assesses the degree to which the different MECCAS levels are communicated by the advertisement. Statements about each

TABLE 11.1
Brand Affect Statements and MECCA Level Elements Within Questionnaire.

Brand Affect Statements

This ad makes me feel even better about using the product/service.
This ad makes me really want to get the product/service.

Message Elements	Consumer Benefits	Leverage Points	Driving Forces
Sound clarity	Dependable service	Trust	Self-esteem
New technology	Save time	Being in control	Peace of mind
Courteous personnel	Worry less	Sense of caring	Security
Takes care of needs	Get more done	Self-assurance	Independence
Fast repair/service	Handle activities better	Being an innovator	
Variety of services	Make life easier	Sense of accomplishment	
Good reputation	Use time better	Sense of belonging	
Access to information	Reduces stress	Family feelings	
Accurate billing	Save money	Making right decisions	
	High quality/fair price	Pride in job well done	
		Sense of Competence	
		Sense of competition	

Note. Executional framework statements are not listed, as they were not a part of this analysis.

TABLE 11.2
Top Five MECCAS Element Scores and Correlations With Brand Affect for Each Ad

Brand Affect	Ad A (N = 70) u = 51		Ad B (n = 68) u = 46		Ad C (n = 70) u = 28		Ad D (n = 69) u = 36		Ad E (n = 76) u = 25		Ad F (n = 63) u = 13	
MECCAS Elements	Mean	Corr.	Mean	Corr.	Mean	Corr.	Mean	Corr.	Mean	Corr.	Mean	Corr.
Message Elements												
Sound clarity	39.7	.52			31.1	.21	14.5	.03				
New technology	60.0	.29			61.4	.21						
Courteous personnel			49.1	.44					36.3	.29	8.3	.00
Takes care of needs	42.9	.33	38.8	.41								
Fast repair/service			49.1	.54			18.0	.33	40.5	.26	9.2	.43
Variety of services	39.1	.32	63.2	.55	32.9	.25	22.6	.33	54.0	.33	7.6	.22
Good reputation	58.3	.25			54.3	.14	34.8	.24	12.6	.32	25.1	.33
Access to information			59.4	.21	28.3	.25	54.8	.25	20.3	.08	7.6	.35
Consumer Benefits												
Dependable service	41.7	.14	58.8	.29	25.7	.36			22.6	.01	12.7	.41
Save time	33.7	.42	28.2	.16	18.6	.34	50.1	.26	22.9	.09		
Worry less			50.0	.39							5.4	.26
Get more done	25.7	.34			18.6	.36	40.6	.30	21.3	.15		
Handle things better	33.7	.08			13.1	.34	36.8	.42	33.2	.17	4.8	.12
Make life easier	38.0	.27	37.3	.26	16.3	.42	38.8	.27	33.7	.18	6.3	.12
Use time better							36.8	.44			3.5	.24
Reduces stress			29.7	.34								

Leverage Points

Trust	46.9	.02	50.8	.57	27.7	.33	15.1	.46	11.3	.17	20.0	.39
Being in control	70.9	.29	54.7	.52	58.6	.37	15.7	.35	22.4	.25	16.5	.26
Sense of caring			66.8	.56								
Self-assurance	34.0	.15									16.5	
Being an innovator			41.8	.36	43.7	.41			12.1	.21		
Accomplishment	43.7	.25			40.6	.33	13.3	.45			25.1	.04
Sense of belonging	74.0	.20										
Family feelings							15.9	.29	29.2	.11	13.3	.35
Making right decision									15.5	.15		
Pride in work			38.8	.46	28.6	.34	17.4	.19			29.5	.06
Sense of competence												
Sense of competition												

Driving Force

Self-esteem	12.2	.05	10.0	.16	9.7	.38	7.2	.23	4.5	.16	3.8	.36
Peace of mind	41.4	.03	23.9	.27	20.9	.47	7.0	.17	4.7	.11	0.0	.00
Security	26.9	.12	47.4	.44	8.9	.53	7.5	.19	7.1	.14	5.1	.02
Independence	16.6	.11	18.8	.25	5.1	.41	17.4	.50	16.8	.11	18.8	.11

individual level component are displayed and the degree to which the ads communicated the component is queried. Table 11.1 shows the different MECCAS levels that were assessed. Reynolds and Trivedi (1989) showed little difference in performance between a two-point and a five-point scale in a similar study. In this case, a three point ordinal scale was used to assess the ratings in the aforementioned statements. Pretesting was performed and the scales were calibrated to values of 0, 60, and 100, rather than assuming equidistant points. The affect questions and MECCAS levels were of similar format and were translated in this fashion.

The final section of the questionnaire is designed to measure the degree to which any two adjacent levels of the MECCAS model are perceived to be associated or connected within the ad. This measure allows us to distinguish ads that communicate a cohesive structural communication of product image from those that do not. The connection measurements were left as values of one, two and three, because the question formats were substantially different from affect and MECCAS communication questions. This scale was determined to be adequate.

Stimuli

This research studied the effects of six ads in the telecommunications market. All ads are for the same corporation. The company is a major supplier of telecommunication services serving several states within the United States. Ads are referred to as *A, B, C, D, E,* and *F*. Four of the ads were intended as corporate image advertising, namely ads *A, B, C* and *F*. The three first Ads (*A, B,* and *C*) share a common executional theme. The other two Ads (*D* and *E*) were intended as product feature oriented. Two hundred and eight adult subjects were selected who lived within the areas serviced by the company and were users of the company's products. Each subject assessed two ads, so there were a total of 416 individual ad assessments. Sample selection and administration of the questionnaire were performed in such a fashion that each ad was assessed with a near equal number of subjects (approximately 70). Sample sizes for each ad can be seen in Table 11.2.

ANALYSIS

The backbone of the analysis rests upon the brand affect measure. As already stated, this measure has shown a reliability of .70. The central goal of the analysis is to study the relationship between the elements of the communication and brand affect generated. Specifically, we are interested in the relationship between structural constructs of the communication and brand affect. To study the structural aspects and their contribution to brand affect, alternative models to predict brand affect are evaluated and compared.

Model Selection and Construction

For each of the ads, analysis of the individual MECCAS levels was then conducted. Means for all concepts at each of the MECCAS levels were produced, and the five highest communicated concepts at each level were retained for analysis. A Pearson's correlation of each of the retained elements in the individual ads to brand affect generated by the ad was then computed. The highest correlated Message Element, Consumer Benefit, Leverage Point, and Driving Force were selected as strategic elements for predicting brand affect, reflecting the theoretical means–end chain bridging from product attributes to personal values.

Three different model constructions were performed. First, a four-variable model was constructed to predict brand affect, where predictor terms were the four components of a means–end chain previously mentioned. This model construction emphasizes only the communication of symbols in the ad and ignores the success of the ad in constructing connections or associations between the MECCAS components. The second model construction consisted of three predictor terms to predict brand affect. In this model, the three predictor terms consisted of association measures between the four levels of association; Message Element to Consumer Benefit, Consumer Benefit to Leverage Point, and Leverage Point to Driving Force. The third model construction consisted of a combination of the first two, containing all four MECCAS levels and all three connections to predict brand affect. Two variations of models two and three were constructed, using alternative measures of connection strength.

Alternative Connection Measures

Connections are the strength of association communicated between levels of the MECCAS model. When we are discussing the connection between two levels, we can use the physical analogy of a two-piered suspension bridge. The strength of any such bridge is dependent on the strength of both piers and the connecting cables. The strength of connections in this model is dependent upon the strength of the communication of the two adjacent MECCAS levels independently, and the strength of the association between the two MECCAS levels. Two alternative constructions of connection measures are examined. The most obvious and basic method of computation of this connection is to simply use the interaction term between two adjacent MECCAS levels, which we will call the MECCAS interaction connection. This assumes that if two concepts are communicated within the ad, they will be associated according to their respective degrees of communication. Alternatively, a second measure of connection is constructed by multiplying the measured association (the strength of the cables in our analogy) times each of the two concepts it is connecting (the strength of the piers of the bridge). We will call this the MECCAS and association connection.

RESULTS

The mean scores for the top five communicated MECCAS elements at each level of abstraction (Message Elements, Consumer Benefits, Leverage Points, and Driving Forces) are shown in Table 11.2 for each ad. As would be expected, Ad *F* scored low on virtually all levels of communication, and had a correspondingly low brand affect score. Conversely, two of the Ads, *A* and *B* scored highly across all levels and showed a corresponding higher level of brand affect. Ads *C* and *D* scored well in communicating Message Elements concerned with product attributes, yet did not translate these attributes into consumer benefits as well as Ads *A* and *B*. Ad *E* communicated Message Elements moderately well, and translated the Message Elements into Consumer Benefits, but failed in establishing personal relevance of the benefits with weakly communicated Leverage Point and Driving Force levels. Individual correlations of each element with brand affect are shown in Table 11.2, and the highest correlated element at each level was selected for model construction for each respective ad.

Regression results for the different model constructions across all six ads are shown in Table 11.3. Brand affect scores ranged from a low of 13 for ad *F* to a high of 51 for Ad *A*. All of the models containing the four MECCAS levels only

TABLE 11.3
Regression Results for Alternative Model Constructions

		R-Square for Model Construction					
		MECCAS Interaction Connection Construction			MECCAS and Associations Connection Construction		
AD	N=	4 MECCAS Only	3 Connections Only	4 MECCAS and 3 Connections	3 Connections Only	4 MECCAS and 3 Connections	Mean Brand Affect
A	70	.322	.414	.440*	.362	.409*	51
B	68	.467	.363	.519	.346	.506	46
C	70	.357	.251	.363	.267	.374	28
D	69	.399	.265	.530*	.200	.483*	36
E	76	.176	.054	.199	.098	.192	25
F	63	.534	.095	.539	.095	.539	13

*These connections contributed significantly when added to the four MECCAS levels to form a seven variabale model.

were significant at alpha $= .05$, and R-square values ranged from .176 (Ad E) to .534 (Ad F). For the three variable models, containing only the three connection variables, five out of six of the models were significant at alpha $= .05$, with only Ad E not significant for either type of connection construction. For the MECCAS interaction connection, R-square values for the three connection model ranged from .054 (Ad E) to .414 Ad A). For the MECCAS and association connection, R-square for the three connection model ranged from .095 (Ad F) to .362 (Ad A). All of the seven variable models containing the four MECCAS levels and the three connections were significant at alpha $= .05$ across all six ads for both constructions of connections. R-square for the seven variable model for the MECCAS interaction construction ranged from .199 (Ad E) to .539 (Ad F), and from .192 (Ad E) to .539 (Ad F) for the associations connections. No notable difference in predictability was shown across the two different connection construction alternatives.

A test was constructed to examine the contribution to R-square of the set of three connection variables when added to the original four variable MECCAS model. The F-test was constructed as follows (Nie, Hull, Jenkins, Steinbrenner, & Brent, 1975, p. 339):

$$F = \frac{\text{(Increase in } R^2 \text{ due to connections)}/3}{(1 - R^2 \text{ for MECCAS only model})/(N\text{-}4\text{-}1),}$$

with 3, and N-5 degrees of freedom (N is the number of observations). Results of the test found that the connections contributed significantly at alpha $= .05$ in only two of the six models, namely Ads A and D. These are the highest scoring (in terms of brand affect) for each of the two intended orientations, corporate image and product-feature oriented, respectively. As is evident in Table 11.3, the lowest scoring two ads seem to have the least contribution from connections in the seven variable model. Of the three ads that share a common executional theme, the ordering of contribution by connections (of either construction) exactly matches the ordering of brand affect generated. Indeed, if Ad D is ignored, there is a one-to-one relationship across all of the five remaining ads between brand affect and contribution by connections.

DISCUSSION

The results confirm Reynolds and Trivedi (1989), indicating significant relationships between the MECCAS levels and affect. The relationship between the structural measures, or connections, and brand affect scores warrants further discussion. The ads in which the connections contributed more unique variance in explaining brand affect were also the ads that scored the highest brand affect. An important point to be emphasized is that this is a relationship between the correlation with brand affect, and *not* with the absolute strength of the connection communicated. Just as in the case of communicating product attribute information, the issue of principal interest is the relevance of the connection, not its strength of communication.

The fact of the contribution by connections being significant in only two of the six cases would be troubling was it not for this relationship to the brand affect score. The amount of affect generated by an ad, which is explicable by MECCAS element measurement, only seems to plateau and incremental gains in the overall brand affect scores are attributable to the structural components of the model. The process could be called an explanation of the "central route" to persuasion (Petty, Cacioppo, & Schumann, 1983), which "views attitude change as resulting from a person's diligent consideration of the information that s/he feels is central to the true merits of a particular attitudinal position" (p. 135).

CONCLUSIONS

Attitude research has influenced advertising research toward investigating independent attributes of objects as the crucial elements in predicting the affect generated by an advertisement. This research supports the importance of attribute communication measures in predicting the brand affect generated by an advertisement; yet it indicates that the structural components of a communication may also be of importance. This importance is magnified when one considers that this contribution by structural components seems to be closely related to differences in brand affect generated by the ad. The semiotic viewpoint of advertising as more than just the communication of concepts but also the structural interrelationships of those concepts coupled with a means–end theoretic approach to product differentiation provides an operational insight into evaluation of advertising strategies.

The importance of the "self" orientation, the basis of structural connections, has been emphasized in the literature recently (Belk, 1988, 1989; Cohen, 1989). Belk (1988) states: "That we are what we have is perhaps the most basic and powerful fact of consumer behavior" (p. 139). Belk (1988) presents that objects have enduring personal meanings to consumers far beyond their functional usages, and can be viewed as extensions of the consumer's self. Cohen (1989) criticized the lack of an operational definition for Belk's "extended self." We think that this work is a step toward operationalization of this relational construct.

Future research can progress in a myriad of directions. Deighton (1984) and Hoch and Ha (1986) showed that affects of consumer's nonadvertising experience can influence their response to advertising. The heterogeneity of a priori product knowledge/attitude may well influence response to specific strategic messages and is a subject for consideration in research. Burke and Srull (1988) studied competitive interference effects in advertising recall. Gollin and Sharps (1988) demonstrated categorical structures to influence recall interference measures for objects. The means–end perspective can provide a basis for understanding the important categorical structures employed by consumers in brand evaluation. Because the categorization process affects interference processes in recall, the methodology for measuring the strategic message communicated by an advertisement discussed here may provide deeper insight into how the product will be categorized and into the competitive effects of advertising on brand recall.

IMPLICATIONS

When designing and/or evaluating advertising, additional insight can be gained by viewing the holistic meaning of the message as opposed to solitary measurement of the components of the advertisement. The MECCAS (Olson & Reynolds, 1983; Reynolds & Craddock, 1988; Reynolds & Gutman, 1984) approach to advertising strategy implies a workable paradigm describing the pathways from product attributes to personal relevance. Correlational analysis of strategic elements of a communication (the MECCAS levels) can provide the basis for a program of proactive diagnosis in the copy development process. Finally, alternative strategies can be compared to determine which has the greatest potential for generating brand affect.

ACKNOWLEDGMENTS

The authors would like to thank Bonnie Ballantyne, Joe Dodson, Jim Schirmer, and Sharon Vercimak for their help in this research.

REFERENCES

Anderson, J. R. (1983). *The architecture of cognition*. Cambridge, MA: Harvard University Press.

Belk, R. W. (1988). Possessions and the extended self. *Journal of Consumer Research, 15*, 139–168.

Belk, R. W. (1989). Extended self and extending paradigmatic perspective. *Journal of Consumer Research, 16*, 129–132.

Burke, R. R., & Srull, T. (1988). Competitive interference and consumer memory for advertising. *Journal of Consumer Research, 15*, 55–68.

Cartwright, D. (1949). Some principles of mass persuasion. *Human Relations, 2*, 253–268.

Cohen, J., & Basu, K. (1987). Alternative models of categorization: Toward a contingent processing framework. *Journal of Consumer Research, 13*, 455–472.

Cohen, J. B. (1989). An over-extended self? *Journal of Consumer Research, 16*, 125–128.

Collins, A. M., & Loftus, E. F. (1975). A spreading activation theory of semantic processing. *Psychological Review, 82*(6), 407–428.

Deighton, J. (1984). The interaction of advertising and evidence. *Journal of Consumer Research, 11*, 763–770.

deSassure, F. (1959). *Course in General Linguistics.* New York: Philosophical Linguistics.

Fodor, J. A., & Pylyshyn, Z. W. (1988). Connectionism and cognitive architecture: A critical analysis. *Cognition, 28*, 3–72.

Friedmann, R. (1986). Psychological meaning of products: Identification and marketing applications. *Psychology and Marketing, 3*(1), 1–16.

Friedmann, R., & Zimmer, M. (1988). The role of psychological meaning in advertising. *Journal of Advertising, 17*(1), 31–40.

Gollin, E. S., & Sharps, M. J. (1988). Facilitation of free recall by categorical blocking depends on stimulus type. *Memory and Cognition, 16*, 539–544.

Gutman, J. (1982). A means end chain model based on consumer categorization process. *Journal of Marketing, 46*, 60–72.

Gutman, J., & Reynolds, T. J. (1979). An investigation at the levels of cognitive abstraction utilized by the consumers in product differentiation. In J. Eighmey (Ed.), *Attitude research under the sun.* Chicago, IL: American Marketing Association.

Hoch, S. J., & Ha, Y. W. (1986). Consumer learning: Advertising and the ambiguity of product experience. *Journal of Consumer Research, 13*, 221–233.

Maslow, A. H. (1963). Fusion of facts and values. *The American Journal of Psychoanalysis, 23*(2), 117–131.

McClelland, J., & Rumelhart, D. (1986). *Parallel Distributed Processing: Explorations in the Microstructure of Cognition: Vol 2. Psychological and Biological Models.* Cambridge, MA: M.I.T. Press/Bradford Books.

McLuhan, M., & Nevitt, B. (1974). Medium meaning message. *Communication, 1*, 27–36.

Mick, D. G. (1986). Consumer research and semiotics: Exploring the morphology of signs, symbols, and significance. *Journal of Consumer Research, 13*, 196–213.

Nie, N., Hull, C., Jenkins, J. Steinbrenner, K., & Brent, D. (1975). *Statistical package for the social sciences* (2nd ed., pp. 339). New York: McGraw-Hill.

Olson, J. C., & Reynolds, T. J. (1983). Understanding consumers cognitive structures: Implications for advertising strategy. In L. Percy & A. G. Woodside (Eds.), *Advertising and consumer psychology.* Lexington, MA: Lexington Books.

Ostlund, L. E., Clancy, K. J., & Sapra, R. (1980). Inertia in copy research. *Journal of Advertising Research, 20*(1), 17–24.

PACT *Committee* (1982). PACT—Positioning advertising copy testing, a consensus credo representing the views of leading american advertising agencies. *Journal of Advertising, 11*(4), 3–29.

Petty, R. E., Cacioppo, J. T., & Schumann, D. (1983). Central and peripheral routes to advertising effectiveness: The moderating role of involvement. *Journal of Consumer Research, 10*, 135–146.

Quillian, M. R. (1969). The teachable language comprehender: A simulation program and theory of language. *Communications of the ACM, 12*, 459–476.

Reynolds, T. J., & Craddock, A. (1988). The application of MECCAS model to the development and assessment of advertising strategy: A case study. *Journal of Advertising Research, 28*(2), 43–54.

Reynolds, T. J., & Gutman, J. (1984). Advertising is image management. *Journal of Advertising Research, 24*, 27–38.

Reynolds, T. J., & Gutman, J. (1988). Laddering theory, method, analysis, and interpretation. *Journal of Advertising Research, 28*, 11–31.

Reynolds, T. J., & Rochon, J. (in press). Strategy-based advertising research: Copy testing is not strategy assessment. *Journal of Business Research.*

Reynolds, T. J., & Trivedi, M. (1989). An investigation of the relationship between the MECCAS model and advertising affect. In P. Cafferata & A. Tybout (Eds.), *Cognitive and affective responses to advertising.* Lexington, MA: Lexington Books.

Rokeach, M. (1973). *The Nature of Human Values.* New York: Free Press.

Rosenberg, M. (1956). Cognitive structure and attitudinal effect. *Journal of Abnormal and Social Psychology, 53,* 367–372.

Shannon, C. E., & Weaver, W. (1949). *The Mathematical Theory of Communication.* Urbana, IL: The University of Illinois Press.

Smith, T. R., Mitchell, A. A., & Meyer, R. (1982). A computational process model of evaluation based on the cognitive structuring of episodic knowledge. In A. A. Mitchell (Ed.), *Advances in Consumer Research* (Vol. 9, pp. 136–143). Ann Arbor, MI: Association for Consumer Research.

12

Observing Information Processing and Memory Development: The Potential Value of EEG in the Study of Advertising

Michael L. Rothschild
University of Wisconsin, Madison

For most of the history of consumer psychology and advertising, information processing and memory development were observed retrospectively, via obtrusive and introspective questioning methods, and for units of analysis that considered the entire message rather than its component parts. Although researchers have made important strides forward using these methods, our knowledge is incomplete. Observations can only take place in the past tense, as if the only views of the passing landscape could come via looking in a rear view mirror. In addition, these observations only occur when our travelling partner chooses to report something of interest to us. As a further limitation, the observations are almost always of the dominant features of the landscape; details are rarely reported.

Another potential way to study information processing is via online recording devices. These tools eliminate the need for retrospection and introspection and, as a result, present a whole new way of observing information processing and memory development. Emerging methods in this area include physiologic measures, hand-held potentiometers; verbal responses based on truncated viewing can be close to online.

Potentiometers have the disadvantage of distracting the consumer from the viewing task and therefore being quite obtrusive; the consumer needs to continuously adjust responses to changes in feelings or some other dependent variable in need of self-assessment. Truncated viewing is expensive in its use of subjects. In this method, consumers are stopped at some point while viewing a stimulus and asked to respond to questions. Although the presence of a physiologic measuring instrument is obtrusive initially, its presence is soon overlooked and the actual data collection becomes unobtrusive. This chapter will focus on one type of physiologic response.

While physiologic techniques were available, in fact, in the past, in practice, rudimentary equipment and knowledge imposed limits that made widespread use impractical and results unreliable. Widely publicized electronic breakthroughs in the development of computing equipment have led to the development of physiologic measurement equipment that is relatively inexpensive and easily useable. The interaction of increased knowledge and technology has led to exciting new developments in physiologic measurement and theory.

The area of brain research has been no different from the general field of physiology. There has been incredible progress in neurophysiology in a number of dimensions over the past decade; consumer research is only now beginning to investigate some of these breakthroughs. Brain research has moved forward on two major fronts: the observation of electrical patterns and chemical changes. Within the former, one can consider electrical patterns themselves or magnetic resonances emanating from the patterns. Within electrical patterns, one can study brief periods of stimulus–response interaction under tightly controlled conditions (evoked response potential [ERP]) or longer time periods with specific electrical frequencies and scalp locations considered (electroencephalogram [EEG]). Both areas have contributed in quite different ways to the extant body of knowledge.

In considering each of these areas of method, the researcher needs to consider the time unit of analysis that will best serve the objectives of the research. As students of advertising and consumer psychology, we must be concerned with a unit of analysis that allows us to observe rapid changes in response variables. Current technology allows this type of observation via electrical patterns in the brain, but does not allow it via chemical changes. Magnetic images allow precise locations of activity to be shown, but, again, do not allow recording of rapid changes. Within electrical patterns, the study of ERPs is limited to simple (e.g., single word, line, or drawing), brief (usually less than 250 milliseconds), unchanging stimuli and therefore can not be used to study responses to television advertising.

This chapter will present a review of the work that our lab has done with respect to EEG. This review will show some of the relevant theory that has emerged with respect to electrical activity in the brain; In virtually all cases, this work is based on the use of brief simple stimuli. We will then show how we have been able to extend this work with respect to a complex, continuous stimulus, such as a television commercial, and how the basic findings hold in the more complex case.

The work to be presented will be divided into two parts for ease of presentation. An $S-O-R$ framework seems appropriate for this presentation. In this framework, S represents the advertising stimulus, O represents the internal processing of information, which is operationalized as changes in electrical activity, whereas R is an observable response such as awareness, knowledge, recognition, affect, or feelings. The paper will consider the first linkage ($S-O$) to examine the effect of the stimulus on the process; the second linkage ($O-R$) considers the relation between this processing and a memory structure that can be examined as well.

Basic research in EEG has been conducted across three major observable dimensions. These are *spatial* (location of the electrical changes as observed at various points on the skull), *spectral* (frequency of the electrical signal observed as part of a complex sine wave generated from the brain) and *temporal* (timing of the patterns with respect to the stimulus). As will be seen, the EEG literature is replete with studies that consider the $S-O$ relation from the spatial and spectral perspectives; here, consumer research can easily borrow from a wide and well established body of literature. The basic literature, perhaps because of its reliance on brief simple stimuli, has neglected the temporal dimension and the $O-R$ relation. As a result, the findings that have emerged from our lab concerning the temporal dimension and $O-R$ are not extensions of basic work, but are novel in their own right.

Consumer researchers and physiologists have been noteworthy in their respective contributions but each has shed little light on the neural mechanisms of real-world information processing and memory development engaged in by a normal population.

A BRIEF INTRODUCTION TO
ELECTROENCEPHALOGRAMS

There are two purposes to this section. First, a few basic findings are presented, which will be assumed to hold across any investigation of EEG, and can be assumed to be useful in the current work without replication. Second, there are findings of import to the current work that need to be established in the context of consumer psychology and that will form the basis of the current work. The work will be presented with respect to the $S-O$ and the $O-R$ relations discussed earlier.

Prior Work as it Relates to the Stimulus–
Electroencephalogram Relation

It is a basic fact that all living animal life emits electrical activity from its brain. What is useful about this fact is that the electrical activity is continuously changing, and, as a result, there is variance in a stream of data; it is this variance that is interesting to the EEG researcher. The electricity varies in its amplitude (power), and does so at different frequencies of a spectrum that ranges from direct current (0 Hz) up to at least 100 Hz. This power also varies in the location in the brain from which it eminates (and the location on the scalp from which it can be measured). These two dimensions are spectral and spatial; in addition, one needs to consider the temporal dimension when dealing with an ongoing stimulus such as a television commercial. Early work in EEG and ERP considered brief stimuli and was less concerned with the temporal dimension; early EEG work related to advertising skirted the temporal issue by aggregating data over long time periods (2 to 30 seconds).

The spectral frequency range most commonly studied when observing a normal population (as opposed to subjects with some sort of pathologic disorder) is alpha (8–13 Hz). One of its major characteristics is that a high level of power is an indicator that the brain (or the location under observation) is at rest. This high level of power results from a synchronization in the firing of neurons during resting. An indicator of cognitive activity is a desynchronization and a lower level of power known as *alpha blocking*. Blocking indicates arousal and/or cognitive activity.

One can observe changes in alpha as a function of changes in environmental stimuli and the passage of time from the onset or change of the stimulus. Whereas the initial drop in power is generally felt to be an involuntary response of an arousing or orienting nature, the nature of the continuation of the blocking is felt to be voluntary. If the environmental change is felt to be important, blocking will continue, otherwise there will be an attenuation and return to a resting level of alpha power.

Variance in EEG can also be observed spatially by observing the different lobes from the front to the rear of the brain or by looking at homologous sites at a particular lobe. There is considerably more research with respect to homologous sites. This work, commonly referred to as hemispheric lateralization is burdened by an oversimplification of early work by the popular press. The popular notion that the brain has two distinct hemispheres that engage in discretely different tasks is naive and incorrect when observing a normal population. This view postulates that the right hemisphere processes visual, musical, and artistic stimuli, and is the center for feeling, holistic, and parallel processes; the left hemisphere is said to process verbal and mathematical stimuli, and is the center for thoughtful, discrete, and serial processes. These views are a vestigial remainder of early EEG studies, which used subjects with surgically severed hemispheres or pathologic disfunction in a hemisphere, and/or simple stimuli, which carefully presented either a pictorial or verbal stimulus. While the basic thrust of the findings still holds, recent work has shown the aforementioned to be a gross oversimplification of the complexities of the interactions between the hemispheres of a normal population responding to real-world stimuli. In addition, the popular view of laterality tends to ignore the different functions served by the different lobes.

More recent work has recognized these complexities; a currently popular model of hemispheric processes is one with a bilateral and parallel view. It hypothesizes that both hemispheres process virtually all information but that each is superior at its specialization. Although hemispheric dominance exists, it can be the result of several causes:

1. *Verbal versus nonverbal stimuli:* Previously discussed.

2. *Level of clarity and complexity of stimulus:* Unclear stimuli are first processed in the right hemisphere; as the stimulus becomes more clear, it is more likely to be processed in the left hemisphere.

3. *Vigilance versus learning mode of receipt:* In this model, the right hemisphere is dominant when the environment is being scanned, but when something of importance occurs, the left hemisphere becomes dominant. In a similar model of facial recognition, it was hypothesized that the right hemisphere is dominant in early processing in order to explicate initial perceptions and classification duties, whereas left dominance occurs later as semantic processing of features occurs.

4. *Visual hemifield of presentation:* Considerable research has shown that stimuli that are first seen in the left visual field will be initially processed in the right hemisphere and vice versa. If a verbal stimulus is presented in the left visual hemifield, it will, therefore, be processed slower and less efficiently than if it had been initially presented in the right hemifield, for the left hemisphere of the brain is more specialized toward verbal stimuli. The issue of visual field is important to consumer processing of print advertising with respect to ad location and layout within the ad, but is less relevant to the processing of television, which normally operates from a fixed central gaze.

Each of these causes of laterality shifts is correct within the confines of its own experimental paradigm. In a real-world setting, each will contribute to laterality, and make laterality difficult to observe. The greater the complexity of a stimulus, the less observable will be the lateral dominance as both hemispheres become implicated in processing.

In EEG studies, data are typically presented in terms of power or dominance. *Power* is operationalized by the *sum* of the electrical voltage across the right and left hemispheres at the lobes under consideration. Low levels of power are indicative of high levels of cognitive activity. *Dominance* is operationalized by the *difference* between the power levels at homologous sites (generally right minus left; often with normalizing corrections added). A negative value (or shift toward a lower value) is indicative of a lower level of power in the right hemisphere, and, therefore, more right processing, and right hemispheric laterality, or dominance.

Prior Work as it Relates to the Electroencephalogram–Memory Relation

Although there is an extensive literature relating to the spatial and spectral components of the stimulus–EEG relation, there is very little prior work that considers any dimension of the EEG–memory relation. Fortunately, though, there is another literature of value. The study of Evoked Response Potentials (ERP) provides valuable insights although the paradigm is quite different from that of EEG research.

In this paradigm, subjects are usually exposed to multiple repetitions (often greater than 100) of the same stimulus. The collected data are then averaged across trials before analysis begins. Data is usually in the form of power without respect to spatial or spectral concerns, but are considered in a temporal dimension. This temporal dimension is also different from what could be useful to the study of real-world stimuli, as the length of exposure is usually less than 250 milliseconds and the period of observation of the electrical patterns is usually less than 650 milliseconds. In addition, stimuli are closely controlled with respect to the visual field of exposure and the characteristics of the stimulus. Although this paradigm is clearly different and not directly relevant to the topic of this paper, the results that have emerged provide useful insights.

Studies have shown that levels of memory are related to patterns of ERP both during (a) the initial exposure period to the stimulus, and (b) the later memory test. There are clear differences between the electrical patterns when stimuli are remembered well as opposed to when the stimuli are poorly remembered. Both of these types of studies show that there is a clear relation between the process (as operationalized by the electrical patterns) and the result (as operationalized by the memory test).

The most relevant EEG study related to performance has shown that attentiveness (as operationalized by EEG) just prior to task instructions was strongly related to goodness of performance on the task.

A BRIEF STATEMENT OF METHOD

The method was similar in the several studies to be discussed. Right and left hemisphere occipital alpha were collected from right-handed adult women as they watched a stimulus videotape. They watched an acclimation tape, filled out a distractor questionnaire, watched the stimulus tape, and completed a questionnaire designed to measure memory of what they had seen. The stimulus tape consisted of programming with nine commercial messages imbedded. Sample sizes were 20 to 25 women per study.

The questionnaire consisted of a series of unaided recall and recognition items. Most relevant to this discussion were the series of recognition items consisting of slides and script lines that may have come from scenes in the target messages. The research stream focused on the incidental learning of commercial messages imbedded in television programming.

The EEG data were Fourier transformed, aggregated every half second, and normalized (Z) within subjects; the data were then aggregated across subjects (median) for each half second at each location. Sixty (half-second) period dependent variable EEG time series were constructed, based on these half-second units for each commercial; dependent variables considered dominance and power in separate sets of models. The time series constructed for the independent stimulus variables were based on nine verbal and nonverbal elements of the audio and video tracks of the videotape.

Time series analysis was used to study the stimulus–EEG relation; the EEG-memory relation was examined, using correlations between the EEG patterns during the first 5 half seconds of the onset of a scene, and recognition of that scene.

A SUMMARY OF RESULTS TO DATE

In this section, results are presented with respect to the linkages of the $S–O–R$ model; EEG applications in a consumer psychology and advertising setting are shown.

Results as they Apply to the Advertising– Electroencephalogram Relation

The goals of this aspect of the work were to establish that the findings from the basic literature discussed previously would hold in the complex setting of viewing televised advertising, and that these findings would be valid. (This section is a summary of work reported upon in more detail in Reeves et al., 1985 and Rothschild, Hyun, Reeves, Thorson, & Goldstein, 1988.)

EEG Changes With Respect to Changes in Television Commercials. The most basic issue to be explored considered whether there was a significant linkage between S and O. One study considered *power* at the occiput as the dependent variable with scene changes and character movement as the independent variables. Alpha change occurred across periods of 3 to 8 seconds during which alpha blocked in response to the onset of the independent variables and then slowly attenuated. Alpha blocking occurred during the first half second after the onset of the independent variable. Thirty-seven percent of the variance in alpha was accounted for by the two independent variables and another 20% of the variance was accounted for due to autocorrelation.

In a second study, occipital *dominance* was the dependent variable and was a function of nine independent variables that covered verbal and nonverbal components of both the audio and video tracks of the television commercials. These variables covered, for example, actors speaking and voice-overs (verbal–audio), sound effects, and nonverbal music (nonverbal–audio), appearance of package and supers (verbal–video), and camera movements, edits, and actor movements (nonverbal–video).

A time-series regression model was developed for each of the nine commercials. Significant portions ($p < .05$) of the variance in dominance scores were explained for six of the nine commercials; marginally significant ($p < .1$) portions were explained in two of the remaining three. Changes in EEG were seen to be a function of changes in the stimulus environment.

Verbal Aspects of the Stimulus Lead to Shifts Toward Left Dominance, Whereas Nonverbal Aspects Lead to Shifts Toward the Right.   Across the nine regression models, there were 26 independent variable cells that made either a significant or a marginally significant contribution. In all cases, the contribution was in the expected direction; that is, the verbal stimulus variables all contributed to left-dominance shifts and the nonverbal components all contributed to a shift toward right dominance. These data confirm that the findings relating to the specialization of the hemispheres hold even with a complex stimulus.

The Hemispheres Change Together.   Even though verbal and nonverbal stimuli cause differing lateral shifts, the correlation of the time series across the hemispheres is also strong. The average correlation across the nine commercial time series models was .62. This is consistent with the notion of parallel or bilateral processing across the hemispheres and is also consistent with the notion that, although the hemispheres seem to have specializations, both hemispheres are involved in all processing and the specialization may be less observable as the complexity of the stimulus increases. There was significantly more bilateral processing (higher correlation) during the rational commercials than during the emotional commercials. The results presented here, in conjunction with those of the previous paragraph, seem to work together to support the earlier literature with respect to what should happen during the processing of a complex stimulus with both verbal and nonverbal components.

Lag Effects Exist Between the Onset of a Stimulus Change and a Shift in Laterality.   The average lag between the onset of the stimulus and an observable hemispheric change was 1180 milliseconds. More interestingly, EEG changes lagged the verbal stimuli by a significantly greater amount than the nonverbal stimuli; this could be an indicator that verbal stimuli are processed differently than nonverbal ones and that EEG changes are more than mere orienting responses.

EEG Data Are Reliable.   Several reliability tests have been performed both within a study and across separate data sets with respect to the $S-O$ relation. Within one study, the time-series correlations were examined for each of the nine commercials and each of the two hemispheres across three different groups of subjects, who were defined by the order in which they saw the commercials. In the 54 different correlations that resulted, over 75% of them were significant

($p < .05$). In spite of the different context effects created by the different orders of the commercials, the data nevertheless showed a strong reliability when examining the relation between changes in the commercial and changes in EEG.

There were also strong similarities in the data across two different studies. As stated earlier, the average correlation across the hemispheres for the nine commercials of one study was .62; in the other study, this correlation was .68. The average lag that was earlier reported as 1180 milliseconds in one study was 1100 milliseconds in the other study when comparable independent variables were considered.

Of the nine commercials examined in one study, three were also used in the other study. The correlations of the 60-point time series plots for each of the three commercials were 0.33 ($p < .01$), 0.48 ($p < .001$), and 0.29 ($p < .02$), respectively. These correlations existed even though the commercials were imbedded in different programs and surrounded by different other commercials. Finally, the $S-O$ relation showed face validity. The patterns of data were consistent with what would be expected, based on the earlier literature based on simpler stimuli and more closely controlled conditions. None of the findings were inconsistent with the literature. It should also be noted that there was no prior data-based literature to support the expectation of what would happen in a complex stimulus environment.

Results as They Apply to the Electroencephalogram–Memory Relation

The goals again were to establish that the findings from the basic literature discussed previously would hold in the complex setting of viewing television advertising, and that these findings would be reliable. While the $S-O$ relation is important in order to establish that EEG does change as a result of its environment, the $O-R$ relation is more important because it gives insights for information processing and memory development theories. This relation can be considered from the perspective of overall EEG–overall learning as well as the perspective of component EEG–component memory. Both will be examined. (This section is a summary of work reported upon in more detail in Rothschild and Hyun 1989; Rothschild, Thorson, Reeves, Hirsch, and Goldstein, 1986.)

Overall Electroencephalogram–Overall Memory.   Other researchers who have investigated the virtues of EEG with respect to advertising have most often focused on an overall view of this issue and the results have been mixed. Weinstein, in one study (Appel, Weinstein, & Weinstein, 1979) found a significant relation, but was unable to replicate it in a second study (Weinstein, Appel, & Weinstein, 1980). Rust (Rust, Price, & Kumar, 1985), Olson and Ray (1983), and Rockey (Rockey, Greene, & Perold, 1980) all showed mixed results with respect to this focus. We have confirmed the equivocality of findings here. In one study, there was a strong negative correlation between overall power and summary measures of recall and recognition. In a second study, these results were not replicated with respect to either power or dominance.

In retrospect, it is easy to explain why this linkage is so tenuous. The virtue of examining EEG is in the microscopic insights yielded with respect to processing. The insights come because there is a high degree of variance occurring within brief time periods. When the data are pooled with respect to time, the variance disappears, and, with it, the benefit of EEG disappears also. It is interesting to note that this phenomenon relates to pooled variance with time periods as short as 2 seconds. The patterns that are reported here are generally not observable when the unit of analysis is 2 seconds or greater in length.

Component Electroencephalogram–Component Memory.   In this analysis, correlations between the two more compact variables are considered. Memory components were derived from the results of a recognition test wherein subjects were asked if they had previously seen slides that may have come from the commercials they had been shown. EEG was considered during the pre-onset period (the 3 half-seconds preceding the onset of a scene), during the onset of a scene (the first 2 half-seconds), and during the following period (the next three half-seconds). Scores were derived for the change in EEG between the pre-onset and onset periods, and between the onset and following periods for both power and dominance. (Change scores were adjusted as per Cohen & Cohen, 1975.) This method yielded the four components of EEG that will be discussed; each of these components could be correlated with the memory score for the scene occurring during the time at which the EEG had been collected. Fig. 12.1 shows these data for well versus poorly recognized components.

There was no significant correlation between *power during the onset period* and memory. Because a power change (alpha blocking) is felt to be involuntary, the change occurring in onset power should occur independent of memory.

Whether alpha blocking continues or not is determined by the interest that the individual has in the stimulus. As a result, *power in the following period* should relate to memory. The data showed a significant negative correlation ($p < .05$) between lagged power and memory based on the 97 observations of slide recognition and EEG. This meant that EEG attenuated rapidly for those scenes that were remembered poorly but that blocking continued into the lagged period for those scenes that were remembered well.

Stronger learning should occur if there is a shift toward right *dominance during the onset period;* this shift would be signified by a negative correlation. The data showed a marginal negative correlation ($p < .08$), indicating a weak relation between this shift to vigilance and enhanced recognition. Several models of EEG and learning described earlier hypothesize that such a shift is necessary for learning to occur.

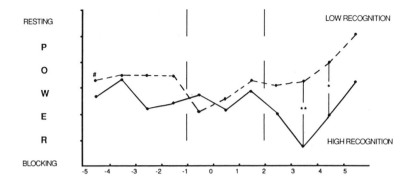

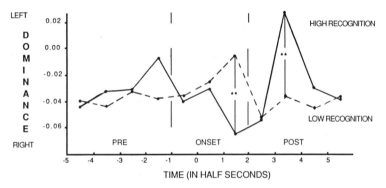

#DATA REPRESENT MOVING AVERAGES OVER TWO TIME POINTS AND ARE PLOTTED
BETWEEN TIME MARKERS

* p < .10
** p < .05

FIG. 12.1.   Patterns of EEG for high and low levels of memory. From Rothschild and Hyun (1990). Reproduced by permission of *Journal of Consumer Research* (March, 1990).

Dominance in the following period should shift to the left as an indicator of a learning type of processing. There was a significant shift ($p < .05$) to the left during the following period. This dominance reversal was an indicator of learning that was manifested in a higher recognition level when it occurred.

High recognition scores were tied to longer periods of alpha blocking and slower attenuation, as well as a shift toward the right hemisphere in the onset period followed by a shift toward the left during the following period. These characteristics of learning were observable when scenes were learned well.

In *low recognition cases,* this pattern did not occur. More rapid attenuation was an indicator that attention was not maintained beyond the initial arousal. In addition, the pattern of dominance shifts differed. When subsequent recognition was poor, there was more likely to be early left dominance followed by a shift to the right. Perhaps this reverse shift was a result of continued attention to the prior scene. The early shift to the left for the target scene that resulted in poor recognition also may have been a late shift to the left for the prior scene, which may have resulted in good learning of it.

In examining the onset and following periods, one can see that the correlations were stronger during the following scenes. Again, this may be due to the impact of a prior scene on processing. The onset period of the target scene may also be the following period of the prior scene. This duality would lead to weaker correlations in the onset periods and would also lead to the shift reversals described in the previous paragraph. These occurrences would not appear elsewhere in the literature because there are no other studies that examine an ongoing stimulus in this same way.

EEG Data are Reliable.   Some of the O–R tests described also have been replicated. In the replication, student subjects saw a series of nine commercials without programming. The commercials were separated by 30 seconds of black during which the subjects had their eyes closed. Whereas the data from the last 20 seconds of each commercial replicated the previous findings, the data from the first 10 seconds did not. Perhaps subjects need to be in a "processing mode" in order to do so; when they had just finished sitting in the dark with their eyes closed, it seemed to take them some time (approximately 10 seconds) to get into a processing mode.

The data from the last 20 seconds of each commercial was consistent with the previously reported findings. There was no relation between onset memory and EEG, but there was a significant relation between following EEG and memory. Lagged power correlated negatively with memory; that is, EEG power attenuated rapidly for those scenes where recognition was poor and remained low for those scenes where recognition was strong. Lagged dominance correlated positively with memory; that is, EEG dominance shifted toward the right for those scenes where recognition was poor and toward the left for those scenes where memory was strong.

DISCUSSION

One virtue of collecting online data at such a micro level is that the researcher can examine dependent variables as they develop through the commercial. Given the combination of sites on the scalp being considered, different sorts of diagnostic plots might emerge. For example, occipital power could show when attention levels were higher and lower during a commercial; dominance shifts could show at what points learning might be more likely to be taking place; frontal site data (not discussed in this chapter) might give insights into affective shifts as the commercial progressed.

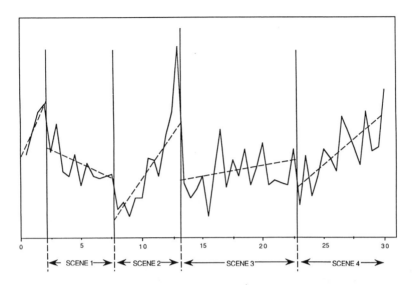

FIG. 12.2   Occipital alpha power for 30-second commercial.

A graphic representation of occipital power data is presented in Fig. 12.2 for a regional hot dog brand. The jagged line is the actual power data, the overlaid smooth line represents the slopes between the vertical lines, and the vertical lines show the demarcations of the epochs; epochs are defined by a specific scoring system but generally are bounded by the periods with the largest drops in power. (This section is a summary of work reported upon in more detail in Rothschild et al., 1986.)

In the commercial in the figure, there are two types of scenes. One type shows children playing baseball; the other shows families at a picnic with the product being roasted and shown through close-up shots along with the package. Scene 1 shows baseball; attention is held well as alpha remains low. Scene 2 sells hotdogs via the picnic; attention is lost as alpha power increases rapidly. In Scene 3, children are again playing baseball and attention is again held well. Finally, in Scene 4, there are more product, package and picnic shots, which do not hold attention well.

It seems that the advertiser knew the value of borrowed interest and knew that children were good at creating this borrowed interest. Unfortunately, the borrowed interest and the product are not coordinated and, as a result, may have competed. Overall, the commercial has two scenes that hold attention quite well, but the product is not being sold at these times. Perhaps a better commercial would have the children more well integrated into the selling of the product.

In future work, we will attempt to develop these diagnostics with respect to dominance as well as power, and also will coordinate this type of plot with the EEG-memory data described previously. Although the main thrust of this chapter dealt with examining theoretic issues of information processing, the analysis shown via Fig. 12.2 may be of great value to practitioners as a commercial diagnostic device.

Most current information processing work exposes a subject to a stimulus (for example a 30-second television commercial) and then asks for retrospective and introspective assessment of the processes that took place within the subject. Furthermore, these evaluations are based on constructs and questions imposed by the researcher upon the subject. The data presented here suggest that an enormous amount of processing occurs during a 30-second commercial and that processing cannot be completely addressed via introspective and/or retrospective assessment of hypothetical constructs. By considering arousal and memory only at the macro level, too much information is lost. The work presented here hopefully will lead to a reassessment of some of the basic concepts of information processing as practiced by those in consumer research.

It is time to pursue a new field that may be termed *micro information processing;* there are currently several other researchers who are also working with physiologic tools and units of time that are smaller than the entire message. Although other tools also can provide insight to processing, EEG has the richest potential, for it can be observed at multiple locations on the scalp and at multiple electrical frequencies at each location. Interpretation of this richer data set may ultimately lead to a better understanding of information processing and learning.

We have not found any other work that links EEG to memory in cases of complex stimuli; neither the EEG nor the memory literature provides this work. Perhaps the greatest contribution of this work to these areas is methodologic; the knowledge of the relationship between EEG, information processing, and memory is not new, but the ability to show these relationships with complex stimuli over time is new. Whereas the simple stimuli used in earlier studies represent static presentations, the current work examines a dynamic stimulus unfolding with the passage of time.

ACKNOWLEDGMENTS

The author thanks Yong Hyun, Esther Thorson, Byron Reeves, Brian Deith, Lisa Qualheim, Robert Goldstein, Richard Davidson, and Judith Hirsch for assistance in various forms; and the University of Wisconsin, Marketing Science Institute, Bruzzone Research, American Broadcasting Company, and Mc-Collum/Spielman Research for financial assistance as this project developed over the past few years.

REFERENCES

Appel, V., Weinstein, S., & Weinstein, C. (1979). Brain activity and recall of TV advertising. *Journal of Advertising Research, 19*(4), 7–15.

Cohen, J., & Cohen, P. (1975). *Applied multiple regression/correlation analysis for the social sciences*. Hillsdale, NJ: Lawrence Erlbaum Associates.

Olson, J., & Ray, W. (1983). *Brain wave responses to emotional versus attribute oriented television commercials*. Working Paper No. 83-108, Marketing Science Institute, Cambridge, MA.

Reeves, B. B., Thorson, E., Rothschild, M. L., McDonald, D., Hirsch, J. E., & Goldstein, R. (1985). Attention to television: Intrastimulus effect of movement and scene changes on alpha variation over time. *International Journal of Neuroscience, 27*(3&4), 241–256.

Rockey, E. A., Green, W. F., & Perold, E. A. (1980). *Attention, memory and attitudinal reactions to television commercials under single and multiple exposure conditions as measured by brain research*. Paper presented at the Advertising Research Foundation's 26th Annual Conference, New York, NY.

Rothschild, M. L., & Hyun, Y. J. (1990). Predicting memory from EEG. *Journal of Consumer Research, 16*(3), 472–478.

Rothchild, M. L., Hyun, Y. J., Reeves, B., Thorson, E., & Goldstein, R. (1988). Hemispherically lateralized EEG as a response to television commercials. *Journal of Consumer Research, 15*(2), 185–198.

Rothchild, M. L., Thorson, E., Reeves, B. B., Hirsch, J. E., & Goldstein, R. (1986). EEG activity and the processing of television commercials. *Communication Research, 13*(2), 102–220.

Rust, R. T., Price, L. L., & Kumar, V. (1985). EEG response to advertisements in print and broadcast media (Working paper No. 85-111). Cambridge, MA: Marketing Science Institute.

Weinstein, S., Appel, V., & Weinstein, C. (1980). Brain activity responses to magazine and television advertising. *Journal of Advertising Research, 20*(3), 57–63.

13 Concluding Remarks

Andrew A. Mitchell
University of Toronto

The chapters in this volume make a number of contributions to our understanding of advertising effects. These contributions fall into the following three general areas: (a) contributions to advertising exposure models, (b) examination of the effects of multiple advertisements for the same brand, and (c) linkages between advertising exposure and choice. The ensuing discussion deals with each area in turn.

ADVERTISING EXPOSURE MODELS

As mentioned in the introduction, our understanding of how the psychological processes that occur during advertising exposure affect attitude formation and change, and the mediators of this relationship, are generally well known. Here message relevance or processing set has been found to affect the type of processing that occurs during advertising exposure. Under high message relevance consumers actively process the information in advertisements with the goal of evaluating the advertised product or service. Under low message relevance or an advertising processing set consumers focus on elements of the advertisement which interests them or require little effort to process. Both the Elaboration Likelihood model and the approaches that focus on goals and processing strategies fit within this framework (e.g., Petty & Cacioppo, 1985; Gardner, 1985; Lichtenstein & Srull, 1985).

Recent research has indicated that the relationship between the mediators of attitude formation and change is best described by the Dual Mediation Model under both a brand or an advertising processing set (e.g., Homer, 1990). According to this model attitude toward the ad has both a direct and an indirect effect on brand attitudes. Indirectly, attitude toward the ad affects, the number of support and counterarguments that are generated, which in turn affect brand attitudes (MacKenzie, Lutz, & Belch, 1986). A review of this general conceptualization of the effects of psychological processing on brand attitudes during advertising exposure can be found in MacInnis and Jaworski (1989).

The research underlying our current understanding of advertising effects indicates that attitudes are relatively easy to change. In contrast, Zanna (Chapter 5) notes that 40 years ago, most research indicated that it was very difficult to change attitudes. In attempting to resolve these differences, Zanna notes that while the earlier research on attitude change generally examined important, ego-involving, social issues (e.g., racial integration), more recent research, tends to examine less important topics such as attitudes toward new razors or facial tissues. He suggests that individuals are likely to be "closed minded" in ego involving situations and proposes measures such as attitude accessibility and the size of the latitude of acceptance as means of determining whether or not a message recipient is "closed minded."

The formation of inferences during exposure to advertisements is an important topic that has been largely ignored in the development of advertising exposure models. In his chapter (Chapter 6), Kardes discusses the two necessary conditions for consumers to form inferences from advertisements. The first condition is that the consumer must be motivated to form an inference and the second is that an inference must be required to make a specific judgment. This suggests that consumers will form inferences in high issue involvement conditions and when an explicit conclusion is not provided in the advertisement. Kardes then discusses when the inferences that are formed may be biased.

There has been considerable research recently examining how positive affect may influence cognitive processes such as recall and decision making. In Chapter 9, Isen discusses recent research on the effects of positive affect on cognitive organization and decision processes. This research indicates that positive affect experienced during advertising exposure may affect choice in a number of different ways. For instance, Isen suggests that when viewing an advertisement, positive affect may influence how consumers categorize the advertised product and may make them more receptive to image enhancing products. In addition, positive affect may cause consumers to think more innovatively about the advertised product and may cause them to create more associations with highly evaluated products and product categories. These effects on the learning of information from advertisements may later influence decision making in a number of ways. For instance, since positive affect caused consumers to think about the product innovatively, this will create many different types of associations. Consequently, this information may be accessed by many different retrieval cues. This increases the likelihood that the brand and the learned information will be retrieved in a given purchase situation. In addition, the innovative thinking will also cause the advertised product to be perceived as relevant for many different situations.

Most of the previous research examining advertising effects has examined the role of informational and emotional advertisements. The former present information about the attributes of the advertised brand, while the latter are designed to evoke an emotional response in the consumer. Deighton and Hoch (Chapter 10) remind us of a third type of advertisement—drama advertisements. These ads use drama or a story to communicate information about the advertised product. Deighton and Hoch argue that with informational advertisements the advertiser has more control over what is communicated, but less control over how consumers react to the communication. For instance, an advertisement that states that a particular model of automobile gets 40 miles per gallon is certain to communicate this information to the consumer, however, the consumer may choose to disbelieve this claim and counterargue against it. On the other hand, a drama advertisement may portray a situation, for instance, where someone is driving on a desolate highway in the appropriate model of automobile and is almost out of gas. The driver becomes increasingly worried when she realizes that she has only one gallon of gas left. She then sees a sign that indicates that there is a gasoline station 35 miles away and gives a sigh of relief because she knows that her automobile gets 40 miles to the gallon. In this situation, it is less likely that the consumer will encode this piece of information, however, at the same time, the consumer is less likely to counterargue against it.

Deighton and Hoch also argue that effective drama advertisements should demonstrate that the advertised product creates emotional feelings and the drama must be relevant to the consumer. They then evaluate four television commercials using these criteria.

Gengler and Reynolds (Chapter 11) discuss a methodology for applying the MECCA model for evaluating television commercials. The MECCA model applies mean-ends analysis to examine the linkages between the message element, consumer benefit, leverage point and driving force. Gengler and Reynolds present evidence that if an advertisement provides the linkages between these different levels to a consumer, the consumer will tend to evaluate the advertised brand higher.

Finally, Rothchild (Chapter 12) discusses the results of a number of studies that examine the relationship between different physical elements of television advertisements and EEG measures. Relationships between verbal elements of commercials (e.g., voice overs), nonverbal elements (e.g., sound effects and music), video elements (e.g., camera movements) and occipital dominance are reported. Verbal elements in the ad seem to cause shifts toward left dominance, while nonverbal elements cause shifts toward right dominance at an average lag of around 1180 multiseconds. Mixed results were found between measures of

EEG and measures of memory (e.g., recognition and recall), however, advertisements that scored poorly on recognition tests seemed to have a different pattern of EEG measures than advertisements that scored highly on recognition tests. The latter advertisements had longer periods of alpha blocking and a shift toward the right hemisphere in the onset period followed by a shift to the left during the following period.

MULTIPLE ADVERTISEMENTS FOR ONE BRAND

Although a number of studies have examined the effects of multiple exposures to a single message (e.g., Cacioppo & Petty, 1979) or to related messages (e.g., Cacioppo & Petty, 1985), most of this research has only examined the effect of advertising repetition within the same medium on attitudes and cognitive responses. In some situations, advertising repetition seems to cause attitudes to have an inverted U shaped relationship (e.g., Cacioppo & Petty, 1979), whereas in other situations advertising repetition has no effect on brand attitudes (e.g., Mitchell & Olson, 1981). In order to understand when advertising repetition will affect attitudes in a particular situation and the effect of advertising in a different medium, a finer grained view of the underlying psychological processes is required.

In this vein, Edell (Chapter 7) discusses the psychological processes that may occur during exposure to a second advertisement, which occurs either in the same or in a different medium. Of particular interest, is the situation where one of the advertisements contains only audio (radio) and the other has both video and audio (television), and when the audio portion of the radio and television advertisements are the same. Under these conditions, exposure to the second advertisement may activate the memory trace of the first advertisement and this activation may interfere with the processing of the second commercial. When the advertisements are in the same medium, the memory trace of the first advertisement seems to reinforce and accentuate the type of processing that occurred during exposure to the first advertisement.

On a related topic, Mitchell (Chapter 8) examines different attitude change processes that occur during exposure to a second message. In this study, subjects executed a brand processing strategy during exposure to advertisements with highly valenced photographs, which were designed to create brand attitudes that are based primarily on attitude toward the ad. These attitudes are then changed by presenting the subjects with information about the brands 2 weeks later.

Regression analysis is used to test a number of models of different attitude change processes. The results indicate that the subjects used an anchor and adjust model in changing attitudes where the previous attitude toward the brand was the anchor and adjustment was based on the new beliefs formed about the brand.

Both of these chapters indicate that prior exposure to advertising for a brand will affect the processing of additional advertisements for the brand. Understanding the effect of previous advertising exposures on the subsequent processing of advertisements for the same brand in the same or different medium is an important research topic that has been largely ignored in previous research examining advertising effects.

ADVERTISING AND CHOICE

A number of the chapters also present different perspectives on extending advertising exposure models to include brand choice processes. The first, by Keller (Chapter 1), develops a framework for understanding when the retrieval of advertising information will affect purchase decisions. In this framework, the same factors that affect encoding processes—motivation, ability and opportunity—are also hypothesized to affect retrieval processes. Keller argues that the level of motivation in the retrieval process is determined by the perceived value of the advertising information, while ability is determined by both the organization of the information in memory and the availability of internal and external retrieval cues. Finally, opportunity is affected by both the amount of distraction in the environment and by time pressure. These three factors affect retrieval processes which are conceptualized as having two dimensions—intensity and direction. Intensity refers to the amount of effort devoted to retrieving the information, while direction refers to the direction of search in memory.

Keller then focuses on the effect of advertising retrieval cues at the point of purchase. These retrieval cues increase the probability that advertising memory traces will be retrieved and influence purchase decisions. The use of these retrieval cues are especially critical when there are both weak and strong linkages between the advertising memory trace and the brand name. The problem with strong linkages occurs when an advertiser makes major changes in an advertising campaign. In these situations consumers are more likely to retrieve the advertising memory traces from the old campaign than from the new campaign when making purchase decisions. When there are weak linkages, the advertising memory trace may not be retrieved in a purchase situation. Keller then discusses the results of a number of studies that support this conceptualization.

Chapter 4 by Herr and Fazio discuss Fazio's process model of how attitudes guide behavior and an extension of this model, the Dual Mode Model. According to the process model, attitude accessibility moderates the relationship between an individual's attitude toward an object and his or her behavior toward that object. Here the accessibility of an attitude is conceptualized as the strength of the link between the representation of the attitude and the object in memory. Attitudes that are highly accessible will generally be activated in most behavioral situations and, therefore, will make the attitude object more salient in the environment and cloud the perceptions of the object. In other words, if an individual has a positive attitude toward an object, then she or he will tend to perceive only positive aspects of the object.

Herr and Fazio argue that the process model is applicable in situations where the individual either lacks the motivation or the opportunity to engage in effortful reasoning and reflection in deciding on a course of action. Here the level of motivation is determined by the individual's "fear of invalidity" in the particular situation. If there is little fear that a poor decision will result in undesirable consequences, then she or he will not be motivated to engage in effortful processing. If on the other hand, the individual fears that a poor decision will lead to undesirable outcomes and, is therefore motivated to engage in effortful processing and has the opportunity to do so, then he will carefully consider the consequences of alternative behavior as defined by the Theory of Reasoned Action (Fishbein & Ajzen, 1975).

The third model, which links advertising exposure and the choice process, the Relevance-Accessibility Model (RAM), is described by Baker (Chapter 2). Baker uses the Level of Representation Model (Greenwald & Levitt, 1985) to explain the effect of motivation at advertising exposure. According to this model, with low motivation only affective reactions toward the brand are stored in memory. This may occur either through frequent exposure to the advertising (e.g., mere exposure) or from affective reactions to the advertisement itself. With moderate levels of motivation, the consumer focuses on the structure of the advertisement thereby forming a memory trace of the advertisement. A consumer may remember, for instance, that an advertisement for a motor oil featured a famous racing driver or an advertisement for a shampoo had a very attractive model. Finally, with high levels of motivation, consumers actively process attribute level information from the advertisement and store this information in memory.

The level of motivation will also vary when choice decisions are made and the type of information used in making a decision will depend on this level of motivation. When motivation is low, consumers will not actively search for information in memory and will, consequently, rely on affective information. With moderate levels of motivation, consumers will tend to retrieve the memory trace of the advertisement and use primarily structural information from the ad in making a choice. Finally, at high levels of motivation they will actively search for and use attribute information about the alternative brands in making a choice.

The key idea in the model is that the appropriate information must be available in memory for a particular brand in order for it to be chosen when the purchase decision is made. In other words, if only attribute information about a particular brand is available in memory and the motivation in the purchase decision is low, then the brand probably will not be selected because consumers will not expend the effort required to retrieve and evaluate alternatives using this information.

Alternatively, if only affective information about the brand is available in memory and the motivation level in the purchase decision is very high, then the affective information will not be used, because the consumer will base his or her decision on attribute information. Consequently, in order for advertising information to have an effect on choice, the level of motivation during advertising exposure must match the level of motivation at the purchase decision. In his chapter, Baker briefly discusses the results of an experiment which provides strong support for this proposition.

The final chapter discussing the link between advertising exposure and choice is by Nedungadi, Mitchell, and Berger (Chapter 3). In discussing this link, the authors first examine the choice process and the factors that may affect it. They conceptualize the choice process as consisting of three stages. These are: (a) generation of alternatives, (b) consideration of alternatives, and (c) selection of an alternative. They hypothesize that both the content of different types of information and its accessibility will affect each stage of the choice process. For instance, they hypothesize that brand accessibility will affect whether or not a brand is retrieved at the first stage. Attitudes and attitude accessibility are most likely to affect whether a brand is considered for choice, while at the choice stage attribute information and its accessibility will generally determine which alternative is selected. They also discuss how motivation and opportunity will affect the different stages of the choice process and potential differences in these stages for memory versus stimulus based choices. Finally, they present the results of a study which demonstrates the benefits of their approach.

TOWARD A MODEL LINKING ADVERTISING EXPOSURE AND CHOICE

As mentioned before, a number of the chapters in this volume present a conceptualization of the link between advertising exposure and choice. These include chapters by Keller (Chapter 1), Baker (Chapter 2), Nedungadi, Mitchell, and Berger (Chapter 3), and Fazio and Herr (Chapter 5). There are many similarities between these conceptualizations, however, there are also important differences. In their conceptualizations, Keller, Fazio and Herr, and Nedungadi, Mitchell and Berger focus primarily on the choice process. Only the framework presented by Baker specifically considers the relationship between advertising exposure and choice.

Since all four conceptualizations examine choice processes, we begin here in examining the similarities and differences. In all four conceptualizations, the level of motivation to retrieve information from memory and to process it to reach a decision plays an important role. In three of the conceptualizations (Fazio and Herr, Keller and Nedungadi, Mitchell and Berger) the opportunity to retrieve information from memory and process it to reach a decision is also considered. In all these conceptualizations motivation is determined by the perceived *cost* of making a poor decision while opportunity is determined by time pressure and distractions in the environment. When either motivation or opportunity are low, the consumer is believed to expend minimal effort in making a choice.

In the MODE Model discussed by Fazio and Herr, when either motivation or opportunity are low, consumers rely on their attitudes toward each of the different alternatives in making a choice. Although Fazio and Herr do not explicitly consider the final stage of the choice process, their model seems to imply that a consumer needs to have formed an attitude toward an alternative brand and the attitude has to be accessible in order for the brand to be considered for choice. If the consumer has not formed an attitude toward a brand and if the attitude is not accessible, then the brand probably will not be considered for choice when either motivation or opportunity is low.

When motivation and opportunity are high, consumers follow the Theory of Reasoned Action (Fishbein & Ajzen, 1975). This would imply that consumers form an attitude toward purchasing a brand based on attribute information and a behavioral intention by also considering the opinions of relevant others toward the particular choice. Although there is evidence that consumers may make direct comparisons between alternatives on different attributes in making a choice, the general notion that consumers actively process information about the alternatives in making a decision under these conditions has received considerable support in the literature (e.g., Sanbonmatsu & Fazio, 1990).

Keller (Chapter 1) focuses on the effects of motivation and opportunity on the retrieval of an advertising memory trace. The implication here is that in most advertising exposure situations, consumers do not actively process the information in the advertisement. Consequently, in order for an advertisement to have an effect in a purchase situation, consumers must retrieve the memory trace of the advertisement in order for it to affect the choice process.

The likelihood of retrieving the memory trace of an advertisement in a given purchase situation depends on the strength of the link between the brand node in memory and the memory trace of the advertisement. If there is a strong link, the memory trace of the advertisement will generally be recalled in a purchase situation. However, when the link is weak, a memory trace of the advertisement will only be retrieved when both motivation and opportunity are high. When motivation and opportunity are low, retrieval cues will be required to increase the likelihood that the advertising memory trace is retrieved. Examples of retrieval cues are scenes from a television advertisement on the package or on display signage.

As discussed previously, Baker (Chapter 2) presents a model that integrates advertising exposure with the choice processes. The critical variables that link these two events are the motivation to process information about the advertised brand during advertising exposure and the motivation to retrieve and process information about alternative brands in making a purchase decision.

In making a choice, Baker hypothesizes that motivation affects both the process and the type of information used in making a choice. With low motivation, consumers make choices using only affective information, whereas with moderate levels of motivation consumers retrieve a memory trace of the advertisement and then rely on heuristics based on the structure of the advertisement (e.g., attractiveness of the model). Finally, with high levels of motivation, consumers actively compare alternatives along different attributes.

At this point, it may be instructive to make a quick comparison between these different conceptual models or frameworks. Keller's framework seems to fit primarily with moderate levels of motivation at both advertising exposure and the purchase decision in Baker's model. At this level, consumers focus primarily on the structure of the advertisement during advertising exposure and are motivated to try to retrieve the advertisement in purchase situations. With low levels of motivation in the purchase decision, however, the use of retrieval cues may allow the advertising memory trace to be retrieved spontaneously or with very little effort. Consequently, advertising memory traces may have an effect at this level.

There are clear parallels between the Baker model and the Fazio and Herr's MODE Model under high levels of motivation in the purchase decision. With both models, consumers use attribute information stored in memory to make a choice. There are fewer parallels under low levels of motivation. Here the MODE Model assumes that consumers use accessible attitudes in making a choice, while the Baker model assumes that consumers have not formed attitudes toward any of the competing brands. Consequently, it might be hypothesized that the MODE Model would hold if highly accessible attitudes have been formed for at least one of the alternatives and Baker's model will hold otherwise.

The fourth model, by Nedungadi, Mitchell, and Berger differs from the other models in that it conceptualizes the choice process as having three stages. The first is an alternative generation stage where the alternatives to be considered are either retrieved from memory or recognized in the purchase environment. At the second stage, a preliminary screening of the alternatives is performed to eliminate unacceptable alternatives. Finally, at the third stage, a choice is made between the remaining alternatives.

Different types of information (brand, attribute levels, and brand attitudes), the content of this information, and its accessibility in memory will affect different stages of the choice process. For instance, the accessibility of a brand will affect whether it is generated as an alternative. The authors hypothesize that the valence and accessibility of brand attitudes of the generated alternatives will be used for screening alternatives, while consumers will generally use attribute information to make a choice.

The authors argue that advertising exposure will affect the content and accessibility of the three types of information. For instance, a large number of studies have demonstrated that advertising exposure will affect brand attitudes (e.g, Petty, Cacioppo, & Schumann, 1983; Mitchell & Olson, 1981) and attitude accessibility (Berger & Mitchell, 1989).

There are also many similarities and differences between this model and the other models. The MODE Model of Fazio and Herr, for instance, fits nicely within this framework. When either motivation or opportunity is low in the purchase decision, consumers may consider only brands with highly accessible attitudes by selecting the brand with the most favorable attitude. When both motivation and opportunity are high, the consumer may actively process attribute information in making a choice. It is also compatible with the Baker model under high and low levels of motivation in the purchase decision, although it does not explicitly consider the latter situation.

Although the Nedungadi, Mitchell, and Berger framework does not explicitly consider the use of memory for advertising messages in the decision process (as in Keller's model), it could easily accommodate this type of information. The framework also does not explicitly differentiate moderate levels of motivation from either high or low levels (as in Baker's model).

Finally, the Nedungadi, Mitchell, and Berger model extends the other models in at least two ways. First, they explicitly consider the alternative generation stage of the choice process. This is important because advertising exposure has generally been found to affect brand accessibility (e.g., Ray & Sawyer, 1971). This means that repeated advertising exposure is required to keep the brand name accessible in the consumer's mind. Second, the model explicitly considers the accessibility of attribute information in memory. Advertising exposure clearly affects the accessibility of attribute information and a growing body of literature indicates its importance in the choice process.

In an attempt to integrate these different conceptual models of how advertising exposure may affect the choice process, it is useful to first consider how information about alternative brands within a product category may be organized in memory. In considering this organization, we will rely primarily on a spreading activation theory of memory (Anderson, 1983). In such a model, a brand within a product category will probably be organized hierarchically with the highest node being the product category node. All the brands in the product category may be linked directly to the product category node or there may be additional layers with brands organized by subcategories (Fig. 13.1). Each of the links in this structure may vary in strength, which will determine the likelihood that a particular brand will be retrieved in a particular situation. The stronger the linkage or linkages between a brand and the product category, the more likely that brand will be retrieved when the product category is cued.

Both Hutchinson (1983) and Nedungadi (1990) present evidence for a multi-layer hierarchical structure for different product categories. Hutchinson (1983) found that the recall of different brands of analgesics by experts tended to cluster by type. This would be expected if these types represented different subcategories in the hierarchical organization. Nedungadi (1990) also found evidence for this type of structure for fast food restaurants, hamburger condiments and alcohol mixers. In this study, priming brands in different subcategories had differential effects on brand recall, consideration, and choice.

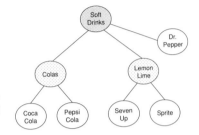

FIG. 13.1. Alternative structures linking brands to a product category.

At the brand level, a number of different types of information may be linked to a brand node. These different types of information include: (a) attribute values and other associations (e.g., types of people who use the brand), (b) attitudes and other types of affect (e.g., moods), and (c) a memory trace of different advertisements for the brand and possible attitudes toward each ad. Some of this information may be organized hierarchically (Fig. 13.2). Again each link may vary in strength, which affects the likelihood that a particular piece of information will be retrieved in a particular situation. In some situations, particular retrieval cues (e.g., a scene from an advertisement) may cue both the brand node and memory trace of the advertisement, which may result in different information being retrieved than if only the brand node were cued.

It is also possible that there may be links between different brands based on attributes or other types of information. For instance, there may be links between the number of miles per gallon that different automobiles obtain. In these situations, consumers may generate alternatives that have specific attribute values (e.g., automobiles that get over 40 miles per gallon).

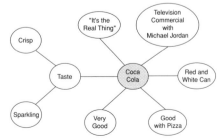

FIG. 13.2. Coca Cola knowledge structure for a hypothetical consumer.

In a particular purchase situation, the motivation and opportunity to avoid the *cost* of making a poor decision will vary. In addition, the amount of information available about the alternatives in the purchase environment will also vary. In some situations, no information about the alternatives is externally available (memory based choice), while in others the names of the alternatives or the actual packages of the alternatives will be available along with other possible retrieval cues (e.g., signage).

The choice process begins with the generation of alternatives. In memory based choice, the alternatives must be generated from memory, while in other situations the names or packages of the alternatives may be available in the environment. In this volume, Nedungadi, Mitchell, and Berger (Chapter 3) present evidence that when the number of alternatives available in the environment is large, the accessibility of the brands may influence which alternatives are considered and chosen. In general, when motivation and opportunity in the purchase decision are high, consumers will probably consider more alternatives.

During the decision process consumers will have a number of alternatives under active consideration (e.g., held in short term or working memory). Some of the information linked to each brand will also be activated for each alternative. What information is activated for each brand will determine how the decision will be made. Because individuals have control over what information is activated in memory, the information used in making a choice will be affected by the accessibility of the information and its perceived value or diagnosticity (Feldman & Lynch, 1988). In some cases, the most diagnostic information will also be the most accessible. This may occur if the same purchase decision has been made many times. Under these conditions, little effort will be required in making a choice. In other situations, the most diagnostic information may be inaccessible. This may occur if the purchase decision is being made for the first time. Under these conditions, the level of motivation and opportunity will determine what information is used. If either motivation or opportunity are low, the consumer may use the most accessible information in making a choice. If motivation and opportunity are high, then the consumer may expend the effort required to retrieve the most diagnostic information.

For many product categories, advertising may be the primary determinant of both how information about the different brands in a product category is organized in memory, and the accessibility of this information. However, in most situations other factors will also affect this organization and the accessibility of the information. As Baker (Chapter 2) points out, the motivation to process the information contained in the advertisement will determine what information is stored in memory for a particular brand and its organization and accessibility. What is important here is the type of information that is linked to the brand node and the accessibility of this information for one brand versus the other alternatives considered in a given situation. For a brand manager, they key is to make sure that the information that a consumer has about your brand is both more

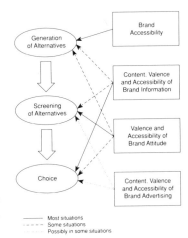

FIG. 13.3. The types and characteristics of the information hypothesized to affect each of the three stages of the choice process.

diagnostic and more accessible than the information about competing brands. Another requirement may be that consumers must have formed an attitude toward your brand, if they have formed attitudes toward competing brands, in order to have your brand considered (see Nedungadi, Mitchell, and Berger, Chapter 3).

A summary of this evolving framework, which contains the three different stages of the decision process and the types and characteristics of the information that may affect each stage is present in Fig. 13.3. In most situations, we believe that brand accessibility will be the primary determinate of the first stage—the generation of alternatives. In some situations, the generation of alternatives also may be affected by the perceived amount of a particular attribute the alternative has or the attitude toward the alternative. For instance, an individual may retrieve the names of restaurants that an individual believes are inexpensive or that s/he likes. This may occur when there are a large number of alternatives.

For the second study, screening of alternatives, we believe that attitudes will be used in most situations. Brands with favorable attitudes that are accessible will pass this screen and will be considered for choice. In some situations, when the motivation to make a good decision is high, screening may be based on more diagnostic information which may be less accessible.

Finally, in most situations, we believe that brand informations will be used to make the final choice. This information is generally the most diagnostic and with only a few brands in the consideration set, it will be relatively easy to compare the attribute values of the brands. In some situations, where motivation to make a good decision is very low, attitudes may be used to make the final choice.

What is unclear in this process is the possible effect of the content, valence and accessibility of brand advertising. Previous research has indicated that if individuals have not previously formed an attitude toward a brand, they may retrieve advertisements from memory to help them form an attitude (e.g., Beattie & Mitchell, 1985). However, if consumers have already formed attitudes toward competing brands, it is unclear if they would go to the effort of retrieving advertisements to form attitudes for brands without attitudes stored in memory. We suspect that in some cases they will if the advertisements are highly accessible and well liked. In these situations, the content and valence of the advertisement may affect either the screening of alternatives or choice.

The framework presented in Fig. 13.3, is primarily for memory based choice. Additional research is needed to determine if it is also appropriate for mixed choice situations.

Future Research

Although the chapters in this volume present the beginnings of a conceptual framework of how advertising exposure affects choice, additional research is clearly needed in order to flesh out this framework. Although there are a large number of research issues that remain to be answered, we will mention only five.

The first issue is the need to obtain a better understanding of how advertising affects the organization of information about brands within a product category in memory. This organization includes both the linkages between each brand and the product category node and the organization of information for each brand. For instance, one might hypothesize that comparative advertising may affect the hierarchical structure linking the brands to the product category node and produce possible linkages between brands along specific attributes.

The second issue concerns the development of a model to explain which alternatives are generated in particular purchase situations. For instance, is generation based entirely on the hierarchical product category structure and the linkages between brands along specific attributes? Under what conditions do consumers use other procedures such as the generation of ad-hoc categories described by Barsalou (1983)?

The need to understand the conditions that determine when consumers retrieve the memory trace of an advertisement and use this information in making a choice is the third issue. Under what conditions will advertising information be diagnostic or will it only be used if it is highly accessible? Under some conditions consumers may simply use an estimate of the amount of advertising for a particular brand as an indication of quality (Kirmani & Wright, 1989).

The fourth issue concerns the possibility of a tradeoff between the accessibility and content of information in affecting choice. Nedungadi, Mitchell and Berger present evidence that in some situations highly accessible information may determine choice even if the content of that information is not very positive.

The final issue is the need to understand decision making in mixed choice situations. In the study reported in the Nedungadi, Berger, and Mitchell chapter, the effects of advertising repetition on consideration and choice were very different in the mixed choice and memory based choice conditions. The question is whether these differences were due to fundamental differences in the structure of the decision processes or simply differences in function relationships.

REFERENCES

Anderson, J. R. (1983). A spreading activation theory of memory. *Journal of Verbal Learning and Verbal Behavior, 22*, 261–295.

Barsalou, L. W. (1983). Ad hoc categories. *Memory and Cognition, 11*, 211–227.

Beattie, A. E., & Mitchell, A. A. (1985). The relationship between advertising recall and persuasion: An experimental investigation" In L. A. Alwitt & A. A. Mitchell (Eds.), *Psychological processes and advertising effects* (pp. 129–156). Hillsdale, NJ: Lawrence Erlbaum Associates.

Berger, I., & Mitchell A. A. (1989). The effect of advertising on attitude accessibility, attitude confidence and the attitude-behavior relationship. *Journal of Consumer Research, 7*, 234–248.

Cacioppo, J. T., & Petty, R. E. (1979). Effects of message repetition and position on cognitive responses, recall and persuasion. *Journal of Personality and Social Psychology, 37*, 97–109.

Cacioppo, J. T., & Petty, R. E. (1985). Central and peripheral routes to persuasion: The role of message repetition. In L. Alwitt & A. A. Mitchell (Eds.), *Psychological processes and advertising effects*. Hillsdale, NJ: Lawrence Erlbaum Associates.

Feldman, J. M., & Lynch, J. G., Jr. (1988). Self-generated validity and other effects of measurement on belief, intention and behavior. *Journal of Applied Psychology, 73*, 421–435.

Fishbein, M., & Ajzen, I. (1975). *Belief, attitude, intention and behavior: An introduction to theory and research*. Reading, MA: Addison-Wesley.

Gardner, M. (1985). Does attitude toward the ad effect brand attitude under a brand evaluation set? *Journal of Marketing Research, 22*, 192–198.

Greenwald, A. G., Leavitt, C. (1984). Audience involvement in advertising: Four levels. *Journal of Consumer Research, 11*, 581–592.

Homer, P. (1990). The mediating role of attitude toward the ad: Some additional evidence. *Journal of Marketing Research, 27*, 78–86.

Hutchinson, J. W. (1983). Expertise and the structure of free recall. In R. P. Bagozzi & A. M. Tybout (Eds.), *Advances in consumer research* (Vol. 10, pp. 585–589). Ann Arbor, MI: Advances in Consumer Research.

Kirmani, A., & Wright, P. (1989). Money talks: Perceived advertising expense and expected product quality. *Journal of Consumer Research, 17*, 160–171.

Lichtenstein, M., & Srull, T. K. (1985). Conceptual and methodological issues in examining the relationship between consumer memory and judgment. In L. Alwitt & A. A. Mitchell (Eds.), *Psychological processes and advertising effects*. Hillsdale, NJ: Lawrence Erlbaum Associates.

Lingle, J. H., & Ostrom, T. M. (1979). Retrieval selectivity in memory-based impression judgments. *Journal of Personality and Social Psychology, 37*, 180–194.

MacInnis, D., & Jaworski, B. J. (1989). Information processing from advertisements: Toward an integrative framework. *Journal of Marketing, 53*, 1–23.

MacKenzie, S., Lutz, R., & Belch, G. (1986). The role of attitude toward the ad as a mediator of advertising effectiveness: A test of competing explanations. *Journal of Marketing Research, 23*, 130–143.

Mitchell, A. A., & Olson, J. C. (1981). Are product attribute beliefs the only mediator of advertising effects on brand attitudes. *Journal of Marketing Research, 18*, 318–332.

Nedungadi, P. (1990). Recall and consumer consideration sets: Influencing choice without altering brand evaluations. *Journal of Consumer Research, 17*, 263–276.

Petty, R. C., & Cacioppo, J. T. (1986). The elaboration likelihood model in persuasion. In L. Berkowitz (Ed.), *Advances in experimental social psychology* (Vol. 19, pp. 123–205). New York: Academic Press.

Petty R. C., Cacioppo, J. T., & Schumann, D. (1983). Central and peripheral routes to advertising effectiveness. *Journal of Consumer Research, 10,* 135–146.

Ray, M. L., & Sawyer, A. G. (1971). Repetition in media models: A laboratory technique. *Journal of Marketing Research, 8,* 20–30.

Sanbonmatsu, D. M., & Fazio, R. H. (1990). The role of attitudes in memory-based decision making. *Journal of Personality and Social Psychology, 59,* 614–622.

Author Index

Subject Index

Ad accessibility, 17, 20-24, 37, 52
  effect of cognitive effort on, 55
  effect of perceived relevance on, 54-57
  influence of motivation on, 52-53
Ad affect,
  effect on brand affect, 297-298
  free floating, 59-61, 68, 80
Ad effectiveness,
  consideration of purchase timing, 54-57
  empirical testing of, 290-299
  information availability, 76
  level relevance, 76
  relative accessibility, 77
Ad exposure,
  and attitudes, 97, 101
  and empathy, 133
  and memory structure, 97, 329
  effect on consideration, 107, 325
  effect on evaluation of other brands, 109-110
  effect of memory structure, 97
  effect on recall, 98, 100, 107, 325
Ad representation, 16, 22
  brand name associations, 22-25
Ad retrieval,
  cue compatibility, 32-34
  effect of the retrieval cue, 31-32, 38-39
Advertising message involvement,
  antecedents, 70-73
  definition, 69-70
  levels, 73-75
Advertising strategies, 284

and affect, 249, 263-265
celebrity endorsement, 134
coordinated media campaigns, 200-201, 204-205
drama advertising, 261-267
explicit vs. implicit conclusions, 173-174
maximizing the effectiveness of, 78-79, 288-289
optimal advertising contribution, 78-79
Affect,
  and incongruence, 241-242, 247, 291
  and memory, 245, 249-252
  and perceived relatedness, 252-253
  and variety seeking, 242, 246
  influence on categorization, 240-241, 247-248, 320
  influence on processing, 240
  influence on self-perception, 248
Affective responses to advertising, 16-17, 203
Anchor and adjustment, 233, 312, 322
Association network model of memory, 13, 17, 289-290
Attention,
  and drama advertising, 278
  and memory biases, 175
  and prior knowledge, 176-177
  as a consequence of involvement, 70-71, 170
  as measured with electroencephalogram, 313-314
  effect of meaningful information on, 52